The Netherlands

Robert L. Collison (Editor-in-chief) is Professor emeritus, Library and Information Studies, University of California, Los Angeles, and was a President of the Society of Indexers. Following the war, he served as Reference Librarian for the City of Westminster and later became Librarian to the BBC. During his fifty years as a professional librarian in England and the USA, he has written more than twenty works on bibliography, librarianship, indexing and related subjects.

John H. Horton is Deputy Librarian of the University of Bradford and currently Chairman of its Academic Board of Studies in Social Sciences. He has maintained a longstanding interest in the discipline of area studies and its associated bibliographical problems, with special reference to European Studies. In particular he has published in the field of Icelandic and of Yugoslav studies, including the two relevant volumes in the World Bibliographical Series.

Ian Wallace is Professor of Modern Languages at Loughborough University of Technology. A graduate of Oxford in French and German, he also studied in Tübingen, Heidelberg and Lausanne before taking teaching posts at universities in the USA, Scotland and England. He specializes in East German affairs, especially literature and culture, on which he has published numerous articles and books. In 1979 he founded the journal *GDR Monitor*, which he continues to edit.

Hans H. Wellisch is Professor emeritus at the College of Library and Information Services, University of Maryland. He was President of the American Society of Indexers and was a member of the International Federation for Documentation. He is the author of numerous articles and several books on indexing and abstracting, and has published *The conversion of scripts* and *Indexing and abstracting: an international bibliography*. He also contributes frequently to *Journal of the American Society for Information Science, The Indexer* and other professional journals.

Ralph Lee Woodward, Jr. is Chairman of the Department of History at Tulane University, New Orleans, where he has been Professor of History since 1970. He is the author of *Central America, a nation divided*, 2nd ed. (1985), as well as several monographs and more than sixty scholarly articles on modern Latin America. He has also compiled volumes in the World Bibliographical Series on *Belize* (1980), *Nicaragua* (1983), and *El Salvador* (forthcoming). Dr. Woodward edited the Central American section of the *Research guide to Central America and the Caribbean* (1985) and is currently editor of the Central American history section of the *Handbook of Latin American Studies*.

VOLUME 88

The Netherlands

Peter King
and
Michael Wintle
Compilers

CLIO PRESS
OXFORD, ENGLAND · SANTA BARBARA, CALIFORNIA
DENVER, COLORADO

British Library Cataloguing in Publication Data

King, Peter K.
The Netherlands. — (world bibliographical series; V.88).
1. Netherlands — Bibliography
I. Title II. Wintle, Michael J. III. Series
016.9492 Z2431

ISBN 1–85109–041–X

Clio Press Ltd.,
55 St. Thomas' Street,
Oxford OX1 1JG, England.

ABC-Clio Information Services,
Riviera Campus, 2040 Alameda Padre Serra,
Santa Barbara, CA 93103, USA.

Designed by Bernard Crossland
Typeset by Columns Design and Production Services, Reading, England.
Printed and bound in Great Britain by
Billing and Sons Ltd., Worcester.

THE WORLD BIBLIOGRAPHICAL SERIES

This series, which is principally designed for the English speaker, will eventually cover every country in the world, each in a separate volume comprising annotated entries on works dealing with its history, geography, economy and politics; and with its people, their culture, customs, religion and social organization. Attention will also be paid to current living conditions – housing, education, newspapers, clothing, etc. – that are all too often ignored in standard bibliographies; and to those particular aspects relevant to individual countries. Each volume seeks to achieve, by use of careful selectivity and critical assessment of the literature, an expression of the country and an appreciation of its nature and national aspirations, to guide the reader towards an understanding of its importance. The keynote of the series is to provide, in a uniform format, an interpretation of each country that will express its culture, its place in the world, and the qualities and background that make it unique.

VOLUMES IN THE SERIES

1 *Yugoslavia*, John J. Horton
2 *Lebanon*, Shereen Khairallah
3 *Lesotho*, Shelagh M. Willet and David Ambrose
4 *Rhodesia/Zimbabwe*, Oliver B. Pollack and Karen Pollack
5 *Saudi Arabia*, Frank A. Clements
6 *USSR*, Anthony Thompson
7 *South Africa*, Reuben Musiker
8 *Malawi*, Robert B. Boeder
9 *Guatemala*, Woodman B. Franklin
11 *Uganda*, Robert L. Collison
12 *Malaysia*, Ian Brown and Rajeswary Ampalavanar
13 *France*, Frances Chambers
14 *Panama*, Eleanor DeSelms Langstaff
15 *Hungary*, Thomas Kabdebo
16 *USA*, Sheila R. Herstein and Naomi Robbins
17 *Greece*, Richard Clogg and Mary Jo Clogg
18 *New Zealand*, R. F. Grover
19 *Algeria*, Richard I. Lawless
20 *Sri Lanka*, Vijaya Samaraweera
21 *Belize*, Ralph Lee Woodward, Jr.
23 *Luxembourg*, Carlo Hury and Jul Christophory
24 *Swaziland*, Balam Nyeko
25 *Kenya*, Robert L. Collison
26 *India*, Brijen K. Gupta and Datta S. Kharbas
27 *Turkey*, Merel Güçlü
28 *Cyprus*, P. M. Kitromilides and M. L. Evriviades
29 *Oman*, Frank A. Clements
31 *Finland*, J. E. O. Screen
32 *Poland*, Richard C. Lewański
33 *Tunisia*, Allan M. Findlay, Anne M. Findlay and Richard I. Lawless
34 *Scotland*, Eric G. Grant
35 *China*, Peter Cheng
36 *Qatar*, P. T. H. Unwin
37 *Iceland*, John J. Horton
39 *Haiti*, Frances Chambers
40 *Sudan*, M. W. Daly
41 *Vatican City State*, Michael J. Walsh
42 *Iraq*, A. J. Abdulrahman
43 *United Arab Emirates*, Frank A. Clements
44 *Nicaragua*, Ralph Lee Woodward, Jr.
45 *Jamaica*, K. E. Ingram
46 *Australia*, I. Kepars

47 *Morocco*, Anne M. Findlay, Allan M. Findlay and Richard I. Lawless
48 *Mexico*, Naomi Robbins
49 *Bahrain*, P. T. H. Unwin
50 *The Yemens*, G. Rex Smith
51 *Zambia*, Anne M. Bliss and J. A. Rigg
52 *Puerto Rico*, Elena E. Cevallos
53 *Namibia*, Stanley Schoeman and Elna Schoeman
54 *Tanzania*, Colin Darch
55 *Jordan*, Ian J. Seccombe
56 *Kuwait*, Frank A. Clements
57 *Brazil*, Solena V. Bryant
58 *Israel*, Esther M. Snyder (preliminary compilation E. Kreiner)
59 *Romania*, Andrea Deletant and Dennis Deletant
60 *Spain*, Graham J. Shields
61 *Atlantic Ocean*, H. G. R. King
63 *Cameroon*, Mark W. Delancey and Peter J. Schraeder
64 *Malta*, John Richard Thackrah
65 *Thailand*, Michael Watts
66 *Austria*, Denys Salt with the assistance of Arthur Farrand Radley
67 *Norway*, Leland B. Sather
68 *Czechoslovakia*, David Short
69 *Irish Republic*, Michael Owen Shannon
70 *Pacific Basin and Oceania*, Gerald W. Fry and Rufino Mauricio
71 *Portugal*, P. T. H. Unwin
72 *West Germany*, Donald S. Detwiler and Ilse E. Detwiler
73 *Syria*, Ian J. Seccombe
74 *Trinidad and Tobago*, Frances Chambers
76 *Barbados*, Robert B. Potter and Graham M. S. Dann
77 *East Germany*, Ian Wallace
78 *Mozambique*, Colin Darch with the assistance of Calisto Pacheleke
79 *Libya*, Richard I. Lawless
80 *Sweden*, Leland B. Sather and Alan Swanson
81 *Iran*, Reza Navabpour
82 *Dominica*, Robert A. Myers
83 *Denmark*, Kenneth E. Miller
84 *Paraguay*, R. Andrew Nickson
85 *Indian Ocean*, Julia J. Gotthold with the assistance of D. W. Gotthold
86 *Egypt*, Ragai N. Makar
87 *Gibraltar*, Graham J. Shields
88 *The Netherlands*, Peter King and Michael Wintle
89 *Bolivia*, Gertrude M. Yeager

For Cora,
with affection and thanks

Contents

ACKNOWLEDGEMENTS xiii

INTRODUCTION xv

GLOSSARY xix

THE COUNTRY AND ITS PEOPLE: 1

GEOGRAPHY 7
General, political and human geography 7
Economic geography 9
Regional geography and the geography of specific regions 10
Physical geography, drainage and reclamation 12
Maps and atlases 14

FLORA AND FAUNA 17

PREHISTORY AND ARCHAEOLOGY 20

HISTORY 23
General works 23
Before the Revolt (ca. 1550) 26
Revolt and Republic (ca. 1550–1795) 27
Modern history (ca. 1795 to the present) 32
Economic history 38

VOYAGES OF DISCOVERY AND THE COLONIES 46

POPULATION 52
Demography 52
Minorities 57

LANGUAGES AND DIALECTS 63
Dictionaries 63
Grammars 67
Language courses and readers 68

General linguistics 71
History of the Dutch language 76

RELIGION 77
Theology 77
History of religion 80
Sociology of religion 85

SOCIAL CONDITIONS 88

SOCIAL SERVICES, HEALTH AND WELFARE 95

POLITICS 101

CONSTITUTION, LEGAL AND JUDICIAL SYSTEM 108
Legal system 108
Constitution 112
Legislation 113

PLANNING AND ENVIRONMENT 116
Planning 116
Environment and pollution 121

FOREIGN RELATIONS 125

THE ECONOMY 131

FINANCE AND BANKING 138

TRADE 144
International trade 144
Commercial history 148

INDUSTRY 150

AGRICULTURE 155

TRANSPORT 159

EMPLOYMENT, MANPOWER, THE LABOUR MOVEMENT AND TRADE UNIONS 163

STATISTICS 168

EDUCATION 170

General education 170
Primary and secondary education 171
Higher education and research 174

SCIENCE AND TECHNOLOGY 178
Scientific achievements 178
Scientists 181

LITERATURE 184
History and criticism 184
Translations 189
Comparative literature 192

THE ARTS 196
The visual arts in general 196
The visual arts: painting 200
The visual arts: graphics 205
The visual arts: architecture and sculpture 206
Design and crafts 208
Music and dance 210
Theatre and film 212

PHILOSOPHY AND THE HISTORY OF IDEAS 214

SPORTS, RECREATION AND CUISINE 221

ARCHIVES, LIBRARIES, GALLERIES AND MUSEUMS 224
Archives 224
Libraries 226
Galleries and museums 227

BOOKS 230

MASS MEDIA 235

PERIODICALS 238

DIRECTORIES 249

BIBLIOGRAPHIES 252

INDEX OF AUTHORS, TITLES AND SUBJECTS 263

MAP OF THE NETHERLANDS 309

Acknowledgements

The preparation of this bibliography was undertaken in the context of the authors' research programme in the Institute of Modern Dutch Studies at the University of Hull, and we would like to express our gratitude to the University authorities for making the necessary resources available to us over a period of two years. A special word of thanks is due to Rinus Penninx, who gave us the benefit of his considerable expertise in the compilation of the section on minority groups. We are indebted to the members of the Computer Centre at Hull University for indispensable assistance with inputting and processing the data, as we are to our secretary Mrs C. Weir. Finally we would like to thank our colleagues and families for the allowances they have made during the course of this project, and Dr Bob Neville of the Clio Press for his helpful and sensitive handling of the final stages.

Peter King
Michael Wintle

The University, Hull.

Introduction

'The Netherlands' is a literal rendering of the Dutch word *Nederlanden*, meaning 'the low(-lying) lands'. It consists of the Dutch and Frisian language area of Europe, often referred to as 'Holland', though this is technically the Dutch name for two important provinces (North and South Holland), which contain both the seat of government (The Hague) and the capital (Amsterdam). One third of the Dutch-speaking peoples of Europe, however, live in the northern half of Belgium, popularly known as Flanders.

The name of the language 'Dutch', like the name of the German language 'Deutsch', means the vernacular, as distinct from Romance or Latin, and, as a language, Dutch is as distinct from German as it is from English. It is by definition the language of major parts of two nations, 'Holland' and 'Flanders', and for this reason we have not employed here the American term 'Netherlandic' to designate either the language or the culture.

With the exception of language, the Netherlands is by no means a complete unknown to outsiders, and a detailed introduction to the country is therefore not a prerequisite to the profitable use of this book. Nevertheless, a few general points can be made which may help to explain certain emphases in the bibliography, concerning the economy, socio-political divisions, the water defences, and the demographic character of the Netherlands.

The 17th century was a Golden Age for the Netherlands in economic as well as cultural terms, during which time the United Provinces functioned as the economic focal point of the world. Thereafter, in the 18th and 19th centuries, although the country remained among the wealthiest, growth was unspectacular, while other nations were in the process of catching up. The Netherlands did not undergo the kind of 'Industrial Revolution' that was witnessed in Britain, Belgium or Germany. In the 20th century, and most particularly after the Second World War, the country has reassumed its leading economic position, and is once again in the forefront of development, based on high-technology industry, a large trading and service sector, and an efficient, export-oriented agriculture. The discovery of natural gas in large quantities under the fields of the province of Groningen has helped pay for one of the most developed welfare states in the world. The recession of the 1980s has, of course, brought its problems, but the Dutch economy is still a great deal healthier than most others, and the standard of living one of the highest in the world.

Socio-political divisions in the Netherlands have traditionally been held to follow vertical (ideological) rather than horizontal (socio-economic) lines. This is not to deny that there are class differences in the Netherlands, but in this essentially bourgeois society they are considerably less pronounced than, for instance, in Britain. Instead, the differences between Roman Catholics, orthodox Calvinists, Socialists and Liberals have seemed to dominate the political world. Although some revision is at present being demanded from Marxist commentators, the generally accepted version is still that these vertical cleavages in Dutch society were so strong that, in the 20th century, a socio-political system was developed called 'vertical pillarization', 'consociation', or *verzuiling*, which allowed each ideological group to live its own life 'from the cradle to the grave' in isolation. Meanwhile, its leaders took on the necessary task of liaising with the leaders of the other 'pillars' in a spirit of compromise, assisted by an extreme form of proportional representation, in order to run the country, so that their rank and file could enjoy a sheltered existence free from interaction with other groups. This system of *verzuiling* has declined rapidly since about 1960, but is still apparent in many aspects of Dutch life, perhaps most noticeably in the media.

The low-lying territory of the Netherlands, partly below sea-level, provides constant problems of drainage, dike-maintenance and salination. The country also gains from its geographical position at the mouth of some of Europe's most important rivers, on the delta of the Rhine, Maas and Scheldt. The extensive canal network further enhances its trading position in Europe. This location has guided the change from an agricultural-commercial economy to a commercial-industrial one, best symbolized by a number of major multinational concerns (Philips, Unilever,

Shell, etc.), and by the post-war development of the Europort, making Rotterdam the largest harbour in the world.

The Netherlands is one of the most densely populated areas on our planet. The shortage of available land for a rapidly expanding population, mushrooming trade and the accompanying infrastructure has created particular problems in this crowded country. Well over fourteen million people live within 33,920 square kilometres. Overcrowding has resulted in the specifically Dutch concept of the *Randstad* (Rim City, City on the Edge) the name given to the conglomerate of large towns in the shape of a horseshoe, running from Amsterdam, Haarlem, Leiden, The Hague, Delft, Rotterdam and through to Utrecht, containing a concentration of population which threatens to become one enormous megalopolis. The vast engineering works, first to close off the Zuyder Zee to form the IJsselmeer, and then to link and protect the Zeeland islands, have also produced urgently needed recreational space, and, in the new polders of the IJsselmeer, agricultural and urban settlements. But in order to provide an acceptable living environment while maintaining the vigorous economy needed to support the standard of living, a high degree of central planning is required: more than is needed or accepted in most other European countries. The well-worn adage, 'God made the world; the Dutch made Holland', is a piece of chauvinism with enough truth apparent in it to anyone who has discovered the Dutch pride in their ingenuity, orderliness and cleanliness.

This necessity for planning and controls accounts for some of the emphases in this bibliography. The mass of literature on planning, government legislation and statistics has made necessary rigorous selection, even in the English-language material. In other subject-areas as well, there are literally thousands of publications in English to choose from, and to select from this multitude a handful of books and articles to inform the general reader, or even the specialist, about Dutch art or Dutch history is a task which calls for the strictest exercise of critical selection. The same applies to Dutch literature and language, although linguistics is now an international subject employing an international language. Often the personal tastes and critical criteria of the selectors have been the deciding factor.

On the other hand, there are areas which are less well represented in the bibliography. That subjects such as flora and fauna, sports and pastimes are thinly represented is not surprising, since there is little in these areas which other European nations do not share with the Dutch.

It is only just that the compilers of such a general bibliography, where such a strong element of selection is involved, should declare their interest. One of the authors is a specialist in the literature and art of the Low Countries, while the other is a socio-economic historian. Our fields of expertise are undoubtedly better represented than some others, and we cannot deny that in certain areas our knowledge of the field amounts to little more than that of the interested layman. On the other hand, both authors are members of the erstwhile Institute of, now Centre for, Modern Dutch Studies at the University of Hull, which consciously concerns itself with all aspects of life in the Low Countries. And we might further argue that people and institutions today, especially in such a country as the Netherlands, are the living participants in a history going back ten centuries or more, and that the past is always part of the present. For this reason, history is implicit if not explicit in almost every item. And this is as it should be in a bibliography published by Clio – the muse of history.

A number of specific points may assist the reader in understanding the way in which the bibliography has been compiled. We would recommend the consultation of three particularly useful general serial publications in English on the Netherlands, namely *Planning and Development in the Netherlands* (1968–82), *Delta* (1958–74), and *Dutch Crossing* (1977– .) (q.v.). For those seeking English translations of Dutch legislation, parliamentary acts, and official reports, the British Library holds a full collection, and its main catalogue and updates should be referred to. In the section on minorities the Frisians have not been included, for the reason that they are, and always have been, an integral part of the indigenous population, with their status recognized and protected in the constitution. We have included very little work written in the Dutch language, but in the instances of indispensable work in Dutch that we have decided to cite, there is an obvious implicit plea for early translations of these major works. A very small number of works in French and German have also been included. Finally, we have endeavoured to concentrate on works readily available either through libraries or booksellers. The cut-off date of research before going to press was early 1987, and thus works published at a later date have only been included as an exception.

Glossary

Amsterdam School	The architects at the beginning of this century who came under the influence of H. P. Berlage.
Dutch School	The artists of the 17th century who abandoned the Italian heroic style of painting for more realistic and domestic themes.
Gemeente	Municipality; local government unit.
Rederijkers	Rhetoricians, a corruption of the French *rhétoriqueurs*, meaning members of the late-medieval Chambers of Rhetoric throughout Flanders and the Netherlands, writing poetry and plays (sometimes for competitions) and providing entertainment at local and national festivals.
Verzuiling	Literally, pillarization, or the division of society into vertical or ideological groups which meet only at government level. For a more detailed explanation, see the introduction.

The Country and its People

1 **Amsterdam 1950–1959.**

Oscar van Alphen. Amsterdam: Fragment, 1985. 109p.

English and Dutch text of the catalogue of an exhibition of twenty photographs of daily life in the city in the 1950s, with biographical notes on the photographers and Remco Campert's reminiscences of the city at that time.

2 **Regional costumes in the Netherlands.**

Valentyn Bing, Braet van Ueberfeldt. Zutphen, The Netherlands: Terra, 1978. 136p. Reprint of the (Dutch) edition of 1857.

Full-page engravings of child and adult figures in the 19th-century costumes of their regions are grouped according to their province and are accompanied by detailed descriptions of daily and formal dress.

3 **Of Dutch ways.**

Helen Colijn. Minneapolis, Minnesota: Dillon, 1980. 240p.

A very readable book, containing what many American tourists might look for in a foreign guidebook. There is a great deal of information on the Netherlands, sometimes quaintly out of date (even in 1980). It includes, somewhat unusually, chapters on 'The Flying Dutchman and other tales', on Dutch cooking recipes and on Dutch settlements in the USA.

4 **Holland: the land and the people.**

Donald Cowie. South Brunswick, Maine: Barnes, 1974. 245p.

A pleasantly written, unpretentious introduction to the Netherlands, obviously highlighting the tourist attractions (with an excellent range of monochrome and colour plates) and pointing out the striking, though often misleading, characteristics of Dutch people. Many amusing, if dubious, conclusions are drawn, and this can therefore be recommended to readers who will not take it too seriously.

5 **Holland on the way to the forum: living in the Netherlands.**
Ab van Dien. Amsterdam: Wetenschappelijke Uitgeverij, 1974. 151p.

A guide to the better understanding of the attitude of the Dutch towards building and living in the 1970s. A catalogue of an exhibition with photographs by Ida Gorter and Sjoerd Holsbergen.

6 **The rough guide to Amsterdam and Holland with a chapter on Luxembourg and selected Belgian cities.**
Martin Dunford, Jack Holland. London: Routledge & Kegan Paul, 1984. Reprinted 1986. 216p. maps.

Contains a chapter on each major locality as well as a section entitled 'Contexts', including chapters on Dutch history, art, language, literature and contemporary society.

7 **Fact sheet on the Netherlands, series E.**
Ministry of Welfare, Health and Cultural Affairs (WVC). Rijswijk, The Netherlands: WVC, 1983–86. 35 leaflets.

This series of brief leaflets (of between 4–8 pages) forms an expanded version of a set of twelve published from 1973–76 under the same title by the predecessor of the WVC, the Ministry of Cultural Affairs, Recreation and Welfare (CRM). The fact sheets provide essential information on a wide variety of subjects coming under the Ministry's supervision. These include minorities, health care, the elderly, youth work, broadcasting, monuments, sport, music, other performing arts, the disabled, drugs, urban renewal, the press, literature, museums, archives and adult education. Series 'E' refers to the publication in English.

8 **24 hours Amsterdam.**
R. Ferdinandusse, photographs by Hans van den Bogaard. London: Thames & Hudson, 1986. 139p.

Photographs taken throughout the day (in May) give a monochrome impression of the cosmopolitan, liberal atmosphere of the city.

9 **Friesland.**
Delta, vol. 8, no. 4 (winter 1965–66), 96p, bibliog. (Special issue).

A special Friesland number containing an introduction posing the problem of Friesland's survival as a minority community with its own language, and essays on Friesland's historical freedom, its changing economy, its facilities for leisure and relaxation, art in Friesland, the Frisian movement, Frisian writers, the threat to the Frisian language, and education in Friesland.

10 **Inside information.**
C. Gelderman-Curtis, R. Niks–Corkum. The Hague: Inside Information, 1980. 2nd ed. 200p.

A detailed vade-mecum for anyone intending to move to the Netherlands, with guidance on removal, registration, house furnishing, daily needs and emergencies, cooking and housekeeping, schools, Dutch customs and etiquette, communications, money matters, clubs and organizations. The information is strictly factual, with numerous addresses, glossaries of terms where needed, and a cross-reference index.

11 **Roaming 'round Holland.**
Patricia Gordon, Sheila Gazaleh–Weevers. Rotterdam: Roaming 'round Holland, 1985. 5th ed. 414p. bibliog.

A sparsely illustrated guidebook with well-researched and uncluttered information on all kinds of interesting places, described according to province, with sections on beaches, amusement centres and zoos, local industries and special annual events. The second half of the book provides varied information for those intending to live in the Netherlands. There is a list of 'background' books and magazines, now rather dated, and an index.

12 **The myth of Sinterklaas.**
A. D. de Groot. *Delta*, vol. 2 (autumn 1959), p. 5–13.

A Jungian interpretation of the folklore surrounding Saint Nicholas and a reference to some of the historic traditions associated with him, some of which contribute to present-day customs in the Netherlands.

13 **The Netherlands in brief.**
Compiled by M. J. M. van Herik, L. Verheijen. The Hague: Ministry of Foreign Affairs, 1984. 54p.

A well-illustrated survey on government, population, education, foreign policy, defence, the economy, finance, agriculture and fisheries, traffic and transport, social policy, health, environmental policy, water control and land reclamation, housing, physical planning, the arts, the media, tourism and sport.

14 **The kingdom of the Netherlands: facts and figures.**
Ministry of Foreign Affairs. The Hague: Government Printing Office, n.d. (1977–).

24 fasciculi on 'Country and people', 'History', 'The kingdom', 'The monarchy', 'Justice', 'Police, civil defence, fire services', 'Finance', 'Economy', 'Agriculture and fisheries', 'Transport and communications', 'Socio-economic system', 'Social security', 'Welfare services', 'Health and environmental protection', 'Housing and physical planning', 'Public works', 'Defence', 'Foreign policy', 'Education and science', 'The arts and the national cultural heritage', 'The mass media', 'The Netherlands Antilles'.

15 **Holland.**
Ruud H.M. Kok, Kees Scherer, photo-selection by Joop van der Liet, translated from the Dutch by Charles Greenwood. Amsterdam: Elsevier, 1983. 159p.

A collection of photographs with accompanying text in Dutch, English, German, French, Spanish and Japanese. The five chapters present the Netherlands in the Golden Age, at work, at play, in politics and as a nation.

16 **Orders and decorations of the Netherlands.**
H. G. Meijer, C. P. Mulder, B. W. Wagenaar. Bussum, The Netherlands: Special Interest Publications, 1985. 2nd rev. ed. 112p.

This lavishly illustrated account covers the history of orders from the Middle Ages to the present day, Royal Family Orders and commemorative medals, Red Cross and life-saving medals, and sections on the protocol of wearing orders and decorations, on the manner of making awards, and on the designers and makers of Dutch insignia.

17 **Living in the Netherlands.**
Jane Meijlink. Haarlem, The Netherlands: Gottmer, 1979. 144p. bibliog.

This is neither an autobiography nor a tourist guide. It is, as the title page states, 'advice and information' primarily intended for those intending to stay for some time in the Netherlands. Hence topics such as rules and regulations, accommodation, insurance, etiquette and pets are dealt with. There are addresses of clubs and societies, and of advisory agencies for education. There is also a list of books and magazines for further reading and an index.

18 **Costumes of Staphorst: a village in the eastern Netherlands.**
C. H. M. Palm. *International Archives of Ethnography*, vol. 50, no. 1 (1964), p. 43–59.

This essay is as much about customs and religion as about costumes. This is understandable since it is the very conservative aspects of religion which make Staphorst an exception to the rapid disappearance of national dress except as a tourist attraction.

19 **Room at last! The Ysselmeer polders described and illustrated.**
The Hague: Ministry of Transport and Public Works, Information Division [n.d.]. 47p.

This outlines the original demands for further land reclamation, the Lely plan, the aims of the Zuyder Zee project and its execution, with a description of the drainage operation and the planning of a polder and the towns within it (Lelystad, Almere and Almere–Haven).

20 **Rotterdam with a green thumb.**
Rotterdam: Rotterdam Information Department, 1970. 72p.

A nicely produced publicity picture-book in full colour, with a text outlining the achievements and policies of the municipality.

21 **Holland in close-up.**
K. Scherer, E. Werkman. Amsterdam: Elsevier, 1981. 2nd imp. 159p.

A 'coffee-table' book in four languages (Dutch, English, German, French) with colour and monochrome illustrations using the kind of photographs of scenes old and new that are favoured in the calendars annually commissioned by the Dutch

Ministries. 5,000 years of history are covered in 8 pages, Dutch art in the same number, and industry in 9. However, it is up to date and has some attractive line-drawings of flora and fauna, and costumes.

22 **A guide to Jewish Amsterdam.**
Jan Stoutenbeek, Paul Vigeveno, consultant editor Joel J. Cahen, translated from the Dutch by Carla van Splunteren. Amsterdam: Jewish Historical Museum; Weesp, The Netherlands: De Haan, 1985. 156p.

The Jewish quarter of Amsterdam was severely damaged in the Second World War, and the remains of it have been further reduced by the construction of new infrastructural projects. This guide gives a short history of the Amsterdam Jews, followed by a series of descriptive 'walks' through what is left of the quarter.

23 **Synthese: twelve facets of culture and nature in South Limburg.**
Heerlen, The Netherlands: Dutch State Mines, 1977. 416p.

This text is in Dutch, English, German and French. The twelve facets described, and handsomely illustrated, are signs from prehistoric times, Roman remains, art and architecture, the *Domus aurea*, Gothic art, Renaissance and post-Renaissance design, the town hall, art in miniature, 'the romanticism of reality', gates and gatehouses, and 'in praise of simplicity'.

24 **Klederdrachten.** (Costumes.)
F .W. S. van Thienen, J. Duyvetter. Amsterdam: Contact, 1962. 87p. (De Schoonheid van Ons Land: Land en Volk).

This standard work, with a Dutch text, has numerous line-drawings illustrating the characteristic shapes of women's and children's head-dresses. There are also colour plates of costumes and jewellery and 184 black-and-white photographs.

25 **Amsterdam canal guide.**
H. Tulleners. Utrecht: Het Spectrum, 1978. 368p. bibliog.

An ingeniously designed book, with line-drawings at the top and (verso) bottom of each page, corresponding to the position of notable buildings on either side of the canals. An introduction describes general architectural features typical of the (17th-century) period of gable construction, with an illustrated list of architectural terms, an outline history of the city, and some amusing statistics.

26 **Lonely but not alone.**
HRH Wilhelmina, Princess of the Netherlands. London: Hutchinson, 1960. 247p.

The autobiography of an octogenarian recalling the court conventions which stifled her early years as a queen and her subsequent reliance on faith to carry her through the fifty years of her reign – through the neutrality of the First World War and her exile during the Second World War, constantly fighting convention, writing her own speeches and determining that her daughter would not inherit the taboos surrounding her own life.

Siertuinen van Nederland en Belgie. (Flower gardens of the Netherlands and Belgium.)
See item no. 77.

The Dutch in London: the influence of an immigrant community.
See item no. 95.

Dances of the Netherlands.
See item no. 870.

Delta: A Review of Art, Life and Thought in the Netherlands.
See item no. 933.

Dutch Heights.
See item no. 938.

Holland Herald.
See item no. 944.

Biografisch woordenboek der Nederlanden. (Biographical dictionary of the Netherlands.)
See item no. 976.

Biografisch woordenboek van Nederland. (Biographical dictionary of the Netherlands.)
See item no. 978.

Nieuw Nederlandsch biografisch woordenboek. (New Dutch biographical dictionary.)
See item no. 980.

Bibliographia Neerlandica.
See item no. 1012.

Het Nederlandse boek in vertaling. (The Dutch book in translation.)
See item no. 1018.

Geography

General, political and human geography

27 **Aardrijkskundig woordenboek der Nederlanden.** (Geographical dictionary of the Netherlands.)
A. J. van der Aa. Gorinchem, The Netherlands: Noorduyn, 1839–51. 13 vols. Reprinted, Zaltbommel, The Netherlands: Europese Bibliotheek, 1976–80. 14 vols. bibliog.

Geographical descriptions from the mid-19th century on all the municipalities and areas of the Netherlands, and on all kinds of general topics to do with the country as a whole. This work is of particular interest to historical geographers.

28 **Netherlands.**
Naval Intelligence Division, written by S. T. Bindoff (et al.). London: HM Stationery Office, 1944. 756p. (Geographical Handbook Series, no. 549).

A wartime handbook produced for use in the British services as a general guide to the country. The information range is vast, covering virtually every subject from a geographical viewpoint. Although obviously dated, it is still a remarkably succinct presentation of useful factual material.

Geography. General, political and human geography

29 **The making of Dutch towns: a study in urban development from the tenth to the seventeenth centuries.**
Gerald L. Burke, foreword by Sir William Holford. London: Cleaver–Hulme Press, 1956. 176p. maps. bibliog.

Based on a dissertation for a London University MSc in estate management, this is a pleasant and interesting introduction to Dutch planning and architecture in urban areas, with many illustrations and maps. An unusual approach is adopted in identifying various types of Dutch towns which grew up before 1700.

30 **The changing countryside: proceedings of the first British–Dutch symposium on rural geography.**
Edited by Gordon Clark, Jan Groendijk, Frans Thissen. Norwich, England: Geo Books, 1984. 349p. maps. bibliog. (International Symposia Series).

This conference was held in Norwich in 1982: about half of the thirty-three articles are concerned with Dutch rural geography, dealing with such themes as standards of living, planning, housing, and politics in rural areas.

31 **Die Beneluxstaaten: eine geographische Länderkunde.** (The Benelux countries: a geographical handbook.)
Hermann Hambloch. Darmstadt, FRG: Wissenschaftliche Buchgesellschaft, 1977. 404p. bibliog.

A general geography on the three nations of the Benelux Economic Union, with sections covering physical, human and economic geography, the various regions in each country, and their environmental problems.

32 **Compact geography of the Netherlands.**
Henk Meijer. The Hague: Ministry of Foreign Affairs, 1983. 4th ed. 43p. maps. bibliog.

A brief but useful introduction, with sections on water control and engineering, demography, the economy, planning and the environment.

33 **Handboek der geografie van Nederland.** (Handbook of the geography of the Netherlands.)
Edited by G. A. M. Mulder. Zwolle, The Netherlands: Tijl, 1949–59. 6 vols. bibliog.

The standard handbook, now rather dated, but still indispensable for reference. Many contributions on all possible subjects.

34 **Patterns of European urbanisation since 1500.**
Edited by H. Schmal. London: Croom Helm, 1981. 309p. bibliog.

The proceedings of an international conference on urbanization which took place in Amsterdam in 1979, and which was dominated by material on the growth of Dutch towns. Much of the material is historical, although geographers were also present; the focus is of course on the Randstad in the west of the Netherlands.

Economic geography

35 **The Netherlands in Western Europe.**
G. A. Hoekveld. *Tijdschrift voor Economische en Sociale Geografie*, vol. 63 (1972), p. 129–48. maps. bibliog.

With a short historical introduction, the author looks at the demographic and economic position of the country in its continental framework. Plenty of maps and data give a useful picture up to 1970.

36 **The new Europe: an economic geography of the EEC.**
G. N. Minshull. London: Hodder & Stoughton, 1985. 3rd ed. 316p. maps. bibliog.

Chapter 14 (p. 218–33) is entitled 'Randstad Holland: the ring city', and forms an introduction to the horseshoe string of conurbations in the west of the country. Attention is focused on the port of Rotterdam.

37 **The Netherlands.**
David A. Pinder. Folkstone, Kent, England: Dawson, 1976; London: Hutchinson, 1978. 194p. maps. bibliog. (Studies in Industrial Geography; Hutchinson University Library).

This most useful study is now unfortunately out of print, but provides the best single volume on the economic geography of the Netherlands in the 1970s. After some attention to the historical and geographical background, Pinder deals with the regional problems and policies of the industrial Netherlands, and then devotes a chapter to each of the six main regions within the country.

38 **Benelux: an economic geography of Belgium, the Netherlands and Luxembourg.**
R. C. Riley, G. J. Ashworth. London: Chatto & Windus, 1975. 256p. maps. bibliog.

An excellent handbook on the Netherlands and its neighbours, with chapters on the historical background, social structure, and the various economic sectors.

39 **A profile of Dutch economic geography.**
Edited by Marc de Smidt, Egbert Wever. Assen, The Netherlands: Van Gorcum, 1984. 201p. maps. bibliog.

This is a collection of various papers given by Dutch economic geographers to the 1984 International Geographers' Union conference. The selection is thus somewhat arbitrary, but this is much helped by a review article on economic geography in the Netherlands by the editors (p. 1–11). The subjects dealt with include regional policy, foreign investment, the labour market, agribusiness, and retailing. It provides a useful collection.

Tijdschrift voor Economische en Sociale Geografie. (Journal of Economic and Social Geography.)
See item no. 972.

Regional geography and the geography of specific regions

40 **Planning and creation of an environment: experience in the Ysselmeerpolders.**
A. K. Constandse, L. Wijers, N. C. de Ruiter. The Hague: Ministry of Housing and Physical Planning, 1964. 89p. maps. bibliog.

Deals with the planning of the Wieringermeer, the North–East Polder and Eastern Flevoland, with a chapter on the regional centre of Emmeloord.

41 **The future of Randstad Holland: a Netherlands scenario study on long-term perspectives for human settlement in the western part of the Netherlands.**
The Hague: Ministry of Housing, 1983. 82p. maps. bibliog.

A ministerial report on planning persectives for this, the most crowded and dense conurbation in the world. A number of influencing factors (demography, the economy, and the like) are enumerated, and an extended prognosis is presented of how the area will look in the year 2010.

42 **Port of Amsterdam.**
G. H. Knap. Amsterdam: De Bussy, 1970. 216p.

Copiously illustrated with monochrome plates, this 'coffee-table' publication has chapters on the harbour economy, technology and modernization, and the men of the River IJ.

43 **The changing face of South Limburg.**
G. R. P. Lawrence. *Geography*, vol. 56 (1971), p. 35–39.

An account of the major changes in Limburg associated with the closing of the state coal-mines there in the 1960s.

44 **Randstad Holland.**
G. R. P. Lawrence. London: Oxford University Press, 1973. 48p. bibliog. (Problem Regions of Europe).

A school textbook on the economic geography of the vast conurbation in the west of the Netherlands. The chapters are concerned with the various regions, the economic sectors, population and planning.

45 **Randstad Holland.**
Henk Meijer. Utrecht: Information and Documentation Centre for the Geography of the Netherlands, 1980. 72p. maps. bibliog.

A short general approach to the geography of the horseshoe-shaped string of cities in the central western area of the country. Planning receives a major chapter, and there are sections on each of the sub-districts.

46 **The south-west Netherlands: Rotterdam Europoort Delta.**
Henk Meijer. The Hague: Ministry of Foreign Affairs, 1978. 2nd ed. 60p. maps. bibliog.

A general section deals with the area's developments and problems, followed by a series of 'excursions' to various parts of this maritime area.

47 **Zuyder Zee: Lake IJssel.**
Henk Meijer. Utrecht: Information and Documentation Centre for the Geography of the Netherlands, 1981. 3rd rev. ed. 72p. map.

An introduction to this vast project of hydraulic engineering, with chapters on the planning of the Lake IJssel project and on each of the various polders or drainage areas.

48 **Changes in the port of Amsterdam.**
D. G. Mills. *Geography*, vol. 63 (1978), p. 209–13. bibliog.

A short account of the modernization of port facilities in the capital since the Second World War. The industrial sector, especially oil, receives attention.

49 **A geographical study of the Dutch-German border.**
Robert S. Platt, translated by E. Bertelsmeier. Münster, FRG: Geographische Kommission für Westfalen, 1958. 88p. maps. bibliog.

This text in English and German is well illustrated, and covers the local geography of the border from the Frisian islands in the north down to the Rhine valley in the south.

Room at last! The Ysselmeer polders described and illustrated.
See item no. 19.

Physical geography, drainage and reclamation

50 **The history of the Dutch coast in the last century.**
W. T. Bakker, D. S. Joustra. The Hague: Ministry of Transport and Public Works, 1970. 15p. maps. bibliog. (Studierapport WWK–70–12).

This research paper sets out to make available various measurements and computations to do with the Dutch coastline, and in particular to investigate the effects of groynes and the motion of gullies in the outer deltas.

51 **Holocene sea level changes in the Netherlands.**
S. Jelgersma. Maastricht, The Netherlands: Van Aelst, 1961. 102p. maps. bibliog.

A study of rises and falls in the sea-level along the Dutch coast since the end of the last Ice Age, based on research surveys in the coastal provinces.

52 **Het klimaat van Nederland gedurende de laatste twee en een halve eeuw.** (The climate of the Netherlands during the last two and a half centuries.)
A. Labrijn. The Hague: Rijksuitgeverij, 1945. 114p. maps. bibliog. (Koninklijk Nederlandsch Meteorologisch Instituut, no. 102; Mededelingen en Verhandelingen, no. 49).

This was Labrijn's doctoral dissertation at the University of Utrecht (1945), and the basis of his research was the unearthing, collation and correction of climatological records going back to ca. 1700. There is a summary in English, and the appendixes on temperature, rainfall, wind direction etc. all have captions in English.

53 **An evaluation of dredging in the western Scheldt (the Netherlands) through bioassays.**
J. M. Marquenie, J. W. Simmers, E. Birnbaum. The Hague: Netherlands Organization for Applied Scientific Research (TNO). 1985. 56p. bibliog.

This report of research sponsored by Delta Service in Middelburg (The Netherlands) gives an account of the success of dredging in this extremely important estuary using biological analysis of samples.

54 **Geological history of the Netherlands: explanation to the general geological map of the Netherlands on the scale of 1:200,000.**
Edited by Antonie J. Pannekoek. The Hague: Staatsdrukkerij, 1956. 147p. maps. bibliog.

This introduction to a series of maps provides a useful short introduction to the geology of the Netherlands. A Dutch version was published simultaneously. A variety of authors contributed chapters on the various geological periods.

55 **Planning and Development in the Netherlands.**
Assen, The Netherlands: Van Gorcum, vol. 4, no. 1 (1970), p. 1–128. bibliog.

This issue of the journal deals with the draining of the Zuyder Zee or Lake IJssel, with the emphasis on planning. There are articles on water management, the administrative organization of the new polders, agricultural and recreational aspects of the new settlements, social developments and institutions.

56 **Rijkswaterstaat Communications.** (Public Works Communications.)
The Hague: Ministry of Public Works, vol. 1 (1959) – vol. 46 (1986). irregular.

This monograph series has been increasingly prolific in recent years, several issues appearing annually. The subject matter varies from the micro-technical (construction of wing-gates) to the broad sweep of planning (structure plan for the IJsselmeerpolders). The texts are all in English, and are useful to anyone interested in drainage, hydraulic engineering, civil engineering, geology and public works in general.

57 **Dredge drain reclaim: the art of a nation.**
J. van Veen. The Hague: Nijhoff, 1948. 165p. maps. Later edition; London: Longmans, 1959; 5th ed. 1962.

An historical sketch of the development of Dutch hydraulic engineering over the ages which is copiously illustrated. The three sections cover the earliest times, the Golden Age of Dutch water engineering, and the post-war period.

58 **Groundwater flow systems in the Netherlands: a groundwater-hydrological approach to the functional relationship between the drainage system and the geological and climatical conditions in a quarternary accumulation area.**
Johannes J. de Vries. Amsterdam: Rodopi, 1974. 226p. maps. bibliog.

A technical exercise for the specialist in groundwater flow systems.

59 **Polderlands.**
Paul Wagret, translated from the French by Margaret Sparks. London: Methuen, 1968. (First published as *Les polders*. Paris: Dunod, 1959).

A general textbook on the marshy areas of northern Europe. The sections concentrating on the Netherlands cover Friesland and Zeeland before 1500, the Dutch 'miracle' of the 17th century (Chapter 3), the 19th century (Chapter 4), and the technological advances of the 20th century, especially those used in the Zuyder Zee project.

Room at last! The Ysselmeer polders described and illustrated.
See item no. 19.

Zuyder Zee: Lake IJssel.
See item no. 47.

Klimaatatlas van Nederland. (Climate atlas of the Netherlands.)
See item no. 63.

The derivation of spatial goals for the Dutch land consolidation programme.
See item no. 604.

The problem of popularising land consolidation in the Netherlands: thirty years of legislative change, 1924–54.
See item no. 605.

Maps and atlases

60 **Atlas van Nederland/Atlas of the Netherlands.**
Compiled by the Foundation for the Scientific Atlas of the Netherlands. The Hague: Government Printing and Publishing Office, 1963–77; with supplements 1978–81. [not paginated].

A series of more than fifty large maps clip-bound into a single volume, with titles, keys and explanatory text in Dutch and English. The various sections contain maps of every conceivable subject, including topography, geology, geomorphology, climate, vegetation, water, settlement, population, agriculture, industry, commerce and planning.

61 **De atlas van Nederland.**
The Hague: Staatsdrukkerij, 1986– . 21 vols in progress.

About ten of the volumes have appeared to date, with twenty-four large pages in each, covering all appropriate subjects. Vol. 21 will be a comprehensive index.

62 **Falk Plan: Nederland autokaart/carte routiere/autokarte/ road map 1:250.000.**
Utrecht; Eindhoven, The Netherlands: Falkplan–Suurland; Antwerp, Belgium: Bruna; Hamburg, FRG: Falk–Verlag, n.d. [ca. 1985]. 28p. map.

This universally available motoring map has a lap-use fold-out format, with town plans, traffic rules, etc.

63 **Klimaatatlas van Nederland.** (Climate atlas of the Netherlands.)
Koninklijk Nederlands Meteorologisch Instituut. The Hague: Staatsuitgeverij, 1972. [not paginated]. maps.

The thirty-four sets of maps are accompanied by a text in Dutch and English with a commentary on the maps.

64 **Collections of maps and atlases in the Netherlands.**
Cornelis Koeman. Leiden: Brill, 1961. 301p. bibliog.

A scholarly and comprehensive work on the history of map collections from the 16th century to the present day, with a chapter on Frederik Muller, the founder of scientific antiquarian bookselling. The second part contains a list of map and atlas collections in the Netherlands with descriptions of the institutions housing them, bibliographical notes on the collections and an index.

65 **Joan Blaeu and his grand atlas.**
Cornelis Koeman. Amsterdam: Theatrum Orbis Terrarum, 1970. 114p.

This gives a short biography of the printer, a description of his printing house and cartographic institute, and the origins and growth of his atlas. The second half of the book is devoted to the Atlas Maior itself with a description of its layout and contents, an account of the extensive damage caused by a fire at the press and the subsequent history of the atlas.

66 **Pictorial atlas of the Netherlands.**
Compiled by the Information and Documentation Centre for the Geography of the Netherlands, University of Utrecht. The Hague: Ministry of Foreign Affairs, 1977. 40p. maps.

The text accompanying the maps is in English. There are also plentiful photographs and diagrams on eighteen topics on the geography of the Netherlands, mainly on the human and social side.

67 **The burning fen.**
Arent Roggeveen, Pieter Goos. Amsterdam: Theatrum Orbis Terrarum, 1971. [not paginated]. maps.

This is a facsimile edition of the original work published in Amsterdam in 1675, with an introduction by Cornelis Koeman, and it is the earliest printed pilot book on the central American coasts. It is therefore of as much interest to the history of printing in the Netherlands as it is to geography.

68 **Het 80.000 straatenboek: met plattegronden van 122 steden en een register met 80.000 straaten.** (The 80,000 street book: with maps of 122 towns and an index with 80,000 streets.)
Rotterdam: Shell; Eindhoven, The Netherlands: Suurland's Vademecum Uitgeversmaatschappij, 1984. 7th rev. ed. 480p.

This extremely useful book of street plans provides the location of 80,000 streets in the towns of the Netherlands and is consultable even without knowledge of the Dutch language. Indexes for each town give simple map-references to virtually every urban street in the country. New editions appear regularly, and the book is available from all newsagents.

69 **The Netherlands in one hundred maps.**
Robert Tamsma. Amsterdam: Royal Dutch Geographical Society, 1977. [not paginated].

These maps, first published in the *Tijdschrift voor Economische en Sociale Geografie* (q.v.) in 1961, present surveys of virtually every conceivable mappable feature in the country.

Atlantes Neerlandici: bibliography of terrestrial, maritime and celestial atlases and pilot books, published in the Netherlands up to 1880.
See item no. 1003.

Flora and Fauna

70 **Animal and man in Holland's past: an investigation of the animal world surrounding man in prehistoric and early historical times in the provinces of North and South Holland.**

A. T. Clason. *Palaeohistoria*, vol. 13 (1967), p. 3–247. maps.

The extensive urban expansion in the Randstad (the conurbation in the west of the country) and the provision of large waterworks for Amsterdam has resulted in many discoveries in the soils below sea-level opened up for deep-foundation building. These are particularly valuable since the higher sandy soils further east have yielded so little. Twenty sites are described and the mammal, bird, fish and molusc remains are illustrated with line-drawings and photographs.

71 **The Netherlands as an environment for plant life.**

W. C. de Leeuw. Leiden: Brill, 1935. 40p. maps.

This paper, presented to the 6th International Botanical Congress in 1935, was prepared by members of the Netherlands Botanical Society and it describes the edaphic, climatic and biotic factors, and the present flora and vegetation which is 'very young indeed'.

72 **The book of tulips.**

Tom Lodewijk, edited by Ruth Buchan. London: Cassell, 1979. 128p.

A lavishly illustrated account of the place of the tulip in art and literature, in various countries and in history. This is followed by a description of the tulip industry in Holland, instructions on how to purchase and cultivate tulips, and appendixes on tulips in America and Britain and lists with flowering times of the various varieties.

Flora and Fauna

73 **Vegetables of the Dutch East Indies**

Jacob Ochse in collaboration with R. C. Bakhuizen van den Brink.

Amsterdam: Asher, 1947. 2nd imp. 1,005p.

This is a revised edition of the original translation, published in 1931, of the Dutch version *Indische groenten*. It includes edible tubers, bulbs, rhizomes and spices in a 'survey of the indigenous and foreign plants serving as pot-herbs and side-dishes'. It is in fact an herbarium, giving for the Latin names of the varieties the Dutch and English equivalents wherever possible. Included is a synopsis of the plants described, with their taxonomic classification, and an extensive register of vernacular names, as well as comprehensive indexes and a list of corrections made to botanical terms in the 1931 edition. This is particularly useful at a time when Indonesian cookery is being taken up in the Netherlands by people who are now able to acquire oriental ingredients.

74 **Hortus Floridus: the four books of spring, summer and winter flowers.**

Crispin van de Pass, translated by Spencer Savage, introduction by Eleanor Sinclair Rhode. London: Minerva, 1974. 2nd imp. [not paginated].

First published in English in 1615, a year after it first appeared in Latin, this new translation contains 100 plates illustrating each flower described according to its flowering season, and this provides a record of what might have been found in a Dutch 17th-century garden. The introduction discusses the popularity at that time of several of the flowers described, with particular reference to the tulip and the tulipomania which followed its introduction.

75 **The poison tree: selected writings of Rumphuis on the natural history of the Indies.**

G. E. Rumphuis, edited and translated by E. M. Beekman.

Amherst, Massachusetts: University of Massachusetts Press, 1981. 260p.

These excerpts from Rumphuis's three-volume *Thesaurus Amboiniensis* (ca. 1670) have been translated as much for their literary as for their botanical value. This is a useful source also to the historian, since considerable background information is included in a work written during Rumphuis's forty years in the Moluccas.

76 **The zoological work of Petrus Camper (1722–1789).**

Robert Paul Willem Visser. Amsterdam: Rodopi, 1985. 207p. bibliog. (Nieuwe Nederlandse Bijdragen tot de Geschiedenis der Geneeskunde en der Natuurwetenschappen, 12).

This doctoral dissertation concentrates on the work of Camper who, with Daubenton, heralded the new school of comparative anatomy investigating exotic animals, the structural uniformity of vertebrates, physical anthropology and fossils.

77 **Siertuinen van Nederland en Belgie.** (Flower gardens of the Netherlands and Belgium.)
Frans W. Wegman. Breda, The Netherlands: Lekturama, 1986. 128p.

An introduction on the history and practical value of pleasure gardens is followed by an illustrated description of a number of fine botanic garden rosaria, country house and castle gardens, and herbaria. It has an index and information on opening times.

The Netherlands as an environment for molluscan life.
See item no. 480.

Dutch elm disease: aspects of pathogenosis and control.
See item no. 609.

Netherlands Journal of Plant Pathology: Tijdschrift over Planteziekten.
See item no. 958.

Netherlands Journal of Zoology.
See item no. 961.

Prehistory and Archaeology

78 **Four linearbandkeramik settlements and their environment: a paleoecological study of Sittard, Stein, Elsloo and Hienheim.**
C. C. Bakels. Leiden: Universitaire Pers, 1978. 248p. maps. bibliog.

This doctoral thesis (Leiden University, 1978) traces the relationship between a prehistoric civilization in South Limburg and its environment, ca. 4500 BC. The appendixes and maps provide ample documentation.

79 **The TRB West group: studies in the chronology and geography of the makers of hunebeds and Tiefstich pottery.**
J. A. Bakker. Amsterdam: University of Amsterdam, 1979. 238p. bibliog.

An expanded and translated version of a Doctor of Science dissertation (University of Amsterdam, 1973). It deals with the civilizations which covered the coastal areas of Western Europe and which built the hunebeds, or megalithic monuments, some of which are to be found in the north and east of the Netherlands. Ample illustrations of every kind abound, and there are many appendixes. 'TRB' stands for 'trechterbeker', and translates as 'Funnel Beaker Peoples', after the pottery they manufactured.

80 **Ex horreo: IPP 1951–1976.**
Edited by B. L. van Beek, R. W. Brandt, W. Groenman–Van Waateringe. Amsterdam: University of Amsterdam, 1977. 302p. bibliog.

This collection of essays, in honour of the twenty-fifth anniversary of the Institute for Prae- and Proto-history (IPP) at the University of Amsterdam, contains eighteen contributions on a wide range of Dutch prehistoric subjects, reflecting the Institute's programme of archaeological research. The articles are mainly concerned with the prehistoric economy, focusing on trade, industry and economic organization.

81 **Roman and native in the Low Countries: spheres and interaction.**
Edited by Roel Brandt, Jan Slofstra. Oxford: B. A. R. International, 1983. 222p. bibliog.

The symposium in 1980, at which these papers were given, reflected the influence of British archaeology on a more theoretically based approach to the Roman period. The common factor in all the papers is the anthropological perspective. The articles range from studies of acculturation to romanization in the frontier areas.

82 **Air photography and Celtic field research in the Netherlands.**
J. A. Brongers. Amersfoort, The Netherlands: Rijksdienst voor het Oudheidkundig Bodemonderzoek, 1976. 147p. maps. bibliog.

This work is based on extensive research, documented fully here, around Vaassen in Gelderland. Celtic field settlements were found in the Netherlands from 1600 onwards. The history of Celtic field research as a discipline is covered in a separate chapter.

83 **The flint material from Swifterbant, earlier Neolithic sites of the northern Netherlands; I: sites S–2, S–4 and S–51; II: final reports on Swifterbant.**
P. H. Deckers. *Palaeohistoria*, vol. 21 (1979), p. 143–80. bibliog.

The three sites, available for excavation when the drainage of the IJsselmeer exposed the Flevo Polder, are described in great detail with numerous diagrams and maps showing the distribution of unburned and burned waste, tools and flint material, and line-drawings of the various flakes, blades and scrapers formed.

84 **Early-medieval Dorestad, an archaeo-petrological study.**
H. Kars. Amsterdam: Casparie, 1984. irr. pag. bibliog.

This doctoral dissertation (Free University, Amsterdam, 1984) applies the archaeological technique of petrology – the analysis of natural stone – to the history of Dorestad, the trade centre of the Netherlands in the early Middle Ages. The thesis is comprised of eight articles already published elsewhere, some of them with co-authors. The technique reveals the way in which Roman building materials were used by subsequent generations, and Kars is able to document the commerce of Dorestad by determining the origin of imported stone.

85 **Pre-Roman urnfields in the north of the Netherlands.**
P. B. Kooi, translated from the Dutch by B. M. van der Meulen–Melrose. Groningen, The Netherlands: Wolters–Noordhoff & Bouma, 1979. 203p. maps. bibliog.

This handsomely illustrated study surveys research to date on the urnfields in some detail, and then focuses on burial rites and pottery types. The fifty years of research chronicled here allow Kooi to draw conclusions about the demography and social habits of the prehistoric societies in the north of the country.

86 **The Low Countries.**
S. J. de Laet. London: Thames & Hudson, 1958. New edition, 1962. 240p. maps. bibliog. (Ancient Peoples and Places, vol. 5).

This is a very detailed and scholarly account of the prehistoric period in present-day Belgium and the Netherlands. It is an excellent technical specialist work, with ample illustration, and is a useful handbook on the subject. It is marred only by a rather poor translation into English.

87 **Mesolithic settlement systems in the Netherlands.**
Theron D. Price PhD thesis, University of Michigan, 1975.

Concerned with the behaviour of mesolithic hunter-gatherer societies, this study concentrates on the subsistence activities of the groups, and their size. Large amounts of data are presented and analysed.

Groundwater flow systems in the Netherlands: a groundwater-hydrological approach to the functional relationship between the drainage system and the geological and climatical conditions in a quarternary accumulation area.
See item no. 58.

Animal and man in Holland's past: an investigation of the animal world surrounding man in prehistoric and early historical times in the provinces of North and South Holland.
See item no. 70.

Middeleeuwse geschiedenis der Nederlanden. (Medieval history of the Low Countries.)
See item no. 100.

Agriculture in pre- and protohistoric times.
See item no. 606.

History

General works

88 **Algemene geschiedenis der Nederlanden.** (General history of the Low Countries.)
Edited by D. P. Blok (et al.). Haarlem, The Netherlands: Van Dishoeck, 1975–83. 15 vols. maps. bibliog.

An entirely new and rewritten version of the earlier standard work, sumptuously but usefully illustrated. The individual contributions from leading experts in their fields are, generally speaking, first class; the shortcoming is in the editing, synthesis and presentation of a comprehensive history of the Low Countries.

89 **History of the people of the Netherlands.**
Petrus J. Blok, translated from the Dutch by O. A. Bierstadt, Ruth Putnam. New York: AMS Press, 1970. Reprinted from the original edition of 1898–1912. 5 vols. maps. bibliog.

This is now very dated, but it is the most detailed account of the whole of Dutch political history in English. The translation is of a poor standard and many of Blok's assertions have now been questioned, but the work is inevitably a useful starting point.

90 **An outline of Dutch history.**
Richard de Burnchurch. Baarn, The Netherlands: Wouter Wagner, n.d. [ca. 1980]. 128p.

This copiously illustrated booklet is an elementary introduction to the main phases of Dutch history from the Middle Ages onwards. Unpretentious, but an adequate first point of departure.

91 **Britain and the Netherlands, vol. 8: Clio's mirror: historiography in Britain and the Netherlands.**
Edited by A. C. Duke, C. A. Tamse. Zutphen, The Netherlands: Walburg Pers, 1985. 238p. bibliog.

A collection of papers delivered to the eighth Anglo–Dutch Historical Conference in 1984 dealing with the science and practice of history in the two countries. There are papers on the historiography of the Dutch Revolt, the Republic, the close of the 18th century, the Second World War, and the work of Fruin, Blok and Geyl.

92 **The Benelux countries: an historical survey.**
F. Gunther Eyck. Princeton, Indiana: Van Nostrand, 1959. 191p. bibliog.

The first half of the book is a very brief history of the Low Countries from Roman times to the 1950s, concentrating on the 19th and 20th centuries. The colonies, and culture, receive minimal treatment. The second half is made up of twenty historical documents, in English, many of which remain useful (for example, in teaching).

93 **Kalendarium: geschiedenis van de Lage Landen in jaartallen.**
(Calendar: a history of the Low Countries, year by year.)
H. P. H. Jansen. Utrecht; Antwerp, Belgium: Het Spectrum, 1971. Reprinted, 1974. 264p.

Covers the period 240000 BC to 1974 AD. This is in effect an elementary 'basic facts' reference work by one of the best Dutch professional historians of his day. Most of the book is arranged chronologically, year by year, with occasional short essays on the main issues, sources, etc., and includes useful appendixes. Belgium is also covered.

94 **The new Cambridge modern history.**
Edited by G. R. Potter (et al.). Cambridge, England: Cambridge University Press, 1957–79. 14 vols. maps. bibliog.

The Netherlands receives regular mention in this standard work, but, as a small country, the coverage is inevitably haphazard except for the 17th century (on which E. H. Kossmann contributes an excellent chapter in vol. IV). The following specific chapters, by a variety of authors, deal exclusively with the Netherlands: vol. I, chapter VIII; vol. III, chapter IX–2; vol. IV, chapter XII; vol. V, chapters VII and XI; vol. IX, chapter XVII–A.

95 **The Dutch in London: the influence of an immigrant community.**
David Ormrod. London: Her Majesty's Stationery Office, 1973. 31p. bibliog.

The Dutch were the most numerous of the aliens in London in the 16th and 17th centuries and tended therefore to take the brunt of the blame for unfair competition and housing shortages, although Elizabeth I, during her reign, had attempted to turn the skills of the Dutch immigrants to improving the economic welfare of the country. In this they were notably successful in the textile and related industries, in brewing, in pottery and in many skilled crafts up to the

18th century, when London depended increasingly on the support of Dutch capital investment.

96 **A short history of the Netherlands.**
Ivo Schöffer. Amsterdam: De Lange, 1973. 200p. bibliog.

The best short survey in English, but unfortunately out of print at the time of writing. Covers the whole period, with useful appendixes on election results since 1922. Schöffer is Professor of History at Leiden University.

97 **Doctoraal scripties geschiedenis 1980–1984.** (Dissertations for the degree of Doctorandus in history 1980–84.)
H. J. Smit. Amsterdam: Swidoc, 1985. 97p. bibliog.

The Doctorandus degree is the first degree taken at Dutch universities, and is (very roughly) equivalent to the Anglo–American Masters degree. This is a list of the 896 dissertations written in part-fulfilment of that degree in history at Dutch universities in the space of 5 years. Every subject within the study of history is covered.

98 **The carriers of Europe: a concise history of Holland.**
F. J. van Wel, translated from the Dutch by N. G. Hazelhoff.
Baarn, The Netherlands: Wereldvenster, 1963. 64p.

A short elementary introduction to the whole of Dutch history, concentrating on the period after 1500.

The Scheldt question to 1839.
See item no. 488.

Holland and Britain.
See item no. 858.

A. A. G. Bijdragen. (Contributions from the Department of Rural History.)
See item no. 925.

Acta Historiae Neerlandicae/Low Countries History Yearbook.
See item no. 927.

Britain and the Netherlands.
See item no. 929.

Dutch Crossing: a Journal of Low Countries Studies.
See item no. 936.

Biografisch woordenboek der Nederlanden. (Biographical dictionary of the Netherlands.)
See item no. 976.

Biografisch woordenboek van Nederland. (Biographical dictionary of the Netherlands.)
See item no. 978.

Dutch medical biography: a biographical dictionary of Dutch physicians and surgeons 1475–1975.
See item no. 979.

Nieuw Nederlandsch biografisch woordenboek. (New Dutch biographical dictionary.)
See item no. 980.

Bibliografie der geschiedenis van Nederland. (Bibliography of the history of the Netherlands.)
See item no. 989.

Historical research in the Low Countries 1970–1975: a critical survey.
See item no. 990.

Historical research in the Low Countries 1981–1983: a critical survey.
See item no. 1004.

Splendid ceremonies: state entries and royal funerals in the Low Countries, 1515–1791.
See item no. 1009.

Repertorium van boeken en tijdschriftartikelen betreffende de geschiedenis van Nederland. (Repertorium of books and periodical articles concerning the history of the Netherlands.)
See item no. 1019.

Before the Revolt (ca. 1550)

99 **The waning of the Middle Ages: a study in the forms of life, thought and art in France and the Netherlands in the fourteenth and fifteenth centuries.**
Johan Huizinga, translated from the Dutch by F. Hopman. Harmondsworth, England: Penguin Books, 1955, various reprints.

This brilliant and entertaining study, originally published in 1924, is enjoying a revival at present, largely because of the praise bestowed upon it by the French 'Annales' school of historians. This work is a true classic, and still rewarding. The theme of the book takes the form of portraying the courtly culture of the period in terms of the chivalric code.

100 **Middeleeuwse geschiedenis der Nederlanden.** (Medieval history of the Low Countries.)
H. P. H. Jansen. Utrecht; Antwerp, Belgium: Het Spectrum, 1965. 6th imp. 1979. 302p.

An unpretentious handbook on a vast subject by a leading academic historian. Covers the period from prehistory to the eve of the Reformation.

101 **The Burgundian Netherlands.**
Walter Prevenier, Wim P. Blockmans, translated from the Dutch by P. King, Y. Mead, picture research by An Blockmans–Delva. Antwerp, Belgium: Fonds Mercator, 1985. 403p. maps. bibliog.

This lavishly and superbly illustrated publication is by two of the foremost scholars of the period (1380–1530), and has comprehensive sections on the ecological, economic, social, political and cultural aspects of the Burgundian era.

102 **Valois Burgundy.**
Richard Vaughan. London: Allen Lane, 1975. 254p. bibliog.

This volume is Vaughan's synthesis of his four major biographical studies, published between 1962 and 1973, of the four great dukes of Burgundy. It pays particular attention to the development of central state institutions and emphasizes dynastic considerations.

The making of Dutch towns: a study in urban development from the tenth to the seventeenth centuries.
See item no. 29.

Roman and native in the Low Countries: spheres and interaction.
See item no. 81.

Early-medieval Dorestad, an archaeo-petrological study.
See item no. 84.

Philip of Leyden: a fourteenth century jurist.
See item no. 438.

Revolt and Republic (ca. 1550–1795)

103 **Venice and Amsterdam: a study of seventeenth-century élites.**
Peter Burke. London: Temple Smith, 1974. 154p. bibliog.

A comparative study of two élites, using a degree of sociological methodology. Work in the Amsterdam municipal archives produces a very readable prosopographical account of the patricians in control of the city in its Golden Age.

104 **The Dutch Republic in Europe in the Seven Years War.**
Alice Clare Carter. London: Macmillan, 1971. 181p. map. bibliog.

A reworking of a thesis for a Masters degree at London University. The book is concerned to show that Dutch neutrality in the Seven Years War was not a result of weakness towards either France or Britain, but a manifestation of a Dutch policy based on Dutch aims.

105 **Guillaume le Taciturne de la 'Généralité' de Bourgogne à la République de Sept Provinces-Unies.** (William the Silent from the Burgundian 'Generality' to the Republic of the Seven United Provinces.)
Yves Cazaux. Paris: Albin Michel, 1970. 379p. map. bibliog.

The biographer divides Orange's public life into four main sections: 'Tolerance' (1553–59), 'Politics' (1560–67), 'Revolution' (1567–76), and 'Democracy' (1577–84).

106 **Ambassadors and secret agents: the diplomacy of the first Earl of Malmesbury at The Hague.**
Alfred Cobban. London: Johnathan Cape, 1954. 255p. map. bibliog.

A biographical study of Sir James Harris in the years 1783–88, during which period he was British minister at The Hague. The book, though now dated, offers clear insights into the world of international diplomacy, and into the Dutch Patriot Revolt of the 1780s.

107 **Calvinist preaching and iconoclasm in the Netherlands 1544–1569.**
Phyllis M. Crew. Cambridge, England: Cambridge University Press, 1978. 221p. bibliog.

Deals with the role and nature of Calvinist ministers in the period leading up to the image-breaking year of 1566. Crew argues that, far from being radical revolutionaries, the ministers achieved their support by appearing as respectable leaders of a legitimate Reform movement.

108 **The Maritime Powers, 1721–1740: a study of Anglo–Dutch relations in the age of Walpole.**
Hugh Dunthorne. New York: Garland Publishing, 1987. 350p. bibliog.

A close-up review of the shifts in the internal policies of Britain and the Netherlands at a time of international tension, which ultimately resulted in the breakdown of an alliance of the two 'Maritime Powers'.

109 **The Netherlands in the seventeenth century.**
Pieter Geyl. London: Benn, 1964. 2 vols. maps. bibliog.

Geyl is perhaps the most famous Dutch historian outside the Netherlands. This work is derived from his *Geschiedenis van de Nederlandse stam* (History of the Dutch people), a work of the 1930s. It is still however a respected narrative account and is constantly referred to in the literature.

110 **The Dutch in the seventeenth century.**
K. H. D. Haley. London: Thames & Hudson, 1972. 216p. map. bibliog.

A generously illustrated account of the 'foundations' of Dutch society, concentrating on economic and political matters, and including a long section on 'Dutch civilization'. Now dated, but still a good introduction to the subject.

111 **An English diplomat in the Low Countries: Sir William Temple and John de Witt 1665–1672.**
K. H. D. Haley. London: Oxford University Press, 1986. 320p. map. bibliog.

Taking a biographical approach and making use of primary material from the Low Countries, France and England, this account of Temple's work comes from the hand of one of our most accomplished historians of the period, and concentrates on the years 1665–72, and Temple's relationship with De Witt.

112 **Gouda in Revolt: particularism and pacifism in the Revolt of the Netherlands 1572–1588.**
C. C. Hibben. Utrecht: HES Publishers, 1983. 298p. bibliog.

A case-study based on a London University PhD thesis, paying particular attention to religion and politics.

113 **Dutch civilisation in the seventeenth century and other essays.**
Johan Huizinga, selected by Pieter Geyl, F. W. N. Hugenholtz, translated by Arnold J. Pomerans. London: Collins, 1968. 288p. bibliog.

This dated but classic essay dwells on the unique aspects of the Dutch Golden Age which distinguish it from other cultural achievements. Other essays are on 'The spirit of the Netherlands' and on historiography.

114 **The Dutch Republic and the Hispanic world 1606–1661.**
Jonathan I. Israel. Oxford: Clarendon Press, 1982. 478p. maps. bibliog.

A chronological account of the later stages of the Dutch Revolt in the wider context of the Spanish Empire. A highly scholarly work, based on extensive original research.

115 **Texts concerning the Revolt of the Netherlands.**
Edited by Ernst H. Kossmann, A. F. Mellink. Cambridge, England: Cambridge University Press, 1974. 295p. bibliog.

A collection of sixty-seven documents from the period 1565–88 covering high politics. The fifty-page introduction contains an excellent assessment of the impact of the events of the Revolt on political theory.

116 **The ideological origins of the Batavian Revolution: history and politics in the Dutch Republic 1747–1800.**
I. Leonard Leeb. The Hague: Nijhoff, 1973. 300p. bibliog.

Emphasizes the international nature of the movements of the period and uses the technique of analysing political vocabulary, concentrating especially on contemporary views of the past.

117 **The rise of the Dutch Republic: a history.**
John Lothrop Motley. London: Dent; New York: Dutton, 1906. 3 vols. bibliog.

A classic work, first published in 1855, in Motley's distinctive style of prose, in the Whiggish tradition of historical writing. Dated, with many inaccuracies and much bigotry, but still highly entertaining and a worthwhile introduction. This has been, for many years, the only synthesis available.

118 **The Dutch Revolt.**
Geoffrey Parker. Harmondsworth, England: Penguin Books, 1979. (First published by Allen Lane, 1977.) 327p. maps. bibliog.

An excellent and highly readable account of the period ca. 1549–1609, with much original research and analysis. Particularly good on the iconoclastic movement, and in its determination to set the Revolt in a European context.

119 **Culture and society in the Dutch Republic during the seventeenth century.**
J. L. Price. London: Batsford, 1974. 260p. map. bibliog.

Perhaps the best single-volume assessment of the achievement of the Dutch Golden Age, concentrating on explaining art and literature in the context of the social and economic background.

120 **Traders, artists, burghers: a cultural history of Amsterdam in the 17th century.**
Deric Regin. Assen, The Netherlands: Van Gorcum, 1976. 214p. bibliog.

A detailed account of the capital's Golden Age, focusing on everything from the psychology of commerce to popular culture. A satisfying study of bourgeois culture, based on extensive archive work. Each chapter is organized around a significant year, in the range 1578–1697.

121 **John de Witt: statesman of the 'true freedom'.**
Herbert H. Rowen. Cambridge, England: Cambridge University Press, 1986. 243p. bibliog.

A short, readable version of the author's major study of De Witt *John de Witt* (Princeton, New Jersey: Princeton University Press, 1978), but not simply an abridgement.

122 **The Low Countries in early modern times: selected documents.**
Edited by Herbert H. Rowen. London: Macmillan, 1972. 291p. bibliog.

An illuminating collection of extracts from the sources covering the period ca. 1500–1800, translated and edited by the biographer of John de Witt (see previous item).

123 **The embarrassment of riches: a history of Dutch civilization in the Golden Age.**
Simon Schama. New York: Knopf; London: Collins, 1987. 325p. bibliog.

A controversial and stimulating analysis of the civilization of the Dutch Golden Age, concentrating on the juxtaposition of great wealth and a Calvinist morality.

124 **Observations upon the United Provinces of the Netherlands.**
Sir William Temple, edited by Sir George Clark. Oxford: Clarendon Press, 1972. 154p. map.

This edition, with an introduction, index, glossary and map by George Clark, was taken from the text of the first edition (London: Gellibrand, 1675. 255p. Available in facsimile from Ann Arbor, Michigan: University Microfilms, 1976). Temple was the British Ambassador at The Hague between 1668 and 1670, and his first-hand account is one of the most illuminating of the century. He gives chapters on the rise of the Republic, government, the people, religion, trade, armed forces, taxes and 'the causes of their fall in 1672'. At the time of publication the English and the Dutch were embroiled in the Third Anglo–Dutch war.

125 **Oldenbarnevelt.**
Jan den Tex, translated from the Dutch by R. B. Powell. Cambridge, England: Cambridge University Press, 1973. 2 vols. map. bibliog.

Translated from the monumental five-volume set in Dutch (Groningen, The Netherlands: Tjeenk Willink, 1960–72), this is a work in the finest and fullest 'life and times' biographical tradition, providing a sound account of the period around 1600.

126 **The Dutch Republic and the civilisation of the seventeenth century.**
Charles H. Wilson. London: Weidenfeld & Nicolson, 1968. 255p. map. bibliog. (World University Library).

An illustrated essay concentrating on the social, cultural and economic aspects of the Republic, with an interesting and unusual chapter on 'Holland and Scotland'.

Migrant labour in Europe 1600–1900: the drift to the North Sea.
See item no. 242.

Judicial violence in the Dutch Republic: corporal punishment, executions and torture in Amsterdam 1650–1750.
See item no. 443.

Leiden university in the seventeenth century: an exchange of learning.
See item no. 675.

Hugo Grotius, a great European 1583–1645.
See item no. 846.

The Anglo–Dutch contribution to the civilization of early modern society: an Anglo–Netherlands symposium.
See item no. 857.

The world of Hugo Grotius (1583–1645: proceedings of the International Colloquium organised by the Grotius Committee of the Royal Netherlands Academy of Arts and Sciences, Rotterdam 6–9 April 1983).
See item no. 859.

Modern history (ca. 1795 to the present)

127 **The Second World War and Dutch society: continuity and change.**
J. C. H. Blom. In: *Britain and the Netherlands*, vol. VI: *War and society: papers delivered to the sixth Anglo–Dutch historical conference*. Edited by A. C. Duke, C. A. Tamse. The Hague: Nijhoff, 1977, p. 228–49. bibliog.

This conference paper deals with the impact of the Second World War on the Netherlands, and examines the degree of continuity between events pre-1940 and post-1945. Blom concludes that the only major change precipitated by the war was in Dutch foreign policy.

128 **The Dutch crisis in the eighteen-forties.**
J. C. Boogman. In: *Britain and the Netherlands: papers delivered to the first Anglo–Dutch historical conference.* Edited by J. S. Bromley, E. H. Kossmann. London: Chatto & Windus, 1960, p. 192–203. bibliog.

Emphasizes the decade as a watershed between the autocracy of William I and the liberalism of Thorbecke, but is also concerned to show that the constitutional revision of 1848 was just one aspect in a decade of general change.

129 **Thorbecke: a liberal statesman; J. R. Thorbecke, challenge and response.**
J. C. Boogman. *Acta Historiae Neerlandicae*, vol. 7 (1974), p. 122–45. bibliog.

An introduction and an essay on the the founder of Dutch liberalism in the 19th century. A general all-round portrait of this politician who dominated the third quarter of the 19th century, and one of the very few in English.

130 **Delta.**
Vol. 13, no. 3 (autumn 1970) (Special issue).

This issue of the journal was devoted to the subject of Dutch history between 1920 and 1970. It includes excellent articles on economic development (by Johan de Vries) and on the Protestant churches (by J. J. Buskes), as well as more general socio-political coverage.

131 **Documents of the persecution of the Dutch jewry, 1940–1945.**
Joods Historisch Museum, Amsterdam. Amsterdam: Athenaeum- Polak, Van Gennep, 1969. Reprinted, 1979. 173p. bibliog.

A publication to accompany an exhibition held in the Jewish Historical Museum in Amsterdam in 1969. Many of the documents are reproduced here in facsimile, and there is a complete catalogue of those which were on display.

132 **Remember Arnhem.**
John Fairlee, introduction by R. E. Urquhart. Aldershot, England: Pegasus Journal, 1978. 235p. maps. bibliog.

This is a lively and authentic account of the events from January 1941 to September 1944, including the prologue to the parachute landings and the heroic, but finally disastrous battle for Arnhem bridge itself. It is well illustrated with photographs and has a comprehensive index of personal names. Fairlee served with the Reconnaissance Corps and is now head of the History Department at Jordanhill College of Education.

133 **Fascism and Nazism in the Netherlands 1929–39.**
Erik Hansen. *European Studies Review*, vol. 11 (1981), p. 355–85. bibliog.

Hansen draws a rigid distinction between Dutch Fascists, who were fragmented, often confessional, but quite harmless, and were keen admirers of the Italian State in the 1930s, and the Dutch National Socialists (NSBers), who looked to Berlin, were highly organized, and likely to become a mass movement. Provides a useful exposition of these movements against a socio-economic backdrop.

134 **Fremdherrschaft und Kollaboration: die Niederlande unter deutscher Bezatzung 1940–1945.** (Foreign rule and collaboration: The Netherlands under German occupation 1940–45.)
G. Hirschfeld. Stuttgart, FRG: Deutsche Verlags–Anstalt, 1984. 311p. bibliog.

A 1980 doctoral dissertation from Dusseldorf, based on research done in 1976 and 1977. Deals explicitly with the concept of collaboration.

135 **The modern Netherlands.**
Frank E. Huggett. London: Pall Mall, 1971. 272p. maps. bibliog.

A convenient general account in English of the modern period, with a useful bibliography of English-language books.

136 **The historiography of the Netherlands in the Second World War.**
L. de Jong. In: *Britain and the Netherlands*, vol. 8: *Clio's mirror: historiography in Britain and the Netherlands*. Edited by A. C. Duke, C. A. Tamse. Zutphen, The Netherlands: Walburg Pers, 1985, p. 215–31. bibliog.

The official Dutch historian of the Second World War, and author of a multi-volume work on the subject, explains the methodological problems of his life's work.

137 **The Low Countries 1780–1940.**
Ernst H. Kossmann. Oxford: Clarendon Press, 1978. 784p. maps. bibliog. (Oxford History of Modern Europe).

This standard work is a masterly synthesis of recent work on the political, social and intellectual history of the Netherlands and Belgium in this period. A new edition of the Dutch version (1976), taking the analysis up to 1980, appeared in 1986: it is to be hoped that an English translation of the update will appear before too long.

138 **Isolation, integration and secularization: a case study of the Netherlands.**
Gerald Larkin. *Sociological Review*, vol. 22 (1974), p. 401–18. bibliog.

A sketch of Dutch society in the 20th century in its vertical arrangement known as *verzuiling*, or vertical pluralism. Larkin's paper, which is a useful first introduction to the subject, argues that Dutch society has not undergone significant secularization, and that this has not harmed its industrialization or modernization in the least.

139 **The Netherlands at war: 1940–1945.**
W.B. Maass. London: Abelard–Schuman, 1970. 264p. maps. bibliog.

A roughly chronological arrangement, with some illustrations. The treatment is popular, and there are better accounts available, like W. Warmbrunn's *The Dutch under German occupation, 1940–1945* (q.v.).

140 **Refugees from Nazi Germany in the Netherlands 1933–1940.**
Bob Moore. Dordrecht, The Netherlands: Nijhoff, 1986. 241p. bibliog.

Arising out of the author's PhD research and based on primary sources, this study deals with the stream of refugees from Germany and Austria flowing into the Netherlands in the 1930s and 1940s, most particularly Jews, Socialists and Communists. Dutch government policy formulation and execution is examined. Despite the admission of 33,000 refugees, apparently there were many who were refused entry.

141 **The Netherlands: an historical and cultural survey, 1795–1977.**
Gerald Newton. London: Ernest Benn, 1978. 312p. bibliog. (Nations of the Modern World).

The ten chapters cover a wide range, including 'The Dutch language', 'Literature', 'The dispersal of Empire', and 'Socialism and women's rights'. Often ill-informed and inaccurate, it is nonetheless readable, and one of the few general studies of the period in English.

142 **Les radicaux aux Pays-Bas (1840–1851).** (Radicals in the Netherlands (1840–51).)
M. J. F. Robijns. *Acta Historiae Neerlandicae*, vol. 5 (1971), p. 103–34. bibliog.

A synopsis by the author of his *Radicalen in Nederland* (Leiden: 1967), this is an intriguing study of party politics in the turbulent decade of the 1840s, and especially of the impact made by radical politicians on King William II, with the ensuing constitutional changes of 1848.

History. Modern history (ca. 1795 to the present)

143 **Patriots and liberators: revolution in the Netherlands 1780–1813.**
Simon Schama. London: Collins, 1977. 745p. maps. bibliog.

A brilliant and forceful narrative, relying on new interpretations of the period, particularly that of the historian C. H. E. de Wit. A highly readable synthesis of existing scholarship, with extensive new work as well. It has become the standard work on the period.

144 **The position of the Jews during the German occupation of the Netherlands: some observations.**
B. A. Sijes. *Acta Historiae Neerlandicae*, vol. 9 (1976), p. 170–92. bibliog.

Originally a paper at a conference in Israel on the rescue of Jews during the Second World War, this essay looks at how the 16,000–19,000 Jews who went into hiding during the war were helped to survive and escape deportation.

145 **Neither resistance nor collaboration: historians and the problem of the 'Nederlandse Unie'.**
M. L. Smith. *History*, vol. 235 (June 1987), p. 251–78. bibliog.

The 'Unie' was a large-scale political organization in the Netherlands during the Second World War, which showed signs both of collaboration with the Germans and of resistance against the occupying forces. On the basis of considerable archive research, Smith shows how most Dutch historians' views of the war experience have been distorted by an obsession with classifying every movement as either 'collaborationist' or as part of the resistance movement.

146 **Anton Mussert and the N.S.B.: 1931–45.**
Lawrence D. Stokes. *History*, vol. 56, no. 188 (Oct. 1971), p. 387–407. bibliog.

Mussert was a leader of the main Fascist Party in the Netherlands, the NSB (National Socialist Union), in the 1930s and during the Second World War, and was executed by the Dutch in May 1946. The activities of the Dutch Fascists and their leader are reliably reported here.

147 **The party structure of Holland and the outer provinces in the nineteenth century.**
Theo van Tijn. In: *Britain and the Netherlands*, vol. IV: *Papers delivered to the fourth Anglo–Dutch historical conference*. Edited by J. S. Bromley, E. H. Kossmann. The Hague: Nijhoff, 1971, p. 176–207. bibliog.

A closely argued article maintaining that liberalism was essentially provincial until the 1870s, when changes in the franchise began to mean the inclusion of the lower middle classes in the political process.

148 **Twenty years in the history of Amsterdam: the social development of the Dutch capital from the mid-nineteenth century to 1876.**
Theo van Tijn. *Acta Historiae Neerlandicae*, vol. 3 (1986), p. 215–46. bibliog.

A synopsis by the author of his doctoral dissertation (Amsterdam University, 1965), which was a seminal exercise in Dutch integrated social history, by which Van Tijn means the history of social groups in relation to one another. All aspects of the city's life come under examination, with special attention to the growth of the labour movement.

149 **The Dutch under German occupation, 1940–1945.**
Werner Warmbrunn. Stanford, California: Stanford University Press, 1963. 338p. map. bibliog.

An expanded version of a 1955 PhD dissertation, this is a rare English-language scholarly work on the subject, and therefore still of value, despite being rather dated. It is concerned with the reaction of the people to the German occupying forces, and makes the important distinction between the two phases of 1940–44, and the 'Hunger Winter' of 1944–45.

Lonely but not alone.
See item no. 26.

Aardrijkskundig woordenboek der Nederlanden. (Geographical dictionary of the Netherlands.)
See item no. 27.

Religion and political development in nineteenth-century Holland.
See item no. 337.

The dynamics of Dutch politics.
See item no. 400.

Consociationalism, center and periphery in the Netherlands.
See item no. 401.

Democratic parties in the Low Countries and Germany: origins and historical developments.
See item no. 424.

Die Niederlande und das deutsche Exil 1933–1940. (The Netherlands and the German exodus 1933–1940.)
See item no. 493.

The origins and consolidation of Dutch social democracy, 1894–1914.
See item no. 633.

Deelname aan het lager onderwijs in Nederland gedurende de negentiende eeuw. (Participation in primary education in the Netherlands in the 19th century.)
See item no. 652.

School and politics in the Netherlands, 1796–1814.
See item no. 656.

Anne Frank: the diary of a young girl.
See item no. 727.

Economic history

150 **Dutch enterprise and the world bullion trade 1550–1800.**
Arthur Attman, translated by Eva Green, Allan Green. Gothenburg, Sweden: Kungl. Vetenskaps- och Vitterhets-Samhället, 1983. 113p. bibliog. (Acta Regiae Societatis Scientarium et Litterarum Gothoburgensis, Humaniora, no. 23).

In the period under consideration precious metals came to Europe mainly from South America to Spain and Portugal. The Dutch were instrumental in the trade which then distributed this bullion around the world, especially to the Orient. Attman assesses the size of the trade and the Dutch role in servicing not only their own trade, but that of England as well.

151 **Dutch capitalism and world capitalism: capitalisme hollandais et capitalisme mondial.**
Edited by Maurice Aymard. Cambridge, England: Cambridge University Press; Paris: Edition de la Maison des Sciences de l'Homme, 1982. 312p. bibliog.

The proceedings of a 1976 Paris conference, concerned with the economic history of the 17th century. The papers are set against a background of W. Wallerstein's theory of a world economic system.

152 **Consumer behaviour and economic growth in the modern economy.**
Edited by Henri Baudet, Henk van der Meulen. London; Canberra, Australia: Croom Helm, 1982. 283p. bibliog.

The printed proceedings of a conference held in 1981 at Groningen University, and a contribution to the 'standard of living debate' amongst economic and social historians around the world. The introduction, conclusion, and a lengthy paper on Dutch 'Food consumption and welfare 1852–1911' (p. 73–108), all by the editors, are of interest in the Dutch field.

153 **Industrialization and economic growth in the Netherlands during the nineteenth century: an integration of recent studies.**
R. W. J. M. Bos. *Low Countries History Yearbook*, vol. 15 (1982), p. 21–58. bibliog.

Bos has produced several articles on the 19th-century Dutch economy: this is a synthesis in English of his main ideas. It takes the form of a review article dealing with recent research, concentrates on capital availability and puts the Dutch economy into its European context.

154 **Academic economics in Holland 1800–1870.**
Irene Hasenburg Butter. The Hague: Nijhoff, 1969. 162p. bibliog. (Studies in Social Life, no. 13).

An original study, concerned in the first place with the growth of economics departments in Dutch universities. Butter also gets involved with the development of economic thought in the Netherlands in the 19th century, particularly on the subject of endemic poverty.

155 **Getting, spending and investing in early modern times: essays on Dutch, English and Huguenot economic history.**
Alice Clare Carter. Assen, The Netherlands: Van Gorcum, 1975. 179p. bibliog.

A collection of various articles by Carter, which have previously appeared elsewhere. The Dutch subjects are centred around public finance in the 18th century, with some attention to foreign policy as well.

156 **Enterprise and history: essays in honour of Charles Wilson.**
Edited by D. C. Coleman, Peter Mathias. Cambridge, England: Cambridge University Press, 1984. 290p. bibliog.

Several of the essays in this Festschrift concern the Netherlands. David Ormrod and Pieter Klein provide papers on the commercial history of the Republic, and H. Baudet writes on Dutch economic interests in the East Indies.

157 **Long-term changes in growth in the Netherlands since the middle of the nineteenth century.**
J. B. D. Derksen. In: *Konjunktur, Krise, Gesellschaft: wirtschaftliche Wechsellagen und soziale Entwicklung im 19. und 20. Jahrhundert.* Edited by Dietmar Petzina, Ger van Roon. Stuttgart, FRG: Klett–Cotta, 1981, p. 23–35. bibliog.

Derksen's subject is the sluggish movement of the Dutch economy towards industrialization, and he uses an econometric approach. The analysis is inconclusive because of inadequate statistical material, but nonetheless provides a sharp insight into Dutch economic development.

158 **The creation of a national Dutch economy, 1795–1909.**
Richard Thomas Griffiths. *Tijdschrift voor Geschiedenis*, vol. 95, no. 4 (1982), p. 513–37. bibliog.

Concentrates on the way in which the transport infrastructure was built up in the 19th century, and on regional imbalances in the economy. There are interesting provincial breakdowns of various indicators for the Dutch economy.

159 **The economy and politics of the Netherlands since 1945.**
Edited by Richard Thomas Griffiths. The Hague: Nijhoff, 1980. 311p. maps. bibliog.

A distinguished group of authors, including the present Prime Minister of the Netherlands, Ruud Lubbers, have provided a wide range of essays on the post-war period. The chapter subjects include the economy, economic policy, counter-inflation policy, natural gas, regional imbalances, the planning service, domestic politics, voting, government formation, the end of Empire, and the EEC. Indispensable.

160 **Industrial retardation in the Netherlands 1830–1850.**
Richard Thomas Griffiths. The Hague: Nijhoff, 1979. 235p. maps. bibliog.

A reworking of a Cambridge University PhD thesis. This is a major work of reassessment in Dutch economic history, maintaining that there was appreciable growth in the period, in contrast to the received wisdom which holds that the 19th century was largely an economic write-off.

161 **The Low Countries.**
Jan Albert van Houtte, L. van Buyten. In: *An introduction to the sources of European economic history 1500–1800*, vol. I: *Western Europe*. Edited by Charles Wilson, G. Parker. London: Weidenfeld & Nicolson, 1977, p. 81–114. bibliog.

This essay concentrates on the urban growth in Amsterdam and Antwerp, and the high status attached to mercantile professions, which ended the remains of feudalism. The authors see the Netherlands as being in a state of decline after 1700.

162 **Economic development of Belgium and the Netherlands from the beginning of the modern era: an essay in compared history.**
Jan Albert van Houtte. *Journal of European Economic History*, vol. 1 (1972), p. 100–20. bibliog.

Master of the summarizing synthesis, Van Houtte describes the Low Countries' economies from the 16th century to the present day. This article contains little hard information, but is a good interpretative introduction to the subject.

163 **An economic history of the Low Countries, 800–1800.**
Jan Albert van Houtte. London: Weidenfeld & Nicolson, 1977. 342p. bibliog.

A revised and expanded version of the bulk of Van Houtte's standard work on the socio-economic history of the Netherlands and Belgium, published (in Dutch) in 1964. Each major chapter has a section on population, agriculture, industry, trade and finance.

164 **Industrial growth in the Netherlands (1850–1914).**
J. A. de Jonge. *Acta Historiae Neerlandicae*, vol. 5 (1971), p. 159–212. bibliog.

A synopsis of the author's doctoral dissertation of 1968, on industrialization, which is the definitive and standard work on the subject. He subjects each manufacturing sector to a detailed scrutiny, and comes to the conclusion that, in so far as one can talk of 'Industrial Revolution' in the Netherlands, it occurred in the 1890s. Previous orthodoxy had favoured the 1860s.

165 **The role of the outer provinces in the process of Dutch economic growth in the nineteenth century.**
J. A. de Jonge. In: *Britain and the Netherlands*, vol. 4: *Papers delivered to the fourth Anglo–Dutch Historical Conference*. Edited by J. S. Bromley, E. H. Kossmann. The Hague: Nijhoff, 1971, p. 208–25. bibliog.

Using figures for taxation on industry, De Jonge shows that the relative backwardness of provinces outside the central Holland area, which was apparent in 1850, had virtually disappeared by 1914.

166 **Depression and policy in the thirties.**
Pieter W. Klein. *Acta Historiae Neerlandicae*, vol. 8 (1975), p. 123–58. bibliog.

A translation of an earlier article in Dutch (1973), suggesting that blame should not so readily be laid at the door of the Dutch leaders for the disaster of the 1930s. Instead Klein looks to the structure of the Dutch economy itself as it had evolved prior to the decade of depression.

167 **Failed transitions to modern industrial society: Renaissance Italy and seventeenth century Holland.**
Edited by Frederick Krantz, Paul M. Hohenberg. Montreal: Interuniversity Centre for European Studies, 1975. 105p. bibliog.

Three papers are included on the Netherlands, by D. Ormrod, K. W. Swart and E. H. Kossmann, as well as commentaries by other historians. The subject matter is the postponed transition from Golden Age to Industrial Revolution.

168 **Long-term trends in income and wealth inequality in the Netherlands 1808–1940.**
J. M. M. de Meere. *Quantum: Historical Social Research*, vol. 27 (July 1983), p. 8–37. bibliog.

The point of departure is Simon Kuznets' work on long-run income distribution patterns. De Meere establishes that inequality increased between 1850 and 1880, declined between 1880 and 1914, grew dramatically during the First World War, and declined again in the interbellum.

169 **The development of the economies of continental Europe 1850–1914.**
Alan Milward, S. B. Saul. London: Allen & Unwin, 1977. 555p. bibliog.

Chapter 3 of this standard work, entitled 'The economic development of Belgium and the Netherlands 1850–1914', is probably the best account of the economic history of the Netherlands in this period in English. The arrangement is by economic sector, and emphasizes the importance of social modernization in the agricultural sector for economic development in general.

170 **Industralization in the Low Countries, 1795–1850.**
Joel Mokyr. New Haven, Connecticut: Yale University Press, 1976. 295p. bibliog.

Mokyr is a cliometrician, or a theoretical economist working on historical material. His aim, in this revised PhD dissertation, is to construct a model of industrialization and test it with the Dutch and Belgian experiences. His model has stood up well since publication; his main conclusion on Dutch industrialization was that high wage levels held back development.

171 **Nederlandsche prijsgeschiedenis.** (Dutch price history.)
Nicolaas Wilhelmus Posthumus. Leiden: Brill, 1943–64. 2 vols. bibliog.

As part of an international enquiry into the history of prices, this large-scale work provides data from 1348 to 1914 for goods on the Amsterdam market and for various items regularly bought in by institutions in Leiden, Utrecht and Amsterdam. The tables have all titles translated into English.

172 **Religious factors in early Dutch capitalism 1550–1650.**
Jelle C. Riemersma. The Hague, Paris: Mouton, 1967. 98p. bibliog. (Studies in the Social Sciences, no. 2).

Taking as a point of departure Max Weber's hypothesis of a causal link between Protestantism and capitalism, Riemersma examines Dutch Calvinist teachings on economic matters in the early Republic. This represents a revealing investigation into contemporary economic thought.

173 **The Dutch economy after 1650: decline or growth?**
James C. Riley. *Journal of European Economic History*, vol. 13, no. 3 (1984), p. 521–69. bibliog.

Riley reviews research on the economy of the late Republic, and pulls the material together very skilfully. The three main hypotheses under consideration are stagnation, decline and growth. Riley's sympathies are with the 'growth' theory, though the conclusions are by no means definite.

174 **Tobacco growing in Holland in the seventeenth and eighteenth centuries: a case study of the innovative spirit of Dutch peasants.**
H. K. Roessingh. *Low Countries History Yearbook*, vol. 11 (1978), p. 18–54. bibliog.

A summary of the author's doctoral dissertation of 1976, and one of the most surprising studies in agricultural history, showing the adaptability and flexibility of what we had always thought were immovably conservative farmers.

175 **Industrialization without national patents: the Netherlands, 1869–1912: Switzerland 1850–1907.**
Eric Schiff. Princeton, New Jersey: Princeton University Press, 1971. 137p. bibliog.

Schiff tests the general hypothesis that a lack of a patent law protecting technological innovations and inventions hinders industrialization, and he uses the Dutch and Swiss experiences as case-studies. In doing so he also provides a brief history of Dutch industry from 1850 to the First World War.

176 **Yield ratios 810–1820.**
B. H. Slicher van Bath. *A. A. G. Bijdragen*, vol. 10 (1963), p. 1–264. bibliog.

This celebrated study uses the brilliant assumption that an increase in yields as measured by the ratio between harvest and seedcorn is a reliable indicator of economic development in a predominantly agricultural economy. Most of the work is a collection of data from all over Europe; much of it is from the Netherlands, from the 9th century to the 19th century.

177 **Barges and capitalism: passenger transportation in the Dutch economy, 1632–1839.**
Jan de Vries. *A. A. G. Bijdragen*, vol. 21 (1978), p. 33–398. bibliog.

De Vries traces the rise and fall of an integrated system of transport in the western Dutch Republic which was, he claims, central to the prosperity of the Golden Age in providing a truly reliable service and nurturing a modern economic mentality.

178 **The decline and rise of the Dutch economy, 1675–1900.**
Jan de Vries. *Research in Economic History*, supplement 3 (1984), p. 149–89. bibliog. (Technique, spirit and form in the making of the modern economies: essays in honor of William N. Parker. Edited by Gary Saxonhouse and Gavin Wright. Greenwich, Connecticut: Jai, 1984).

In this Festschrift for W. N. Parker, De Vries reviews recent work on the economic history of the 18th and 19th centuries which bridge the gap between the economic Golden Ages of the 17th and the 20th centuries. He produces hypothetical national income data from all manner of sources, and backs them up with other economic indicators including some impressive figures on wages, concluding that Dutch per capita income in the late 17th century was probably much higher than we had thought, but that it declined thereafter until after the French Revolution.

179 **The Dutch rural economy in the Golden Age, 1500–1700.**
Jan de Vries. New Haven, Connecticut: Yale University Press, 1974. 316p. bibliog. (Yale Series in Economic History).

De Vries points to the fundamental strength of Dutch agriculture as the basis for the economic success of the Golden Age. Employing new technology, Dutch farmers took advantage of basic food imports from elsewhere to move into profitable cash crops, increasing productivity and earnings, and releasing labour to trade and industry.

180 **The Netherlands economy in the twentieth century: an examination of the most characteristic features in the period 1900–1970.**
Johan de Vries. Assen, The Netherlands: Van Gorcum, 1978. 135p. bibliog.

De Vries has written a great deal on this subject and is a recognised expert. His approach is not sectoral, but looks at the economic structure, the economic cycle, and economic policy. Although there is plentiful use of statistics and economic jargon, this is an approachable handbook, limited only by its end-point in 1970.

Wealth and property in the Netherlands in modern times.
See item no. 352.

At spes non fracta: Hope & Co., 1770–1815: merchant bankers and diplomats at work.
See item no. 541.

The post-war financial rehabilitation of the Netherlands.
See item no. 552.

International government finance and the Amsterdam capital market 1740–1815.
See item no. 556.

Report on the agriculture of the Kingdom of the Netherlands.
See item no. 602.

Productivity of land and agricultural innovation in the Low Countries (1250–1800).
See item no. 612.

International Review of Social History.
See item no. 948.

Select bibliography of works in English on the economic history of the Netherlands from the sixteenth to the nineteenth century.
See item no. 997.

Voyages of Discovery and the Colonies

181 **The Dutch retreat from empire.**
H. Baudet. In: *Britain and the Netherlands in Europe and Asia: papers delivered to the third Anglo–Dutch historical conference.* Edited by J. S. Bromley, E. H. Kossmann. London: Macmillan, 1968, p. 207–33. bibliog.

A factual account of the Dutch loss of the East Indies, concluding that it was probably for the economic good of the Netherlands.

182 **All of one company: the VOC in biographical perspective.**
Edited by Leonard Blussé. Utrecht: HES, 1986. 230p. bibliog.

This Festschrift for Professor M. A. P. Meilink–Roelofsz contains a number of essays written by her pupils at the Centre for the History of European Expansion at Leiden University. All the contributions discuss the relationship of various individuals to the East India Company (VOC), all of them lower functionaries or their Asian counterparts. This throws considerable, if fragmentary, light on dealings with China, Japan, India, the East Indies and Yemen.

183 **Johan Maurits van Nassau–Siegen 1604–79: a Humanist prince in Europe and Brazil: essays on the tercentenary of his death.**
Edited by E. van den Boogaart (et al.). The Hague: Johan Maurits van Nassau Stichting, 1979. 538p. bibliog.

A very substantial collection of articles on Maurits' life and times, concentrating on various aspects of his venture in Brazil. There is also a major section on his impact on architecture. This work is luxuriously illustrated.

184 **The Dutch seaborne empire 1600–1800.**
Charles R. Boxer. London: Hutchinson, 1965. Reprinted 1977. 326p. bibliog. maps. (History of Human Society).

This is the classic account in English of the Dutch colonial empire in its age of glory, and moreover remains highly readable more than twenty years on.

185 **Some remarks on the cultivation system in Java.**
C. Fasseur. *Acta Historiae Neerlandicae*, vol. 10 (1978), p. 143–62. bibliog.

A very useful and authoritative summary of the historical debate on the infamous 'cultuurstelsel', or system of compulsory crop cultivation organized by the Dutch colonial authorities in the middle decades of the last century. Fasseur is at pains to point out the regional diversity in the operation of this profitable régime.

186 **Netherlands India: a study of plural society.**
J. S. Furnivall. Cambridge, England: Cambridge University Press, 1939. Reprinted 1967. 502p. bibliog. maps.

This still remains a standard work on the colonial history of the Dutch East Indies. The early chapters comprise a chronological treatment of the subject, followed by a wide-ranging analysis of the politics, economy and society of 'Netherlands India' in the 1930s.

187 **The birth of New York: Nieuw Amsterdam 1624–1664.**
Edited by Roelof van Gelder. Amsterdam: Amsterdams Historisch Museum, 1982. 44p.

The catalogue of an exhibition held by the New York Historical Society in 1982, and at the Historical Museum in Amsterdam the following year, on the Dutch years of colonial rule in New York.

188 **The Dutch impact on Japan (1640–1853).**
Grant Kohn Goodman. Leiden: Brill, 1967. 242p. map. bibliog.

In the years covered by this study, Japan had virtually no contact with the outside world except the Chinese and the Dutch. This study examines the Dutch colony in Japan and the influence of the West, through the Dutch, on Japanese science and culture.

189 **Trading companies in Asia 1600–1830.**
Edited by J. van Goor. Utrecht: HES, 1986. 167p. map. bibliog.

A collection of essays which is the product of a workshop of colonial historians held in Utrecht in 1983. The papers concern coffee cultivation in the East Indies, the East India Company and relations between the native principalities of the East Indies, the Dutch and the Japanese, and the British in Java from 1811 to 1816.

190 **The Dutch in the Caribbean and on the Wild Coast 1580–1680.**
Cornelis C. Goslinga. Assen, The Netherlands: Van Gorcum, 1971. 647p. bibliog. maps.

An impressive standard work on the history of overseas expansion in central and southern America in the early colonial period. Goslinga's style is that of the traditional historical narrative, and there are substantial appendixes of statistical material and key documents.

191 **The Dutch in the Caribbean and in the Guianas, 1680–1791.**
Cornelis C. Goslinga, edited by Maria J. L. van Yperen. Assen, The Netherlands: Van Gorcum, 1985. 712p. bibliog.

A sequel to Goslinga's *The Dutch in the Caribbean and on the Wild Coast 1580–1680* (q.v.). It traces the start of the demise of the second West India Company, and the early years of the Dutch trading and farming associations in the Antilles and the Guianas.

192 **A short history of the Netherlands Antilles and Surinam.**
Cornelis C. Goslinga. The Hague: Nijhoff, 1979. 198p. bibliog. map.

This history of the Dutch West Indies covers mainly the Dutch colonial period, but is also concerned with Spanish and British interludes in the islands and on the mainland. Chapters on the discovery of oil and bauxite, and on economic and political developments of the 20th century, complete this useful handbook.

193 **New York historical manuscripts: Dutch.**
Translated and annotated by Arnold J. F. van Laer, edited with additional indexes by K. Scott, K. Stryker–Rodda. Baltimore, Maryland: published under the direction of the Holland Society of New York by the Genealogical Publishing Co., 1974. 4 vols. bibliog.

This collection of translated, annotated and printed documents comprises the Register of the Provincial Secretary, New York State, from 1660 to 1688 (vols. I, II and III), and the Council Minutes from 1638 to 1649 (vol. IV). These volumes are reproduced from typed transcripts in the New York State Library, and include indexes. These four volumes form part of a much larger series, containing land papers (1980), the Kingston Papers (1976) and other manuscripts useful to the historian of the Dutch period in New York.

194 **The Dutch come to Korea.**
Gari Ledyard. Seoul: Royal Asiatic Society in conjunction with Taewon Publishing Co., 1971. 231p. bibliog. map.

A fascinating account of the little-known visit by a ship of the Dutch East India Company to Korea in 1653. Hendrik Hamel wrote a first-hand account of the thirteen-year sojourn, which is printed here as an appendix.

195 **The trauma of decolonization: the Dutch and West New Guinea.**
Arend Lijphart. New Haven, Connecticut; London: Yale University Press, 1966. 303p. bibliog. (Yale Studies in Political Science, 17).

An account and analysis of the Dutch withdrawal from West Irian or New Guinea by a distinguished political scientist. New Guinea excited very strong feeling amongst the Dutch at a time when the rest of their possessions in the Indonesian archipelago were being removed from their control.

196 **Changing economy in Indonesia: a selection of statistical source material from the early nineteenth century up to 1940.**
Initiated by W. M. F. Mansvelt, re-edited and continued by P. Creutzberg. The Hague: Nijhoff, 1975–80. 6 vols.

The six volumes cover the following subjects: export crops, 1816–1940 (vol. 1), public finance, 1816–1939 (vol. 2), expenditure on fixed assets (vol. 3), rice prices (vol. 4), national income (vol. 5), and money and banking (vol. 6). Provides a useful collection of basic data.

197 **The Dutch contribution to the European knowledge of Africa in the seventeenth century: 1595–1725.**
Marvin Thomas Ouwinga. Ann Arbor, Michigan; London: Microfilms International, 1979. 317p. bibliog. maps.

This PhD dissertation examines the means by which the Dutch accumulated their knowledge of Africa throughout the 17th century, and gives a detailed account of the means by which this knowledge was disseminated throughout Europe, including maps which appear in an appendix, and are unfortunately often unreadable in their exo-graphic reproduction.

198 **Cape of Good Hope, 1652–1702: the first fifty years of Dutch colonisation as seen by callers.**
Edited by R. Raven–Hart. Cape Town: Balkema, 1979. 2 vols. bibliog.

A collection of eye-witness reports, well translated, and providing great depth of detail as well as the necessary general background.

199 **The Dutch explorations, 1605–1756, of the north and northwest coast of Australia: extracts from journals, log-books and other documents relating to these voyages.**
Edited by Willem C. H. Robert. Amsterdam: Philo Press, 1973. 197p. bibliog. maps. (Contributions to a Bibliography of Amsterdam and the South Sea Islands, Supplement 2).

Contains a substantial analytical introduction (p. 3–84) by the editor of this highly varied series of fifty-five translated documents.

200 **Australia unveiled: the share of the Dutch navigators in the discovery of Australia.**
G. Schilder, translated from the German by Olaf Richter. Amsterdam: Theatrum Orbis Terrarum, 1976. 424p.

Covers the period 1606–44, tracing the growth of a concept of 'Australia' through the voyages of Dutch mariners in the 17th century. The work is in two parts: an account of the voyages, and an analytical collection of maps of the period.

201 **Dutch colonial policy and the search for identity in Indonesia 1920–1931.**
E. J. M. Schmutzer. Leiden: Brill, 1977. 178p. bibliog.

An analysis of policy in the period of the Ethical Policy in the Dutch East Indies, and particularly illuminating on the response of public and political opinion at home.

202 **Dutchmen on the bay: the ethnology of a contractual community.**
Lawrence J. Taylor. Philadelphia: University of Pennsylvania Press, 1983. 206p. bibliog.

Concerns the history of a Dutch immigrant community around West Sayville, Long Island (USA), mainly in the period 1840–1900. The Dutch were shell-fishermen, originating in the Scheldt river estuary in Zeeland, The Netherlands. A micro-study of community history concentrating on such cohesive influences as religion and kin relationships.

203 **The Japanese civilian internment camps during the Second World War.**
D. van Velden. *Acta Historiae Neerlandicae*, vol. 4 (1970), p. 234–75. bibliog.

A synopsis by the author of her doctoral thesis of 1963. Her analysis of the traumatic experience of the interned Dutch in the East Indies during the Second World War relies heavily on first-hand accounts and memoires. A reliable introduction.

204 **Dutch capital in the West Indies during the eighteenth century.**
J. P. de Voort. *Low Countries History Yearbook*, vol. 14 (1981), p. 85–105. bibliog.

A rare analysis of the financial involvement of Dutch investors in the plantations of the West Indian colonies. The investments were, as a rule, far from successful.

205 **The Netherlands as an imperial power in south-east Asia in the nineteenth century and after.**
S. L. van der Wal. In: *Britain and Netherlands in Europe and Asia: papers delivered to the third Anglo–Dutch historical conference*. Edited by J. S. Bromley, E. H. Kossmann. London: Macmillan, 1968, p. 191–206. bibliog.

Points out the influence of other colonial empires, for example the British, on Dutch policy towards the East Indies.

206 **The Netherlands and the partition of Africa.**
H. L. Wesseling. *Journal of African History*, vol. 22 (1981), p. 495–509. bibliog.

A clear account of the Dutch involvement in the celebrated 'scramble'. The Dutch role was apparently strictly limited, because of interests elsewhere, namely the East Indies. The Dutch commercial role in the Congo is interestingly highlighted.

207 **Post-imperial Holland.**
H. L. Wesseling. *Journal of Contemporary History*, vol. 15 (1980), p. 125–42. bibliog.

Wesseling examines the decolonization process and aftermath in the Netherlands. The New Guinea question, the economic effects of the loss of the colonies, and the crisis of conscience in the 1970s are all extensively investigated.

A critical survey of studies on Dutch colonial history.
See item no. 993.

Population

Demography

208 **Regional differences in marital fertility in the Netherlands in the second half of the nineteenth century.**
John D. Buissink. *Population Studies*, vol. 25 (1971), p. 353–74. bibliog.

Buissink examines the considerable variety in the rate of reproduction within marriage in the 1850s between the various Dutch provinces. He offers religion as an explanation: Roman Catholics were far less modern in their demographic behaviour.

209 **The Low Countries.**
Paul Deprez. In: *European demography and economic growth*. Edited by W. R. Lee. London: Croom Helm, 1979. p. 236–83. bibliog.

This article covers the demographic history of both Belgium and the Netherlands in the 19th and 20th centuries. There are twenty-four pages of statistics; the analysis of the Dutch figures is largely concerned with technical problems to do with the quality of the data.

210 **Regional differences in social mobility patterns in the Netherlands between 1830 and 1940.**
Henk van Dijk, J. Visser, E. Wolst. *Journal of Social History*, vol. 17 (1984), p. 435–52. bibliog.

The authors' working hypothesis is that industrialization relates to an increased degree of social mobility. They put it to the test in research projects in Rotterdam, Eindhoven and several other towns and rural areas in the

Netherlands. It was concluded that although Rotterdam conforms to the expected pattern, the other areas behave in no predictable manner in this respect.

211 **Migration and settlement 5: Netherlands.**
Paul Drewe. Laxenburg, Austria: International Institute for Applied Systems Analysis, 1980. 79p. bibliog.

Taking the five major planning regions of the Netherlands, Professor Drewe tries to establish relationships between multi-regional demographic developments and regional policy. He examines closely the effects of social and economic factors on migration and commuting.

212 **Population changes and economic developments in the Netherlands: an historical survey.**
J. A. Faber (et al.). *A. A. G. Bijdragen*, vol. 12 (1965), p. 47–114. bibliog.

Using all manner of sources, the authors devise estimates for the population of the Netherlands from 1500 to the end of the 18th century, when the first reliable censuses were taken.

213 **Demographic research and spatial policy: the Dutch experience.**
Edited by Henk ter Heide, Frans J. Willekens. London: Academic Press, 1984. 410p. maps. bibliog. (Studies in Population).

In seventeen substantial papers the whole set of issues to do with population developments and physical planning necessities are discussed. All forms of migration are considered and projections are made for the future.

214 **Population increase in the Netherlands.**
E. W. Hofstee. *Acta Historiae Neerlandicae*, vol. 3 (1981), p. 43–125. bibliog.

Hofstee is the most important figure in Dutch historical demography this century, and for many years has held a chair at the University of Wageningen. His publications in English are few and far between, however. He is the author of the 'Hofstee thesis', which seeks to explain regional imbalances in demographic behaviour in the Netherlands from 1800 to the present day in terms of a theory of modern social attitudes being 'diffused' gradually across the country from the coastline landwards from about 1850 onwards. Although his theory has met with much opposition, it has dictated the parameters of discussion since he first formulated it in the 1950s. This is quite an early version: for a later, refined form, see *The modernization of the demographic pattern: the case of the Netherlands* (q.v.).

215 **The modernization of the demographic pattern: the case of the Netherlands.**

E. W. Hofstee. *Bevolking en Gezin* [Brussels; Voorburg, The Netherlands], no. 3 (1985), p. 213–28. bibliog.

A rare English-language presentation of the 'Hofstee thesis', described in the previous item. This version was prepared in 1975, although not published until ten years later.

216 **The promise of American life: social mobility in a nineteenth century immigrant community, Holland, Michigan, 1847–94.**

Gordon W. Kirk. Philadelphia: American Philosophical Society, 1978. 164p. bibliog.

Kirk's subject is one particular community of Dutch emigrants in the 19th century, who settled in western Michigan, but retained a large degree of their Dutch characteristics. He concentrates on the structure of occupations in the community and on wealth mobility.

217 **Population growth and urban systems development: a case study.**

G. A. van der Knaap. Boston, Massachusetts; The Hague: Nijhoff, 1980. 237p. maps. bibliog. (Studies in Applied Regional Science, 18).

Taking the Dutch urban system as a case-study, this work looks at the interrelationship between growth in the towns and increases in population, concentrating on the effect of transport systems and examining television ownership in particular as an illuminating variable.

218 **Dutch immigrant memoires and related writings.**

Edited with a foreword by Henry S. Lucas. Assen, The Netherlands: Van Gorcum, 1960. 2 vols. bibliog.

One of many published collections of letters and memoires by Dutch migrants to the New World, concentrating on the 19th century. Dutch texts and English translations are printed side by side. A fascinating collection of documents, ranging from farmers' diaries to the 'bacon letters' encouraging friends and relatives to join the pioneers. Probably the best of this genre of publication, of which there have been several in the last thirty years.

219 **Netherlands survey on fertility and parenthood motivation 1975: country report, world fertility survey.**

Edited by H. G. Moors. Voorburg, The Netherlands: Netherlands Interuniversity Demographic Institute (NIDI), 1982. 183p. bibliog.

This report summarizes the most important data and analyses concerning a major survey of Dutch fertility in 1975, conducted by members of the NIDI, CBS (Central Bureau for Statistics) and the Institute of Sociology at Utrecht University. There are three sections: the first deals with methodology; the second with the principal data and a brief explanation of trends; and the third is a series of short analytical reports by the original authors.

220 **Child spacing and family size in the Netherlands.**
H. G. Moors. Leiden: Stenfert Kroese, 1974. Doctoral dissertation, Leiden University, 1974. 193p. bibliog.

This analysis of Dutch fertility in the 1950s and 1960s is a complex demographic exercise, establishing relationships between family size and such variables as religion, socio-economic status, and contraception.

221 **The demographic transition in the Netherlands.**
William Petersen. *American Sociological Review*, vol. 25 (1960), p. 334–47. bibliog.

Seeks to explain the rapid fall in the death rate in the Netherlands which took place after 1870, and fluctuations in the birth and fertility rates which occurred that the time. Petersen follows Professor E. W. Hofstee in his analysis, subscribing to his theory of a diffusion of modernization. This article covers the period from 1600 to 1960 in broad terms, and is interesting on the social control of reproductive processes in traditional Dutch society.

222 **Planned migration: the social determinants of the Dutch–Canadian movement.**
William Petersen. Berkeley, California: University of California Press, 1955. 273p. bibliog. (University of California Publications in Sociology and Social Institutions, vol. 2).

Mainly concerned with the emigration wave from the Netherlands to Canada between 1930 and 1950, paying particular attention to religious factors.

223 **Population mobility in the Netherlands, 1880–1910: a case study of Wisch in the Achterhoek.**
Mike L. Samson. Uppsala, Sweden: Acta Universitatis Upsaliensis, 1977. 180p. maps. bibliog. (Studia Historica Upsaliensia, no. 87).

A detailed study of a village near the German border in the period of agricultural crisis and recovery after 1880. A wide spectrum of social and economic variables are considered for their effects on population mobility.

224 **Models of contemporary Dutch family building.**
Gigi Santow. Voorburg, The Netherlands: Netherlands Interuniversity Demographic Institute, 1977. 34p. bibliog.

This working paper examines contraceptive usage and the delay of the first birth in Dutch marriages, in order to construct a model of Dutch family-building structures in the 1970s.

225 **The Dutch in America: immigration, settlement, and cultural change.**

Edited by Robert P. Swierenga. New Brunswick, New Jersey: Rutgers University Press, 1985. 303p. maps. bibliog.

A varied collection of papers first presented to a conference entitled 'Dutch immigration 1782–1982' in Philadelphia in 1982. The introduction and the first chapter on the overall picture of Dutch emigration, both by Swierenga himself, are very useful indeed. Chapter two, by Pieter Stokvis, on Dutch international migration, is less lucid but also useful. In the other chapters, the religion and culture of the Dutch in America tend to dominate.

226 **The population and economy of the preindustrial Netherlands.**

Jan de Vries. In: *Population and history from the traditional to the modern world.* Edited by R. I. Rotberg and T. K. Rabb. Cambridge, England: Cambridge University Press, 1986, p. 101–22. bibliog.

An attempt to apply the dynamic model of economic-demographic interaction developed by E. A. Wrigley and R. S. Schofield in their *Population history of England* (Cambridge, Massachusetts: 1981) to the Netherlands in the 17th and 18th centuries, despite the fact that the Dutch data do not lend themselves to family reconstruction techniques, but rather to macro-demographic analyses at the local level. De Vries provides the basic demographic series for the period, and some data on real wages from 1550 to 1850, and pleads for a more regional approach than Wrigley and Schofield have adopted in their national model.

227 **Dutch emigration to North America 1624–1860: a short history.**

Bertus Harry Wabeke. New York: Netherlands Information Bureau, 1944. 160p. bibliog. (Booklets of the Netherlands Information Bureau, no. 10).

Now dated, but it does cover the earlier period of emigration up to 1800, whereas most recent works tend to concentrate on the 19th and 20th centuries.

Patterns of European urbanisation since 1500.
See item no. 34.

The Dutch in London: the influence of an immigrant community.
See item no. 95.

Rural migrants in urban setting.
See item no. 349.

Population and family in the Low Countries, vols I–IV.
See item no. 367.

National population bibliography of the Netherlands, 1945–1979.
See item no. 1011.

Minorities

228 **Immigration and the formation of minority groups: the Dutch experience 1945–1975.**
Hans van Amersfoort, translated from the Dutch by R. Lyng. Cambridge, England: Cambridge University Press, 1982. 234p. bibliog.

The standard work in English on this subject by an academic specialist who has since been appointed to a chair at the University of Amsterdam. The first part is a theoretical exercise in sociology, building an analytical model for the study of adaptation of minority groups. The second and more substantial part is a research report on the Eurasian Indonesians, the Moluccans, the Surinamese and 'guest labour'. The extent of 'absorption' of minorities into Dutch society ranges from the highly successfully integrated Eurasian Indonesians to the still distinctive minority of 'guest labour', which comprises mainly Turks and Moroccans.

229 **The Dutch plural society: a comparative study in race relations.**
Christopher Bagley. London: published for the Institute of Race Relations by the Oxford University Press, 1973. 293p. bibliog.

A now dated but still useful study of the way in which the Dutch deal with problems concerning immigration minorities, and providing comparisons with Britain. The groups dealt with are the Indonesian immigrants, and the first wave of West Indians (mainly Surinamese). Bagley goes on to examine concepts of what 'deviance' and 'social control' mean in the Netherlands, and to look at racial prejudice there. The whole is set against a background model of the Dutch plural society.

230 **Wooden shoes and baseball bats: a study of sociocultural integration of Americans in The Hague.**
Victoria J. Baker. Leiden: Instituut voor Culturele Anthropologie en Sociologie der Niet–Westerse Volken, 1983. 158p. bibliog.

This study is a dissertation produced for a Doctorandus degree at Leiden University, and is based on interviews with a sample of 50 of the 2,400 strong American population in The Hague. This empirical material is combined with a considerable body of theory. The line of approach taken deals with such issues as 'The American national character', culture shock, and a sociographic sketch of the expatriots. One interesting result of this study is that the longer the American individual remains in The Hague, the more disparaging he or she is likely to become about the Dutch.

231 **Can the train ever be stopped again? Developments in the Moluccan community in the Netherlands before and after the hijackings.**
Dieter Bartels. *Indonesia*, vol. 41 (1986), p. 23–45. bibliog.

This article provides a good historical analysis of the arrival of the Moluccan community as soldiers of the Dutch Colonial Army (KNIL) in the 1950s, and indeed construes their further developments in the Netherlands in the light of that military tradition. Attention is focused on the differences between the various generations of Moluccans in the Netherlands. The hijackings were terrorist actions in the Netherlands by extreme Moluccan pressure groups in 1975 and 1977 which had the object of setting up an independent Moluccan Republic in the Indonesian archipelago.

232 **The hustler culture of young unemployed Surinamers.**
W. E. Biervliet. In: *Adaptation of migrants from the Caribbean in the European and American metropolis*. Edited by H. E. Lamur, John D. Speckmann. Amsterdam; Leiden: Department of Anthropology, University of Amsterdam; Department of Caribbean Studies, University of Leiden, 1978, p. 191–201. bibliog.

In the mid-1970s, Biervliet took part in a research project on Surinamese youth who had recently arrived in Amsterdam, and concentrated on the attempts to earn a living via the unofficial sectors on the part of those largely excluded from the conventional economy by their lack of qualifications.

233 **The integration of ethno-cultural minorities: a pluralist approach: the Netherlands and Canada: a comparative analysis of policy and programme.**
Hubert Campfens. The Hague: Government Publishing Office, 1980. 241p. bibliog.

A report of research which is most revealing in its examination of Dutch policy on minorities. The direct comparison with Canada, a nation with equally significant minorities but with a very different current situation, allows Campfens to be quite critical of Dutch policy – or rather the lack of it – and to suggest a long list of considerations to be borne in mind by the Dutch in formulating policy and programme objectives.

234 **The underdevelopment of ex-colonial immigrants in the metropolitan society: a study of Surinamers in the Netherlands.**
Vernon A. Domingo. PhD thesis, Clark University, Massachusetts, 1980. Available from Ann Arbor, Michigan: University Microfilms International, 1980. 309p. maps. bibliog.

Contains a short history of the 'underdevelopment' of Surinam from 1600 onwards, an account of the migration to the Netherlands mainly in the 20th century, and then comprises a study of the Surinamese community in Rotterdam in the mid-1970s.

235 **Minorities and policy-making in the Netherlands: South Moluccans and other aliens in comparative perspective.**
J. E. Ellemers. *The Netherlands' Journal of Sociology*, vol. 15 (1979), p. 97–122. bibliog.

The author provides as much information on the Moluccans as is available, and by comparing the group's problems with brief accounts of Eurasian Indonesian repatriates, Surinamese and foreign workers, he hopes to persuade the reader that the Moluccan 'problem' is not an isolated one, but should be seen in the context of the general issue of minorities. A postscript is provided to take account of the events of 1979.

236 **Immigrant ethnic minorities in the Netherlands.**
Han B. Entzinger (et al.). *Planning and Development in the Netherlands*, vol. 13, no. 1 (1981), 140p. [Special issue.] bibliog.

This collection of essays is concerned mainly with the formulation of policy on immigrant minorities in the Netherlands, the first contribution being 'The contours of a general minorities policy' by M. J. A. Penninx (p. 5–26). Topics covered by the other five papers include the labour market, research on ethnic minorities, social policy formulation and minority leaders' views on government policy.

237 **The Netherlands.**
Han B. Entzinger. In: *European immigration policy: a comparative study*. Edited by Tomas Hammar. Cambridge, England: Cambridge University Press, 1985, p. 50–88. bibliog.

Focuses on the legislation on immigration in the Netherlands, especially since the Second World War, and also deals with the legal side of the naturalization of foreign nationals. The main area under consideration is Dutch government policy in this matter.

238 **Adjustment after migration: a longitudinal study of the process of adjustment by refugees to a new environment.**
Jacques Ex, foreword by F. J. T. Rutten. The Hague: Nijhoff, 1966, 110p. bibliog. (Publications of the Research Group for European Migration Problems, no. 13).

An investigation based on interviews with Eurasian refugees from Indonesia, trying to illuminate the settlement process of those who left Indonesia after it became a Republic independent of the Netherlands. There is much attention to social science methodology.

239 **Foreigners in our community: a new European problem to be solved.**
Edited by Hans van Houte, Willy Melgert. Amsterdam; Antwerp: Keesing, (1971). 202p. bibliog.

A congress of the Netherlands United Nations Association and the Anne Frank Foundation in 1971 produced this collection of papers, which is particularly strong on West Indian immigration to the Netherlands in the 1960s. The article by H. van Amersfoort (p. 50–65) is of particular interest.

240 **Zigeuners, woonwagenbewoners en reizenden: een bibliografie.**
(Gypsies, caravan-dwellers and travellers: a bibliography.)
Jeanne Hovens, Pieter Hovens. Rijswijk, The Netherlands: Ministry of Cultural Affairs, Recreation and Social Welfare, 1982. 120p.

An unannotated collection of 1,000 articles and books dealing with gypsies and tinkers the world over, but with a generous share on the Netherlands. The listing is alphabetical, rather than thematic, but an index – an English translation is included – provides reasonable access.

241 **Decolonization and racial conflict: the Indonesian–Dutch experience.**
O. Hong Lee. *Cultures et Developpement: Revue Internationale*, vol. 6 (1974), p. 829–50. bibliog.

This article covers the integration of Eurasian Indonesian repatriates in the Netherlands in the 1950s, and argues that the Dutch reputation for toleration and well-planned assimilation is not entirely deserved.

242 **Migrant labour in Europe 1600–1900: the drift to the North Sea.**
Jan Lucassen, translated by D. A. Bloch. London: Croom Helm, 1987. 339p. maps. bibliog.

A translation of a Utrecht University doctoral dissertation of 1984. Lucassen depicts several ‘systems’ of migrant labour in Europe, concentrating on the ‘North Sea system’, the coastal strip from northern France to Germany, which attracted hordes of migrant labour from inland areas. The principal source is a Napoleonic survey of migration throughout most of Europe in 1811. This highly original work forms an interesting background to the 20th-century issues of migrant labour.

243 **Nieuwkomers: immigranten en hun nakomelingen in Nederland 1550–1985.** (Newcomers: immigrants and their descendants in the Netherlands 1550–1985.)
Jan Lucassen, Rinus Penninx. Amsterdam: Meulenhoff, 1985. 176p. bibliog.

This study, by a social historian and an anthropologist, was commissioned in conjunction with an exhibition in 1985 in the Amsterdam Historical Museum on immigrant communities in the Netherlands. The direct juxtaposition of present day ‘guest labour’ communities with the history of immigrant groups over four centuries is extremely refreshing, and the book begs a translation into English in the near future. The authors examine the issues from many innovative angles, concentrating as much on the behaviour of the host nation as on the immigrant groups themselves. Some very apposite black-and-white illustrations, mostly from the Amsterdam exhibition, complement the text.

244 **The import of labour: the case of the Netherlands.**
Adriana Marshall. Rotterdam: Rotterdam University Press, 1973. 177p. bibliog.

Basing her work on an historical economic model which assumes an increasing labour force as necessary to continued economic growth, Marshall concludes that the import of labour is no worse for indigenous workers than most other growth-sustaining policies in a capitalist society. The contribution of foreign workers to an economy – the Netherlands is used as a case-study – is juxtaposed with the condition and experience of the imported workers themselves, and Marshall finds plenty of evidence of restrictive and discriminating policy and practice. The problems presented by immigrant labour in the early 1970s have changed considerably in the recession of the 1980s, especially in the Netherlands, but this nevertheless remains a worthwhile study.

245 **Migration, minorities and policy in the Netherlands: recent trends and developments. Report for the Continuous Reporting System on Migration (SOPEMI) of the Organisation for Economic Co-operation and Development (OECD).**
Philip J. Muus. Amsterdam: Institute for Social Geography, University of Amsterdam, 1986. 93p. bibliog.

A substantial statistical appendix provides the material for this up-to-date analysis of minorities issues, which appears annually. There are chapters on migration flows, demographic developments, Dutch residents abroad, the labour market and minorities policies.

246 **Overzicht onderzoek minderheden. Deel I: onderzoek minderheden 1980–1985: een geselecteerde bibliografie.** (Survey of research on minorities. Part I: research on minorities 1980–1985: a select bibliography.) **Deel II: samenvattingen van verslagen van achttien interdepartmentale onderzoeksprojecten met betrekking tot minderheden.** (Part II: summaries of reports from eighteen interdepartmental research projects concerning minorities.)
Adviescommissie Onderzoek Minderheden, Annemarie Cottaar, Wim Willems. The Hague: Ministry of Home Affairs, Ministry of Welfare, 1985. 235p. bibliog.

The bibliographical section contains a generous though unannotated selection (807 items) on all aspects of research in the period 1980–85, divided thematically and serviced by an index (p. 110ff.). The 18 report summaries cover areas including the labour market, language teaching, housing, racism and return migration.

247 **Ethnic minorities: A. Report to the Government. B. Towards an overall ethnic minorities policy: preliminary report.**
Rinus Penninx. The Hague: Netherlands Scientific Council for Government Policy (WRR), 1979. 170p. bibliog. (Reports to the Government, no. 17).

Penninx, the author of Part B, was commissioned in 1978 to write a report which encompassed a survey of the Moluccans, Surinamese and Antilleans, and the communities in the Netherlands from the Mediterranean countries, and which suggested a comprehensive policy for ethnic minorities in the future. The report was submitted to the Dutch government, was adopted more or less completely, and has been the basis for minorities policy in the 1980s.

248 **Moroccan workers in the Netherlands.**
W. A. Shadid. Leiden: 1979. 342p. bibliog. Doctoral dissertation, Leiden University, 1979.

The methodological aspects of this thesis receive a large proportion of attention; the research itself is based on structured interviews with a sample of Moroccan workers in the Netherlands, from which the author attempts to determine the degree and nature of the migrants' integration into mainstream Dutch society in the 1970s.

249 **Allochtonen in Nederland: beschouwingen over de gerepatrieerden, Molukkers, Surinamers, Antilleanen, buitenlandse werknemers, Chinezen, vluchtelingen, buitenlandse studenten in onze samenleving.** (Visitors in the Netherlands: studies concerning the repatriated, Moluccans, Surinamese, Antilleans, foreign workers, Chinese, refugees, foreign students in our society.)
Edited by H. Verwey–Jonker. The Hague: Staatsuitgeverij, 1971. rev. ed. 1973. 267p. bibliog.

Organized under the auspices of the Ministry of Culture, Recreation and Social Work, this collection of essays was conceived as a 'reader' on the subject of minorities in the Netherlands and has now become a standard work, although it is rather dated.

Ethnic minorities and Dutch as a second language.
See item no. 288.

Education and training for migrants in the Netherlands.
See item no. 648.

Languages and Dialects

Dictionaries

250 **Travels through the lexicon.**
H. Baetens Beardsmore, D. Goyvaerts. Ghent, Belgium: Story–Scientia, 1982. 195p.

A reliable English–Dutch word list with phrases related to the semantic fields of the words given under such headings as 'Clothing', 'Occupation' and 'Climate'. Its purpose is to extend the user's vocabulary within identified topics.

251 **Wolters' ster woordenboek Nederlands/Engels en Engels/Nederlands.** (Wolters' star dictionary Dutch/English and English/Dutch.)
Compiled by H. de Boer, E. G. de Bood. Groningen, The Netherlands: Wolters–Noordhoff, 1984. 2 vols.

A simplified (school) edition of the standard two-volume Wolters' dictionary, *Engels woordenboek* (q.v.), including a supplement with thematically ordered groups of words.

252 **Woordfrequenties in geschreven en gesproken Nederlands.** (Word frequencies in written and spoken Dutch.)
Edited by P. C. uit den Boogaart. Utrecht: Oosthoek, Scheltema & Holkema, 1975. 471p.

The 720,000 words were taken from the texts of newspapers and 'weeklies', family magazines, popular scientific journals, novels and ghost stories, and from discussions with more and less educated informants, and the frequencies are subdivided according to these headings.

253 **Engels woordenboek.** (English dictionary.)
Compiled by K. ten Bruggenkate, J. Gerritsen, N. E. Osselton, assisted by W. Zandvoort. Groningen, The Netherlands: Wolters–Noordhoff, 1986. 19th imp. 2 vols.

Until the publication of Van Dale's two-volume dictionary (q.v.), this was the standard two-way dictionary for English users. It is intended for the Dutch reader, so it does not give the gender nor pronunciation of Dutch words, nor the declination of verbs. It is fairly reliable on idiom, has a good range of vocabulary and is easy to use and pleasant to handle.

254 **Nederlands–Engels woordenboek voor landbouwwetenschappen.** (Dutch–English dictionary of agriculture.)
T. Huitenga. Leiden, The Netherlands: Nederlandsche Uitgeversmaatschappij, 1976. 600p.

An exemplary technical dictionary including specialist terms in related disciplines: botany, engineering, ecology, biology and veterinary science.

255 **Translation guide: Dutch–English.**
T. Huitenga, J. J. van Moll. Apeldoorn, The Netherlands: Van Walraven, 1981. 390p.

A very reliable register of current idiomatic usage, defining words in context and thus providing a more readable (though more selective) survey of words in context than the conventional dictionary as well as comparative commentaries on some untranslatable institutions such as municipalities and comprehensive schools.

256 **Van AAB tot ZOO.** (From AAB to ZOO.)
D. Janssen. Hasselt, Belgium: Heideland–Orbis, 1978. 2nd rev. ed. 179p.

A paperback dictionary of acronyms, abbreviations, international car registrations, chemical elements, etc.

257 **Spreektaal: woordfrequenties in gesproken Nederlands.** (Spoken language: word frequencies in spoken Dutch.)
Edited by E. D. de Jong. Utrecht: Bohn, Scheltema & Holkema, 1979. 144p.

An introduction describes the range and balance of informants used. 117 recordings, from a total of 245, formed the basis of the frequency analysis of the 120,000 words in the basic corpus. The frequency of all the words is divided into sub-groups according to the formality/ informality of the conversation and the sex, age group and educational/social background of the informant.

258 **Kramer's Nederlands woordenboek.** (Kramer's Dutch dictionary.)
Amsterdam: Elsevier, 1983. 618p.

A pocket Dutch–English and English–Dutch dictionary with a fairly comprehensive coverage of contemporary language and idiom, though its spelling does not always conform to the official spelling list and it is not always accurate in distinguishing between English and American English.

259 **Glossary of land resources: English, French, Italian, Dutch, German, Swedish.**
Compiled by Gordon Logie. Amsterdam: Elsevier, 1984. 303p. (International Planning Glossaries, no. 4).

The fourth volume in the series, covering soils, ownership of land, climate, agriculture, forestry, recreation, urbanization and pollution.

260 **In so many words.**
B. H. Loof. Groningen, The Netherlands: Wolters–Noordhoff, 1985. [not paginated].

An English–Dutch and Dutch–English dictionary for trade, industry and social services, intended for those in general business, for office use and for translators and interpreters.

261 **Dictionary of electrical engineering.**
Compiled by Y. N. Luginsky (et al.). Deventer, The Netherlands: Kluwer Technische Boeken, 1985. 479p.

A five-language dictionary giving English, French, German, Dutch and Russian equivalents of some 8,000 terms in electro-technology and related areas. English is the key language with indexes of the other languages for cross-reference. The gender of nouns is given.

262 **Dictionary of scientific and technical terminology: English, German, French, Dutch, Russian.**
Compiled by A. S. Markov (et al.). The Hague: Nijhoff, 1984. 496p.

Approximately 9,000 English scientific terms with their Dutch equivalents.

263 **Illustrated dictionary of mechanical engineering: English, French, German, Dutch, Russian.**
Compiled by V. V. Schwartz (et al.). The Hague: Nijhoff, 1984. 416p.

Comprises 14 chapters grouping approximately 4,000 terms in metal-processing techniques, and illustrated with drawings of the process or component in the English headword.

264 **Van Dale, groot woordenboek Engels–Nederlands, groot woordenboek Nederlands–Engels.** (Van Dale, larger English–Dutch, Dutch–English dictionaries.)
Edited by W. Martin, G. A. J. Tops, with assistance from many contributors. Utrecht; Antwerp: Van Dale Lexicografie, 1984, 1985. 2 vols.

Apart from being by far the most extensive two-way English dictionary, including much more technical terminology than the 'general usage' modes referred to in the introduction, it introduces a number of lexicographic innovations: high-frequency words are given a frequency index, the various meanings of the lemmata are related to contextualised phrases by number coding, and the context of these words are further identifiable by decimal coding indicating the grammatical category of the word associated with them. There is also a copious list of proverbs and a grammatical compendium. The small type-face could be improved.

265 **De haventolk.** (The harbour book.)
Compiled by P. Versnel. Rotterdam: Stichting Vervoer- en Havenopleiding, 1984. [not paginated].

A dictionary of Dutch port terminology translated into English, German and French.

266 **Wolters' beeld-woordenboek Engels en Nederlands: Wolters' illustrated English and Dutch dictionary.**
Groningen, The Netherlands: Wolters–Noordhoff, 1986. 872p.

This was compiled with the cooperation of the compilers of Duden and the Oxford dictionaries and follows the same method as the Duden *Bildwörterbücher*. The most important items in a wide range of topics are arranged thematically, and the headings with their vocabularies are given English translations. An alphabetical index enables this to be used as a two-way dictionary.

A bibliography of Netherlandic dictionaries: Dutch–Flemish.
See item no. 992.

A guide to foreign language grammars and dictionaries.
See item no. 1025.

Grammars

267 **Studies in functional grammar.**
Simon C. Dik. London: Academic Press, 1980. 245p. bibliog.

A general application of the theory of functional grammar to a number of general linguistic problems. It includes specific studies of the Dutch causative construction, and a comparison of English and Dutch predicate formation.

268 **Dutch reference grammar.**
Bruce C. Donaldson. The Hague, Nijhoff, 1981. 275p. bibliog.

This is not a reference grammar but a grammar for intermediate use adding a great deal of useful information to works such as Shetter's *Introduction to Dutch* (q.v.) in a traditional form with excellent cross-references to enable reasonably easy access, but with a number of serious omissions.

269 **Introduction to Dutch.**
W. Z. Shetter. Leiden: Nijhoff, 1984. 5th rev. ed. 245p.

This is an expanded and slightly re-ordered version of a grammar that has proved very valuable through a number of revisions since its first publication nearly thirty years ago. It follows the orthodox method of dividing the grammar into chapter sections, each followed by practice sentences, some of which still lack idiomatic spontaneity (la plume de ma tante!). Finally there are a number of reading, dictation and translation passages.

270 **Frisian reference grammar.**
Pieter Meijes Tiersma. Dordrecht, The Netherlands: Foris, 1985. 157p. bibliog.

An excellent and much-needed, straightforward description of the origins, location, status and grammar (pronunciation, spelling, morphology and syntax) of the language spoken by about half of the 500,000 inhabitants of the province, and understood by very nearly all of them. There are a number of texts with English translations.

A guide to foreign language grammars and dictionaries.
See item no. 1025.

Language courses and readers

271 **Idiomata Neerlandica.**

F. J. A. Ballegeer. Kortrijk–Heule, Belgium: UGA, 1981. 159p.

Language exercises for intermediate and advanced Dutch courses with instructions in four languages. The exercises test the use of prepositions governed by verbs, the use of common verbs with varying prefixes, the use of derivatives from verb forms and derivation from given roots, the comprehension by paraphrase of fixed expressions, and the meaning of idiomatic phrases and their application. There are cloze tests involving unfamiliar words, tests requiring discrimination between semantically or phonologically related words and translation exercises. The guidance of a tutor is likely to be needed.

272 **Dutch course.**

F. Bulhof (et al.). Austin, Texas: University of Texas, 1980. 3rd rev. ed. 2 vols.

An audio-lingual elementary course for English speakers. It assumes assistance from a tutor though it is readily adaptable for self-instruction. The first volume takes the student fairly rapidly through the elementary grammar by analysing and tabulating structures in the dialogues and prose passages. The second volume contains a number of short reading and translation texts with grammatical notes and exercises.

273 **Dutch and Afrikaans.**

London: Centre for Information on Language Teaching and Research (CILT), 1986. 85p.

A very comprehensive guide for teachers, learners, training officers and others concerned with the provision and use of resources for learning Dutch or Afrikaans. It has an introductory descriptive chapter of the Dutch and Afrikaans languages, lists of embassies and national tourist offices, organizations and centres, a select, descriptive list of teaching, learning and resource materials, lists of libraries and special collections, specialist booksellers and subscription agents, and film distributors. There is also full information on radio broadcasts, on opportunities for learning Dutch and Afrikaans and on the various examinations and certifications available. Further back-up is available from the Centre itself in Regent's College, Regent's Park, London.

274 **Hugo's Dutch in three months: simplified language course.**

Jane Fenoulhet. London: Hugo's Language Books, 1983. 190p.

Twenty lessons, nineteen on grammar followed by vocabulary lists, a few written exercises and drills for practice, and a short conversation passage with English translations. The first lesson is on pronunciation, the descriptions of which should be used in conjunction with the cassette provided. Within the limitations presumably imposed by the publishers, this is a vast improvement on the earlier editions and indeed shows welcome departures from other Hugo language courses.

275 **Spelen met taal.** (Playing with language.)
A. van der Geest, W. Swüste. 's-Hertogenbosch, The Netherlands: Malmberg, 1979. 3rd imp. 167p.

A collection of 129 language games intended for children but certainly adaptable for use with adults. There is a place for this even in conventional teaching, and it is an essential component of intensive language courses.

276 **Hedendaagse Nederlandse leesteksten voor volwassen buitenlanders.** (Contemporary Dutch reader for adult foreigners.)
W. Geurtsen. Wageningen, The Netherlands: Centrum voor Talenonderwijs, Landbouwhogeschool, 1980. 141p.

This is intended for those who have already followed an elementary course with a vocabulary of about 1,000 words, and it offers a range of texts varying in difficulty on a number of aspects of present-day life in the Netherlands, for use preferably in a language class.

277 **English self-study supplement to Levend Nederlands.**
Jan Hulstijn, Michael Hannay. Amsterdam: Free University, Amsterdam, 1982. 2nd ed. 162p.

This should be used with some caution. Not all the translations are entirely acceptable and some of the grammatical formulations are confusing or questionable.

278 **Nederlandse teksten met verklaring en oefeningen.** (Dutch texts with explanations and exercises.)
B. Joosten, J. Wilmots. Diepenbeek, Belgium: Wetenschappelijk Onderwijs Limburg, 1979. 76p. (DONA Series).

Ungraded texts from children's writing, essays, advertisements and poems, with questions directed at testing comprehension, extending the vocabulary and developing awareness of style. A separate key booklet is provided.

279 **Hoe leer je een taal? De Delftse methode.** (How do you learn a language? The Delft method.)
A. G. Scaron, F. Montens. Meppel, The Netherlands: Boom, 1984. 2 vols.

This basic course consists of texts of increasing length followed by cloze tests and vocabularies in English, French, Turkish, Indonesian and Arabic. It is designed for intensive use and, following the method described in the first booklet, has achieved striking results with learners resident in the Netherlands in establishing and retaining vocabulary and grammar, acquired by repetition and self-correction.

280 **Praatpaal.** (Talking point.)
Anneke Schoenmakers. London: Stanley Thornes, 1981. 144p.

An elementary Dutch course for English adult learners with rules and definitions to supplement the direct method approach in texts such as *Levend Nederlands* (q.v.). In 28 lessons, with tutor assistance, the user is assumed to acquire a competence for conversing on everyday matters with a vocabulary stock of some 3,500 words.

281 **Reading Dutch: fifteen annotated stories from the Low Countries.**
Compiled by William Z. Shetter, R. Byron Bird. Leiden: Nijhoff, 1985. 176p.

Each extract from contemporary Dutch prose and poetry is preceded by brief details of the author and explanatory notes, and followed by an extensive Dutch–English glossary, with some grammatical information. The texts, of an intermediate standard, are chosen for their literary merit and their relevance to present-day life in the Netherlands.

282 **Levend Nederlands.** (Living Dutch.)
Edited and compiled by J. L. M. Trim, J. Matter, with collaboration from various other contributors. Cambridge, England: Cambridge University Press, 1984. 2nd rev. ed. 222p.

This is an audio-visual course of twenty-four units, with cassettes and film strip, which has been well-received in a wide range of teaching situations for a number of years. It follows the conventional pattern of dialogues followed by drills and 'homework', with instructions for use in various languages, including English. It covers the full range of grammar and vocabulary for everyday usage, but it is now becoming a little dated, and though it claims to be universal, its background is essentially middle class and its appeal is primarily to university students.

283 **A Dutch reader.**
J. K. Williams. London: Stanley Thornes, 1981. 102p.

Graded texts from a really elementary standard up to about A-level, varying from children's verse to essays, short stories and newspaper articles. English translations are given of words not included in the English Universities Press Dutch dictionary; the layout is good and it is enhanced with lively illustrations.

General linguistics

284 **Automatic semantic interpretation: a computer model of understanding national language.**
Jan van Bakel. Dordrecht, The Netherlands: Foris, 1984. 176p. bibliog.

A two-stage system of syntactic analysis and semantic interpretation of Dutch sentences.

285 **Dutch morphology.**
G. Booij. Dordrecht, The Netherlands: Foris, 1981. 181p. bibliog.

This study of word formation in generative grammar contributes to a field of great importance to the foreign student since it deals with stress and syllabification and hence pronunciation and spelling.

286 **Sound structures: studies for Antonie Cohen.**
Edited by M. van den Broecke, V. van Heuven, W. Zonneveld. Dordrecht, The Netherlands: Foris, 1983. 318p. bibliog.

This contains H. Schultink's survey of Cohen's contribution to scholarship at Utrecht and articles by various colleagues on voice adaptation, echoes in transmission, speech errors, acquisition of consonant clusters, production and perception, mispronunciations, evaluation of intonation, voice quality, sentence accent, Dutch diphthongs, syntax, voice assimilation and the velar nasal, and the intelligibility of Dutch and English three-digit numbers.

287 **The sounds of English and Dutch.**
Beverley Collins, Inger Mees. Leiden: Brill. Vol. 1, 1984. 2nd ed. Vol. 2, 1982. bibliog.

The theoretical first volume establishes in well-illustrated simple terms the meaning and application of the terminology needed to deal with articulation, assimilation, stress, deviation, phonetic transcription and phonetic and phonemic contrasts, with passages for phonemic transcription in English and Dutch. The second volume, which should be used in conjunction with cassettes that may be obtained from the English Department at Leiden University, contains annotated transcriptions of standard and dialectal English and Dutch dictation passages and allophonic descriptions.

288 **Ethnic minorities and Dutch as a second language.**
Edited by Guus Extra, Ton Vallen. Dordrecht, The Netherlands: Foris, 1985. 266p. bibliog. (Studies on Language Acquisition, 1).

A collection of articles on the acquisition of Dutch as a second language by foreign minorities in the Netherlands, particularly Turks and Moroccans. It includes Anne Vermeer on the variations in fluency between different ethnic groups, Anne Kerkhoff and Ton Vallen on the influence of cultural backgrounds on language learning, and a number of contributions on the teaching of a second language.

289 **Characteristics and recognizability of vocal expressions of emotion.**
Renée A. M. Governia van Bezooijen. Dordrecht, The Netherlands: Foris, 1984. 164p. bibliog.

An investigation of the characteristics of vocal expressions of emotion in Dutch as a function of sex, age and culture in Dutch men and women, boys and girls and adults from Taiwan and Japan.

290 **Syllable structure and stress in Dutch.**
Harry van der Hulst. Dordrecht, The Netherlands: Foris, 1984. 260p. bibliog.

A study in metrical philology to examine the question of how to describe suprasegmental phenomena, syllable structure and stress, and their interrelationship.

291 **Monitor use by adult second language learners.**
J. H. Hulstijn. Meppel, The Netherlands: Krips Repro, 1981. 200p. bibliog. Doctoral dissertation, Amsterdam Free University, 1980.

This lists the Krashuis Monitor Theory against the error analysis of thirty-two adult learners of Dutch in the Netherlands (half of them English) who were required to apply inversion rules and verb-final rules in Dutch. The students performed better when concentrating on grammar rather than on information and the English students performed very unfavourably in the verb-final tests by comparison with other students with SVO (subject, verb, object) first languages.

292 **The problem of presentative sentences in modern Dutch.**
Robert S. Kirsner. Amsterdam: North-Holland Publishing Co., 1979. 215p. bibliog.

On the basis of his method of form-content analysis, Kirsner establishes a lucid and cogent alternative to Kraak's analysis of 'existential' phrases, concluding that a far more coherent view of a language can be obtained by examining the invariant signals of invariant meanings than by working with other theoretical constructs. Thus he is making a Sausurian case for treating the basic units of grammar as signals of meaning.

293 **Vowel contrast reduction: an acoustic and perceptual study of Dutch vowels in various speech conditions.**
F. J. Koopmans–Van Beinum. Amsterdam: 1980. 163p. bibliog. Doctoral dissertation, University of Amsterdam, 1980.

This is essentially a study comparing vowel pronunciation in various speech situations on the basis of acoustic measurements (comparing, for example, duration with emphasis) and showing that vowels in unaccented positions tend towards neutralization.

294 **Linguistics in the Netherlands.**
Conferences of 1972–73, edited by A. Kraak (Assen, The Netherlands: Van Gorcum, 1975, 294p.); conferences of 1977–79, edited by Wim Zonneveld, Fred Weerman (Dordrecht, The Netherlands: Foris, 1980, 483p.); conferences of 1980–82, edited by Saskia Daalder, Marinel Gerritsen (Amsterdam: North Holland, 1980, 1981, 1982); conferences of 1983–84, edited by Hans Bennis, W. U. S. van Lessen Kloeke (Dordrecht, The Netherlands: Foris, 1983, 1984); conference of 1985, edited by Hans Bennis, Frits Beukema (Dordrecht, The Netherlands: Foris, 1985. 234p.).

These volumes contain papers read at conferences, including a variety of English-language articles on theoretical and applied aspects of contemporary Dutch, e. g. on Dutch as a subject-verb-object language, Dutch word stress, the use of Dutch auxiliaries, who-questions in Dutch, the development of Dutch negation; the verbal specifier in Dutch.

295 **Dialects and dialectology in the Dutch language area.**
Jaap J. de Rooij. *Dutch Crossing*, vol. 13 (1981), p. 61–74. bibliog.

A lucid account of the historical background to the distinctions between northern and southern dialects which exposes the fallacy of alluding to Flemish as a language distinct from Dutch, and tracing the history of Dutch dialectology from Kloeke (1887–1963) and Blancquaert (1894–1964) to the present day.

296 **Speech punctuation: an acoustic and perceptual study of some aspects of speech prosody in Dutch.**
Jaap J. de Rooij. Helmond, The Netherlands: Wibro, 1979. 172p. bibliog.

A doctoral dissertation of 1942 which has remained the standard work on the subject. It investigates the contribution of speech prosody to the recognition of words and word groups. Acoustic and perceptual measurements are derived from a number of experiments. Since speech patterns do not always conform to punctuation in written language, the contribution to meaning provided by speech pauses and pitch contours is examined, in order to discover the relevance of clear prosodic boundaries for speech communication.

297 **Meaning and lexicon: proceedings of the second international colloquium on the interdisciplinary study of the semantics of natural language held at Cleves, 30 August–2 September 1983.**
Edited by Pieter A. M. Seuren. Dordrecht, The Netherlands: Foris, 1985. 509p. bibliog.

These papers discuss lexical semantics as part of psycholinguistics, as well as pragmatics, lexicography and descriptive grammar.

298 **The voiced-voiceless distinction and assimilation in Dutch.**
Iman Hans Slis. Helmond, The Netherlands: Wibro, 1985. 175p. bibliog.

A reprint of seven articles published between 1969 and 1985, on the factors regulating voiced-voiceless distinction, on articulation measurement and effort, and on assimilation, with short chapters added which discuss effort (un)voicing, and line patterns in assimilation.

299 **Language and language attitudes in a bilingual community: Terherne (Friesland).**
J. F. Smith. Groningen, The Netherlands: Stabo-All-Round, 1980. 299p.

This investigates the present state of language usage in Terherne, and in particular whether or not a positive correlation exists in this community between 'language attitudes and language use' on the one hand, and on the other 'the degree of maintenance or displacement of Frisian by Dutch in Terherne'.

300 **Use and function of accentuation: some experiments.**
J. M. B. Terken. Helmond, The Netherlands: Wibro, 1985. 128p. bibliog. Doctoral dissertation, Leiden University, 1985.

An investigation of the difference in accentuation in phrases expressing known and fresh information. The material was tested by asking informants to describe the changes in graphic illustrations presented to them. Secondly, informants were asked to describe the effect of accentuation and lack of accentuation in sentences heard by them. The conclusions are that context is a significant factor.

301 **The syllable in Dutch: with special reference to diminutive formation.**
Mieke Trommelen. Dordrecht, The Netherlands: Foris, 1984. 188p. bibliog. (Publications in Language Sciences, 15).

Morphophonological description of the syllable within a metrical phonological model.

302 **Loss of inflection in the Dutch language.**
J. van der Velde. PhD thesis, University of Iowa, 1982. 168p. bibliog.

A diachronic study, based on literary and non-literary texts of the 13th, 14th and 15th centuries. It is easier to establish the deflection in spoken (and written) Dutch than it is to deduce causes, but phonetic law and, hence, analogy must be the two main contributory factors. The conclusion that 'the general situation in the spoken language at the end of that period is quite comparable to modern standard Dutch' is, however, only a hazardous surmise.

303 **Linguistic theory and the function of word order in Dutch: a study on interpretive aspects of the order of adverbial and noun phrases.**
Arie Verhagen. Dordrecht, The Netherlands: ICG Printing, 1986. 288p. bibliog.

This doctoral dissertation discussing the general question of how to analyse the relationship between formal aspects and resultant interpretations, leads to an analysis of the description of adverbial phrases in generative grammar. The author's own analysis of the relationship between the position of adverbial phrases and the interrelation of sentences takes him on to his own model for describing the sequence of what is traditionally referred to as subject and object.

304 **A semantic analysis of temporal elements in Dutch and English.**
J. de Vuyst. Doctoral dissertation, Groningen University, The Netherlands, 1984. 144p. bibliog.

This points out the deficiencies in an interval semantics description and constructs an accessibility model in which the relation between the event (reality) and the situation (its representation) is established along a time axis.

Current Research in the Netherlands.
See item no. 932.

Dutch Crossing: a Journal of Low Countries Studies.
See item no. 936.

Dutch Studies.
See item no. 939.

Tijdschrift voor Nederlands en Afrikaans. (Journal for Dutch and Afrikaans.)
See item no. 973.

Bibliografie van de Nederlandse taal- en literatuurwetenschap. (Bibliography of Dutch language and literature.)
See item no. 982.

Bibliografie van de geschriften op het gebied van de Nederlandse taalkunde uit de periode 1691–1804. (Bibliography of writings on Dutch language from the period 1691–1804.)
See item no. 1002.

Guide to Netherlandic studies: bibliography.
See item no. 1006.

History of the Dutch language

305 **The Dutch language: a survey.**
Pierre Brachin, translated from the French by Paul F. Vincent. Cheltenham, England: Stanley Thornes, 1985. 150p. bibliog.

This compact and well-informed history of the language, first published as *La langue neerlandaise: essai de présentation* in 1977, was written for the general reader, and in tracing the development of the language, discusses the differences in usage in Holland and Belgium, and compares Dutch with German and, in an appendix, Afrikaans.

306 **A linguistic history of Holland and Belgium.**
Bruce Donaldson. Leiden: Nijhoff, 1983. 200p. bibliog.

A systematic account of contemporary Dutch (p. 3–81), external influences on the language (p. 85–116) and an internal history (p. 119–83). Though of broader scope than Brachin's history of the language (q.v.), it does not supercede it, because although it covers phonology and the synchronic analysis more fully, Brachin is useful for information on modern Belgian Dutch, and both studies fail to deal with syntactic developments.

307 **Dutch: the language of twenty million Dutch and Flemish people.**
Omer Vandeputte, English adaptation by P. F. Vincent, T. J. Hermans. Rekkem, Belgium: Stichting 'Ons Erfdeel', 1981. 64p. bibliog.

With its bibliography of some of the most recent dictionaries, grammars, language courses and works on the Dutch language, this is a useful introduction for first-year university students and anyone interested in European languages.

Bibliografie van de geschriften op het gebied van de Nederlandse taalkunde uit de periode 1691–1804. (Bibliography of writings on Dutch language from the period 1691–1804.)
See item no. 1002.

Religion

Theology

308 **Light and enlightenment: a study of the Cambridge Platonists and the Dutch Arminians.**
Rosalie L. Colie. London: Cambridge University Press, 1957. 162p. bibliog.

Covers the interaction between liberal Protestant theologians of 17th-century England, and the followers of Arminius in the Netherlands, such as the Remonstrants, and later on, Spinoza.

309 **The development of Dutch Anabaptist thought and practice from 1539–1564.**
William Echard Keeney. Nieuwkoop, The Netherlands: B. de Graaf, 1968. 247p. bibliog.

A study mainly to do with Anabaptist theology, concentrating on its theory and principles rather than on its deeds. A useful introduction on the use of terminology.

310 **Calvinism: six Stone Lectures.**
Abraham Kuyper. Amsterdam; Pretoria, South Africa: Höveker & Wormser, 1899. 275p.

The great Calvinist theologian and political leader gave these lectures in 1898 on a tour of the United States. They represent perhaps the most concentrated expression of all his work, giving the Dutch neo-Calvinist's view of what it meant – and to some extent, still means – to be a Calvinist in politics, in religion, in education, in the arts and in the sciences.

311 **Principles of sacred theology.**
Abraham Kuyper, introduction by B. B. Warfield, translated by J. H. de Vries. Grand Rapids, Michigan: Baker Book House, 1980. 683p.

Originally published in 1898 under the title *Encyclopaedia of sacred theology: its principles*, this is an abridged version of Kuyper's theological magnum opus. Kuyper's neo-Calvinist theology was the basis of the religious and political movement which spawned the Protestant Christian Democrat movement in the Netherlands.

312 **A new catechism: Catholic faith for adults.**
Translated from the Dutch by Kevin Smyth. New York: Crossroad, 1982. 2nd imp. 574p.

A new translation of the controversial catechism offering a 'Catholic faith for adults', originating in 1966 during a period of turbulent renewal in Dutch Roman Catholicism. An earlier translation was published in London (Burns & Oates, 1967).

313 **Reformed thought and scholasticism: the arguments for the existence of God in Dutch theology, 1575–1650.**
John Platt. Leiden: Brill, 1982. 249p. bibliog. (Studies in the History of Christian Thought, 29).

The subject is pursued by means of examining the work of Melancthon, the abridgements of Calvin's *Institutes*, the various arguments presented by orthodox Dutch theologians especially in their commentaries on the Heidelberg Catechism and the Belgic Confession, and the disputes between the Remonstrants and Contra-Remonstrants in the early 17th century.

314 **The Eucharist.**
Edward Schillebeeckx, O.P., translated from the Dutch by N. D. Smith. London: Sheed & Ward, 1968. 160p.

An example of the prolific work of this renowned and controversial Roman Catholic theologian from Nijmegen. It is perhaps his best known work, and deals with a new approach to faith centred on the reality of the presence of Christ in the Eucharist.

315 **Bible and theology in the Netherlands: Dutch Old Testament criticism under Modernist and conservative auspices 1850 to World War I.**
Simon J. de Vries. Wageningen, The Netherlands: Veenman, 1968. 152p. bibliog.

A study of Dutch Calvinist theology in the 19th century, focusing on the struggle between progressives and conservatives. Chapter two contains a useful summary of Church history in the period.

316 **Towards a reformed philosophy: the development of a Protestant philosophy in Dutch Calvinistic thought since the time of Abraham Kuyper.**
William Young. Grand Rapids, Michigan: P. Hein, 1952. 157p. bibliog.

A complex and difficult work, but valuable in attempting to set out the ideas of orthodox Calvinistic religious-based philosophy, founded on the work of its titanic leader in the 19th century, Kuyper. The philosophy culminates, according to Young, in the 'Wetsidee', or religious philosophical synthesis.

Religious factors in early Dutch capitalism 1550–1650.
See item no. 172.

La crise religieuse en Hollande: souvenirs et impressions. (The religious crisis in Holland: recollections and impressions.)
See item no. 323.

Dutch Anabaptism: origin, spread, life and thought (1450–1600).
See item no. 331.

Variants within Dutch Calvinism in the sixteenth century.
See item no. 336.

Pillars of piety: religion in the Netherlands in the nineteenth century 1813–1901.
See item no. 340.

Studies in the posthumous work of Spinoza: on style, earliest translation and reception, earliest and modern edition of some texts.
See item no. 833.

Spinoza's political and theological thought.
See item no. 839.

Hugo Grotius, a great European 1583–1645.
See item no. 846.

The world of Hugo Grotius (1583–1645: proceedings of the International Colloquium organised by the Grotius Committee of the Royal Netherlands Academy of Arts and Sciences, Rotterdam 6–9 April 1983).
See item no. 859.

History of religion

317 **Arminius: a study in the Dutch Reformation.**
Carl Bangs. Nashville, Tennessee: Abingdon Press, 1971. 382p. map. bibliog.

A scholarly biography, based on extensive archive research, of this leading theologian of liberal Calvinism in the late 16th century. The sections are labelled 'Student', 'Pastor', 'Professor', and the study concentrates on the great theological battles he fought towards the end of his life.

318 **Mental, religious and social forces.**
H. Bavinck. The Hague: Ministry of Agriculture, Industry and Commerce, 1915. 63p. (A General View of the Netherlands, no. XVII).

A very brief and dated but reliable account of Dutch Church history since the Reformation, concentrating in more detail on the 19th century. It also deals briefly with the literature and art of the Netherlands before 1914.

319 **Mythical aspects of Dutch anti-Catholicism in the nineteenth century.**
J. A. Bornewasser. In: *Britain and the Netherlands*, vol. 5: *Some political mythologies: papers delivered to the fifth Anglo–Dutch historical conference*. Edited by J. S. Bromley, E. H. Kossmann. The Hague: Nijhoff, 1975, p. 184–206. bibliog.

A well-informed account of religious bigotry, inevitably concentrating on the April Movement of 1853, the Protestant whiplash reaction to the re-establishment of a Catholic episcopal hierarchy in the Netherlands.

320 **Thorbecke and the churches.**
J. A. Bornewasser. *Acta Historiae Neerlandicae*, vol. 7 (1974), p. 146–69. bibliog.

A study of Johan Rudolph Thorbecke's ideas, thoughts and theories about religion and the Dutch churches. A sensitive study of intellectual history, based on archival material, covering the middle decades of the 19th century when this liberal statesman dominated Dutch politics.

321 **Dutch Calvinism in modern America: a history of a conservative subculture.**
James D. Bratt. Grand Rapids, Michigan: Eerdmans, 1984. 329p. bibliog.

Covers the period from the emigrant movement of orthodox Calvinists from the Netherlands in the 19th century, through three stages of American development, up to the 1970s.

322 **The English Reformed Church in Amsterdam in the seventeenth century.**
Alice Clare Carter. Amsterdam: Scheltema & Holkema, 1964. 238p. bibliog.

The subject is the English-language congregation of the Dutch Calvinist Church in the capital, which was often at loggerheads with the other English institutions in the city. Based on the archives of the Begijnhof Church (the chapel of a Beguinage, or community of laywomen), the book portrays this pious community with affection and intimacy.

323 **La crise religieuse en Hollande: souvenirs et impressions.** (The religious crisis in Holland: recollections and impressions.)
Daniel Chantepie de la Saussaye. Leiden: De Breuk & Smits, 1860. 202p. bibliog.

Chantepie was a minister of the Dutch Calvinist Church, serving the Walloon (French-speaking) congregation at Leiden in the 1850s, then moving to Rotterdam in 1862, and to Groningen Univeristy as professor of theology in 1872. He was the founder of the 'Ethical Movement' in theology, which combined a Calvinist orthodoxy with a socially conscious humanism. In this work, he was concerned to highlight what he saw as the tragic split between the orthodox and the liberals in Dutch Calvinism.

324 **Dutch Jews in a segmented society.**
H. Daalder. *Acta Historiae Neerlandicae*, vol. 10 (1978), p. 175–94. bibliog.

A race through the history of the Jewish community in the Netherlands since 1796, looking at their social and political life, and mainly concerned with Jewish participation in the famous 'pillarized' or segmented Dutch society. The background motif is of course the fate of Dutch Jews in the Second World War.

325 **Britain and the Netherlands**, vol. 7: **Church and State since the Reformation: papers delivered to the seventh Anglo–Dutch historical conference.**
Edited by A. C. Duke, C. A. Tamse. The Hague: Nijhoff, 1981. 249p. bibliog.

The seventh Anglo–Dutch historical conference, held at Sheffield in 1979, produced a crop of papers on the history of Dutch religion, namely: J. A. Bornewasser's 'Introductory essay', A. C. Duke on the early Reformation in Dutch towns; N. Mout on the 'Family of Love', G. Groenhuis on Calvinism and national consciousness in the Dutch Revolt; J. A. Bornewasser on the State's authority over the churches, 1795–1853; and J. Bank on Dutch Catholicism, 1920–1970.

326 **Guillaume Groen van Prinsterer and his conception of history.**
J. L. van Essen. *Westminster Theological Journal*, vol. 44 (1982), p. 204–49.

Mrs van Essen has been involved in editing Groen's papers for publication in the Rijks Geschiedkundige Publicatiën (RGP) series, and this is a translation of some lecture material she used at the Evangelical College in Amersfoort. There is a biographical sketch of Groen, followed by an analysis of his historical thought, which was centred on the presence and role of God in the affairs of mankind.

327 **Memorbook: a history of Dutch Jewry from the Renaissance to 1940.**
Mozes H. Gans, translated by A. J. Pomerans. Baarn, The Netherlands: Bosch & Kenning, 1977. 852p.; London: George Prior, 1978. bibliog.

A fascinating and comprehensive account, lavishly illustrated with 1,100 black-and-white photographs.

328 **The Church in Holland.**
John Horgan. *Dublin Review*, no. 512 (summer 1967), p. 115–40.

A collection of short articles reprinted from *The Irish Times* (February 1967), trying to rationalize and place an optimistic complexion on the bewildering events engulfing Dutch Roman Catholicism in the 1960s. The sections concern 'The resurgent Church', 'Reshaping the Liturgy', 'Shalom' (an ecumenical movement), 'Ecumenical activity', 'Voices of the people', and 'A crisis of authority?'.

329 **The Dutch dissenters: a critical companion to their history and ideas.**
Edited by Irvin B. Horst. Leiden: Brill, 1986. 233p. bibliog. (Kerkhistorische Bijdragen no. 13).

A collection of thirteen articles concerned mainly with the Anabaptists. There are several chapters on Menno Simons, as well as one by L. G. Jansma on the social background to the Anabaptist Movement (p. 85–104). The editor provides a substantial bibliography of recent studies on the early Reformation in the Netherlands (p. 207–24).

330 **The Old Catholic Church of the Netherlands.**
M. Kok. Utrecht: 1948. [Not paginated].

A pamphlet on the history and birth of the Jansenist Old Catholic Movement. Very brief, and dated, but substitutes are lacking.

331 **Dutch Anabaptism: origin, spread, life and thought (1450–1600).**
Cornelius Krahn. The Hague: Nijhoff, 1968. 303p. bibliog.

A history of the Anabaptists against a background of a general history of the Low Countries, with a chapter on Melchior Hofmann. Slightly ageing standard work on this early pre-Mennonite period.

332 **Abraham Kuyper and the rise of neo-Calvinism in the Netherlands.**
Justus M. van der Kroef. *Church History*, vol. 17 (1948), p. 316–34.

Dated, but useful: a biographical study of the Christian Democrat politician Kuyper, who dominated Dutch politics from the 1880s up to the First World War. Kuyper was also an internationally renowned theologian, the founder of a university, and a journalist and publicist without equal.

333 **Austin Friars: history of the Dutch Reformed Church in London, 1550–1950.**
J. Lindeboom, translated from the Dutch by D. de Iongh. The Hague: Nijhoff, 1950. 208p. bibliog.

An entertaining narrative of the Dutch Church in the heart of the City of London from the foundation and the influence of Johannes à Lasco in the 16th century to the post-war construction of the bombed church building.

334 **Dutch Jewish history: proceedings of the [second] symposium on the history of the Jews in the Netherlands, November 28 – December 3, 1982, Tel-Aviv – Jerusalem.**
Edited by J. Michman, T. Levie. Tel-Aviv: Tel-Aviv University; Jerusalem: Hebrew University of Jerusalem, 1984. 568p. bibliog.

Michman himself contributes an essay on Dutch Jewish historiography, and twenty-seven further papers cover almost all conceivable aspects of the subject.

335 **Ecclesia reformata: studies on the Reformation.**
W. Nijenhuis. Leiden: Brill, 1972. 220p. bibliog. (Kerkhistorische Bijdragen, no. 3).

Six of the nine articles collected here have been previously published elsewhere. Several of the contributions are on various aspects of Calvin's theology, and one of the new papers is on the conflict between Presbyterian and Episcopalian theologians at the Synod of Dordt between 1618 and 1619.

336 **Variants within Dutch Calvinism in the sixteenth century.**
W. Nijenhuis. *Acta Historiae Neerlandicae*, vol. 12 (1979), p. 48–64. bibliog.

Nijenhuis argues that there was a rich variety in Calvinist theology and thought long before the celebrated divisions of the 17th century. He highlights the presence of a liberal Calvinism before the emergence of the Arminian dispute.

337 **Religion and political development in nineteenth-century Holland.**
James W. Skillen, S. W. Carlson–Thies. *Publius*, vol. 12, no. 3 (summer 1982), p. 43–64. bibliog.

A generally reliable account, with notes packed with useful references to English-language work on the subject. The authors are unashamed admirers of the Dutch confessional parties, but, nevertheless, the analysis is still useful.

338 **Religion and trade in New Netherland: Dutch origins and American development.**
G. L. Smith. Ithaca, New York: Cornell University Press, 1976. 266p. bibliog.

Concerned with 17th-century trade and emigration, and more particularly with the lasting effects of Dutch origins on early American society. The author argues that religious toleration, as practised by the Amsterdam patricians running the West India Company, was crucial in its influence on the early forms of American religious pluralism.

339 **Dutch Puritanism: a history of English and Scottish Churches of the Netherlands in the sixteenth and seventeenth centuries.**
Keith L. Sprunger. Leiden: Brill, 1982. 485p. bibliog.

An overall history on English-language congregations in the Netherlands, 1550–1700, concentrating on the 'Puritan' or strict Calvinist links with England, Scotland and America. An impressive work of research based on extensive archive sources.

340 **Pillars of piety: religion in the Netherlands in the nineteenth century 1813–1901.**
Michael J. Wintle. Hull, England: Hull University Press, 1987. 91p. map. bibliog. (Occasional Papers in Modern Dutch Studies, 2).

Based on secondary sources in Dutch, this guide provides a synthesis of Dutch-language work to date on Dutch church history of the 19th century, for those who do not read Dutch. The theme is the confrontation between progressive and conservative trends in the various denominations.

A guide to Jewish Amsterdam.
See item no. 22.

Calvinist preaching and iconoclasm in the Netherlands 1544–1569.
See item no. 107.

Documents of the persecution of the Dutch jewry, 1940–1945.
See item no. 131.

Light and enlightenment: a study of the Cambridge Platonists and the Dutch Arminians.
See item no. 308.

The development of Dutch Anabaptist thought and practice from 1539–1564.
See item no. 309.

Bible and theology in the Netherlands: Dutch Old Testament criticism under Modernist and conservative auspices 1850 to World War I.
See item no. 315.

Iconography of the Counter-Reformation in the Netherlands: heaven on earth.
See item no. 762.

Biografisch woordenboek der Nederlanden. (Biographical dictionary of the Netherlands.)
See item no. 976.

Biografisch woordenboek van Nederland. (Biographical dictionary of the Netherlands.)
See item no. 978.

Godsdienst en kerk in Nederland, 1945–1980; een geannoteerde bibliografie van sociaal-wetenschappelijke en historische literatuur over de godsdienstige en kerkelijke ontwikkelingen in Nederland. (Religion and church in the Netherlands, 1945–1980: an annotated bibliography of social-scientific and historical literature on the religious and ecclesiastical developments in the Netherlands.)
See item no. 1023.

Sociology of religion

341 **'Verzuiling': a confessional road to secularization: emancipation and the decline of political Catholicism, 1920–1970.**
Jan Bank. In: *Britain and the Netherlands*, vol. 7: *Church and State since the Reformation: papers delivered to the seventh Anglo–Dutch historical conference*. Edited by A. C. Duke, C. A. Tamse. The Hague: Nijhoff, 1981, p. 207–30. bibliog.

This article is concerned with the growth, development and decline of the Dutch system of vertical pluralism, or 'verzuiling', using the focus on the Roman Catholic pillar of society to investigate the precise workings of the system.

342 **The 'kleine luyden' as a disturbing factor in the emancipation of the orthodox Calvinists (Gereformeerden) in the Netherlands.**
Lodewijk Brunt. *Sociologia Neerlandica*, vol. 8 (1972), p. 89–102. bibliog.

A translation of an article which originally appeared in the *Sociologische Gids* (1972, p. 49–58). A very perceptive piece, pointing out crucial divisions within the group usually loosely referred to as 'orthodox Calvinists'. The term 'kleine luyden' literally means 'small people', and refers to the lower middle class.

343 **The evolution of Dutch Catholicism, 1958–1974.**
John A. Coleman. Berkeley, California: University of California Press, 1978. 328p. bibliog.

An account of the tumultuous events of the 1960s in which the author argues that the changes amounted to an adaptive reaction rather than a disintegration, as the Dutch Church moved away from the 'cradle-to-grave' organizational structure.

344 **The deferred revolution: social experiment in church innovation in Holland, 1960–1970.**
Walter Goddijn. Amsterdam: Elsevier, 1975. 202p. bibliog.

Goddijn, a leading Catholic sociologist of religion in the Netherlands, adds his contribution to an explanation of the radicality of Dutch Catholicism in the 1960s, which culminated in a degree of conflict with Rome by the end of a turbulent decade.

345 **Lowland highlights: church and oecumene in the Netherlands.**
Edited by J. A. Hebly. Kampen, The Netherlands: Kok, 1972. 134p. bibliog.

A useful collection of papers on the history of the Dutch churches up to the 1970s, focusing on ecumenical trends but by no means excluding other matters. The Reformation, Church and State relations, Protestant and Catholic theology, the churches and social issues, missionary work: all these accompany the general discussions of Dutch claims to the title of an 'ecumenical model' in church matters.

346 **Those Dutch Catholics.**
Edited by Michel van der Plas, H. Suèr, preface by D. Fisher, translated from the Dutch by T. Westow. London: Geoffrey Chapman, 1967. 164p.

A collection of eight essays from various hands which sets out to explain to the outside world, and perhaps to themselves, what Roman Catholics in the Netherlands thought they were doing in the 1960s in the wake of Vatican II.

347 **The case of Dutch Catholicism: a contribution to the theory of the pluralistic society.**
J. M. G. Thurlings. *Sociologia Neerlandica*, vol. 7 (1971), p. 118–36. bibliog.

A short summary of Thurlings' *De wankele zuil* (The tottering column) (1971). He attempts to explain Dutch Catholic behaviour and experience by evolving a model of pluralist society and of the emancipation of various groups within it. Catholic development from 1800 to 1970 is dealt with.

348 **The preacher and the farmers: the Church as a political arena in a Dutch community.**
Jojada Verrips. *American Anthropologist*, vol. 75 (1973), p. 852–67. bibliog.

An account of religious conflict in a central Dutch village, given the pseudonym 'Muusland' in the text, but drawing very heavily on the author's research in the village of Ottoland in the province of South-Holland. The conflict between mainstream Calvinists and the orthodox Church is subjected to an original analysis in the light of national economic and theological developments.

Isolation, integration and secularization: a case study of the Netherlands.
See item no. 138.

Catholic power in the Netherlands.
See item no. 399.

Catholic emancipation in the Netherlands.
See item no. 413.

Godsdienst en kerk in Nederland, 1945–1980; een geannoteerde bibliografie van sociaal-wetenschappelijke en historische literatuur over de godsdienstige en kerkelijke ontwikkelingen in Nederland. (Religion and church in the Netherlands, 1945–1980: an annotated bibliography of social-scientific and historical literature on the religious and ecclesiastical developments in the Netherlands.)
See item no. 1023.

Een voorlopige bibliografie over het thema 'verzuiling'. (A provisional bibliography on the theme 'vertical pluralism'.)
See item no. 1024.

Social Conditions

349 **Rural migrants in urban setting.**
G. Beijer. The Hague: Nijhoff, 1963. 327p. bibliog.

An analysis of the literature on the problem arising from the internal migration from rural to urban areas in twelve European countries (1945–61). The chapter on the Netherlands (p. 170–204) reveals that despite efforts to improve facilities in the rural environment, the migration to the towns continues, with consequent problems which cannot be satisfactorily analysed and explained.

350 **Social stratification and the aged in the Netherlands: the aged as a minority category.**
G. P. A. Braam. *The Netherlands' Journal of Sociology*, vol. 20 (1984), p. 98–114. bibliog.

This sketch of the social position of the elderly in Dutch society is dominated by the hypothesis that the aged form some kind of underprivileged minority of low social position.

351 **Country monograph 1982 on the human settlements situation and related trends and policies in the Netherlands.**
Ministry of Housing, Physical Planning and Environment. The Hague: Ministry of Housing, 1982. 75p.

This is a report submitted to the United Nations Committee on Housing, and covers physical planning of settlements, urban renaissance policy, and the impact on housing of energy conservation.

352 **Wealth and property in the Netherlands in modern times.**
Henk van Dijk. Rotterdam: Erasmus University, 1980. 28p. maps. bibliog. (Centrum voor Maatschappijgeschiedenis, Information Bulletin, no. 8).

Taking the period from the mid-19th century up to the 1960s, Van Dijk looks at the distribution of wealth by examining taxation returns, showing the regional differentiation within the country. There are additional appendixes (not paginated) with specific information on the taxation sources used.

353 **The mood of the country: new data on public opinion in the Netherlands on nuclear weapons and other problems of peace and security.**
Philip P. Everts. *Acta Politica*, vol. 17 (1982), p. 497–553. bibliog.

A follow-up to an article by the same author in the same periodical in 1981, analysing the results of opinion polls to gauge how truly representative certain radical views on security issues actually are. The questions covered are all to do with defence and security policy options, levels of expenditure, and the like.

354 **The future of old housing stock in the Netherlands.**
Ministry of Housing and Physical Planning. The Hague: Information Service, [1970]. 73p.

A memorandum submitted by the Ministry to the Lower Chamber of the Dutch parliament in September 1968, and then revised. It deals with the importance of maintaining old housing, and emphasizes the role to be played by private enterprise, by the municipal authorities, and by the central government.

355 **A Dutch community: social and cultural structure and process in a bulb-growing region of the Netherlands.**
Ivan Gadourek. Leiden: Stenfert–Kroese, 1956; Groningen, The Netherlands: Wolters, 1961. 2nd ed. 556p. bibliog.

Gadourek, at the time a young refugee sociologist from Czechoslovakia, spent several months living in the community of Sassenheim in the bulb-growing region north of The Hague in 1950 and 1951. His participatory research based on hundreds of interviews provides data on the administrative, religious, economic, domestic, cultural and recreational aspects of social relations. Gadourek uses the data to establish relationships between the various variables under examination.

356 **Social change as redefinition of roles: a study of structural and causal relationships in the Netherlands of the 'seventies'.**
Ivan Gadourek. Assen, The Netherlands: Van Gorcum, 1982. 522p. bibliog.

A major work of reassessment on social conditions in the 1970s, taking full account of theories of social change. There is a statistical analysis of forty variables to do with everything from educational level to views on the desirability of social change.

357 **The Netherlands Association for Sexual Reform: a study in the sociology of social movements.**
N. J. J. van Greunsven. PhD thesis, Catholic University of America, Washington, DC, 1971. 289p. bibliog.

The Netherlands Association for Sexual Reform (Nederlandse Vereniging voor Sexuele Hervorming, NVSH) was founded as a successor to the Neo-Malthusian League in 1946, and concentrated primarily on making birth control socially acceptable. This thesis gives an account of its evolution. Since the early 1970s its leadership has become more outspokenly radical on sexual matters, and its membership has tended to decline.

358 **The Dutch solution to the problem of a residential environment.**
H. P. Heeger. *Planning and Development in the Netherlands*, vol. 11, no. 1 (1979), p. 3–16.

This article by a professional transport planner concerns the concept of the 'woonerf', or 'residential environment'. This involves the severe restriction of automobile traffic (not a ban) in residential areas, so that cars, cycles, walkers, and children can all use the streets together. In 1976 the 'woonerf' became a legal concept in the form of a ministerial order; since then it has become a common feature of Dutch residential planning.

359 **The history of the women's movement in the Netherlands.**
H. P. Hogeweg–De Haart. *The Netherlands' Journal of Sociology*, vol. 14 (1978), p. 19–40. bibliog.

Starting with some political pamphlets at the end of the 18th century, the author traces the women's movement through the 19th century and the extraordinary campaign in the 1930s for and against the right of married women to work. There is coverage of the post-war period, and a look to the future. A useful synopsis.

360 **Family life in the Netherlands.**
K. Ishwaran. The Hague: Keulen, 1959. 291p. bibliog.

A Leiden University doctoral dissertation examining the rural and the urban family, family organization, roles and authority, youth and expectations; all in the light of the Netherlands in the 1950s.

361 **Rural community studies in the Netherlands.**
A. J. Jansen, J. P. Groot. In: *Rural community studies in Europe: trends, selected and annotated bibliographies, analyses*, vol. 2. Edited by J–L. Durand–Drouhin, L–M. Szwengrub. Oxford: Pergamon Press, 1982, p. 1–36. bibliog.

Two sociologists from the Agricultural University at Wageningen provide a sketch of developments in the Dutch rural economy and society before and after the Second World War, including the so-called 'industrialization of the countryside'. There follows a sketch of the Dutch discipline of 'sociography' up to the 1950s, evolving thereafter into modern community studies. Section II is a fully annotated bibliography of local studies in the Netherlands since the 1930s, and this very useful review article ends with an in-depth analysis of one particular local study: J. Boer, *Dorp in Drenthe* (Village in Drenthe) (Meppel, The Netherlands: Boom, 1975. 365p.).

362 **The deeply rooted: a study of a Drenthe community in the Netherlands.**
John Y. Keur, Dorothy L. Keur. London: University of Washington Press, 1955. Reprinted, 1966. 208p. bibliog. (Monographs of the American Ethnological Society).

A now classic anthropological study which seeks to establish the relationship between the natural environment and the cultural development of Anderen, a small rural village in the east of the country. Isolation is the keynote.

363 **Current issues in anthropology: the Netherlands.**
Edited by Peter Kloos, H. J. M. Claessen. Rotterdam: Anthropological Branch of the Netherlands Sociological and Anthropological Society, 1981. 252p. bibliog.

A collection of review articles covering Dutch anthropology in the years 1970–80, with chapters on the basic anthropological subdivisions. An appendix lists the main anthropological institutions in the Netherlands.

364 **Enforced marriage in the Netherlands: a statistical analysis in order to test some sociological hypotheses.**
G. A. Kooy, M. Keuls. Wageningen, The Netherlands: Landbouwhogeschool, 1967. 53p. maps. bibliog.

Based on Central Bureau of Statistics (CBS) official figures rather than new fieldwork, the conclusions of this now rather dated study concern the importance of religion as a determining variable in enforced marriages (marriages preceded by a premarital pregnancy). Levels are also found to be affected by degrees of urbanization and education.

365 **Soldiers and students: a study of right- and left-wing radicals.**
Rob Kroes. London: Routledge & Kegan Paul, 1975. 174p. bibliog. (International Library of Sociology).

A sociological model-building exercise, with most of the documentation taken from Dutch military resistance to Indonesian independence, and from student radicalism in Amsterdam University in 1970.

366 **The Dutch family in the 17th and 18th centuries: an explorative-descriptive study.**
Bertha Mook. Ottawa: University of Ottawa Press, 1977. 100p. bibliog.

A brief survey of family life, looking at parent-child relationships, youth, courtship, marriage, and love.

367 **Population and family in the Low Countries, vols I–IV.**
Edited by H. G. Moors (et al.). Various publishers, 1976–84; vol. 4: Voorburg, The Netherlands; Brussels: Netherlands Interuniversity Demographic Institute and the [Flemish] Population and Family Study Centre, 1984. 201p. bibliog.

A series of monographs and essay collections on all aspects of demography and family studies in the Netherlands and Belgium. To date, the most recent is volume 4 (1984), which includes articles on marriage and cohabitation, Turkish and Moroccan women, and one-person households.

368 **Policy for the elderly in the Netherlands.**
M. Mootz, J. M. Timmermans. *Planning and Development in the Netherlands*, vol. 11, no. 1 (1979), p. 58–82.

This article by two government planners deals briefly but comprehensively with the following aspects of policy for the elderly: demographic developments from 1960, housing, socio-economic status, and social activities. It produces recommendations for government policy, particularly on housing provision and financial assistance.

369 **Conduct unbecoming: the social construction of police deviance and control.**
Maurice Punch. London, New York: Tavistock, 1985. 249p. bibliog.

Punch presents his research into deviance and corruption in the Amsterdam police force in the period 1976–80, with a comparative look at police work in New York and London.

370 **Policing the inner city: a study of Amsterdam's Warmoesstraat.**
Maurice Punch. London: Macmillan, 1979. 231p. map. bibliog.

A research project on the Amsterdam police, arranged after the author had been discouraged from setting up similar projects in Britain. As well as discussing the police, the book tells us a great deal about social life in the major Dutch city in the mid-1970s.

371 **The changing class structure and political behaviour – a comparative analysis of lower middle-class politics in Britain and the Netherlands.**
C. S. Rallings, R. B. Andeweg. *European Journal of Political Research*, vol. 7 (1979), p. 27–47. bibliog.

A comparative study of white-collar worker political behaviour, which is shown to be undramatic and undecisive, hovering between working class and middle class options.

372 **Women in the Netherlands: past and present.**
M. G. Schenk. Baarn, The Netherlands: Wereldvenster, 1956. 64p.

Though now very dated, this book was widely distributed in the 1950s and it gives a useful impression of the part played by women in an economy less industrialized than now, in a society more domestic and pluriform than today. There are a number of photographs of women leaders, female committees and women in training and at work.

373 **Values affecting women's position in society.**
I. J. Schoonenboom, H. M. in 't Veld–Langeveld. *Planning and Development in the Netherlands*, vol. 8, no. 1 (1976), p. 17–33. bibliog.

The authors look at the historical development of Dutch feminism, the formulation of new patterns of values since the 1960s, and various policy options. They advocate participation by men and women in each others' labour markets, and legislation against discrimination.

374 **Research on homosexuality in the Netherlands.**
C. J. Straver. *The Netherlands' Journal of Sociology*, vol. 12 (1976), p. 121–37. bibliog.

Argues that the famous Dutch tolerance is actually very limited towards homosexuals, and that what tolerance exists is of recent origin. Reviews research done in the 1960s and early 1970s.

375 **Summary of the report on urbanization in the Netherlands.**
The Hague: Ministry of Housing and Physical Planning, 1976. 14p. map.

This is a summary of part 2 of a mid-1970s report on physical planning. It outlines developments to that date, and lays out the policy options for the planning of urban life in the future.

376 **The division of labour in Dutch families with preschool children.**
L. W. C. Tavecchio (et al.). *Journal of Marriage and the Family*, vol. 46 (1984), p. 231–42. bibliog.

A research group from Leiden University looks at roles in young Dutch families, and finds that although there is a strong ideal of equality between the sexes, especially in the higher social classes, the reality seldom matches the ideal.

377 **Planning the emancipation of women?**
Paula Wassen–Van Schaveren. *Planning and Development in the Netherlands*, vol. 8, no. 1 (1976), p. 4–16.

A report on the Commission for Emancipation (of women) set up by the Dutch government in 1974. The Commission's activities are outlined, including the formulation of a five-year plan for the emancipation of women.

Holland on the way to the forum: living in the Netherlands.
See item no. 5.

Fact sheet on the Netherlands, series E.
See item no. 7.

The kingdom of the Netherlands: facts and figures.
See item no. 14.

The future of Randstad Holland: a Netherlands scenario study on long-term perspectives for human settlement in the western part of the Netherlands.
See item no. 41.

Population mobility in the Netherlands, 1880–1910: a case study of Wisch in the Achterhoek.
See item no. 223.

The Dutch welfare state.
See item no. 382.

Factors in the growth of the number of disability beneficiaries in the Netherlands.
See item no. 383.

Comparative social policy and social security: a ten-country study.
See item no. 388.

Dutch prisons: important lessons for the British.
See item no. 442.

Dutch governmental planning and the moods of particular times.
See item no. 461.

Income distribution: analysis and policies.
See item no. 559.

The derivation of spatial goals for the Dutch land consolidation programme.
See item no. 604.

The Netherlands' Journal of Sociology.
See item no. 960.

Sociologia Neerlandica.
See item no. 968.

WVC Documentatie. (WVC Documentation.)
See item no. 975.

Social Services, Health and Welfare

378 **Lunacy reform in the Netherlands: State care and private initiative.**
Hans Binneveld. *Centrum voor Maatschappijgeschiedenis*, vol. 12 (1987), p. 165–87. bibliog.

Deals with the development of mental health care in the Netherlands, mainly in the 19th century. The most interesting and progressive initiatives came from confessional groups, most particularly the orthodox Calvinists.

379 **'Force of order and methods': an American view into the Dutch directed society.**
Maurice Blanken. The Hague: Nijhoff, 1976. 174p. maps. bibliog. (Studies in Social Life).

An investigation into planning in the Netherlands in the 1960s. There are chapters on the economy, the health service, housing, physical planning, the environment and education.

380 **Towards the austerity state: cutting down and pruning in the welfare state.**
Peter B. Boorsma. *Planning and Development in the Netherlands*, vol. 12, no. 1 (1980), p. 32–57.

The inaugural lecture of the Professor of Public Finance at Twente University. The author assumes the need for major spending cuts in the welfare state, and lays out the various technical alternatives for achieving the reductions. It is an unimpassioned analysis, arguing for a proper strategic policy of cuts instead of 'muddling through with the present corrective policy'. For the translation and publication of his lecture in *Planning and Development*, Boorsma has added an 'Introduction' (p. 24–31) explaining Dutch budgetary mechanisms.

381 **Limits to the welfare state: an inquiry into the realizability of socioeconomic and political desiderata in a highly industrialized society.**
G. J. van Driel, J. A. Hartog, C. van Ravenzwaaij. Boston, Massachusetts; The Hague: Nijhoff, 1980. 182p. bibliog.

This is a highly complex exercise in computer-model-building, known as input-output relations. The region covered is the Benelux and parts of West Germany and northern France.

382 **The Dutch welfare state.**
Amsterdam: Elsevier, 1983. 137p. bibliog.

This is a special issue of *Contemporary Crises*, vol. 7 (1983), p. 95–232, containing Martin Moerings, 'Protest in the Netherlands: developments in a polarised society'; Han Janse de Jonge, Ties Prakken, Theo de Roos, 'Action and law in the Netherlands'; B. Buiting, Nico Jög, 'Criminal justice in the Netherlands 1970–1980'; C. Kelk, 'The humanity of the Dutch prison system and the prisoner's consciousness'; Frans Koenraadt, 'Forensic psychiatric expertise and enforced treatment in the Netherlands'; Nico Jög, 'Organisational change and fundamental rights in the Dutch army, 1966–1976'; Koos Dalstra, 'The South Moluccan minority in the Netherlands'. The last article in the collection, by M. C. P. M. van Schendelen, 'Crisis of the Dutch welfare state' calls into question the actual existence of any 'crisis' in the welfare state.

383 **Factors in the growth of the number of disability beneficiaries in the Netherlands.**
Han Emanuel. *International Social Security Review*, vol. 33 (1980), p. 41–60. bibliog.

The author was Economic Secretary to the Dutch Social Security Council, and, thus, well informed. The subject is the rising number of those declared unfit for work (excluding the effects of accidents and occupational disease) from 1960 to 1978, when there were more than 400,000 claimants.

384 **Health in the Netherlands: publications in foreign languages.**
Edited by the Department of Documentation and Library, Ministry of Welfare, Health and Cultural Affairs (WVC). Rijswijk, The Netherlands: WVC, 1985. 4th ed. 120p. bibliog.

This most useful bibliography on health matters is concerned mainly with works in the English language, but some pieces in French and German are also listed. The arrangement is thematic, by subject, and there is an alphabetical index for easy access. Contains no annotations.

385 **New trends in social welfare policy in the Netherlands.**
G. Hendriks. The Hague: Government Publishing Office, 1978. 90p.

A collection of four papers presented by the author in the mid-1970s, on social welfare policies, local authorities and citizens' participation, community work and voluntary work. Hendriks was the Director-General of Social Development at the Ministry of Cultural Affairs, Recreation and Social Welfare (CRM).

386 **A perspective on governmental housing policies in the Netherlands.**
Otto J. Hetzel. The Hague: Ministry of Housing, Physical Planning and Environment, 1983. 35p. bibliog.

An historical perspective is adopted in this short account of housing policies. The focus falls on the 1970s, with new government measures for finance in housing. The bibliography refers to works in English.

387 **Family allowance and tax relief for children in the Netherlands.**
W. P. Huizing. *International Social Security Review*, vol. 29 (1976), p. 378–91. bibliog.

This article, by a senior civil servant, explains the complex and generous system of allowances, and comments on plans to integrate tax relief and benefits in this area.

388 **Comparative social policy and social security: a ten-country study.**
P. R. Kaim–Caudle. London: Martin Robertson, 1973. 357p. bibliog.

Concerns social policy in New Zealand, Great Britain, Germany, Austria, Denmark, Australia, Ireland, Canada, the United States and the Netherlands. There are informative separate sections on Dutch pensions, Dutch unemployment insurance and family endowment, as well as general comparative sections which concern the Dutch in passing.

389 **Savings through innovative care provision in the Dutch welfare state.**
Adrian de Kok. Voorschoten, The Netherlands: Ministry of Welfare, Health and Cultural Affairs (WVC), 1985. 20p. bibliog.

De Kok is head of Research and Development at the Welfare Ministry in the Netherlands, and this paper lays out a ten-year policy option for the care sector of the welfare state. There is a survey of welfare provision, an account of the approaches taken by the three main Dutch political parties to the problem, and the message is that severe cuts are necessary but should be implemented with some sensitivity.

390 **The societal state: the modern osmosis of state and society as presenting itself in the Netherlands in particular: a case study of a general trend.**
Paul E. Kraemer. Meppel, The Netherlands: Boom, 1966. Doctoral dissertation, University of Leiden, 1966. 210p. bibliog.

A sociological study of the growth of society and state in the Netherlands towards each other, resulting in our modern welfare state. Contains a helpful sketch of Dutch history from 1850 to the 1960s.

391 **Voluntary agencies in the welfare state.**
Ralph M. Kramer. Berkeley, California: University of California Press, 1981. 334p. bibliog.

A study of voluntary help for the mentally and physically handicapped in the United States, England, the Netherlands and Israel in the mid-1970s, in the context of debates about the desirability of public welfare services in the Americas. The Dutch case-study is presented in Chapter I (p. 19–36).

392 **The development of socio-medical care in the Netherlands.**
A. Querido. London: Routledge & Kegan Paul, 1968. 118p. bibliog.

A historical treatment from the Middle Ages to the 1960s, concentrating on the 19th and 20th centuries. All the relevant legislation is listed, and as such this rather dated book retains its usefulness. There is an appendix of demographic information.

393 **A reappraisal of welfare policy: summary of the twenty-second report to the government.**
Netherlands Scientific Council for Government Policy (WRR). The Hague: WRR, 1982. 53p.

A translated summary of a major report by this quango on physical health care, out-patient mental health care, care of the elderly, and adult education. The report concludes with recommendations for government policy, especially concerning the desired relationship between the government and the private sector.

394 **Liberal policing in the interventionist state.**
P. van Rheenen. *Police Studies*, vol. 8, no. 2 (1985), p. 93–96.

Instead of decentralizing police administration regionally, the author argues that the shift from government according to principles towards legislating for feasibility should be reflected in a change towards structuring policing according to the sectors of control that are needed.

395 **The bureaupolitics of policing: the Dutch case.**
U. Rosenthal. *Police Science Abstracts*, vol. 12, no. 5 (Sept.–Oct. 1984), p. 1–14. bibliog.

The bureaucratic organization of the police force results, the author argues, in power struggles between departments, in which the police manipulate political power.

396 **Social security in the Netherlands.**
Compiled by Dutch members of the International Social Security Association. *International Social Security Review*, vol. 23 (1970), p. 3–61. bibliog.

A full survey of the system as it existed in 1970, listing the relevant legislation and all its provisions; still the basis of the Dutch system.

397 **Health care facilities and work incapacity: a comparison of the situation in the Netherlands with that in six other West European countries.**
J. Soeters, R. Prins. *International Social Security Review*, vol. 38 (1985), p. 141–56. bibliog.

The subject is industrial absenteeism within the health care service in the Netherlands. Generally the Dutch system is supported, though some modifications are suggested.

398 **The use of a health education planning model to design and implement health education interventions concerning AIDS: the application of the PRECEDE-framework (Green, 1980) for the situation in the Netherlands and the USA.**
M. Stadlander (et al.). Maastricht, The Netherlands: Rijksuniversiteit Limburg, 1985. 31p. bibliog. (GVO Cahiers, no. 3).

This is the text of a paper given to an international conference on problems related to AIDS held in Atlanta (Georgia) in April 1985, and concerns proposals for health education programmes specifically designed to counteract the spread of AIDS.

In so many words.
See item no. 260.

Policy for the elderly in the Netherlands.
See item no. 368.

Policing the inner city: a study of Amsterdam's Warmoesstraat.
See item no. 370.

Policy development: a study of the Social and Economic Council of the Netherlands.
See item no. 423.

Child care and protection in the Netherlands.
See item no. 431.

Criminal justice in the Netherlands.
See item no. 437.

Dutch prisons: important lessons for the British.
See item no. 442.

Sensory assessment and chemical composition of drinking water.
See item no. 486.

The Netherlands' Journal of Sociology.
See item no. 960.

WVC Documentatie. (WVC Documentation.)
See item no. 975.

Politics

399 **Catholic power in the Netherlands.**
Herman Bakvis. Kingston, Ontario; Montreal: McGill–Queen's University Press, 1981. 240p. bibliog.

An examination of Dutch Catholic politics since 1945. It comprises a full analysis of the Catholic community, the Catholic Party, theological upheavals in the 1960s, and the decline of the Catholic vote in the 1960s and 1970s.

400 **The dynamics of Dutch politics.**
Robert C. Bone. *Journal of Politics*, vol. 24 (1962), p. 23–49. bibliog.

Statistical data on the period 1945–59 provide the basis for a sound account of post-war politics. A valuable asset is the long historical run-up taken by the author, which also makes the article of use to students of the 19th and 20th centuries.

401 **Consociationalism, center and periphery in the Netherlands.**
Hans Daalder. In: *Mobilization, center-periphery structures and nation-building: a volume in commemoration of Stein Rokkan.* Edited by Per Torsvik. Bergen, Norway: Universistetsforlaget, 1981, p. 181–240. bibliog.

An amalgam of several previous papers, this study traces the development of Dutch state structure from the 16th century onwards, examining the urban-rural balance in politics and the evolution of religious communities, and the formative period for the Dutch political structure between 1848 and 1919.

402 **Extreme proportional representation – the Dutch experience.**
Hans Daalder. In: *Adversary politics and electoral reform*. Edited by S. E. Finer. London: Wigram, 1975, p. 223–48. bibliog.

Daalder gives an account of the introduction of proportional representation (PR) in 1917, and goes on to discuss political instability and party alignment in this light. The Dutch PR system is very 'pure', with one single (national) constituency and a very low 0.67% threshold. Daalder suggests some reforms and directions which might counteract the adverse effects of the system.

403 **On building consociational nations: the cases of the Netherlands and Switzerland.**
Hans Daalder. *International Social Science Journal*, vol. 23 (1971), p. 355–70. bibliog.

In looking at the way in which nations devise political systems to deal with their internal rifts and divisions, Daalder examines geopolitical factors, the similarities and differences between the two countries in question, and concludes by asking whether consociationalism might not be a luxury affordable only by small nations.

404 **Dutch parliamentary election study 1982: an enterprise of the Dutch political science community.**
C. van der Eijk (et al.). Amsterdam: C. T. Press for the Dutch Interuniversity Election Study Workgroup, 1983. 450p. bibliog.

The sixth of a series of national election studies – the others refer to the elections of 1967, 1971, 1972, 1977 and 1981. The research for this study is based on post-election interviews, and re-interviews with those approached for the study of the 1981 election. There is much attention to methodology, and many tables and appendixes are provided.

405 **Electoral change in the Netherlands: empirical results and methods of measurement.**
C. van der Eijk, Broer Niemöller. Amsterdam: C. T. Press, 1983. 440p. bibliog. Doctoral dissertation, University of Amsterdam, 1983.

The 'empirical results' are election results in the Netherlands in the period from 1945 to 1983, concentrating on 1971 to 1981. The study goes beyond an analysis of the political results, and deals with Dutch voters' psychological behaviour as well. There is overt concern for methodological problems in 'empirical' studies.

406 **Elite images of Dutch politics: accommodation and conflict.**
S. J. Eldersveld, J. Kooiman, T. van der Tak. Ann Arbor, Michigan: University of Michigan Press; The Hague: Nijhoff, 1981. 266p. bibliog.

A detailed analysis, based on interviews in 1973 with 120 Dutch politicians and senior civil servants, of the Dutch élite's view of its own functions and characteristics. Insights emerge about the functioning of the Dutch political system, and there is some contribution to theoretical works on élites.

407 **Party politics and performance: the case of Dutch cities.**
R. C. Fried. *Acta Politica*, vol. 15 (1980), p. 61–110. bibliog.

This study of parties in city politics concludes that the partisan nature of local party politics is exaggerated. The data are taken from the 1960s and 1970s, while an implicit comparison with US local government is always in the background.

408 **The other Western Europe: a political analysis of the smaller democracies.**
Earl H. Fry, Gregory A. Raymond. Santa Barbara, California; Oxford: ABC–Clio, 1983. 288p. bibliog. (Studies in International and Comparative Politics, vol. 14).

Chapter III of this study is on the Benelux nations, and includes an historical view of Dutch politics, as well as an analysis of political culture today.

409 **The Dutch political parties and the May 1986 elections.**
Ken Gladdish. *Government and Opposition*, vol. 21, no. 3 (summer 1986), p. 317–37. bibliog.

A full analysis of Dutch politics since the war from the standpoint of oppositional dynamics, with a short section on the 1986 election results.

410 **Parlement en kiezer: jaarboek.** (Parliament and voter: yearbook.)
P. Goossen, G. G. J. Thissen. Leiden: Nijhoff. Latest edition: vol. 68 (Session 1984–85), 1986. 311p. bibliog.

An annual almanac for parliamentary matters containing lists of ministries since 1848, Cabinet Members since 1945, Members of Parliament, and similar information, including a survey of parliamentary business in the relevant year. No index is included.

411 **Benelux conference: September 1977.**
J. L. Heldring (et al.). Hull, England: University of Hull, 1977. 88p. bibliog.

The papers read at this conference at Hull University cover subjects including Dutch foreign policy, Dutch politics, the Dutch economy and economic policy, and post-war economic development. There are also papers on Belgium and Luxembourg.

412 **Six European states.**
Stephen Holt. London: Hamilton, 1970. 414p. bibliog.

Part 6 of this politics textbook deals with the Netherlands. The political system is described, showing the role of the monarchy, the constitutional set-up, and the importance of religion. Local government and the judiciary are also dealt with.

413 **Catholic emancipation in the Netherlands.**
Gerlof D. Homan. *Catholic Historical Review*, vol. 52 (1966/67), p. 201–11. bibliog.

A conveniently simple introduction to a very complex subject. Roman Catholic grievances of the 19th century are catalogued, together with the legislation which has alleviated their situation.

414 **Influencing mass political behaviour: elites and political subcultures in the Netherlands and Austria.**
Joseph J. Houska. Berkeley, California: Institute of International Studies, 1985. 198p. bibliog. (Research Series, no. 60).

A comparative study of élites and their functioning in two countries. The growth of the Dutch system is explained, concentrating on organizational developments. Electoral behaviour is the subject of the main research, and data are provided in the appendixes.

415 **The libertarian movement in the Netherlands.**
Rudolph de Jong. *Anarchist Review*, vol. 1, no. 5 (1981), p. 56–69. bibliog.

Traces the history of the Anarchists in Dutch society from the 19th century to the 1970s. De Jong gives only a brief glimpse, but his references provide the key to further investigation; a useful introduction.

416 **Pillars of sand: a Marxist critique of consociational democracy in the Netherlands.**
R. A. Kieve. *Comparative Politics*, vol. 13 (1981), p. 313–37. bibliog.

Criticizing the use of the field of Dutch politics as a testing ground for theories of political stability, Kieve points to breakdowns in order as well as to the importance of class issues in the Netherlands. He claims that the ideological rifts in the Netherlands have been exaggerated, and the main section is entitled, significantly, 'The failure of the politics of accommodation'.

417 **The politics of accommodation: pluralism and democracy in the Netherlands.**
Arend Lijphart. Berkeley, California: University of California Press, 1975. 2nd ed. 231p. bibliog.

The first edition of this major synthesis on the Dutch polity appeared in 1968. Lijphart's analysis of Dutch politics has now become the orthodoxy, and indeed has come under the kinds of attacks launched by the new guard on the old. He has made immortal the image of Dutch society divided into ideological 'pillars', connected only by the machinery of government: 'verzuiling', or vertical pluralism. The second edition carries a new Chapter 10, dealing with the disintegration of the pillarized society in the late 1960s and early 1970s.

418 **Verkiezingsprogramma's 1986: verkiezingen voor de tweede kamer der Staten-Generaal, 21 mei 1986.** (Election manifestos 1986: elections for the second chamber of the States General, 21 May 1986.)

Edited by I. Lipschits. The Hague: Staatsuitgeverij, 1986. 527p.

The election manifestos of the eleven contesting political parties for the May 1986 elections. An index is provided. A similar volume, *Verkiezings programma's 1981*, with the same editor and publisher, appeared for the elections of that year (477p.).

419 **Confessional attachment and electoral behaviour in the Netherlands.**

W. E. Miller, P. C. Stouthard. *European Journal of Political Research*, vol. 3 (1975), p. 219–58. bibliog.

Based on two surveys of 1970 and 1972, the article examines the effect of secularization on Dutch political adherence. As the confessional vote declines, just as many go to secular parties of the right as to the left, and the socialist threat is kept at bay.

420 **Local elites and the structure of political conflict: parties, unions and the action groups in the Netherlands.**

Thomas R. Rochon. PhD thesis, University of Michigan, 1980. 258p. bibliog.

This is a rather opaque study of local Dutch politics and the ways in which conflict arises at that level. There is some useful information, but it is very hard to extract from behind the barrage or smoke-screen of social-science terminology.

421 **Consociationalism, pillarization and conflict management in the Low Countries.**

Edited by M. C. P. M. van Schendelen. *Acta Politica*, vol. 19, no. 1 (Jan. 1984), p. 1–178. bibliog. (Special issue).

Examines various political science models of consociationalism in the empirical context of the Low Countries. It contains a systematic bibliography on the subject (p. 161–74). Belgium also receives good coverage. A. Lijphart himself contributes a retrospective article (p. 9–18).

422 **Does consociationalism exist?**

I. Scholten. In: *Electoral participation: a comparative analysis.* Edited by Richard Rose. London: Sage, 1980. p. 329–54. bibliog.

The author, who was working on a PhD at the time of writing, rejects the concept of consociationalism in explaining Dutch political life in the 20th century, and instead points to a corporatist tradition amongst the 'pillars' or ideological groups in the Netherlands.

423 **Policy development: a study of the Social and Economic Council of the Netherlands.**

Wazir Singh. Rotterdam: Rotterdam University Press, 1972. 210p. bibliog.

Singh has not used Dutch sources for this essay, but has based his study on a questionnaire sent to all the members of the Social and Economic Council (SER). It is an examination of the process of policy creation as practised by the SER in its heyday: its influence is arguably on the decline in the 1980s.

424 **Democratic parties in the Low Countries and Germany: origins and historical developments.**

Willem Verkade. Leiden: Universitaire Pers, 1965. 331p. bibliog.

Covering Belgium, Germany and the Netherlands, this is a most useful guide to the growth of modern political parties, being especially strong on the development of modern political liberalism.

425 **The Dutch Labour Party: a social democratic party in transition.**

Steven B. Wolinetz. In: *Social democratic parties in western Europe*. Edited by W. E. Patterson, A. H. Thomas. London: Croom Helm, 1977, p. 342–88. bibliog.

Traces the development of the Dutch parliamentary Socialists since the First World War, and explains the place of religion and class in the Dutch party system. The 'New Left' movement is examined, and certain dilemmas for the Dutch Socialists are outlined.

426 **Party re-alignment in the Netherlands.**

Steven B. Wolinetz. PhD thesis, Yale University, 1973. 237p. bibliog.

Based on parliamentary election results, 1918–72, and on interviews, this thesis examines the proliferation of small parties in the Netherlands in the 1960s. Wolinetz points to the disintegration of Roman Catholic cohesion and to the introduction of youth to politics as explanations for the decline of strong subcultural political attachments.

The economy and politics of the Netherlands since 1945.

See item no. 159.

'Verzuiling': a confessional road to secularization: emancipation and the decline of political Catholicism, 1920–1970.

See item no. 341.

The case of Dutch Catholicism: a contribution to the theory of the pluralistic society.

See item no. 347.

The changing class structure and political behaviour – a comparative analysis of lower middle-class politics in Britain and the Netherlands.
See item no. 371.

Bi-lingual codebooks of the questionnaire The Dutch member of parliament 1979/80.
See item no. 446.

Democracy and foreign policy.
See item no. 487.

Political union: a microcosm of European politics 1960–1966.
See item no. 489.

Dutch organised agriculture in international politics.
See item no. 608.

The origins and consolidation of Dutch social democracy, 1894–1914.
See item no. 633.

Studies in the posthumous work of Spinoza: on style, earliest translation and reception, earliest and modern edition of some texts.
See item no. 833.

Acta Politica: Tijdschrift voor Politicologie. (Acta Politica: Journal for Political Science.)
See item no. 928.

Keesing's Contemporary Archives.
See item no. 951.

Een voorlopige bibliografie over het thema 'verzuiling'. (A provisional bibliography on the theme 'vertical pluralism'.)
See item no. 1024.

Constitution, Legal and Judicial System

Legal system

427 **Geweld in onze samenleving.** (Violence in our society.)
Edited by G. A. van Bergeijk, R. W. Jongman, S. J. Steenstra. The Hague: Staatsuitgeverij, 1978. 270p. bibliog.

This contains the papers read to the First Congress of the Netherlands Society of Criminology at Amsterdam in 1975. The current importance of this topic would justify a translation of some of these contributions.

428 **Public legal services: a comparative study of policy, politics and practice.**
Jeremy Cooper. London: Sweet & Maxwell, 1983. 320p. bibliog.

This compares the provision of legal community services in the Netherlands, the United States and the United Kingdom. It shows how the government-sponsored Legal Aid and Law Centres in Holland differ from the much less rationalized local initiatives in Britain and the more systematic promotion by a Legal Services corporation in the United States and it also analyses the different programmes and activities of the services in the three countries, with a detailed description of the Amsterdam Bureau voor Rechtshulp, the Brent and Manchester Law Centres and the Oregon Legal Services.

429 **Legal Services for the poor in the Netherlands.**
Jeremy Cooper. *New Law Journal*, vol. 130, no. 5940 (1980), p. 119–21.

A useful, factual description of the provision of legal aid through nineteen local, private offices entirely subsidized by central government funds. There are also lawyers' collectives, recognized by the Ministry of Justice and the Bar.

430 **Patterns of criminality and law enforcement during the Ancien Régime: the Dutch case.**

H. Diederiks. *Criminal Justice History*, vol. 1, 1980. p. 157–74. bibliog.

This gives the results of research by a group of criminologists who examined the apparently conflicting evidence of sentences during the 18th century and contemporary views of the legal system. By comparison with standards throughout Europe, they conclude that the wealth of the minority affected the severity of punishment for robbery and banditry, that sodomy was unusually harshly treated, but that on the whole, most sentences were humane.

431 **Child care and protection in the Netherlands.**

J. E. Doek, S. Slagter. Amsterdam: Stichting voor het Kind, 1979. 63p.

A survey of the history and development of child care, the law and child protection, statutory and voluntary provisions, child care outside the home, and the future of child care.

432 **The origins and consequences of Dutch penal policy since 1945.**

D. Downes. *British Journal of Criminology*, vol. 22, no. 4 (Oct. 1982), p. 325–62. bibliog.

A comparison of the Dutch and British penal systems shows a greater increase in the 1970s for driving offences in the Netherlands, but a more tolerant attitude to convicts and ex-convicts, but that there, too, the system is under severe pressures which require a remedy.

433 **Seventeenth-century Leyden law professors and their influence on the development of the civil law: a study of Bronchorst, Vinnius and Voet.**

R. Feenstra, C. J. D. de Waal. Amsterdam: North Holland Publishing Company, 1975. 124p. bibliog.

A mainly bibliographical study which gives an idea of what the three professors taught their students and how their works were spread outside the Netherlands.

434 **Introduction to Dutch law for foreign lawyers.**

Edited by D. C. Fokkema, J. M. J. Chorus, E.H. Hondius, E. C. Lisser. Deventer, The Netherlands: Kluwer, under the auspices of the Netherlands Comparative Law Association, 1978. 700p. bibliog.

The contributions by various specialists fall under the headings: 'Dutch legal system', 'Private law', 'Criminal law', 'Constitutional law', 'Fiscal law', 'Economic law', 'Labour law', 'International law', and 'Legal philosophy'. There is a selective bibliography of Dutch law (of publications in Dutch and French), a list of useful addresses and an index.

435 **The jurisprudence of Holland.**
Hugo de Groot, translated by Robert Warden Lee. Aalen, FRG: Scientia–Verlag, 1977. 2 vols. Volume I contains the text and translation of notes. Volume II provides a commentary.

The commentary is extensive and detailed and there is a very useful index of Dutch and English terms.

436 **Adat law in Indonesia.**
Edited and with an introduction by B. ter Haar, E. Adamson Hoebel, A. A. Schiller. New York: AMS Press, 1979. 280p.

This American translation of the greater part of Ter Haar's standard work of 1939 includes the editors' introduction on the place of Adat law in the legal system and on its ethnological background, and Ter Haar's study of its social organization, its effect on land rights and land transactions, its obligations and its personal and private applications.

437 **Criminal justice in the Netherlands.**
L. H. C. Hulsman. *Delta*, vol. 16, no. 4 (winter 1973–74), p. 7–19.

A review of the liberal reforms that made the Netherlands the country with the smallest prison population, and an analysis of the factors which maintain a relatively favourable position among most countries experiencing an increasing crime rate. These are: comprehensive social services and financial benefits, an extensive network of youth centres, well-supported alternatives to prison sentences, and the short terms imposed.

438 **Philip of Leyden: a fourteenth century jurist.**
P. Leupen. The Hague: Leiden University Press; Zwolle, The Netherlands: Tjeenk Willink, 1981. 300p. bibliog.

A study of Leyden's life and treatise 'De cura republicae et sorte principantis'.

439 **The Netherlands Business Corporation code.**
Chicago, Illinois: Commerce Clearing House, 1977. 71p. (Common Market Reports, no. 318, 20 May 1977).

An American translation of the code which deals with the corporation, its shares, capital, general meeting of shareholders, management and supervision of management, board of overseers of a large business corporation, investigation of a corporation's affairs and dissolution; the closed corporation and its general regulations, shares, meetings of shareholders, management and dissolution.

440 **International law in the Netherlands.**
Edited by H. F. van Panhuys, W. P. Heere, J. W. Josephus Jitta, Ko Swan Sik, A. M. Stuyt. Alphen, The Netherlands: Sijthoff & Noordhoff; Dobbs Ferry, New York: Oceana Publications, 1978. 537p.

This is the only volume to have appeared so far, and has four chapters on international law and foreign relations in the past; three chapters on the law of international rivers, jurisdiction over the Continental Shelf and international fisheries law; and three chapters on the Netherlands' participation in the international legal system. Two further volumes are planned, all of them published under the auspices of the T. M. C. Asser Institute in The Hague.

441 **Access to justice in Holland.**
E. Rothfeld, J. C. Houtappel. In: *Access to justice: a world survey*. Edited by M. Cappalletti, B. Garth. Milan; New York: Guiffre Oceana; Alphen, The Netherlands: Sijthoff, 1978, vol. 1, bk. 2, p. 581–94. bibliog.

A summary of access to justice in Holland, it outlines the judicial system and, since there is no direct access to the courts, gives information on the various procedures using legal representatives, with further information on ways of reducing the costs of legal proceedings and a forecast of likely future developments.

442 **Dutch prisons: important lessons for the British.**
Richard Smith. *British Medical Journal*, vol. 288 (March 1984), p. 847–850.

The Dutch not only spend three times as much per prisoner as the English do, but have shorter sentences and succeed in keeping the costs the same since they only have one third the number of prisoners. Yet they have reduced their prison population without invoking a rise in the crime rate, though that has been increasing rapidly in other countries.

443 **Judicial violence in the Dutch Republic: corporal punishment, executions and torture in Amsterdam 1650–1750.**
P. C. Spierenburg. Doctoral dissertation, University of Amsterdam, 1978. 247p. bibliog.

This sets the judicial procedures in Amsterdam against the general state of the northern provinces after the Dutch Revolt. The analysis shows that violence actually increased after 1650 even though there had been a reaction against violence before then. The author attributes this to the emergence of a new aristocracy.

The kingdom of the Netherlands: facts and figures.
See item no. 14.

Liberal policing in the interventionist state.
See item no. 394.

The bureaupolitics of policing: the Dutch case.
See item no. 395.

The rules of physical planning in the Netherlands.
See item no. 467.

Hugo Grotius, a great European 1583–1645.
See item no. 846.

The world of Hugo Grotius (1583–1645: proceedings of the International Colloquium organised by the Grotius Committee of the Royal Netherlands Academy of Arts and Sciences, Rotterdam 6–9 April 1983).
See item no. 859.

Netherlands International Law Review.
See item no. 955.

Netherlands Journal for Legal Philosophy and Jurisprudence and Proceedings of the Netherlands Association for the Philosophy of Law.
See item no. 957.

Benelux abbreviations and symbols: law and related subjects.
See item no. 981.

Constitution

444 **Parliament in the Netherlands.**
Introduction by D. Dolman. The Hague: Government Publications Office, 1982. 3rd ed. 61p.

An adaptation, with illustrations, of the official publication *Al meer dan vijfhonderd jaar* (More than five hundred years) (1976), outlining the history and present constitution of the Dutch parliament.

445 **European electoral systems handbook.**
Edited by G. Hand, Jacques Georgel, Christoph Sasse. London: Butterworth, 1979. 252p.

Chapter eight, on the Netherlands (by Dick Seip) outlines the history of the system, the method of voting, the elections and the organization and financing of the parties, candidacy and election results.

446 **Bi-lingual codebooks of the questionnaire The Dutch member of parliament 1979/80.**
Edited by J. L. van der Pauw, A. J. van Marlen. Rotterdam: Erasmus University Press, 1981. 392p.

A survey, in Dutch and English, carried out by the Department of Political Science in the Faculty of Social Sciences at Erasmus University, on the functions and practice of Dutch MPs.

447 **The parliament of the Kingdom of the Netherlands.**
Ernst van Raalte. London: Hansard Society for Parliamentary Government, 1959. 216p. bibliog.

Despite its date this is still a reliable and authoritative study of the development of the parliamentary system from 1848 to the present day, the state of the parliamentary system now, the organization of power of the States General, and the organization and procedures in the work of parliament. The short bibliography and notes refer to Dutch-language texts, and there is a general index.

448 **Current trends in local power and authority in the Netherlands.**
Alex Reinders, Ron Verhoef. *Polish Round Table Yearbook*, vol. 7 (1976–77), p. 231–68.

This article outlines the development of local government from its early origins; and the activities of local, municipal and provincial government; the legal system and its impact on the relationship between the various levels of local government; the municipal organization; territorial and functional committees; municipal finances; and likely developments.

Legislation

449 **A modern European company law system: commentary on the 1976 Dutch legislation.**
J. M. M. Maeijer. Alphen, The Netherlands: Sijthoff & Noordhoff, 1978. 382p.

A full survey of the considerable changes in Dutch company law between 1971 and 1977 due to the introduction of worker participation and the requirements of EEC directives. Appendixes contain translations of the Resolution of the Social and Economic Council on Rules relating to Public Offers and Mergers of 1975 and the statutes of a typical large company and of a smaller company.

450 **Corporate law of the Netherlands and of the Netherlands Antilles.**
S. W. van der Meer. Zwolle, The Netherlands: Tjeenk Willink, 1976. 6th ed. 126p.

A short introduction draws attention to the main differences between Roman (hence Dutch) law and common law and to the pending revision of the Netherlands Civil Code in the year this translation of the 'Civil Code, Legal Entities' was published. Unfortunately, the translation was not prepared in consultation with an English lawyer, and it must therefore be treated with some caution.

451 **The Netherlands Civil Code, Book 6: the Law of Obligations.**
Edited by the Netherlands Ministry of Justice. Leiden: Sijthoff, 1977. 654p.

This is a 'draft text and commentary', and its main purpose is to serve students of comparative law, and its commentary thus deals with comparative aspects of the Code. Though 'not to be considered an official translation', the translation reads well (for a legal document) and has been approved by the then Professor of Comparative Law at Lancaster University. The extensive commentary and notes make this a valuable text book on law, and it is only unfortunate that it is the draft rather than the final text of Book 6 to which so much scholarly attention has been given.

452 **Dutch company law.**
P. Sanders. London: Oyez, 1977. 277p.

Written for businessmen and professional advisers, it covers the main features of company law with chapters on formation and registration, shares and loan capital, share and other securities, shareholders' rights, the board of management, the supervisory board, general meetings, annual accounts, amendment of the articles of association, dissolution and winding up, groups of companies, the 'Besloten Vennootschap' (closed corporation), large companies, the works council, mergers and takeovers.

453 **Dutch business law.**
Steven R. Schuit, Jan M. van der Beek, Bonne K. Raap.
Deventer, The Netherlands: Kluwer, 1978. 567p.

A member of the Amsterdam Bar, an accountant and a tax consultant and partners in their firms explain the legal system in the Netherlands with particular reference to the differences between the Dutch, American and British law. It contains chapters on juridical structure and legal proceedings, moratorium and bankruptcy, the free professions, choice of law, jurisdiction and enforcement of foreign judgements, contracts in general, real estate transactions, agents and distributors, company law, accounting and auditing requirements, enterprise councils, mergers and take-overs, EEC and Dutch competition law, investment incentives and business regulations, exchange control, banking institutions and finance companies, capital raising and financing contracts, foreign trade, oil and gas, industrial and intellectual property rights, product regulations and liability, insurance practice, zoning, building and environmental regulations, labour, social security, and taxation.

454 **Planning between law and legislation.**

H. van der Sluys. *Planning and Development in the Netherlands*, vol. 14 (1982), p. 68–100. bibliog.

Since modern law is derived from legal practice rather than legislation, the attempt to link planning with legislation causes some surprise. But modern administrative law has become highly complex in the Netherlands. Moreover, many administrative measures are of a discretionary nature, making judgements in law very difficult. As a result, appeal procedures have had to be introduced. Hence, physical planning should rely on exercising existing powers rather than trying to impose some form of external organization on the decision-making system.

455 **Dutch/English company law.**

Floris O. W. Vogelaar, Martin G. Chester. Deventer, The Netherlands: Kluwer, 1973. 104p.

'A comparative review' by solicitors of the Supreme Courts in the Netherlands and Britain. It deals with different types of companies, the formation of a company, share and loan capital administration and management, meetings of shareholders, worker participation, investigation into a company's affairs, amendment of the constitution, winding-up and take-over codes.

Chemical Substances Act.
See item no. 472.

Regulations concerning protection of the soil.
See item no. 483.

Waste Substances Act.
See item no. 484.

Netherlands Corporate Tax Act 1969.
See item no. 554.

The new Netherlands airport zoning act.
See item no. 625.

Educational developments in the Netherlands, 1984–1986.
See item no. 649.

Primary Education Act (The Netherlands).
See item no. 655.

University education in the Netherlands.
See item no. 677.

Broadcasting in the Netherlands.
See item no. 917.

Planning and Environment

Planning

456 **Amsterdam: the planning and development in a nutshell.**
Amsterdam: Department of Public Works, Urban Development Section [n.d.], 16p.

An illustrated outline of the city's growth since 1600 and plans for its development towards the end of this century.

457 **A study of the spatial planning process in Britain and the Netherlands.**
David M. Dunham. Amsterdam: Planning and Demographic Institute of the University, n.d. [1971], 69p. bibliog.

A chapter on the theory of planning is followed by chapters on planning in Britain and planning in the Netherlands. The results of planning in the two countries are not compared, but there is a close comparison of the influence and the impact of political decisions in planning.

458 **Public planning in the Netherlands.**
Edited by Ashok K. Dutt, Frank J. Costa. Oxford: Clarendon Press, 1985. 256p. bibliog.

This contains articles by Peter Hall on Dutch urban planning within the perspective of European development, Seve Hamnett on the political framework and development objectives of post-war Dutch planning, Andreas Faludi and Peter de Ruijter on the theoretical and institutional framework of Dutch planning, A. E. J. Morris on the historical roots of Dutch city planning and urban form, J. Nieuwenkamp on national physical planning, J. M. Timmermans and J. W. Becker on social planning, A. van Delft and A. Kwaak on national development and economic policy since 1945, F. van der Sluys and G. van Evert on planning for urban renewal in The Hague, Ashok K. Dutt on the Delta works, Ashok K. Dutt and Frank J. Costa on the evolution of land use and settlement policies in Zuyder Zee project planning, C. van der Wal on the new towns of the IJsselmeerpolders and Ashok K. Dutt and Frank J. Costa on Dutch planning in the next century.

459 **Information systems for integrated regional planning and policy making in the Netherlands.**
J. van Est, J. Scheurwater, H. Voogd. Delft, The Netherlands: Technische Hogeschool, 1982. 18p.

A paper in the form of a planning memorandum, 1983–86, given at the Conference on International Working on Regional Information Systems in Austria. The implementation and evaluation of plans relies on the collaboration of provinces and municipalities, but the information systems themselves may be very unreliable and rely too heavily on quantitative rather than qualitative analysis.

460 **Feature service.**
Amsterdam: Gemeente Amsterdam, Bureau Voorlichting.

News-sheets are issued from time to time on a wide range of topics concerning Amsterdam: water supply, urban development, economic and financial activities, medical, commercial, tourist facilities, etc.

461 **Dutch governmental planning and the moods of particular times.**
P. den Hoed. *Planning and Development in the Netherlands*, vol. 14, no. 1 (1982), p. 33–48.

A comparison of the state of government planning in 1960, 1970 and 1980 in order to assess the interaction between planning and its effects on the social environment. A shift is noted from central co-ordinated planning in the 1960s to greater flexibility and local autonomy in the 1980s.

462 **Relations between central and local government in the Netherlands.**
Andries Hoogerwerf. *Planning and Development in the Netherlands*, vol. 13 (1981), p. 215–36. bibliog.

Though the autonomy of municipalities is guaranteed by the constitution, this is effectively limited in a number of ways, not least by the extent of financial control from central government. To challenge this the Union of Netherlands Municipalities constitutes a formidable pressure group, as the government traditionally strives for decentralization. However, in the absence of empirical research, policy decisions continue to be haphazard and arbitrary.

463 **Nuclear facilities in Dutch border areas.**
H. Huisman. *Planning and Development in the Netherlands*, vol. 14 (1982), p. 205–30.

Since Germany and Belgium already have nuclear power stations near the Dutch border, which are indispensable for their energy needs, the question whether the Netherlands should retain, close down or increase its nuclear capacity is academic. What is essential, however, is the provision of adequate trans-frontier consultations and safety measures.

464 **The next twenty-five years: a survey of future developments in the Netherlands.**

The Netherlands Scientific Council for Government Policy (WRR). The Hague: WWR, 1978. 197p. (Reports to the Government, no. 15).

The anticipated developments are forecast according to two alternatives representing reasonable expectations for the future. From general assumptions the survey moves to propositions based on less certain forecasts and then offers two scenarios: labour, economy, space and environment in the two proffered alternatives.

465 **Regional information systems and impact analysis for large-scale energy development.**

Peter Nijkamp. Amsterdam: Faculty of Economics, Amsterdam Free University, 1983. 35p.

A survey of information systems with regard to energy policies leads to the conclusion that regional analyses of requirements must precede any large-scale energy policy. This should have a clear policy orientation and the spatial dimensions of large-scale energy development must be carefully monitored.

466 **A policy-oriented survey of the future: towards a broader perspective.**

Netherlands Scientific Council for Government Policy (WRR). The Hague: WRR, 1983. 80p.

This is a summary of the Council's twenty-fifth report to the government giving a coherent statement on the factors governing planning decisions, viewed from a number of perspectives: labour, social, consumption requirements, environment, educational and cultural requirements, foreign policy and administration.

467 **The rules of physical planning in the Netherlands.**

The Hague: Ministry of Housing and Physical Planning, 1976. 37p.

This briefly describes the bodies involved in physical planning and the instruments for this planning at state, provincial and local level, with an outline of the government's physical planning policy. Appendixes deal with procedures, and central and regional decision-making.

468 **Flexibility and commitment in planning.**

David Thomas (et al.). The Hague: Nijhoff, 1983. 269p. bibliog.

A general comparison of local government, planning and development in the Netherlands and England, with case-studies of planning in Leiden and Oxford providing conclusions on general features of planning in both countries, on problems of local planning in both countries with a comparative analysis, and recommendations for future practice. There are illustrations, a glossary of Dutch words and an index.

469 **Dutch planning pioneers and the conservation movement: a forgotten tradition in urban and regional planning in the interwar period.**

Arnold van der Valk. Amsterdam: Institute for Planning and Demography, Amsterdam Free University, 1982. 13p.

A paper delivered to a conference on 'Dutch architecture in the inter-war period' treats pioneering work on nature conservation and urban planning as the watershed in the late development of urban planning resulting in the National Plan of 1942.

470 **Issues and tendencies in Dutch regional planning.**

H. Voogd. In: *Regional planning in Europe*. Edited by R. Hudson, J. R. Lewis. London: Pion, 1982, p. 112–26. bibliog. (London Papers in Regional Science).

A reconsideration as a somewhat critical supplement to earlier work by Bigh (1973) and Hamnett (1975), showing up weaknesses in regional planning which is in a transitional phase from 'blueprint' to 'process' planning as the problem of conflicting demands (residence, industry, environment) becomes increasingly acute.

Planning and creation of an environment: experience in the Ysselmeerpolders.
See item no. 40.

The future of Randstad Holland: a Netherlands scenario study on long-term perspectives for human settlement in the western part of the Netherlands.
See item no. 41.

Demographic research and spatial policy: the Dutch experience.
See item no. 213.

The Dutch solution to the problem of a residential environment.
See item no. 358.

Policy for the elderly in the Netherlands.
See item no. 368.

Summary of the report on urbanization in the Netherlands.
See item no. 375.

'Force of order and methods': an American view into the Dutch directed society.
See item no. 379.

Towards the austerity state: cutting down and pruning in the welfare state.
See item no. 380.

Policy development: a study of the Social and Economic Council of the Netherlands.
See item no. 423.

Planning between law and legislation.
See item no. 454.

Economic policy and planning in the Netherlands, 1950–1965.
See item no. 510.

Central Economic Plan.
See item no. 515.

Multi-criteria analysis and regional decision-making.
See item no. 516.

Fluctuations and growth in a near full employment economy: a quarterly economic analysis of the Netherlands.
See item no. 517.

Dutch regional economic policy: a review of contents and evaluation of effects.
See item no. 522.

Dilemmas in regional policy.
See item no. 525.

Port modernisation: the lesson of Rotterdam–Europort.
See item no. 573.

The derivation of spatial goals for the Dutch land consolidation programme.
See item no. 604.

The problem of popularising land consolidation in the Netherlands: thirty years of legislative change, 1924–54.
See item no. 605.

'Livability' of the environment in terms of traffic in the Netherlands.
See item no. 621.

The new Netherlands airport zoning act.
See item no. 625.

Main lines of the informatics stimulation plan.
See item no. 650.

The role of the documentation in educational planning.
See item no. 654.

Dutch architecture after 1900.
See item no. 797.

Planning and Administration.
See item no. 964.

Planning and Development in the Netherlands: a Periodical on the Initiative of the Netherlands Universities Foundation for International Co-operation (NUFFIC).
See item no. 965.

Summary of the Annual Report of the National Physical Planning Agency.
See item no. 971.

Environment and pollution

471 **Acidification in the Netherlands: effects and policies.**
The Hague: Ministry of Housing, Physical Planning and Environment, 1986. 2nd rev. ed. 8p.

A brief survey of the problem and requisite solutions to eliminate the threat to aquatic and terrestrial ecosystems, soil, surface water and materials. See also *Cultural property and air pollution*, and *Indicative multi-year programme to control air pollution, 1985–1989* (q.v.).

472 **Chemical Substances Act.**
The Hague: Ministry of Housing, Physical Planning and Environment, 1986. 30p.

A translation of the 1985 Act to protect 'man and the environment against dangerous substances and preparations'. It regulates notification, testing, reporting, investigation, packaging and labelling, and legal penalties. See also *Environmental innovation in small firms* (q.v.).

473 **Environmental hygiene and urban and village renewal.**
The Hague: Ministry of Housing, Physical Planning and Environment, 1986. 270p. bibliog.

This looks briefly at housing, business firms, traffic, amenities and administration in residential areas.

474 **Environmental innovation in small firms.**
The Hague: Ministry of Housing, Physical Planning and Environment, 1986. 8p. bibliog.

This is the draft final report of an EEC project prepared by the Institute of Economic Geography in the University of Amsterdam. It is intended to contribute to the international research project on training and advisory needs in the environmental field. It is based on information taken from twenty-eight small firms adopting 'clean technology', and it finally makes policy recommendations. See also *Chemical Substances Act* (q.v.).

475 **Environmental program of the Netherlands.**
The Hague: Ministry of Housing, Physical Planning and Environment, 1985. 169p.

This integrates the several planning documents presented to parliament in the preceding years and results from a memorandum sent to the Lower Chamber 'More than the sum of its parts'. The previous programmes remain in force except where explicitly stated in this document. The English version has a valuable introduction outlining the administrative structure responsible for environmental affairs in the Netherlands. See also *Chemical Substances Act* and *Waste Substances Act* (q.v.).

476 **Environmental programme of the Netherlands, 1985–1989, concerning waste substances.**
The Hague: Ministry of Housing, Physical Planning and Environment, 1986. 124p.

This is an extension of the policy intentions in the earlier multi-year programme, outlining the current state of affairs and the future policy, with appendixes on wastes and public health, wastes and employment, components of wastes and developments in the number of processing plants in individual provinces. See also *Netherlands indicative multi-year programme for chemical waste* and *Waste Substances Act* (q.v.).

477 **Cultural property and air pollution.**
J. F. Feenstra. The Hague: Ministry of Housing, Physical Planning and Environment, 1984. 142p. bibliog.

This surveys the damage done to monuments, art objects, archives and buildings due to air pollution, and attempts to give an economic valuation of the damage caused. The damage already done is estimated at about Dfls. 660 m. and preventive maintenance is estimated to cost Dfls. 10 m. per annum. See also *Acidification in the Netherlands: effects and policies* (q.v.), and the following item.

478 **Indicative multi-year programme to control air pollution, 1985–1989.**
The Hague: Ministry of Housing, Physical Planning and Environment, 1984. 15p.

A summary of the progress made in implementing the policies drawn up for 1984–88. It considers the substances affected by the policy, general effects of air pollution and the effects of the policy on administrations and organizations. See also *Acidification in the Netherlands: effects and policies* and *Cultural property and air pollution* (q.v.).

479 **Annoyance in the dwelling environment due to cumulative environmental noises: a literature study.**
H. M. E. Miedema. The Hague: Ministry of Housing, Physical Planning and Environment, 1985. 51p. bibliog.

A theoretical study of the effects of noise as an inconvenience, with models for describing the total annoyance due to two different sources of noise and establishing the effects of masking noise, with an appendix on a computer program for determining masked or unmasked loudness.

480 **The Netherlands as an environment for molluscan life.**
Basteria: Tijdschrift van de Nederlandse Malacologische Vereniging, vol. 23, supplement 1 (July 1959). 174p.

This special issue of *Basteria* contains the following articles: W. S. S. van Benthem Jutting, 'The history of the study of Dutch recent Mollusca'; Ingvar Kristensen, 'The coastal waters of the Netherlands as an environment for Nudibranchia'; C. O. van Regteren Altena, 'The Netherlands beach as a cemetry for Mollusca'; W. S. S. van Benthem Jutting, 'Ecology of brackish water Mollusca in the Netherlands' and 'Ecology of freshwater Mollusca in the Netherlands'; M. F. Mörzer Bruijns, C. O. van Regteren Altena and L. J. M. Butot, 'The Netherlands as an environment for land Mollusca'.

481 **Netherlands indicative multi-year programme for chemical waste.**
The Hague: Ministry of Housing, Physical Planning and Environment, 1985. 171p. bibliog.

A translation of the policy document sent to parliament in 1984, containing a description of Dutch chemical waste policy for 1985 and an indication of that policy for the following four years.

482 **Recycling and clean technologies.**
The Hague: Ministry of Housing, Physical Planning and Environment, 1985. 15p.

The increase in industrial waste necessitates this government policy of reducing all waste by recycling where possible. The present level of waste disposal at 28 million tons per annum includes 5 million tons of domestic waste, 7 million tons of building and demolition waste and 5 million tons of sludge from waste-water treatment. See also *Waste Substances Act* (q.v.).

483 **Regulations concerning protection of the soil.**
The Hague: Ministry of Housing, Physical Planning and Environment, 1986. 32p.

This is the amended bill of the Soil Protection Act passed by the Upper House of parliament in 1985. It makes general provisions for protecting the soil, and states the financial provisions, official powers and penal provisions. See also *Environmental program of the Netherlands* (q.v.).

484 **Waste Substances Act.**
The Hague: Minstry of Housing, Physical Planning and Environment, 1984. 29p.

A translation of the Act of June 1977 containing regulations concerning domestic refuse, unroadworthy motor vehicles and other categories of waste.

485 **Environmental Protection.**
G. J. R. Wolters (et al.). *Planning and Development in the Netherlands*, vol. 9, no. 2 (1979). 186p.

This special number of the journal contains contributions by G. J. R. Wolters on 'Standards for our environmental protection'; K. F. Roltshäfer and D. J. Flaman on 'Indicative multi-year programmes', giving a survey of the type of legislation envisaged for protection of the environment and an assessment of the success of previous planning; M. C. in 't Anker and M. Burggraaff on 'Environmental aspects in physical planning', outlining the application of Environment Impact Assessment (EIA) and considering how this can be integrated into future planning; S. J. Timmenga on 'The new Netherlands airport zoning act'; J. W. Fornier on 'Managing the natural environment in agricultural areas', on the third 'green report' concerning 'the relationship between agriculture and the safeguarding of nature and rural scenery'; and J. W. Becker on 'Public opinion and environment 1970–1975', discussing an environmental survey which indicated in 1972 that there was in general satisfaction that government legislation was adequate.

486 **Sensory assessment and chemical composition of drinking water.**
Bastiaan C. J. Zoeteman. The Hague: Van der Gang, 1978. 151p. bibliog.

Although this doctoral dissertation deals with technical aspects of testing drinking water and analysing its composition, the study is based on the situation in the Netherlands where (due to river pollution) the quality of the water is notoriously varied, and the layman may derive comfort from the fact that this study favours his untrained powers of judgement above the scientist with his sophisticated instrumentation.

Foreign Relations

487 **Democracy and foreign policy.**
P. R. Baehr. *Acta Politica*, vol. 18 (1983), p. 37–62. bibliog.
Examines the desirability in theory, and the feasibility in reality, of democratic influences on Dutch foreign policy. Surveys of public opinion are used.

488 **The Scheldt question to 1839.**
S. T. Bindoff. London: Allen & Unwin, 1945. 238p. map. bibliog.
A dated but still useful account of the diplomatic history concerning the Scheldt River, from the 13th century up to the final secession of Belgium in 1839.

489 **Political union: a microcosm of European politics 1960–1966.**
Susanne J. Bodenheimer. Leiden: Sijthoff, 1967. 229p. bibliog.
Based on interviews with political figures in the original Common Market countries, in Britain and the United States, the study is concerned with the Common Market in its early years, focusing on the Dutch attitudes to political union and in particular their handling of Britain's application to join the club.

490 **The Netherlands in the European scene, 1813–1913.**
J. C. Boogman. In: *Britain and the Netherlands in Europe and Asia: papers delivered to the third Anglo–Dutch historical conference*. Edited by J. S. Bromley, E. H. Kossmann. London: Macmillan, 1968. p. 138–59. bibliog.
An account of changes in approaches to foreign policy, arguing for 1848 as a landmark signifying a change from intractable attempts to regain the glories of the 17th century, towards acceptance of small power status with goals of neutrality and abstention.

491 **The quest for security: some aspects of Netherlands foreign policy 1945–1950.**
Samuel I. P. van Campen. The Hague: Nijhoff, 1957. 314p. bibliog. Doctoral dissertation, University of Amsterdam, 1957.

A detailed account of the post-war period, arranged chronologically year by year, concentrating on the major issue of the German question, and paying attention to integration policies. A large body of appendixes presents important documents of the period (p. 163–304).

492 **Neutrality or commitment: the evolution of Dutch foreign policy 1667–1795.**
Alice Clare Carter. London: Edward Arnold, 1975. 118p. bibliog.

Carter examines the Dutch policy of non-alignment in foreign affairs in the 18th century, and argues that it was not a product of weakness, as has been contended by previous writers, but was a developed strategy expressly designed to further the Republic's political and economic fortunes.

493 **Die Niederlande und das deutsche Exil 1933–1940.** (The Netherlands and the German exodus 1933–1940.)
Edited by Kattinka Dittrich, Hans Würzner. Königstein, FRG: Athenäum, 1982. 251p. bibliog.

A collection of essays in German, mostly by Dutch scholars, on German emigrants or refugees in the Netherlands in the 1930s. The papers are the product of a symposium held in Leiden in 1981.

494 **Anglo–Dutch relations and European unity, 1940–1948.**
Janet Eisen. Hull: University of Hull, 1980. 60p. bibliog. (Occasional Papers in Modern Dutch Studies, no. 1).

Based on ministerial archive sources in Britain and the Netherlands, this essay concentrates on the failure of total European unity, and the realization of unity in Western Europe instead.

495 **European and Atlantic co-operation: the Dutch attitude.**
Internationale Spectator, vol. 19, no. 8 (April 1965), p. 433–692. (Special issue).

A series of twenty-one essays on the Dutch role in NATO in all its aspects, including several contributions to do with economic integration in the EEC. Interesting documentation of how the Dutch saw their position in the world in the 1960s.

496 **Public opinion, the churches and foreign policy: studies of domestic factors in the making of Dutch foreign policy.**
Philip P. Everts. Leiden: P. Everts, 1983. 427p. bibliog. Doctoral dissertation, Leiden University, 1983.

A comprehensive analysis of recent developments, concentrating on the period of the 1970s and early 1980s. The author focuses on the increasing importance of public opinion in the formulation of foreign policy, and takes as his major case-study the religious pressure groups and their campaign against nuclear weapons.

497 **The German factor: a survey of sensitivity and vulnerability in the relationship between the Netherlands and the Federal Republic: summary of the twenty-third report to the government.**
Netherlands Scientific Council for Government Policy (WRR). The Hague: WRR, 1982. 42p.

A translated summary of a major report by this powerful quango. With a background of German occupation of the Netherlands in the war, this report looks at how the Dutch can reduce their sensitive vulnerability to their major trading partner. A multilateral approach to problem-solving is recommended.

498 **The Ottoman Empire and the Dutch Republic: a history of the earliest diplomatic relations 1610–1630.**
A. H. de Groot. Leiden; Istanbul: Nederlands Historisch–Archaeologisch Instituut, 1978. 417p. bibliog.

Much of this large study concerns Turkish history rather than the Netherlands, but there is a considerable treatment of the Dutch in the Levant (Eastern Mediterranean) in this period, and especially on the diplomatic work of Cornelis Haga, Dutch ambassador to the Empire 1612–29.

499 **The implementation of international sanctions; the Netherlands and Rhodesia.**
Pieter Jan Kuyper. Alphen, The Netherlands: Sijthoff & Noordhoff, 1978. 358p. bibliog.

A case-study of one nation's implementation of sanctions agreed by the United Nations. The considerable research, consisting of archive work and interviews, was carried out in the mid-1970s, and despite the great idealism in Dutch foreign policy, Kuyper concludes that in actual fact a 'sanguine realism' prevailed. Sanctions have not, it seems, been a successful measure.

500 **The foreign policy of the Netherlands.**
Edited by J. H. Leurdijk. Alphen, The Netherlands: Sijthoff & Noordhoff, 1978. 356p. bibliog.

This collection of essays concentrates on the development of Dutch security policy. Part I is a general essay by P. R. Baehr, Part II discusses the background of the 19th and early 20th centuries up to 1948, Parts III and IV cover the post-war period, examining the Dutch position in Europe, NATO, and other international bodies.

501 **Two hundred years of Netherlands–American interaction.**
Edited by M. J. G. Reichenbach–Consten, Abraham Noordergraaf. No publisher: printed by Dorrance & Company Inc., Bryn Mawr, Pennsylvania 19010. US, 1985. 128p.

The publication of a lecture series held in 1982 at the University of Pennsylvania, for the Dutch Studies Program there, to mark the bicentenary of Dutch–American relations. The speakers were very distinguished, and their subjects cover a wide range of Dutch foreign policy areas.

502 **A bilateral bicentennial [papers presented to the bicentennial conference on Dutch–American relations, held in Amsterdam, May–June 1982].**
Edited by J. W. Schulte–Noordholt, R. P. Swierenga. *Bijdragen en Mededelingen betreffende de Geschiedenis der Nederlanden*, vol. 97 no. 3 (1982), p. 389–669. bibliog.

A mixed collection of fourteen papers from the conference on Dutch–American relations since 1782, some of the best being on Dutch emigration to the United States, the Dutchness of the Roosevelts, the work of J. L. Motley, and on economic and financial ties between the two nations. An index completes this highly useful special issue of the periodical.

503 **The Netherlands–Bulgaria: traces of relations through the centuries: material from Dutch archives and libraries on Bulgarian history and on Dutch contacts with Bulgaria.**
Compiled by J. Slot (et al.). Sofia, Bulgaria: State Publishing House 'Semtemvri', 1981. 52p.

Compiled to celebrate the 1300th anniversary of the Bulgarian State, this richly illustrated work deals with six different aspects of Dutch–Bulgarian relations, from trade to the establishment of Bulgarian independence, with a series of illustrations for each topic.

504 **Foreign policy adaptation.**
Steve M. Smith New York: Nichols; Aldershot, England: Gower, 1981. 152p. bibliog.

Originating in a PhD dissertation for Southampton University, this is an attempt to test the 'adaptive behaviour theory' of foreign policy developed by J. N. Rosenau by taking the foreign policies of Britain and the Netherlands from 1945 to 1963 as case-studies. The three main areas of focus on Dutch policy in this period are European integration, West European security and the Dutch East Indies.

505 **The role of small countries in the international politics of the 1860s: the Netherlands and Belgium in Europe.**

C. A. Tamse. *Acta Historiae Neerlandicae*, vol. 9 (1976), p. 143–69. bibliog.

The congress diplomacy of the 19th century downgraded the smaller nations of Europe in international affairs: in this elegantly written article, Tamse examines Dutch and Belgian reactions in the 1860s.

506 **Dutch foreign policy since 1815: a study in small power politics.**

Amry Vandenbosch. The Hague: Nijhoff, 1959. 318p. bibliog.

Vandenbosch describes the relegation of the Netherlands from world power status in the 18th century to being a minor force in the 19th century, and with it the growing aversion on the part of the Dutch to power politics right up to the Second World War. There is special attention to the colonial question, and to relations with Belgium and Germany.

507 **Tuscany and the Low Countries: an introduction to sources and an inventory of four Florentine libraries.**

Henk T. van Veen. Florence, Italy: Centro Di, 1985. 182p.

The four libraries referred to are the Biblioteca Medicea Laurenziana, Moreniana, Riccardiana and Marucelliana, and the presence of so many Dutch publications is explained in a historical introduction describing the relations between Tuscany and the United Provinces up to the accession of Cosimo III, during his reign and after his death. There is an index of manuscripts and of names.

508 **Peace, profits and principles: a study of Dutch foreign policy.**

J. J. C. Voorhoeve. The Hague; Boston, Massachusetts; London: Nijhoff, 1979. 378p. map. bibliog.

This is concerned with post-war trends in Dutch foreign policy, and has major sections on security policy, integration into Benelux and Europe, and the Netherlands' worldwide policies on human rights and overseas development. This standard work concludes with a substantial systematic bibliography on the subject.

509 **Aloofness and neutrality: studies on Dutch foreign relations and policy-making institutions.**

Cornelis B. Wels. Utrecht: HES, 1982. 232p. bibliog.

A motley and mixed collection of essays, for the most part already published elsewhere, translated and collated to make up a doctoral dissertation. There is a general history of Dutch foreign relations 1813–1945, a chapter on the colonies, an essay on the development of policy institutions 1580–1980, and on the consular service.

The Dutch impact on Japan (1640–1853).
See item no. 188.

The mood of the country: new data on public opinion in the Netherlands on nuclear weapons and other problems of peace and security.
See item no. 353.

Benelux conference: September 1977.
See item no. 411.

Sir Constantine Huygens and Britain 1596–1687, vol. I: **1596–1619.**
See item no. 834.

Internationale Spectator.
See item no. 949.

The Economy

510 **Economic policy and planning in the Netherlands, 1950–1965.**
James G. Abert. New Haven, Connecticut; London: Yale University Press, 1969. 282p. bibliog.

A history of Dutch planning in this period, focusing on the policy-making process as it is delimited by economic constraints. In an appendix a model is constructed, while in the main body of the book special attention is given to the government's attempts at an incomes policy.

511 **Netherlands.**
R. Barents. In: *Discipline communautaire et politiques économiques nationales/Community order and national economic policies: colloque organisé par des revues de droit européen et l'Institut d'Études européennes, Bruxelles, 19–20 mai 1983.* Antwerp: Kluwer, 1984, p. 275–314. bibliog.

A comprehensive essay covering economic policy 1973–83, legislation in the same period, subsidies and fiscal premiums from the Dutch state, and Dutch economic law within an EEC context. The main development in the decade after the oil crisis was the extension of economic policy and law to cover long-term developments.

512 **Implementing regional economic policy: an analysis of economic and political influences in the Netherlands.**
Cornelis P. A. Bartels, Jacob H. van Duijn. *Regional Studies*, vol. 18, no. 1 (1984), p. 1–11. bibliog.

An investigation of economic and political factors affecting the implementation of Dutch regional policy. Political issues are found to be unimportant; economic influences do indeed take their toll, though short-term effects tend to be cyclical.

513 **Price effects in input-output relations: a theoretical and empirical study for the Netherlands, 1949–1967.**
P. M. C. de Boer. Utrecht: Elinkwijk, 1981. 145p. bibliog.

A highly technical exercise in economic analysis, using data from the Dutch economy in the 1950s and 1960s in assembling economic models.

514 **The volume of payments and the informal economy in the Netherlands 1965–1982: an attempt at quantification.**
W. C. Boeschoten, M. M. G. Fase. Amsterdam: De Nederlandsche Bank; Dordrecht, The Netherlands: Nijhoff, 1984. 75p. bibliog. (Monetary Monographs, no. 1).

An attempt to measure the size of the informal economy in the Netherlands by means of Fiege's transaction method. The informal economy is defined as that part of GNP which is not registered but which involves monetary transaction. Exchange is therefore excluded from the definition. Conclusions are tentative, but it is certainly clear that the informal economy is considerable, and that it has been growing apace, especially since 1976.

515 **Central Economic Plan.**
Voorburg, The Netherlands: Central Planning Office. annual.

The government's economic plan for the coming year is also published in English, with extensive documentation from the Central Planning Office.

516 **Multi-criteria analysis and regional decision-making.**
Ad van Delft, Peter Nijkamp. Leiden: Nijhoff, 1977. 135p. bibliog.

A theoretical exercise by a professional planner and by an academic, but using as an illustration for their model the case of the Maasvlakte, a reclaimed development area at the mouth of the Rhine. The authors are concerned with the economics of regional development planning.

517 **Fluctuations and growth in a near full employment economy: a quarterly economic analysis of the Netherlands.**
N. Driehuis, foreword by C. A. van den Beld. Rotterdam: Rotterdam University Press, 1972. 272p. bibliog.

A model-building exercise based on data from the Central Bureau of Statistics in the period 1951–68. Driehuis was a staff economist working for the Central Planning Office.

518 **The Dutch economy: recent developments and prospects: March 1986.**
Federation of Netherlands Industry (VNO). The Hague: VNO, 1986. 28p.

A general survey of economic development in the Netherlands, with attention to budgetary policy, industry policy, youth employment, wages, domestic and foreign demand, prices, monetary developments, and prospects for the coming year.

519 **The Economist.**

London: Economist Newspaper. weekly.

Regular items on Dutch politics and the Dutch economy; periodically *The Economist* publishes a major survey on the Netherlands, the most recent of which was 'Ruffles on the calm: a survey of the Dutch economy', in the issue of 30 January, 1982. These editorial surveys are usually very critical – a change from much of the material sponsored by the Dutch government.

520 **The Economist Intelligence Unit Analysis of Economic and Political Trends every Quarter: Country Report: Netherlands.**

London: Economist Intelligence Unit (EIU). quarterly.

A publication of approximately 20p. with brief articles and quantitative information on the country's economic outlook, economic structure, a political review of economic matters, economic trends (in graph form) and foreign trade. Its title prior to 1986 was *EIU Quarterly Economic Review of the Netherlands*.

521 **The Economist Intelligence Unit: Country Profile: Netherlands 1986–87.**

London: Economist Intelligence Unit (EIU), 1986. annual.

A series of approximately sixty pages, giving brief information on politics, demography, the economy, national accounts, the various economic sectors, wages, finance, trade, currency, etc.

522 **Dutch regional economic policy: a review of contents and evaluation of effects.**

Hendrik Folmer, Jan Oosterhaven. Groningen, The Netherlands: Institute of Economic Research, Faculty of Economics, State University, 1980. 28p.

This is a research memorandum (no. 18) to the Polish–Dutch Seminar on regional policies, experiences and prospects held at Warsaw in April 1980. It is a report on policy developments since the Second World War, showing the effects on unemployment, migration, regional disparity, on industrialization and on building.

523 **Road to recovery: the Marshall Plan, its importance for the Netherlands and European co-operation.**

H. M. Hirschfeld (et al.). The Hague: Ministry of Foreign Affairs, 1954. 212p.

This exercise in public relations contains essays by distinguished academics, industrialists and politicians on various aspects of post-war recovery and the beginnings of economic integration. There are many illustrative graphs, and some key texts on the subject are laid out in the appendixes, together with a chronology of important events in the Organisation for European Economic Co-operation (OEEC).

524 **An investment guide to the Netherlands.**
The Hague: Ministry of Economic Affairs, 1984.

A package of eight pamphlets in a single binder, totalling about 200 pages. It is issued in several different languages, with information particularly relevant to the country at which it is directed. The version intended for the United Kingdom includes the following booklets: 'How Dutch tax law affects investors', 'Taxation, accounting and auditing in the Netherlands', 'Business entities and company law in the Netherlands', 'Banking, finance and government incentives in the Netherlands', 'Trading in the Netherlands', and 'Labour relations in the Netherlands'.

525 **Dilemmas in regional policy.**
Edited by A. Kuklinski, J. G. Lambooy. Berlin: Mouton, 1983. (Regional Planning Series, vol. 12).

This volume is the result of Polish and Dutch academic co-operation. After a theoretical first section on the problems of regional policy, with several Dutch papers included, there follows a section (p. 227–348) on 'Experiences and prospects in the Netherlands', which looks at socio-economic policy, integral regional policy, and environmental problems.

526 **De Nederlandsche Bank n.v.: Quarterly Bulletin.**
Dordrecht, The Netherlands: Nijhoff. quarterly.

The bulletin is published about three months after the calendar quarter it concerns; thus the review of the Dutch economy in the second quarter of 1986 is published in September of that year. There is a short review of the economy (15–20p.), and various articles on banking and financial matters of topical interest. The bulletin is used as the basis for the Bank's *Annual Report* (q.v.). There is a large statistical annex to each issue.

527 **De Nederlandsche Bank n.v.: Annual Report Presented to the General Meeting of Shareholders.**
Dordrecht, The Netherlands: Kluwer–Nijhoff. annual.

The annual report is compiled from the *Quarterly Bulletin* (see the previous item), and is presented to the bank's AGM each spring, covering the events of the previous calendar year. The Nederlandsche Bank is a government bank, and the report covers the national economy in all its financial aspects, with sections on economic trends, trade, monetary developments, the money markets, and banking in general, as well as a report on the bank's own activities. There is a large statistical annex.

528 **Nederlandse ondernemingen en hun financiële kenmerken: Dutch companies and their financial characteristics 1980.**
Rotterdam: Dun and Bradstreet, 1980. 213p.

This 1980 edition was the fourth annual issue, listing 500 Dutch companies ranked by profits, sales, and number of employees. The text and diagrams are in Dutch and English, and after the basic quantitative data, individual chapters are devoted to each economic sector.

529 **The Netherlands economic and cultural documentation.**
Compiled by Nederlands Economisch Cultureel Archief. [Amsterdam]: n.p. [n.d.]. 8 folio vols, 1 (1952)–7 (1962) + 8 [n.d.].

This sumptuous manifestation of 'Holland Promotion', with (for the 1950s) lavish photographic illustration and a text in six languages, has short chapters on almost every conceivable article produced by the Dutch from tulip bulbs to hotels. More than an account of the Netherlands in the 1950s, it is an eloquent testimony to how the Dutch wanted to see themselves at that time. Indexes are included.

530 **Netherlands Investment News.**
The Hague: Ministry of Economic Affairs. Vol. 7, no. 3 (fall 1986).

A brief broadsheet (about four pages) which appears quarterly, containing news and information intended in the first place for American investors in the Netherlands. Compiled by Gavin Anderson & Company, Inc., an agent of the Dutch government in the United States. There are articles on topical economic issues to do with the Netherlands, details of investment conferences, etc.

531 **Netherlands: OECD economic survey 1985/1986.**
Organisation for Economic Co-operation and Development. Paris: OECD, 1986. 97p.

The OECD produces these reports each year; the most recent one being in March 1986. An excellent and objective analysis, with sections on industrial performance, budgetary and monetary conditions, demand trends, productivity, the labour market, trade, the balance of payments, and the outlook for the next year. There is a substantial statistical annex.

532 **Interregional input-output analysis and Dutch regional policy problems.**
Jan Oosterhaven. Aldershot, England: Gower, 1981. 209p. bibliog.

A study of regional economics, this work sets out to examine the success with which the technique of input-output analysis can be applied to Dutch interregional economic problems. Primarily theoretical, the main case-study is the relocation of the PTT (Postal and Telecommunications Service) from The Hague to Groningen.

533 **Review of the Netherlands Economy: Bank Mees and Hope N.V.**
Amsterdam: Economic Research Department of Bank Mees & Hope N.V. Every two months.

A brief report (usually eight pages), from a leading Dutch bank, on the economy, with the latest statistical indicators, the trade position, prices developments, and analysis of the money and capital markets.

534 **Right in the center: the Netherlands foreign investment review.**
Industrial Commission of the Netherlands. [New York:] Gavin Anderson & Co. [1986]. 25p.

Produced under the auspices of the Dutch Ministry for Economic Affairs, this publicity brochure is designed to attract foreign investment, particularly from the United States. Information on strikes, wage rates, inflation, foreign investment to date (the Dutch claim the highest per capita investment in Europe), R & D, etc. is provided.

535 **Input-output experiments: the Netherlands 1948–1961.**
C. B. Tilanus. Rotterdam: Rotterdam University Press, 1966. 141p.

A technical exercise in economic analysis, using Dutch data because the Netherlands – with its massive Central Bureau of Statistics – was the only country with such a detailed level of information available.

536 **Economic policy in practice: the Netherlands 1950–1957.**
C. Weststrate. Leiden: Stenfert Kroese, 1959. 212p. bibliog.

Intended for the general reader abroad, this close analysis devotes its four main chapters to four principal economic policy goals in the period: full employment, price stability, a stable balance of payments, and the equitable distribution of wealth. Now dated but still worth reading on the period.

Academic economics in Holland 1800–1870.
See item no. 154.

The economy and politics of the Netherlands since 1945.
See item no. 159.

The Netherlands economy in the twentieth century: an examination of the most characteristic features in the period 1900–1970.
See item no. 180.

Limits to the welfare state: an inquiry into the realizability of socioeconomic and political desiderata in a highly industrialized society.
See item no. 381.

Benelux conference: September 1977.
See item no. 411.

Dutch company law.
See item no. 452.

Dutch business law.
See item no. 453.

Country profile: Netherlands: export Europe.
See item no. 565.

De Economist: Driemandelijks Tijdschrift – Quarterly Review.
See item no. 941.

European Economic Review.
See item no. 942.

Arts and economics.
See item no. 1017.

Finance and Banking

537 **The use and extent of replacement value accounting in the Netherlands.**
R. K. Ashton, K. Raymond. London: Institute of Chartered Accountants in England and Wales, 1981. 207p.

This describes the theory and practice of financial reporting in the Netherlands and analyses the results of the authors' survey, with particular reference to the effect of replacement cost accounting on reported profits and stock market valuation. The authors intend in future research to compare the efficacy of the Dutch systems with the British.

538 **Banking and finance in the Netherlands.**
Bank -en Effectenbedrijf: bi-monthly periodical, vol. 9. no. 2 (3 Sept. 1960). 58p.

Dated of course, but a good guide to financial institutions and practices in the late 1950s. Includes articles by a variety of experts, on the stock exchange, the balance of payments, money markets, capital markets, agriculture banks, savings banks, and banking in general.

539 **Geld door de eeuwen heen: geschiedenis van het geld in de Lage Landen.** (Money throughout the centuries: the history of money in the Low Countries.)
Bert van Beek, Hans Jacobi, Marjan Scharloo, photographs by Kees Jansen. Amsterdam: Pampas Associates, 1984. 160p. bibliog.

There is no English language general history or guide to Dutch numismatics. This attractive publication in Dutch fulfils that role, with chapters on money in the Netherlands from the earliest times to the present day. The work is richly illustrated, adequately indexed, and also covers Belgium and Luxembourg.

540 **Monetary policy in the Netherlands in the post-Smithsonian era.**
Hans W. J. Bosman. Tilburg, The Netherlands: Société Universitaire Européenne de Recherches Financières (SUERF), 1984. 23p. (SUERF Series, no. 43A).

This paper examines the role of the Netherlands Bank in the formulation and execution of monetary policy, especially in the period of the Second World War.

541 **At spes non fracta: Hope & Co., 1770–1815: merchant bankers and diplomats at work.**
M. G. Buist. The Hague: Nijhoff, 1974. 716p. bibliog.

An example of the old-fashioned Dutch doctoral dissertation, representing twenty years of research in the archives of this famous merchant bank. Besides a history of the bank's activities, there are interesting studies of the techniques of floating major foreign loans in the Netherlands.

542 **Netherlands adjusting to change: supplement to 'Euromoney', October 1986.**
Barry Cohen, (et al.). London: Euromoney Publications, 1986. 49p.

Amongst several advertisement articles for various Dutch finance houses, the editors of *Euromoney* have put together an informative survey of many aspects of Dutch monetary and financial matters. Deregulation of the stock markets, the views of the executive secretary of the Amsterdam stock exchange, savings banks, the postbank, multinationals, and the port of Rotterdam are amongst the subjects covered.

543 **Instruments of money market and foreign exchange market policy in the Netherlands.**
Emile den Dunnen. Dordrecht, The Netherlands: Nijhoff, 1985, 91p. (Monetary Monographs, no. 3).

Den Dunnen works for the Nederlandsche Bank, and this edition is a translation of the original version in Dutch of 1984. His concern is the means available to major financial institutions to counteract 'undesirable movements' in the exchange money markets especially since the massive growth of international capital flows from the 1970s onwards. Each chapter deals with a set of 'instruments' available to the makers of monetary policy.

544 **Bank solvency regulation and deposit insurance in the U.S. and the Netherlands.**
W. Eizenga, Ian H. Giddy. Tilburg, The Netherlands: Société Universitaire Européenne de Recherches Financières (SUERF), 1979. 18p. (SUERF Series, no. 27A).

The paper is concerned with the need for the regulation of banking operations, and concludes that more protection is necessary in the field of solvency.

545 **The independence of the Federal Reserve System and of the Netherlands Bank: a comparative analysis.**
W. Eizenga. Tilburg, The Netherlands: Société Universitaire Européenne de Recherches Financières (SUERF), 1983. 17p. (SUERF Series, no. 41A).

This comparison of the instruments of monetary policy in the United States and the Netherlands examines the precise nature of the 'independence' of these institutions.

546 **The financial relationship between central and local government.**
The Hague: Ministry of Finance [1986].

Outlines the possible sources of revenue for municipal and provincial government in the Netherlands, variously from local taxation, central government and special funds.

547 **An inflation-adjusted tax system: a summary of the report on the elimination from the Dutch tax system of the distorting effects of inflation.**
H. J. Hofstra. The Hague: Government Publishing Office, 1978. 75p.

Hofstra and others presented a full report on this subject to the Minister of Finance and to the Dutch Parliament in 1977; this is an English abridgement.

548 **Managerial accounting and analysis in multinational enterprises.**
Edited by H. P. Holzer and H. M. Schoenfeld. Berlin; New York: De Gruyter, 1986. 270p.

Besides general essays on accounting and several case-studies, this volume contains a detailed analysis of performance evaluation techniques in N. V. Philips Gloeilampenfabriek in Eindhoven.

549 **ISMO 1985: fraud and abuse in relation to taxation, social security and government subsidies in the Netherlands: a summary of the ISMO report 1985.**
The Hague: Ministry of Finance, 1985. 73p.

In 1979 the Dutch government set up an interdepartmental steering group (ISMO) on fraud from the Ministries of Finance, Social Affairs, Justice, and the Environment. This report summary tries to estimate the size and nature of fraud and the black economy.

550 **Exchange rate policy, monetary policy, and Dutch–German cooperation.**
Pieter Korteweg. Tilburg, The Netherlands: Société Universitaire Européenne de Recherches Financières (SUERF), 1980. 28p. (SUERF Series, no. 30A).

In the light of the European Monetary System agreement, Korteweg seeks to define the monetary policies necessary to ensure exchange rate stability, especially between the guilder and the Deutschmark.

551 **The market for money and the market for credit: theory, evidence and implications for Dutch monetary policy.**
Pieter Korteweg, Peter D. van Loo. Leiden: Nijhoff, 1977. 105p. bibliog.

The authors construct a new economic model for the financial sector of a national economy, and put it to the test with Dutch financial data from the years 1961–74.

552 **The post-war financial rehabilitation of the Netherlands.**
Pieter Lieftinck. The Hague: Nijhoff, 1973. 49p.

This paper by the Finance Minister of the post-war period concerns the financial stabilization of the country in the period 1945–52, and the monetary policies necessary to achieve it.

553 **The Netherlands Budget Memorandum (Abridged).**
The Minister of Finance. The Hague: Ministry of Finance. annual.

Each year the Minister of Finance publishes this English abridgement of his budget for the coming year. Aims and objectives are spelt out, and appendixes provide the quantitative data.

554 **Netherlands Corporate Tax Act 1969.**
Chicago, Illinois: Commerce Clearing House, 1970. 48p. (Common Market Reports, no. 149, 8 December, 1970).

An English translation of the act with an introduction surveying the main aspects of Netherlands corporate taxation and comparing it with the Corporate Tax Ordinance of 1942. The act itself covers tax liability, tax base for resident taxpayers, tax base for non-resident taxpayers, offsetting of losses, rates, assessment and liability, complementary provisions, transitional and final provisions, the Income Tax Act of 1964 and the Ordinance for Prevention of Double Taxation.

555 **Netherlands taxes.**
Information Department, Ministry of Finance. The Hague: Ministry of Finance, 1981. 29p.

An information pamphlet describing the way in which Dutch taxation works, but not a guide for the individual tax payer. An introduction to the general contours of the system.

556 **International government finance and the Amsterdam capital market 1740–1815.**
James C. Riley. Cambridge, England: Cambridge University Press, 1980. 365p. bibliog.

A fascinating study of the organizational chain which linked small-time investors in the Dutch Republic with spendthrift governments and monarchs the world over in the 18th century. The Dutch would not lend to domestic entrepreneurs, suggests Riley, because rates of return were higher abroad.

557 **The Dutch contribution to replacement value accounting theory and practice.**
P. J. van Sloten, translated by R. A. Schmid. Lancaster, England: University of Lancaster International Centre for Research in Accounting, 1981. 65p. bibliog.

An attempt to publicise to the outside world the Dutch academic work on accounting, especially focusing on the work of Theodore Limperg (1879–1961), a leading Dutch accountant who conducted important work on replacement value accounting between the World Wars.

558 **Risks at sea: Amsterdam insurance and maritime Europe, 1766–1780.**
Frank C. Spooner. Cambridge, England: Cambridge University Press, 1983. 306p. bibliog.

A history of the insurance world of Amsterdam based on extensive research into primary material, covering a period when the Republic was slipping into decline.

559 **Income distribution: analysis and policies.**
Jan Tinbergen. Amsterdam: North-Holland Publishing Co., 1975. 170p.

A synthesis of Tinbergen's articles and essays on this subject from the first half of the 1970s. As with most of this renowned Dutch economist's work, its application is more or less universal rather than specifically Dutch, but this work is chosen to represent his prolific output because of the use of Dutch data on price equations, welfare, and other facets of income distribution economics.

560 **Value-added tax in the Netherlands.**
Information Department of the Ministry of Finance. The Hague: Staatsuitegeverij, 1979. 27p.

A layman's guide to the principal features of the Dutch tax, taxable transactions, exemptions, special and formal regulations, with an explanation of the categories liable to taxation and those entitled to make provisional tax deductions.

561 **Economic and financial reporting in England and the Netherlands: a comparative study over the period 1850–1914.**
H. G. A. Vissink. Assen, The Netherlands: Van Gorcum, 1985. 426p. bibliog. (Aspects of Economic History: The Low Countries, vol. 5).

Covers the introduction of economic and financial periodicals in the two countries against a background of industrial development.

The kingdom of the Netherlands: facts and figures.
See item no. 14.

Getting, spending and investing in early modern times: essays on Dutch, English and Huguenot economic history.
See item no. 155.

Towards the austerity state: cutting down and pruning in the welfare state.
See item no. 380.

The Netherlands Business Corporation code.
See item no. 439.

Dutch business law.
See item no. 453.

Dutch/English company law.
See item no. 455.

De Nederlandsche Bank n.v.: Quarterly Bulletin.
See item no. 526.

De Nederlandsche Bank n.v.: Annual Report Presented to the General Meeting of Shareholders.
See item no. 527.

Bibliografie van het Nederlandse belastingwezen. (Bibliography of the Dutch tax system.)
See item no. 995.

Trade

International trade

562 **Getting off to a good start in European Trade.**
Jack Bax. Rotterdam: The City of Rotterdam [n.d.]. 46p.

A publicity description, lavishly illustrated, of the facilities at the ports of Rotterdam and Europoort.

563 **Rotterdam, Rijnmond, poort van Europa.** (Rotterdam, Rhine estuary, port of Europe.)
Ivo Blom. Rotterdam: Phoenix & Den Oudsten, 1983. 188p.

A book of colour photographs with short descriptions in four languages, preceded by an introduction in Dutch, German, English and French tracing the commercial history and architectural development in a city now characterized as a city on the move.

564 **Commerce and industry in the Netherlands: a base for business operations in Europe.**
Amro Bank. Amsterdam: Amsterdam–Rotterdam Bank, 1976. 7th ed. 67p.

A brief introduction on the Netherlands for would-be European businessmen, outlining the basic structure of Dutch geography, trade, industry, labour relations, banking, insurance, taxes, and general conditions.

565 **Country profile: Netherlands: export Europe.**
London: Exports to Europe Branch of Department of Trade and Industry (DTI), Jan. 1986. rev. ed. 104p. map.

An official publication intended to facilitate the work of British exporters to the Netherlands. A general account of the country, its people and politics is followed by substantial chapters on Dutch industry and trade, on doing business in the Netherlands, import regulations, warehousing, marketing, and organizations assisting British firms. A practical handbook for the exporter.

566 **Anglo–Dutch trade flows 1955–75: their effects on, and consequences for, Dutch port development and planning.**
Frank Deakin. PhD thesis, University of Hull, England, 1978. 456p. bibliog.

Using figures for trade between the Netherlands and Great Britain from 1955 to 1975 as a database, Deakin attempts to determine the effects of this trade on the industrialization and port development in the Netherlands. His conclusions are to the effect that Rotterdam has provided a model which is by no means satisfactory for the rest of the Netherlands.

567 **Dutch companies and their financial details.**
Rotterdam: Dun & Bradstreet, 1978. 182p.

This gives a commentary on trends and activities throughout the year (1979) showing the performance of all the companies for which details were available, divided between industrials, trading companies, transport companies, banks, insurance offices and miscellaneous service companies. A comparative analysis shows the turnover, profits and number of employees of the 200 largest companies.

568 **The Netherlands–British trade directory 1985.**
Edited by Koenraad van Hasselt. London: The Netherlands–British Chamber of Commerce [1985]. 164p.

This annual publication is in essence a list, with addresses, of companies affiliated to the Chamber. The members are listed both alphabetically and in a classified system. There are also short articles on the Netherlands, dealing with the country and the people, and various aspects of the Dutch economy.

569 **Hints to exporters: the Netherlands.**
British Overseas Trade Board. London: HMSO, 1985. 47p.

Provides general information for British businessmen seeking to export to the Netherlands, on such subjects as geography, climate, social customs and people. There is also hard economic information, for instance, on import and exchange control.

570 **The port of Rotterdam in figures.**
Edited and compiled by P. Lodder. Rotterdam: Chamber of Commerce and Industry for Rotterdam and the Lower Maas, 1986. 80p. annual.

The statistics for 1984, derived from the annual returns of the Central Bureau of Statistics (CBS) are in the following groups: sea navigation (details of vessels, cargoes, passengers and comparative figures), pipeline, navigation on the Rhine, road transport, railway transport, aviation. These reviews are published annually early in the second year after the year covered by the report.

571 **Trade relations between large and small countries: equal or inequal?**
C. W. A. M. van Paridon, J. W. Nelson. *Planning and Development in the Netherlands*, vol. 14, no. 2 (1982), p. 184–204. bibliog.

A general examination of the commercial relationship between large and small countries, but the case-study is specifically on trade relations between the Netherlands and West Germany.

572 **Community attitude as a limiting factor in port growth: the case of Rotterdam.**
David A. Pinder. Rotterdam: Rotterdam University Economisch Geografisch Instituut, 1980. 29p. bibliog. (Working Papers, Series A, no. 80–82).

The rising intolerance ultimately resulting in the outright rejection of the development plan for the Europoort in the year 2000 is, the author states, only symptomatic of a general fall in society's tolerance levels towards industrialization.

573 **Port modernisation: the lesson of Rotterdam–Europort.**
Frans Posthuma. *Delta*, vol. 12, no. 1 (spring 1969), p. 48–58. bibliog.

An introduction to the history of the development of Rotterdam and its adminstrative structure, followed by a description of the post-war modernization which has made it the largest port in the world. The exploitation of handling, storage and even manufacturing facilities for a market of 160 million people requires ongoing forward planning by the port authority and private enterprise.

574 **Rotterdam Europoort: general information.**
Rotterdam: De Havenkoerier, 1985. 80p. [annual.]

Reprinted from the annual yearbook called 'The Harbour Courier' ('Havencourier'), these reports contain useful information on all the port activities, including transport, banking, port promotion, offshore activities, insurance and education.

575 **Rotterdam: the gateway to Europe.**
Edited by J. Schraver. Rotterdam: Donker, 1948. 259p. maps. bibliog.

This history of the port and trade of Rotterdam is the standard work, covering the period up to the mid-19th century, Rotterdam in the modern transport system, the port and trade between 1882 and 1940, its destruction in the war, reconstruction and cross-river links after the war, and details of activities since the war, including tuggage and shipbuilding. The text is well illustrated with plates, maps and diagrams.

In so many words.
See item no. 260.

The Netherlands Business Corporation code.
See item no. 439.

A modern European company law system: commentary on the 1976 Dutch legislation.
See item no. 449.

Corporate law of the Netherlands and of the Netherlands Antilles.
See item no. 450.

Dutch company law.
See item no. 452.

Dutch business law.
See item no. 453.

Dutch/English company law.
See item no. 455.

Netherlands Corporate Tax Act 1969.
See item no. 554.

Holland Industrial.
See item no. 945.

Holland Quarterly.
See item no. 946.

In Touch with the Dutch.
See item no. 947.

Rotterdam Europoort Delta.
See item no. 967.

Commercial history

576 **Das goldene Delta und sein eisernes Hinterland 1815–1851: von niederländisch-preussischen zu deutsch-niederländischen Wirtschaftbeziehungen.** (The golden Delta and its iron hinterland 1815–51: from Dutch–Prussian to German–Dutch economic relations.)
Joachim F. E. Bläsing. Leiden: Stenfert Kroese, 1973. 276p. bibliog.

A standard work in German on the Rhine trade in a period when the Dutch were obliged gradually to release their control over the trade with the various German states. There is a summary in Dutch.

577 **Dutch–Asiatic shipping in the 17th and 18th centuries.**
Edited by J. R. Bruijn, F. S. Gaastra, I. Schöffer. The Hague: Nijhoff, 1979. 3 vols. bibliog. (Rijks Geschiedkundige Publicatiën, Grote Serie, nos 166 and 167).

Together these volumes provide a virtually complete record of all the voyages, from the Netherlands to the Dutch East Indies and back, between the first expedition under Cornelius Houtman in 1595 and the last voyage of the East India Company, which returned in 1795. Volume I describes the sources and methodological problems, volume II covers outward-bound voyages, and volume III deals with homeward-bound trips.

578 **A primer of Dutch seventeenth century overseas trade.**
D. W. Davies. The Hague: Nijhoff, 1961. 160p. maps. bibliog.

An introduction for those unfamiliar with Dutch scholarship, arranged by trading areas rather than by product type. Dated but still very useful.

579 **Dutch–asiatic trade 1620–1740.**
Kristof Glamann. Copenhagen: Danish Science Press; The Hague: Nijhoff, 1958. 334p. bibliog.

This classic study based on the accumulation of years of archive research presents an analysis of the trade which underlay the Dutch prosperity in its Golden Age. Most of the twelve chapters deal with one particular commodity, such as pepper, sugar, or coffee. There are substantial appendixes summarizing the source material.

580 **Dutch trade with Russia from the time of Peter I to Alexander I: a quantitative study in eighteenth century shipping.**
Jake V. T. Knoppers. Montreal: Interuniversity Centre for European Studies (ICES), 1976. 3 vols. bibliog. (ICES Occasional Papers, no. 1).

A quantitative study on a very large scale. Volumes 2 and 3 are taken up entirely with statistical data in appendixes.

581 **Sweden's trade with the Dutch Republic 1738–1795: a quantitative analysis of the relationship between economic growth and international trade in the eighteenth century.**
Thomas J. Lindblad. Assen, The Netherlands: Van Gorcum, 1982. 200p. bibliog.

Examines the changes in the 18th century attendant on the beginnings of Swedish protectionism (from 1738) and the rising Dutch export of capital (from 1765), against a general background of declining Dutch commercial success. There is a large statistical appendix.

582 **The interactions of Amsterdam and Antwerp with the Baltic region, 1400–1800: De Nederlanden en het Oostzeegebied, 1400–1800.**
Edited by W. J. Wieringa (et al.). Leiden: Nijhoff, 1983. 199p. bibliog.

This collection forms the proceedings of the third conference of the Association Internationale d'Histoire des Mers Nordiques de l'Europe, held in 1982. There are papers on the grain trade, the money and bullion flows, shipbuilding, and many other subjects.

583 **Free trade and protection in the Netherlands 1816–30: a study of the first Benelux.**
Harold R. C. Wright. Cambridge, England: Cambridge University Press, 1955. 251p. bibliog. (Cambridge Studies in Economic History).

Though dated, this study is still a reliable account of the economic history of the Netherlands, which included present-day Belgium in the period 1816–30. The emphasis is on government policy on tariffs.

Trading companies in Asia 1600–1830.
See item no. 189.

Religion and trade in New Netherland: Dutch origins and American development.
See item no. 338.

Industry

584 **Industrial policy and shipbuilding: changing economic structures in the Low Countries 1600–1980.**
C. A. de Feyter. Utrecht: HES, 1982. 352p. bibliog.

This 1982 Rotterdam University doctoral dissertation chronicles the history of an entire industrial sector in the course of nearly four centuries. The theoretical side is substantial; the great scandal of the collapse of the giant Dutch shipbuilding conglomerate RSV came just too late for inclusion.

585 **Unilever overseas: the anatomy of a multinational 1895–1965.**
D. Keith Fieldhouse. London: Croom Helm; Stanford: The Hoover Institution Press, 1978. 620p. bibliog.

Not an official or sponsored history, this work concentrates on the overseas activities of Unilever, and in particular sets out to test hypotheses on the effects of direct investment on third world countries, especially in colonial or ex-colonial territories. It is largely based on material kept in the Unilever archives. A very fair and non-dogmatic assessment.

586 **Holland's industries stride ahead: the new Netherlands of the 1960's.**
Horace George Franks. Federation of Netherlands Industries, 1961. 242p. bibliog.

A popular account of Dutch industry as it surged ahead in the boom of the 1950s. This public relations exercise on behalf of the country's employers is copiously illustrated with black-and-white photographs.

587 **History of the Royal Dutch.**
F. C. Gerretson. Leiden: Brill, 1953–57. 4 vols. maps.

This translation of the Dutch 'Geschiedenis der Koninklijke' is a monumental work of scholarship by a respected historian, chronicling the history of the Royal Dutch Company or Shell Oil as it was later to become, from its foundation up to the eve of the First World War. Strangely, no references to archive or printed material are provided. Includes illustrations.

588 **The history of N. V. Philips' Gloeilampenfabrieken**, vol. I: **The origin of the Dutch incandescent lamp industry.**
A. Heerding, translated by D. S. Jordan. Cambridge, England: Cambridge University Press, 1986. 343p. bibliog.

The first part of a projected three-volume history of this major Dutch multinational covers the Dutch electrical industry in the 1880s prior to the foundation of Philips in 1891.

589 **Industry in the Netherlands: its place and future. Reports to the Government 18, 1980.**
Netherlands Scientific Council for Government Policy (WRR). The Hague: WRR, 1982 (English ed.). 284p.

An examination of policy options by this powerful quango. It pleads for more active trade policies, innovative management in small firms, and environmental planning for industry, as well as for a number of more specific policies.

590 **Industrial mobility and migration in the European community.**
Edited by L. H. Klaassen, W. T. M. Molle. Aldershot, England: Gower, 1983. 438p. maps. bibliog.

Chapter 8 (p. 254–300), entitled 'The Netherlands', by W. T. M. Molle, examines business relocation processes. There are sections on the effects on donor and receiving regions. The editors are associated with the Netherlands Economic Institute in Rotterdam.

591 **Wooden shoes: their makers and their wearers.**
H. Noorlander. Arnhem, The Netherlands: Open Air Museum; Zutphen, The Netherlands: Uitgeverij Terra, 1978, 76p. bibliog. (Monographs of the National Folk Museum: The Netherlands Open Air Museum, vol. 2).

An account, with a strong historical slant, of the folklore and artisan skills surrounding the clog-making industry.

592 **45 years with Philips: an industrialist's life.**
Frits Philips. Poole, England: Blandford Press, 1978. 280p.

First published in Dutch in 1976, this autobiography of one of the scions of this famous industrial family is a very personalized and informal account of the years from 1930 to 1975, laid out chronologically.

593 **Oil refining in the Netherlands and Belgium: growth, crisis and restructuring.**
David A. Pinder. *Dutch Crossing*, vol. 30 (1986), p. 76–92. map. bibliog.

A perceptive account of the impact of plummeting oil prices on the extensive refining industries located in the Low Countries, concentrating, of course, on Rotterdam.

594 **Fifty years of Unilever 1930–1980.**
W. J. Reader. London: Heinemann, 1980. 148p. bibliog.

A popular account of the fortunes of the Anglo–Dutch multinational since the merger of the constituent British and Dutch firms in 1930. Hardly a critical work, but well illustrated and providing some quantitative data. In the final chapter Reader attempts to evaluate Unilever's role in the world, both socially and financially.

595 **The development of Dutch industry in relation to government policy measures and plans.**
A. Stikker, F. J. H. van Woerkom. *Planning and Development in the Netherlands*, vol. 12, no. 2 (1980), p. 146–83.

Stikker was president of the huge RSV engineering conglomerate in 1980 (since the victim of much-publicized financial scandals), and Van Woerkom was one of Stikker's senior planners. These captains of industry paint a bleak picture of Dutch industrial performance in the 1970s, and of prospects for the 1980s. A strong plea is entered for government assistance, for example in the form of profits from natural gas.

596 **Dutch shipbuilding before 1800: ships and guilds.**
Richard W. Unger. Assen, The Netherlands; Amsterdam: Van Gorcum: 1978. 216p. map. bibliog.

This monograph covers the fortunes of this peculiarly Dutch industry in the pre-industrial period. Unger concentrates on the provinces of Holland and Zeeland, and deals extensively with ship design from 1400 to 1800. Eighteen 'guild letters' or charters are reproduced in appendixes.

597 **From keystone to cornerstone: Hoogovens Ijmuiden 1918–1968: the birth and development of a basic industry in the Netherlands.**
Johan de Vries. *Acta Historiae Neerlandicae*, vol. 6 (1973) p. 112–45. bibliog.

A condensed but substantial version of this distinguished business historian's full-length account in Dutch of the modern steel industry, *Hoogovens IJmuiden 1918–1968* (1968).

598 **The history of Unilever: a study in economic growth and social change.**
Charles H. Wilson. London: Cassell, 1954. 2 vols. bibliog.

This is the classic and standard work on the history of this major Anglo–Dutch multinational, and a pioneering work of business history. Vol. 1 covers the English firm of Lever Brothers 1851–1929, vol. 2 covers the Dutch firms of Jurgens and Van den Bergh 1854–1929, and the last part of vol. 2 deals with the merged Unilever, 1929–45.

599 **Unilever 1945–1965: challenge and response in the post-war industrial revolution.**
Charles H. Wilson. London: Cassell, 1968. 290p. bibliog.

This is, in effect, the third volume to complement the previous item, Wilson's *The history of Unilever*. The treatment is slightly different, paying less attention to individual 'captains of industry', and putting more emphasis on the structural growth of this worldwide Anglo–Dutch multinational.

600 **Energy policy in the Netherlands.**
P. de Wolff. *Planning and Development in the Netherlands*, vol. 13, no. 2 (1981), p. 161–90. bibliog.

Deals with the energy situation since the major government White Paper of 1974, showing the enormous increase in the production of natural gas.

The kingdom of the Netherlands: facts and figures.
See item no. 14.

The Netherlands.
See item no. 37.

Benelux: an economic geography of Belgium, the Netherlands and Luxembourg.
See item no. 38.

Industrialization without national patents: the Netherlands, 1869–1912: Switzerland 1850–1907.
See item no. 175.

In so many words.
See item no. 260.

The Netherlands Business Corporation code.
See item no. 439.

Dutch/English company law.
See item no. 455.

Nuclear facilities in Dutch border areas.
See item no. 463.

Industry

Regional information systems and impact analysis for large-scale energy development.
See item no. 465.

Managerial accounting and analysis in multinational enterprises.
See item no. 548.

Commerce and industry in the Netherlands: a base for business operations in Europe.
See item no. 564.

Friendship and Fellowship: recent developments in Fokker aircraft.
See item no. 685.

Holland Industrial.
See item no. 945.

Holland Quarterly.
See item no. 946.

In Touch with the Dutch.
See item no. 947.

Maandstatistiek van de Industrie. (Monthly Bulletin of Industrial Statistics.)
See item no. 954.

Molenbibliografie. (Bibliography on mills.)
See item no. 1015.

Agriculture

601 **Agricultural science in the Netherlands (including the former guide 'Wageningen: Centre of Agricultural Science') 1985–1987.**
Wageningen, The Netherlands: International Agricultural Centre. [1985.] 352p.

Compiled as a guide to agricultural research and teaching in the Netherlands for visitors from abroad, this handbook describes the work of each department at the Agricultural University in Wageningen, the faculty of Veterinary Medicine at the University of Utrecht, and various other agricultural research institutions. The information was compiled in December 1984 as a guide to activities in the period 1985–87.

602 **Report on the agriculture of the Kingdom of the Netherlands.**
H. M. Jenkins. *Parliamentary Papers: Reports from Commissioners, Inspectors and Others*, vol. 16 (1881), p. 638–713.

Jenkins toured the Netherlands to examine the state of its agriculture at the onset of the great agricultural crisis of the late 19th century, and produced a very detailed report of a wide range of Dutch localities for the benefit of the British legislators.

603 **Agricultural geography.**
Peter Laut. Melbourne: Nelson, 1968. Reprinted 1973. 2 vols. bibliog. maps.

Pages 220–60 of volume 2 concern the Netherlands, and provide a full account of Dutch agriculture in the 1960s.

604 **The derivation of spatial goals for the Dutch land consolidation programme.**
David A. Pinder. Rotterdam: Rotterdam University Economisch Geografisch Instituut, 1980. 23p. bibliog. maps. (Working Paper Series A, no. 80–3).

Deals with the land reallocation policy in certain areas since the war, and concludes that, despite government emphasis on the economic benefits of land consolidation, the policy has usually been led by considerations of social factors.

605 **The problem of popularising land consolidation in the Netherlands: thirty years of legislative change, 1924–54.**
David A. Pinder. Rotterdam: Rotterdam University Economisch Geografisch Instituut, 1979. 21p. bibliog. (Working Paper Series A, no. 79–1).

Follows land reallocation legislation from 1920 onwards, examining the Acts of 1924, 1934, 1938, 1947 and 1954. It appears that the 1954 Act was heavily dependent on previous legislation, and that the key factor in getting consolidation going was the injection of large-scale government subsidies.

606 **Agriculture in pre- and protohistoric times.**
J. M. G. van der Poel. *Acta Historiae Neerlandicae*, vol. 1 (1966), p. 159–70. bibliog.

Concentrating on the technological advances in agriculture apparent from archaeological evidence, Van der Poel summarizes the conclusions of research work prior to the 1960s on this subject. This article is a translated synopsis by the author of an article in Dutch of 1961.

607 **A free farmer in a free state: a study of rural life and industry.**
John William Robertson–Scott. London: Heinemann, 1912. 335p. maps.

A contemporary account of Dutch agriculture around the turn of the century, now dated and in any case popularized and somewhat superficial. The chapters concern the various agricultural regions of the country.

608 **Dutch organised agriculture in international politics.**
Alan David Robinson. The Hague: Nijhoff, 1961. 192p. bibliog.

This makes a penetrating study of the interrelationship between agricultural associations and the Ministry in the Netherlands and of the relationship between Dutch agricultural representatives and policy-makers in the EEC. It concludes that the interaction of interested parties in domestic and foreign policies has resulted in fruitful political action though 'outside the Netherlands the political activities of Dutch organised agriculture have had little effect.'

609 **Dutch elm disease: aspects of pathogenosis and control.**
Rudolph J. Scheffer. Wageningen, The Netherlands: 1984. Doctoral dissertation, Agricultural University of Wageningen, 1984. 89p. bibliog.

This study both describes the general state of knowledge on Dutch elm disease, and also goes into considerable detail on combatting the disease. Nearly all the chapters are reprinted from articles previously published elsewhere and four of them are co-authored with other scientists.

610 **A reconsideration of the origins of the agricultural co-operative.**
J. A. van Stuijvenburg. *Low Countries History Yearbook*, vol. 13 (1980), p. 114–32. bibliog.

The article is not based on new research, but rather on a re-analysis of the beginnings of the co-operative movement at the end of the 19th century. Van Stuijvenburg's argument places relatively little emphasis on the great agricultural crisis in the 1880s as a stimulant to co-operative formation, but looks more towards defects in the market mechanism, the increase in agricultural production, and a changing mentality amongst the farmers themselves.

611 **Agriculture in the Netherlands.**
J. Veldman, translated by R. R. Symonds. *Bulletin Algemene Sociale Geografie*, series 1, vol. 10 (Sept. 1974). Utrecht: Geografisch Instituut, 1974. 111p. bibliog.

A general survey with an historical perspective, with chapters on the various agricultural regions of the country, the agricultural industrics, horticulture, government policy, the co-operatives, and a selection of the most recent (pre-1974) literature on the subject.

612 **Productivity of land and agricultural innovation in the Low Countries (1250–1800).**
Edited by Herman van der Wee, Eddy van Cauwenberghe. Leuven, Belgium: Leuven University Press, 1978. 187p. bibliog.

A series of contributions based on long-term quantitative data to do with the agricultural economy. The data series concern tithes, land rents and land prices. Several of the essays are on Belgium.

613 **De economische outwikkeling van de Nederlandse landbouw in de negentiende eeuw, 1800–1914.** (The economic development of Dutch agriculture in the 19th century, 1800–1914.)
Jan L. van Zanden. Utrecht: HES, 1985. 461p. bibliog. (HES Studia Historica, vol. 13). Also published as *A. A. G. Bijdragen*, vol. 25, p. 1–461.

There is a summary in English to this brilliant analysis, which formed the author's 1985 doctoral dissertation at Wageningen University. A wealth of quantitative data forms the basis of this definitive study of the place of agriculture in the growing Dutch economy.

Agriculture

The kingdom of the Netherlands: facts and figures.
See item no. 14.

The changing countryside: proceedings of the first British–Dutch symposium on rural geography.
See item no. 30.

Yield ratios 810–1820.
See item no. 176.

The Dutch rural economy in the Golden Age, 1500–1700.
See item no. 179.

Nederlands–Engels woordenboek voor landbouwwetenschappen. (Dutch–English dictionary of agriculture.)
See item no. 254.

Glossary of land resources: English, French, Italian, Dutch, German, Swedish.
See item no. 259.

Rural community studies in the Netherlands.
See item no. 361.

A. A. G. Bijdragen. (Contributions from the Department of Rural History.)
See item no. 925.

Historia Agriculturae.
See item no. 943.

Netherlands Journal of Agricultural Science.
See item no. 956.

Netherlands Journal of Plant Pathology: Tijdschrift over Planteziekten.
See item no. 958.

Bibliografie van de Nederlandse landbouwgeschiedenis. (Bibliography of Dutch agricultural history.)
See item no. 988.

Transport

614 **The three seaports of the Low Countries in the nineteenth century, Amsterdam, Antwerp and Rotterdam.**
Henk van Dijk. Rotterdam: Erasmus University, 1980. 16p. bibliog. maps.

Besides dealing with the shipping and transport of these three ports, Van Dijk examines the deployment of technology, the occupational and social structure of the populations, and spatial developments. A useful short summary of the information available.

615 **The determinants of transport mode choices in Dutch cities: some disaggregate stochastic models.**
François X. de Donnea. Rotterdam: Rotterdam University Press, 1971. 229p. bibliog.

Concentrating on Amsterdam and Rotterdam, Donnea's study establishes an econometric model of the consumer's choice of transport in Dutch cities.

616 **Holland transport.**
The Hague: Ministry of Transport and Public Works, 1979. 32p. [Information sheets].

Lightweight but informative hand-out on the achievements of Dutch public transport in the 1970s. The accompanying information sheets have about four pages each on subjects including the parks, civil aviation, research, bicycles, containers, dredging, haulage, consultancy, shipping, push-barges, rail, shipbuilding, etc.

617 **An optimizing medium-term planning model for the Netherlands railways.**

Augustinus A. A. Holtgrefe. Rotterdam: Rotterdam University Press, 1975. 167p. bibliog.

This doctoral dissertation from Rotterdam University is based on research conducted by the Dutch State Railways (Nederlandse Spoorwegen) Research and Planning department, and applies a complex optimum decision rule to railway planning.

618 **Interpreting and valuing transport's role in social well-being: an international conference held 12–15 April 1983, Noordwijk, Netherlands.**

The Hague: Ministry of Transport and Public Works, 1983–84. 2 vols. bibliog.

The impact of transport systems – both positive and negative – on people's well-being is the subject of these conference papers. Vol. 1 consists of introductory papers; vol. 2 is the conference report.

619 **Dutch military aviation.**

Paul A. Jackson. Leicester: Midland Counties Publications (Aerophile), 1978. 134p.

A short history of the Dutch air force, information on the various squadrons, photographs of aircraft, lists of battle orders and an appendix on Dutch squadrons serving with the RAF and FAA in the Second World War.

620 **Structural outline plan civil aerodromes (SCA).**

Y. M. D. Kentie. *Planning and Development in the Netherlands*, vol. 12, no. 2 (1980), p. 116–45. bibliog.

A review of civil airport provision in the country and of the volume of traffic in 1980. There are prognoses of traffic levels up to the year 2000, and in planning air transport policy alternatives for the future. Considerable attention is paid to noise levels.

621 **'Livability' of the environment in terms of traffic in the Netherlands.**

The Hague: Ministry of Housing, Physical Planning and Environment, 1983. 39p. bibliog.

This paper is concerned with the efforts of planners to reconcile reasonable standards of living and housing with the needs of the transport sector in a modern densely populated society. The period since 1945 comes under examination, with the focus on 'sympathetic' policies of the 1970s and early 1980s.

622 **Deregulation.**
H. Raben. The Hague: Ministry of Transport and Public Works, 1980. 13p.

This is the text of a paper given at the first Dutch colloquium on international air transport, and pleads for a sharp reduction in the restrictions and regulations governing international air transport.

623 **Relations in civil aviation between the Netherlands and the United States.**
The Hague: Ministry of Transport and Public Works, 1982. 9p.

A report by the staff of the Information Section at the Ministry on this important sector of Dutch international transport.

624 **Service levels of urban public transport: a series of documents on a study commissioned by the Ministry of Transport and Public Works of the Netherlands.**
The Hague: Ministry of Transport and Public Works, 1980. 4 vols.

A full account of a report of a round table meeting on the subject in The Hague in January 1980. Vol. 1 introduces the report, vol. 2 is a report of the meeting, vol. 3 is the first interim report, and vol. 3A is an appendix.

625 **The new Netherlands airport zoning act.**
S. J. Timmenga. *Planning and Development in the Netherlands*, vol. 11, no. 2 (1979), p. 146–78. maps.

New revised aviation legislation came into effect on 1 October 1978, and is designed to avoid the mistakes made in planning the flight paths to Schiphol airport (Amsterdam), which pass over residential and green-belt areas. Timmermans explains the Act's provisions.

The kingdom of the Netherlands: facts and figures.
See item no. 14.

Port of Amsterdam.
See item no. 42.

Changes in the port of Amsterdam.
See item no. 48.

Barges and capitalism: passenger transportation in the Dutch economy, 1632–1839.
See item no. 177.

De haventolk. (The harbour book.)
See item no. 265.

Anglo–Dutch trade flows 1955–75: their effects on, and consequences for, Dutch port development and planning.
See item no. 566.

The port of Rotterdam in figures.
See item no. 570.

Oil refining in the Netherlands and Belgium: growth, crisis and restructuring.
See item no. 593.

Rotterdam Europoort Delta.
See item no. 967.

Employment, Manpower, the Labour Movement and Trade Unions

626 **The Labour Plan and the Social Democratic Workers' Party.**
R. Abma. *Low Countries History Yearbook*, vol. 14 (1981), p. 154–81. bibliog.

A translation of an article in Dutch from *Bijdragen en Mededelingen betreffende de Geschiedenis der Nederlanden* (1977). It concerns the introduction to the Netherlands of Hendrik de Man's 'Plan Socialism' in the 1930s.

627 **Geschiedenis van de Nederlandse arbeidersbeweging in de 19e eeuw.**
(History of the Dutch labour movement in the 19th century.)
Edited by J. M. W. Binneveld. The Hague: Nijhoff, 1978. 207p. bibliog. (Geschiedenis in Veelvoud, vol. 3).

Part of a series published by Nijhoff intended for university students of history, comprising the seminal articles in the field, and extracts of the major monographs. The material is arranged in five 'themes', namely the origins of the labour movement, parliamentary versus anti-parliamentary factions, organizations and tactics, social democracy, and the confessional labour organizations.

628 **The volume and composition of structural unemployment in the Netherlands, 1950–1980.**
H. van der Burg, S. K. Kuipers, J. Muysken, C. de Neubourg, A. H. van Zon. The Hague: Staatsuitgeverij, 1982. 90p.

The title article in the symposium contributing to a national programme of research into the labour market is contributed by Kuipers and Muysken. Other articles discuss output and employment growth in the post-war period, qualitative structural unemployment between 1955 and 1989, and policy implications.

629 **The co-operative movement in the Netherlands: an analysis.**
Nationale Co-operatieve Raad. The Hague: Nationale Co-operatieve Raad, 1956. 103p. map.

The co-operative movement in the Netherlands has been of the greatest importance, especially in the agricultural sector. This publicity operation in the post-war growth period is designed to explain the Dutch system to outsiders, and has chapters on co-operatives for credit, purchasing, marketing, processing, and consumers.

630 **Women in small businesses: focus on Europe.**
Edited by Rik Donckels, Jane N. Meijer. Assen, The Netherlands: Van Gorcum, 1986. 91p.

This contains (p. 65–78) a chapter, 'Contributing wife: partner in business', on the Netherlands where there are practically no women solely in charge of small businesses. The result of a survey shows that they have a very uncertain status in society, although in one third of the firms the wife assists the husband, and may even put up much of the capital.

631 **Industrial democracy in the Netherlands: a seminar.**
P.H. van Gorkum (et al.). Meppel, The Netherlands: Boom, 1969. 122p. bibliog.

This work is somewhat dated, but is useful because it was written at the end of a period of great stability and positive development in industrial relations, before the disillusion and bitterness of the late 1970s and 1980s set in. Ample attention is given to such institutions as works councils, and the whole leglislated system of PBO (Publiekrechtelijk Bedrijfsorganisatie), or public industrial relations.

632 **The future of the quaternary sector.**
H. de Groot. *Planning and Development in the Netherlands*, vol. 12, no. 2 (1980), p. 103–15.

Deals with the prospects for employment in the government-financed non-commercial sector (education, health, public administration, etc.). Points to dangers in the future, which now in the mid–1980s are being realised, of declining resources and overstaffing.

633 **The origins and consolidation of Dutch social democracy, 1894–1914.**
Erik Hansen. *Canadian Journal of History*, vol. 12, no. 2 (Dec. 1977), p. 145–77. bibliog.

Examines the various strands of development within the Dutch socialist movement before the First World War, in both its trade union and political party wings.

634 **Wages and employment in the E.E.C.**
Dewi–Davies Jones. London: Kogan Page, 1973. 159p. bibliog. (PE Briefing Guide to the EEC).

Chapter 5 (p. 82–92), concerns the Netherlands, and provides basic data and information current in the early 1970s on industrial relations, trade unions, conditions of employment, and social security. The information is taken from EEC publications rather than Dutch sources, and is now rather dated.

635 **The miners' general strike in the Dutch province of Limburg (21 June–2 July 1917).**
R. Jurriens. *Low Countries History Yearbook*, vol. 14 (1981), p. 124–53. bibliog.

A translation of an article in the *Economisch- en Sociaal-Historish Jaarboek* of 1979, this article portrays the strike as a struggle not only between capital and labour, but also between Christian (Roman Catholic) and Socialist organized labour.

636 **Manpower and social policy in the Netherlands.**
Organisation for Economic Co-operation and Development (OECD). Paris: OECD, 1967. 301p. maps. (Reviews of Manpower and Social Policy, no. 6).

Now rather dated, but a very thorough and comprehensive survey of the area. The OECD completed this exercise in several member countries, and the systematic approach adopted concentrates on policies, programmes and administrative procedures.

637 **Prospects for reforming the labour system: summary of the twenty-first report to the government.**
Netherlands Scientific Council for Government Policy (WRR). The Hague: WRR, 1981. 39p.

Translated summary of a major report to the government by this powerful quango. Its authors take a selection of ten radical ideas for reform, and examine their implications: a reduction in working hours, part-time work, study-leave, wage differential rearrangements, improving the quality of work, voluntary work, wages for the home-maker, alternative employment, a basic income, and using government financial controls to alter consumption patterns. All are recommended except two, and the whole is undertaken against a background of serious levels of unemployment.

638 **Manpower planning in the Netherlands in perspective.**
J. M. M. Ritzen. *Planning and Development in the Netherlands*, vol. 9 (1977), p. 27–49. bibliog.

Quite a technical exercise in manpower planning, using as a basis the demand for and supply of university courses in the Netherlands in 1980 and 1990.

639 **Education and manpower forecasts.**
R. Ruiter. *Planning and Development in the Netherlands*, vol. 3 (1969), p. 66–185.

When forecasts are made, education, manpower and economic estimates are subjected to time series and cross-section analysis. The repeated errors in forecasting suggest that these analyses are faulty, are not checked frequently enough and do not allow for other indicators, such as intuition. But forecasts are unavoidable and policy-makers must depend on them, particularly since educational goals are in conflict (development of the individual's potential vis à vis manpower requirements).

640 **The Netherlands Works Councils Act.**
Translation of the Act by S. R. Schuit, R. M. Pais, T. R. Offervanger. Chicago, Illinois: Commerce Clearing House, 1982. 56p. (Common Market Reports, no. 454).

A translation of this legislation, which is of considerable importance to foreign companies investing in the Netherlands. Both the organizational aspects of works councils, involving their membership and finances, and the substantive rules, governing when and how the works councils should be consulted, are fully covered.

641 **A contribution to the scientific study of the history of trade unions.**
Theo van Tijn. *International Review of Social History*, vol. 21 (1976), p. 212–39. bibliog.

Van Tijn, Professor of Social and Economic History at Utrecht University, strives to develop a model for 'successful' trade union evolution, 'success' being defined as recognition by the employers of the union's exclusive rights to negotiate the sale of its members' labour. Empirical material is drawn from the Dutch diamond-cutting, printing, and cotton industries. A list of factors affecting union success is tabled.

642 **Labor relations in the Netherlands.**
John P. Windmuller. Ithaca, New York: Cornell University Press, 1969. 469p. bibliog.

An excellent and clear account of the subject covering the situation in the 1960s, with early chapters providing perhaps the best account of the history of the labour movement in all its facets. The bibliography is particularly useful.

Policy development: a study of the Social and Economic Council of the Netherlands.
See item no. 423.

A modern European company law system: commentary on the 1976 Dutch legislation.
See item no. 449.

Dutch company law.
See item no. 452.

Industrial mobility and migration in the European community.
See item no. 590.

Labor relations in the Netherlands: a bibliography.
See item no. 996.

Statistics

643 **1899–1979: tachtig jaren statistiek in tijdsreeksen.** (Eighty years of statistics in time-series.)
Compiled by the Central Bureau of Statistics (CBS). The Hague: Staatsuitgeverij, 1979. 229p.

This is the third commemorative publication to honour the foundation of the CBS in 1899, previous volumes appearing in 1969 and 1959. The period covered is the 20th century, and there are brief chapters on all aspects of statistics covering public life in the Netherlands. An index and a list of CBS major publications are of assistance.

644 **Benelux statistieken/statistiques: tijdreeksen/series retrospectives 1948–1974.** (Benelux statistics: time-series 1948–1974.)
Brussels: Secretariat General of the Benelux Economic Union, 1975. 137p. bibliog.

A handy comparative set of tables for Belgium, Luxembourg and the Netherlands. The chapters cover geography, population, health, housing, and various others aspects of the society and economy of the Low Countries.

645 **Résumé statistique des Pays-Bas 1850–1881: publication de la Société de Statistique des Pays-Bas.** (Statistical summary of the Netherlands 1850–1881: publication of the Statistical Society of the Netherlands.)
The Hague: Smits, 1882. 179p.

These 19th-century statistics leave a great deal to be desired, but there is quantitative material here on most aspects of government finance and some demographic subjects.

646 **Systematic list of publications 1986.**
Netherlands Central Bureau of Statistics (CBS). Voorburg, The Netherlands: CBS, 1986. 56p.

This is strictly speaking a commercial catalogue, but is a good reference handbook. It provides a complete list of official annual statistical publications in English and in Dutch.

The port of Rotterdam in figures.
See item no. 570.

Jaarcijfers voor het Koninkrijk der Nederlanden, Rijk in Europa. (Annual Statistics for the Kingdom of the Netherlands, European Division.)
See item no. 950.

Maandschrift van het CBS. (Monthly Bulletin of the CBS.)
See item no. 953.

Maandstatistiek van de Industrie. (Monthly Bulletin of Industrial Statistics.)
See item no. 954.

Netherlands Official Statistics: Quarterly Journal of the Central Bureau of Statistics.
See item no. 962.

Statistical Yearbook of the Netherlands.
See item no. 969.

Statistisch Zakboek. (Statistical Pocketbook.)
See item no. 970.

Education

General education

647 **The Dutch education system.**
Ministry of Education and Science. Zoetermeer, The Netherlands: Ministry of Education and Science, 1986. 479p. bibliog.

A comprehensive overview of the structure from the Ministry itself, including the role of government and local authorities, the employment of staff, the various kinds of schooling, the universities, adult education and inspectorate and advisory boards. There are statistics on government expenditure and take-up.

648 **Education and training for migrants in the Netherlands.**
The Hague: Ministry of Education and Science, 1976. 21p. (Docinform 310).

The survey falls into two main sections: policy aspects, research, experimentation legislation; and statistics. At the time education was provided for the children of over a quarter of a million migrants, the majority of whom were Turkish, Moroccan and Spanish.

649 **Educational developments in the Netherlands, 1984–1986.**
Zoetermeer, The Netherlands: Ministry of Education and Science, 1986. 29p. (Docinform 330E).

This report to the fortieth International Conference on Education in Geneva is based on Education Reports of 1983 and 1984 and it outlines the system and summarizes developments, new educational legislation and proposed future policy.

650 **Main lines of the informatics stimulation plan.**
Ministries of Education and Science, Economic Affairs, Agriculture and Fisheries. Zoetermeer, The Netherlands: Ministry of Education and Science [n.d.]. 14p.

A computer title for a straightforward account of the government's investment of Dfls. 1.7 billion in information technology in a five-year plan (1984–88), under five main headings: information, education, research, private, and public sectors.

651 **Organization and structure of education in the Netherlands.**
The Hague: Ministry of Education and Science, 1974. 23p. (Docinform 298E).

Chapters cover the historical development of the present structure, the types of general education available, vocational and technical education at the secondary level and continuing education. A valuable appendix lists English equivalents of terms and acronyms.

Education and manpower forecasts.
See item no. 639.

Sport and physical education in the Netherlands.
See item no. 860.

Primary and secondary education

652 **Deelname aan het lager onderwijs in Nederland gedurende de negentiende eeuw.** (Participation in primary education in the Netherlands in the 19th century.)
Hans Knippenberg. Amsterdam: Koninklijk Nederlands Aardrijkskundig Genootschap; Instituut voor Sociale Geografie, Universiteit van Amsterdam, 1986. 266p. bibliog. (Nederlandse Geografische Studies, no. 9).

There is an English summary to this analysis of national developments and regional differences in primary school activities. The variations are examined in their social and geographical contexts and statistics and comments are assembled from school inspectors' reports.

653 **New educational provision for the 16 to 18 age group in the Netherlands.**
Zoetermeer, The Netherlands: Ministry of Education and Science, 1985. 23p. (Docinform 326E).

A description of the genesis and structure of an experimental short course in senior secondary vocational education (KMBO) running since 1979, with some twenty-seven full-time and a number of part-time projects now under review.

654 **The role of the documentation in educational planning.**
K. I. L. M. Peters. *Planning and Development in the Netherlands*, vol. 3 (1969), p. 52–65. bibliog.

The documentation centre established by the Minister of Education and Science provides information to those making decisions in the planning process in order to achieve integration in planning. This is particularly necessary in a situation of mixed state and private (confessional) education.

655 **Primary Education Act (The Netherlands).**
Zoetermeer, The Netherlands: Ministry of Education and Science, 1984. 19p.

Summaries of the Primary Education Act (1981) and the Primary Education Transition Act (1983) are preceded by a history of the genesis of a reform called 'a massive operation, unparallelled in the history of education in the Netherlands'. The acts provide a framework rather than detailed provisions to enable developments to keep pace with the need for change.

656 **School and politics in the Netherlands, 1796–1814.**
S. Schama. *Historical Journal*, vol. 13 (1970), p. 589–610. bibliog.

An interesting treatment of educational reform in the Netherlands under French occupation, revealing that its generating force and eventually successful implementation was entirely Dutch.

657 **Schools inspectorate in the Netherlands.**
Zoetermeer, The Netherlands: Ministry of Education and Science, 1984. 41p. (Docinform 328E).

This outlines the duties and methods, the structure and the activities of the schools inspectorate, showing the radical reorganization in the 1970s, and projecting new developments.

658 **Training teachers and head teachers for pre-primary schools in the Netherlands.**
The Hague: Ministry of Education and Science, 1971. 12p. (Docinform 281E).

This is a revision of Docinform 260 (1970), incorporating the amendment (1971) to the Royal Decree of 1968, containing directives for the training of teachers and head teachers in infant schools.

659 **The subject technology in Dutch education.**
Jenne van der Velde. Eindhoven, The Netherlands: University of Technology [n.d.] [ca. 1987]. 20p. bibliog.

This paper, read at a conference on pupil attitudes towards technology, outlines the place of technology in secondary education and the function of the National Institute for Curriculum Development, before describing the Institute's proposals for modifications in the teaching of the subject.

660 **The planning of non-university education.**
H. Veldkamp *Planning and Development in the Netherlands*, vol. 3 (1969), p. 27–38.

In the history of educational planning, a new and important departure was the establishment, in 1966, of the Foundation for Educational Research. This advises the government on the successes and failures in the implementation of its educational policy of restructuring.

661 **Vocational education in the Netherlands.**
Netherlands Ministry of Education and Science. Berlin: European Centre for the Development of Vocational Training (CEDEFOP), 1986. 19p.

A large part of the Dutch government budget is allocated to a very wide range of educational facilities for some 4.3 million pupils and students of whom over one million are in vocational training. This describes the system and outlines the types of vocational and apprenticeship training.

662 **Functions of planning for secondary education in the Netherlands.**
A. L. M. van Wieringen. *Planning and Development in the Netherlands*, vol. 14 (1982), p. 140–159. bibliog.

The main issues in recent planning are considered with respect to the political, organizational and substantive functions of planning, distinguishing between the various levels of planning (local and national). The analysis shows trends and weaknesses in the present situation.

663 **Bilingual education in Friesland.**
Edited by Koen Zondag. Franeker, The Netherlands: Wever, 1982. 311p. bibliog.

These papers read at the International Conference on Bilingual Education held at Leeuwarden in 1982 discuss the history of the educational system in the Netherlands and Friesland and of the Frisian language and its present status, public opinion on education in Frisian, the objectives of bilingual schools, ethnicity and language, teacher training in a bilingual province.

ETV in the Netherlands: specifically ETV programmes.
See item no. 920.

Higher education and research

664 **The development of planning for the Dutch university system: a review.**
Joris E. J. van Bergen. *Planning and Development in the Netherlands*, vol. 12 (1980), p. 3–23. bibliog.

In recognizing the paradox of conflicting demands of high cost efficiency, higher demand and diminishing resources, the article reviews the relationship between government and universities and planning development in the 1970s in relation to the five-year plan for 1980–85.

665 **Arts in research: the structural position of research in post-secondary music and drama education.**
M. Boon, A. Schrijnen–Van Gastel. Amsterdam: Dr E. Boekman Foundation; The Hague: Government Publications Office, 1981. 75p.

The background history to the present situation is outlined and the central topic of research commissioned to investigate the effectiveness and the needs of after-school music and drama education is combined with useful information on the present structure of this type of education, on teacher training and on the location and activities of the various centres.

666 **The restructuring of university education in the Netherlands.**
Sije van den Bosch. *Higher Education and Research in the Netherlands*, vol. 24, no. 3/4 (summer/autumn 1980), p. 14–17.

A brief outline of the Pais proposal for a two-phase university degree structure and selection procedures to cope with an increasing demand for university places with a falling budgetary provision.

667 **Research policy: an impossible imperative.**
H. B. G. Casimir. *Delta*, vol. 16, no. 2 (summer 1973), p. 5–14.

An attack on government interference in the activities of 'freelance' scholars, which, however, admits that modern science needs substantial funding, and hence government support. The article then describes the support from the various research councils in the Netherlands.

668 **Distance learning: on the design of an open university.**
T. M. Chang, H. F. Crombag, K. F. J. M. van der Drift, J. M. Moonen. Boston, Massachusets; The Hague; London: Kluwer–Nijhoff, 1983. 195p. bibliog.

A discussion of the available means, functions and costs of an open university in the Netherlands.

669 **Counterpart.**

The Hague: NUFFIC (Netherlands Universities Foundation for International Co-operation), 1986. 24p. bibliog.

Five articles discuss the international dimension in higher education and research in the Netherlands, describing Wageningen as the first university to use English in regular courses, referring to the Dutch contribution to international science, describing the new centre in Maastricht for the development of policy management, predicting the future requirements of development studies and research, describing a new technique of wire-lacing used in construction in developing countries, and outlining the work of the traffic academy for third world developments.

670 **Athenae Batavae: the University of Leiden 1575–1975.**

Edited by R. E. O. Ekkart. Leiden: University Press, 1975. 111p. bibliog.

The compiler's aim was to construct a 'pictorial running commentary' on the university during its four centuries of activities, showing its growth from a handful of students to some 16,000 today. It is, as one might expect, a sober but also very entertaining memorial volume.

671 **Distance higher education and the adult learner.**

Edited by Ger van Enckervoort, Keith Harry, Pierre Morin, H. G. Schütze. Assen, The Netherlands: Van Gorcum, 1986. 228p. bibliog.

These are edited papers presented at a conference at Heerlen in 1984. There are three parts: an introduction on distance higher education for adults, outlining general problems and technical innovations; a section on the aims and organization of distance higher education in the Netherlands and other OECD countries; and a section on the learning process and the selection of media, including a chapter on the Dutch open university.

672 **International education: the Dutch system.**

Hans Enklaar. *Higher Education and Research in the Netherlands*, vol. 25, no. 3/4 (summer/autumn 1981), p. 41–53.

A description of the activities of NUFFIC, the Netherlands Foundation for International Co-operation and its Institute of Social Studies. NUFFIC is also the publisher of the journal in which this article appears.

673 **The establishment of an open university in the Netherlands.**

The Hague: Government Publications Office, 1981. 22p.

A policy report by the Ministry of Education and Science based on the proposals by the Open University Planning Committee.

674 **Lijst van docenten in de neerlandistiek aan buitenlandse universiteiten en ledenlijst IVN.** (List of teachers of Dutch Studies at foreign universities and membership list IVN (International Association for Dutch Studies).)
The Hague: IVN, 1987. 113p.

This lists the names and university (and often home) addresses of all those teaching Dutch language, literature, art history and history at universities outside the Netherlands and Belgium. The address list is divided by country.

675 **Leiden university in the seventeenth century: an exchange of learning.**
Edited by T. H. Lunsingh Scheurleer, G. H. Posthumus Meyjes. Leiden: University Press; Brill, 1975. 496p. bibliog.

A handsomely illustrated and authoritative work by eminent scholars on the early years of the university and the contribution of foreign professors to its studies, on Lipsius between the Renaissance and Baroque, and Theodoor Craanen's school of mechanics. There are essays on Arabic scholarship, on Bible studies, the Arminian debate, *le Collège Wallon*, classical philology, philological experiments, medicine, experimental physics, chemistry, publishing, the library, and academic relations between Sweden and Holland.

676 **Trends in research and development in the Netherlands.**
N. J. Tempel, J. E. van Dam. Zoetermeer, The Netherlands: Ministry of Education and Science, 1986. 41p. bibliog.

This is a retrospective report on 'the influence of national science policy between 1973 and 1986'. It covers research in energy, remote sensing, space, marine and maritime studies, environment, toxicology, biotechnology, micro-electronics, information technology, materials, health, behavioural and social sciences, demography and the labour market.

677 **University education in the Netherlands.**
The Hague: Documentation Department, Ministry of Education and Science. 1970. 45p. (Docinform 262).

An outline of the reorganization of university administration resulting from the highly controversial bill of 1970 introducing the so-called democratization of the system. The measure was certainly more radical than similar reforms elsewhere in Europe, and though recent events have substantially affected the courses available at universities as shown in Annex II of this document, the administrative structure is still maintained.

678 **Higher education in the Netherlands.**
Edited by W. Vollmann. Bucharest: UNESCO, 1985. 72p. (Monographs on Higher Education).

This describes the system of higher education, its funding, students and student numbers and the services provided by the universities and open university.

Sections on administration, qualifications and admission (including foreign students), teaching and research, are supplemented by statistical appendixes.

The development of Dutch science policy in international perspective, 1965–1985.
See item no. 679.

ETV in the Netherlands: specifically ETV programmes.
See item no. 920.

Counterpart: The International Dimension of Higher Education in the Netherlands: Bulletin of the Netherlands Universities Foundation for International Co-operation (NUFFIC).
See item no. 931.

Current Research in the Netherlands.
See item no. 932.

Dutch Theses: a List of Titles of Theses Submitted to Dutch Universities.
See item no. 940.

Science research and public policy making.
See item no. 1021.

Science and Technology

Scientific achievements

679 **The development of Dutch science policy in international perspective, 1965–1985.**
Stuart S. Blume. The Hague: Raad van Advies voor het Wetenschapsbeleid (RAWB), 1985. 81p. (Achtergrondstudies 14).

This report to RAWB assumes that science is the motor of progress and proposes a science and technology policy for the Netherlands, with the structural changes needed to make this effective. 'In the eighties', the author argues, 'science has become the source of strategic opportunity', and industrial innovation must be the highest priority in research and development.

680 **Guess work: the discovery of the electron spin.**
Samuel A. Goudsmit. *Delta*, vol. 15, no. 2 (summer 1972), p. 77–91.

The account of how Goudsmit and his colleague George Uhlenbeck discovered, in 1926, a new interpretation of the hydrogen spectrum which could only be accounted for by positing a spinning electron.

681 **The growth of science in the Netherlands in the seventeenth and early eighteenth centuries.**
W. D. Hackmann. In: *The emergence of science in Western Europe*. Edited by M. Crosland. London: Macmillan, 1975, p. 89–111. bibliog.

This provides a survey of the material available on this subject in Dutch.

682 **The Dwingeloo Radio Observatory.**
H. C. van de Hulst. *Higher Education and Research in the Netherlands*, vol. 3, no. 3 (1969), p. 3–9.

A description of the radio telescope and receivers and the mode of operation introduces an account of the scientific aims and of some of the early results from the telescope.

683 **Observationes anatomicae collegii privati Amstelodamensis.**
(Anatomical observations from the Private College in Amsterdam.)
Facsimile with an introduction by G. A. Lindeboom.
Nieuwkoop, The Netherlands: De Graaf, 1975. 37p. + 45p. + 53p.
(Dutch Classics in History of Science, no. 19).

The text of *Annotata anatomica* and *Observationes anatomicae*, published in 1667 and 1673 by members of the Private College in Amsterdam, are provided with an introduction on the society, its members and activities, and notes and an index to the texts.

684 **Offshore drilling and the Dutch.**
Huibert V. Quispel. *Delta*, vol. 12, no. 1 (spring 1969), p. 5–15.

The ability of Dutch marine engineers to meet rush-order delivery targets on North Sea oil rigs gained them a leading position in this field, in which they held the patent for self-elevating mobile platforms, and developed a production of floating cranes with a capacity of up to 1,000 tons.

685 **Friendship and Fellowship: recent developments in Fokker aircraft.**
H. A. Somberg. *Delta*, vol. 12, no. 1 (spring 1969), p. 44–47.

An account of the further development of the F27 Friendship, 'the most successful propeller-turbine powered airliner', to the F28 Fellowship with its twin jets, a cruising speed of 525 mph and an unusual degree of stabilty at slow speeds, enabling landing in distances down to 500 ft.

686 **The Dutch windmill.**
Frederick Stokhuyzen. Bussum, The Netherlands: Van Dishoeck, 1966, 3rd ed. 128p. bibliog.

Written by the former chairman of the Association for the Preservation of Windmills, this describes the development of the windmill from the early 13th century, for grinding corn, pumping water and sawing wood, with some of the thousand remaining (and restored) windmills still in service. The ten types of mill are described, with excellent line-drawings and monochrome photographs.

687 **The land of Stevin and Huygens.**
D. J. Struik. Dordrecht, The Netherlands: Reidel, 1981. 162p. bibliog. (Studies in the History of Modern Sciences, no. 7).

A sketch of science and technology in the Dutch Republic during the Golden Age. The author's own translation of his original text of 1958, revised in 1979, traces the emergence of the new science from the transition in the earlier years of the Republic to Stevin, Descartes, Christiaan Huygens and Boerhaave. There are two bibliographies, one of publications in English, the other of literature in Dutch and other languages.

688 **Europe's longest span: the Eastern Scheldt bridge.**
H. J. Stuvel. *Delta*, vol. 9, nos 1/2 (spring/summer 1966), p. 98–108.

After the restoration of the dikes following the storm flood of 1953 that cost 1,835 lives, the Delta Plan was conceived to ensure that similar freak conditions could never again have the same result. The largest undertaking in this scheme was the bridge spanning the Scheldt estuary over a distance of three miles across deep tidal waters. This article describes the methods used in its construction.

689 **Contrasts in near-similarity.**
Robert Walgate. *Nature*, no. 309 (1984), p. 491–510. bibliog.

A comparative review of science in Belgium, Luxembourg and the Netherlands, which shows the considerable differences within an economic union as clearly defined as Benelux.

Dictionary of electrical engineering.
See item no. 261.

Dictionary of scientific and technical terminology: English, German, French, Dutch, Russian.
See item no. 262.

Illustrated dictionary of mechanical engineering: English, French, German, Dutch, Russian.
See item no. 263.

Regional information systems and impact analysis for large-scale energy development.
See item no. 465.

Dutch shipbuilding before 1800: ships and guilds.
See item no. 596.

Main lines of the informatics stimulation plan.
See item no. 650.

The subject technology in Dutch education.
See item no. 659.

Trends in research and development in the Netherlands.
See item no. 676.

Current Research in the Netherlands.
See item no. 932.

Dutch Theses: a List of Titles of Theses Submitted to Dutch Universities.
See item no. 940.

Holland Industrial.
See item no. 945.

Holland Quarterly.
See item no. 946.

Netherlands Journal of Agricultural Science.
See item no. 956.

Netherlands Journal of Plant Pathology: Tijdschrift over Planteziekten.
See item no. 958.

Netherlands Journal of Sea Research.
See item no. 959.

Netherlands Journal of Zoology.
See item no. 961.

Bibliographie Néerlandaise historique-scientifique des ouvrages importants dont les auteurs sont nés aux 16e, 17e et 18e siécles, sur les sciences mathématiques et physiques, avec leur applications.
(Dutch historical-scientific bibliography of the major works of authors born in the 16th, 17th and 18th centuries on the mathematical and physical sciences, and their applications.)
See item no. 984.

Scientists

690 **Dutch pioneers of science.**
Leo Beek. Assen, The Netherlands: Van Gorcum, 1985. 181p. bibliog.

This contains illustrated chapters on Mercator, Stevin, Snellius, Huygens, Van Leeuwenhoek, Swammerdam, Boerhaave, Van 's-Gravensande, Van der Waals, Van 't Hoff, Lorentz, Eijckman, Einthoven, Zeeman, and Debije. There is a fairly extensive bibliography (mainly of Dutch-language works) and an index of proper names.

691 **Studies on Christiaan Huygens.**
Edited by H. J. M. Bos, M. J. S. Rudwick, H. A. M. Snelders, R. P. W. Visser. Lisse, The Netherlands: Swets & Zeitlinger, 1980. 321p. bibliog.

These papers delivered in 1979 at the Symposium on the Life and Work of Huygens include a biographical sketch, chapters on Huygens' contacts with

France and England, on his problems with Cartesianism, and on his work on astronomy, mechanics, light theory, instrumentation, navigational measurement and music. There is a summary of the symposium and an index.

692 **Vening Meinesz and the sciences of the earth.**
B. J. Collette. *Delta*, vol. 2, no. 1 (spring 1959), p. 27–35.

Meinesz carried out the first gravity survey of the Netherlands in the 1920s, and later of the oceans. His ultimate theory of isostasy revolutionized ideas about the formation of mountains and the equilibrium of compression forces.

693 **Descartes et le cartesianisme hollandais.** (Descartes and Dutch Cartesianism.)
E. J. Dijksterhuis, Cornelia Sevrurier, Paul Dibon, Hendrik J. Pos, Jean Orabel, C.–Louise Thijssen–Schoute, Genevieve Lewis. Paris: Presses Universitaires de France; Amsterdam: Editions Françoises d'Amsterdam, 1950. 309p. bibliog. (Publications de l'Institut Français d'Amsterdam).

This collection of essays by various contributors is as much about Descartes as about Cartesianism in the Netherlands, though three chapters are particularly relevant: Paul Dibon's commentary on Descartes' letter of December 1649 to Constantijn Huygens, Jean Orabel's chapter on Descartes and the United Provinces, and Mrs Thijssen–Schoute's on Cartesianism in the Low Countries. There is an index of proper names.

694 **Darwin and our forefathers: Dutch reactions to the theory of evolution 1860–1875: a field survey.**
J. G. Hegeman. *Acta Historiae Neerlandicae*, vol. 7 (1974), p. 170–220. bibliog.

This article reviews Darwin's theory itself and notes the problems caused by its reception in a field dominated by Opzoomer's dualistic approach to scientific perception and the related theological opposition. This is compared and contrasted to Darwin's reception in Britain and the United States.

695 **Jewish physicians in the Netherlands, 1600–1940.**
Hindle S. Hes. Assen, The Netherlands: Van Gorcum, 1980. 206p. bibliog.

This contains short biographies of over 700 Jewish physicians, and an index of those born between 1600 and 1910.

696 **Boerhaave's correspondence.**
Edited by G. A. Lindeboom. Leiden: Brill, 1962–64. 2 vols. (Analecta Boerhaaviana, nos 3 and 5).

Correspondence with Cox Macro, William Sherard, Hans Sloane, Richard Mead, Cromwell Mortimer, Joannes Baptista Bassand, and people in Eastern Europe, France, Germany, Switzerland, Italy and Portugal is reprinted with translations of the Latin texts but with no translations from the French. The second volume contains indexes of persons, personal names and correspondence.

697 **Herman Boerhaave: the man and his work.**
G. A. Lindeboom. London: Methuen, 1968. 452p. bibliog.

The first half of this biography covers the man's life, his childhood, student years, academic career and his legacy to others; the second half studies his thought – his philosophical and theoretical medical views, his work as a clinician, botanist and chemist. There are indexes of persons and subjects.

698 **Boerhaave's men, at Leyden and after.**
E. A. Underwood. Edinburgh: [n.p.], 1977. 227p. bibliog.

This is an account of the careers of the British graduates who studied under Boerhaave. Over 700 English-speaking students sat at Boerhaave's feet during his 37 years at Leiden, and this is an attempt to do justice to the master by tracing the successful careers of as many of his pupils as could be discovered. No less than 23 of them became Fellows of the Royal Society. There is a general index.

Biografisch woordenboek der Nederlanden. (Biographical dictionary of the Netherlands.)
See item no. 976.

Biografisch woordenboek van Nederland. (Biographical dictionary of the Netherlands.)
See item no. 978.

Dutch medical biography: a biographical dictionary of Dutch physicians and surgeons 1475–1975.
See item no. 979.

Nieuw Nederlandsch biografisch woordenboek. (New Dutch biographical dictionary.)
See item no. 980.

Literature

History and criticism

699 **Man of rancour: J. J. Slauerhoff.**
E. M. Beekman. *Dutch Crossing*, vol. 5 (1978), p. 32–42.

A discussion of Slauerhoff's poetry and prose in relation to his unsettled life.

700 **Nijhoff, Van Ostaijen, 'De Stijl'.**
Edited by Francis Bulhof. The Hague: Nijhoff, 1976. 136p. bibliog.

A collection of six essays on 'Modernism in the Netherlands and Belgium in the first quarter of the 20th century'. Bulhof's introduction defines modernism; J. Brandt Corstius discusses the international context of Dutch literary modernism, 1915–1930; A. van Elslander surveys Flemish literature in the first decades of the 20th century; Paul Hadermann writes on Paul van Ostaijen and *Der Sturm*; Egbert Krispyn discusses the relationship between literature and *De Stijl*; Robert P. Welsh considers geometric abstraction in Theo van Doesburg's work; and A. L. Sötemann defines Martinus Nijhoff's poetry in its European context as non-spectacular modernism.

701 **Closure in the modern Dutch novel.**
Carol Dickinson. *Dutch Crossing*, vol. 23 (1984), p. 70–92. bibliog.

Closure as a feature of fictional writing is discussed as a question of literary theory, and various types of closure in Dutch writing are reviewed (temporal, spatial, cyclical), and devices such as restrospection or narrator-withdrawal, and, in present-tense narratives, implied retrospection, enabling the author to round off his story. There is a substantial bibliography of primary and secondary sources.

702 **Mariken van Nieumeghen.**

Hans van Dijk. *Dutch Crossing*, vol. 22 (1984), p. 27–37. bibliog.

Following the indications in the play that Mariken, the obvious protagonist, also relates closely to Mary, the second Eve, Van Dijk argues that the play contains an intentional universal allegory of the salvation of mankind.

703 **Literary history, modernism, and postmodernism.**

Douwe W. Fokkema. Amsterdam; Philadelphia: Benjamin, 1984. 63p. bibliog. (Utrecht Publications in General and Comparative Literature).

In its review of modernist hypotheses, it considers literary conventions in the work of Ter Braak and Du Perron, and post-modernist conventions in that of W. F. Hermans, Krol, and Nooteboom. Modernist authors (including Du Perron and Ter Braak) are distinguished from post-modernists (including Hermans) on the evidence of a contrastive analysis of semantic and syntactic characteristics, following the theories of the Russian formalists and recent studies in reception and semiotics.

704 **From Wolfram and Petrarch to Goethe and Grass.**

Edited by D. H. Green, L. P. Johnson, Dieter Wuttke. Baden–Baden, Germany: Koerner, 1982. 642p. bibliog. (Saecula Spiritalia, no. 5).

This contains a number of articles on Dutch literature: W. Vermeer on Janus Gruterus, W. P. Gerritsen on Coornhert's translation of Boëthius, P. K. King on Petrarch and the Dutch movement of 1880, and A. L. Sötemann on poetics and periods in literary history.

705 **The enlightened authorship of Jacob Campo Weyerman (1677–1747).**

A. J. Hanon. *Dutch Crossing*, vol. 15 (1981), p. 3–25. bibliog.

An article to rehabilitate a neglected or misunderstood unorthodox spokesman of the Enlightenment, in his journals, plays (one of which places an atheist on the stage for the first time in the Netherlands), pamphlets and biographies. His work attacked personalities, Catholicism and medical practice, but also extolled the personality of the artist expressed in the so-called realistic painting of the Golden Age. It is followed by T. Broos's translation of a fragment of Weyerman's prose.

706 **The individual.**

Maarten 't Hart. *Dutch Crossing*, vol. 23 (1984), p. 2–9.

The author, discussing his own work, believes that the dominant themes in his fiction, the relationship between an older man and a boy, unrequited love, and marriage, can all be identified as expressions of loneliness and alienation in the human condition.

707 **Vondel on translation.**
Theo Hermans. *Dutch Crossing*, vol. 26 (1985), p. 39–72. bibliog.

A commentary on the Renaissance views on translating in so far as they are represented by Vondel in the prefaces and dedications to the translations from Latin and Greek over a period of fifty-five years.

708 **Preliminaries to the study of the comic drama of the Rhetoricians.**
Wim Hüsken. *Dutch Crossing*, vol. 22 (1984), p. 49–59. bibliog.

Since medieval poetics tell us nothing about the structure of the farces, Hüsken's investigation suggests that the answer to this should be sought in the changes that occur when a character is added to the *dramatis personae*.

709 **The dramatic structure of the Dutch morality.**
Willem M. H. Hummelen. *Dutch Crossing*, vol. 22 (1984), p. 17–26. bibliog.

A comparison of two moralities, the biblical *Naaman princhе van Sijrien* (Naaman Prince of Syria) and the secular *'sMenschen Sin en Verganckelijk Schoonheit* (Man's inclination and passing beauty), to show that the Dutch morality can be considered as drama of what Klotz calls the 'open form' *Geschlossene und offene Form im Drama* (1969), in which revaluation plays an important if not dominant part.

710 **Multatuli.**
Peter K. King. New York: Twayne Publishers, 1972. 185p. bibliog. (Twayne World Authors Series. no. 219).

This monograph on the personality of the author, Eduard Douwes Dekker, and his work, provides a commentary with close reference to the texts (with translations of all quotations) of *Max Havelaar*, *Minnebrieven* (Love letters), *Ideeën* (Ideas), *Woutertje Pieterse* (Walter Peters) and *Millioenen-studiën* (Studies of millions).

711 **Vondel: a prophet in his own country.**
Peter K. King. *Dutch Crossing*, vol. 11 (1980), p. 66–81. bibliog.

A discussion of four plays, *Joseph in Dothan*, *Lucifer*, *Jeptha* and *Adam in ballingschap*, to indicate how the essentially human dilemmas in the tragedies transcend the biblical mythology on which they are based.

712 **Gezelle and Multatuli: a question of literature and social history.**
Peter K. King. Hull: Hull University Press, 1978. 27p.

An inaugural lecture suggesting that the apparent relationship between literature and its social environment is complex and often misleading.

713 **A lamb to slaughter.**
Dirk Ayelt Kooiman, Jan Montyn. *Dutch Crossing*, vol. 23 (1984), p. 45–53.

The author of *Montyn* (*A lamb to slaughter* in Adrienne Dixon's translation, London: Souvenir Press, 1984) and the man whose biography it is, discuss the genesis of this book and answer questions about it.

714 **Literature of the Low Countries.**
Reinder P. Meijer. Cheltenham, England: Stanley Thornes, 1978. 2nd imp. 402p. bibliog.

An enlarged revision of the first edition (1971). A thoroughly reliable and readable history of Dutch-language literature from the earliest texts to the present day, with some reference to English literature for comparison. It is the only textbook in English covering the whole field (though necessarily selectively).

715 **The literary theories of Daniel Heinsius: a study of the development of his views on literary theory and criticism during the period from 1602 to 1612.**
J. H. Meter. Assen, The Netherlands: Van Gorcum, 1984. 433p.

A study of the classical and Humanist sources for the *Tragoediae constitutione* and other treatises.

716 **Mirror of the Indies: a history of Dutch colonial literature.**
Rob Nieuwenhuys. Amherst, Massachusetts: University of Massachusetts Press, 1982. 329p.

A translation, edited and abridged by E. M. Beekman, of the substantial history of fictional and non-fictional writing in Dutch on the East Indies by an ex-colonial, under the original title *Oost–Indische spiegel* (1972).

717 **Life and works of Gerardus Joannes Vossius (1577–1649).**
C. S. M. Rademaker. Assen, The Netherlands: Van Gorcum, 1981. 462p. bibliog. (Republica Literaria Neerlandica, no. 5).

This, the expanded version of a doctoral dissertation, is really a study of Vossius and his circle. It is therefore not just the biography of a leading Renaissance scholar, but an important contribution to the history of learning, and a study of Dordrecht and Leiden in the early 17th century.

718 **Silt and sky: men and movements in modern Dutch literature.**
Annie H. M. Romein–Verschoor. Port Washington, Wisconsin: Kennikat, 1969. 98p. bibliog.

Essays by a historian on recent writers for whom the authoress claims European or world status, starting with the 1880 movement: Gorter, Van Eeden, Van Looy, Henriette Roland Holst–van der Schalk, Boutens, Dèr Mouw, Heijermans,

Roland Holst, Marsman, Du Perron, Van Schendel, Huizinga, Vestdijk and others.

719 **Janus Secundus.**
G. Schoolfield. Boston; New York: Twayne Publishers, 1980. 177p. bibliog.

A monograph consisting of a biography and commentary on the earlier and occasional poetry, the elegies, *Basia* and other poetry with blank verse translations of the passages referred to.

720 **Argumentative aspects of rhetoric and their impact on the poetry of Joost van den Vondel.**
Marijke Spies. *Dutch Crossing*, vol. 9 (1979), p. 100–06.

A discussion of Vondel's application of the *ars oratoria* in his poem in praise of the new Amsterdam town hall.

721 **Rainy realism? Some contemporary Dutch fiction.**
Paul F. Vincent. *Dutch Crossing*, vol. 15 (1985), p. 34–45. bibliog.

An incisive if necessarily discursive review of recent writing in Holland and Belgium establishing what is meant by an academist style and agreeing with Ton Anbeek (in *De Gids*, 1981) that there is a contemplative and introspective tone in much recent fiction that emphasizes the lack of breadth. He refers in fact to many more works than are shown in his own bibliography (p. 45).

722 **50 Dutch and Flemish novelists.**
J. de Wit. Merrick, New York: Cross-Cultural Communications, 1979. 200p. bibliog.

Some of the biographical notes, summaries and translated excerpts from fiction by Dutch and Flemish authors as published in *Writing in Holland and Flanders* (q.v.) are collected here. The collection is intended to interest publishers in commissioning translations, but the interested reader will gain some impression of recent fiction from this anthology.

The Netherlands: an historical and cultural survey, 1795–1977.
See item no. 141.

Bibliografie van de Nederlandse taal- en literatuurwetenschap.
(Bibliography of Dutch language and literature.)
See item no. 982.

Translations

723 **Adam International Review**, vol. 41 (1979), nos 410–412.
Edited by Miron Grindea. London. 96p.

Translations of prose and poetry (mainly post-1960) with short essays on Hermans and Wolkers. The whole of Hermans' television play *Periander* (1974) is translated into French, extracts from *Nooit meer slapen* and Mulisch's *Voer voor psychologen* and tales by Henk Romijn Meijer, Maarten 't Hart and Mary Dorna, as well as poems by twelve Dutch poets, are translated into English.

724 **Chapel road.**
Louis–Paul Boon, translated by Adrienne Dixon. New York: Twayne, 1972. 338p. (The Library of Netherlandic Literature, no. 1).

This is the first in the series of literary translations entitled *The Library of Netherlandic Literature*, edited by Egbert Krispyn. *De kapellekensbaan*, of which this is a translation, is probably the most important of the works selected for this series, since the author was a serious candidate for the Nobel Prize. Others in the series are: *Modern stories from Holland and Flanders* (1973, 283p.); Anna Blaman, *A matter of life and death* (1974, 235p.), a translation of *Op leven en dood* by Adrienne Dixon; Frederik van Eeden, *The deeps of deliverence* (1974, 292p.), a translation of *Van de koele meren des doods* by Margaret Robinson; Marnix Gijsen, *Lament for Agnes* (1975, 97p.), a translation of *Klaaglied om Agnes* by W. James–Gerth; (this and subsequent volumes are published by Twayne at Boston, Massachusetts); Marcellus Emants, *A posthumous confession* (1975, 193p.), a translation of *Een nagelaten bekentenis* by J. M. Coetzee; Stijn Streuvels, *The long road* (1976, 160p.), a translation by Edward Crankshaw of *Langs de wegen*; Bert Schierbeek, *Shapes of the voice* (1977, 301p.), a selection from his work translated by Charles McGeehan; *Memory and agony: Dutch stories from Indonesia* (1979, 260p.), collected and introduced by Rob Nieuwenhuys and translated by Adrienne Dixon.

725 **The Spanish Brabanter: a seventeenth century Dutch social satire in five acts.**
Gerbrand Adriaenz Bredero, translated by H. Dixon Brumble. Binghampton, New York: Center for Medieval and Earlier Renaissance Studies, 1982. 137p. (Medieval and Renaissance Texts and Studies, no.2).

An acting, metrical translation of a difficult, largely dialectal text. The English is sometimes too sonorous for the coarser parts of the dialogue, but a happier compromise between readability and Renaissance language could not have been achieved. There is an excellent introduction on Bredero and his work.

726 **Reynard the Fox and other medieval Netherlands secular literature.**
Edited and introduced by E. Colledge. Leiden: Sijthoff; London: Heinemann; New York: London House and Maxwell, 1967. 194p.

This contains Colledge's prose translation of *Karel ende Elegast* and a passage from *Walewein*, A. J. Barnouw's very skilful verse translation of the original (extant) version of *Vanden Vos Reynaerde* (with a bibliography), and Colledge's prose translation of the 'Abel spel' *Lanceloet van Denemerken* and the farce *Nu noch*.

727 **Anne Frank: the diary of a young girl.**
Anne Frank. London: Pan, 1968. 224p.

Even the expurgated edition of this very personal and sometimes intimate account of a Jewish girl's thoughts and expectations, while she was in hiding during the German occupation of the Netherlands, became a best seller as much because of her remarkably mature writing as because of the cause she represents.

728 **Dutch interior: post-war poetry of the Netherlands and Flanders.**
Edited by James S. Holmes, William J. Smith, introduction by Cees Buddingh'. New York: Columbia University, 1984. 324p.

Translations from various hands of forty-five poets in four periods: pre-experimentalists, and the generations of the 1950s, 1960s, and 1970s. Buddingh' gives a short survey of Dutch poetry since the war, and there are biographical notes on the poets and translators.

729 **Language is my world.**
Compiled, edited and with an introduction by Eugene van Itterbeek. Leuven, Belgium: Leuvense Schrijversactie, 1982. 2nd rev. ed. 230p.

Texts in Dutch, French and English, translated by Bert Decorte, Maddy Baysse, Scott Rollins, Theo Hermans (et al.), of essays and poems 'about the poet in his own country', including work by Bernlef, Buddingh', Claus, Van Herreweghen, Jonckheere, Roland Jons, R. Kopland, Kouwenaar, Eric van Ruysbeek and Lucien Stassaert.

730 **New worlds from the lowlands.**
Compiled and introduced by Manuel van Loggem, foreword by Isaac Asimov. Merrick, New York: Cross-Cultural Communications, 1982. 223p.

An anthology of modern Dutch literature, translated by Wanda Boeke, Adrienne Dixon, Greta Kilburn, Ria Leigh–Loohuizen, Scott Rollins and John Rudge of work by Blijstra, Belcampo, Boon, Carmiggelt, Carl Lans, Van Loggem, Lampo, Leonard Olga, Rodenko, Wolkers, Wim Burkunk, Marty Olthuis, Mulisch, Raes, Ruyslinck, Claus, Frank Herzen, Kees Simhoffer, Chapkis, Anton Quintana, Gerben Hellinga, Paul van Herck, Hamelink, Bob van der Goen, Ton van Reen, Peter Cuijpers, Eddy C. Bertin, Julien C. Raasveld, Jaap Verduyn, Patrick Conrad, Karel Sandor, and Bob van Laerhoven.

731 **Experimental Dutch writing in English translation.**
Yann Lovelock. *Dutch Crossing*, vol. 10 (1980), p. 45–57. bibliog.

This survey attributes the radical experiments of the post-war generation of poets to their anger and bitterness seeking to purge language of its hypocrisies. Though in the mainstream of the European quest for a new aesthetic, the Dutch poets went their own way and established their own integrity. There is also a useful bibliography of books and journals containing the translations referred to.

732 **Insulinde: selected translations from Dutch writers of three centuries on the Indonesian archipelago.**
Edited by Cornelis Niekus Moore. Honolulu, Hawaii: The University Press of Hawaii, 1978. 188p. bibliog. (Asian Studies at Hawaii, no. 20).

Excerpts from writings ranging from Bontekoe to Dermoût, with short introductions on the authors and their work and a bibliography of translations of literary works on Indonesia.

733 **A selection of early Dutch poetry.**
Translated by Peter Morris. Wolverhampton, England: Black Knight Press, 1982. 40p.

Translations of poetry by Vondel, Bredero, Hooft, Cats, Spieghel, Roemer Visscher, Van der Noot, Margaret of Austria, De Harduyn and Hadewijch.

734 **Max Havelaar or the coffee auctions of the Dutch Trading Company.**
Multatuli [E. Douwes Dekker], translated by Roy Edwards, introduction by D. H. Lawrence, postscript by E. M. Beekman. Amherst, Massachusetts: University of Massachusetts Press, 1982. 352p. (Library of the Indies).

This is a re-issue of Roy Edwards's excellent annotated translation of 1967 together with D. H. Lawrence's well-known essay accompanying an earlier translation. Beekman's 'afterword' sketches the colonial background to the novel which, despite its English editions of 1868, 1927 and 1967, has still failed to achieve the recognition it deserves, though Penguin have announced its inclusion in their Classics series, due to be published late in 1987.

735 **The waterman.**
Arthur van Schendel, translated by Neline C. Clegg. Leiden: Sijthoff; London: Heinemann; New York: London House and Maxwell, 1963. 171p. (Bibliotheca Neerlandica).

This was one of the first volumes to appear in a promising enterprise to produce a series of Dutch literary 'classics' in translation under the title *Bibliotheca Neerlandica*. Unfortunately incompetent marketing resulted in the premature cessation of publication. The series includes: Gerard Walschap, *Marriage* and

Ordeal, 1963, 234p. (A. Brotherton's translation of *Trouwen* and *Celibaat*); Herman Teirlinck, *The man in the mirror*, 1963, 182p. (a translation of *Zelfportret of het galgemaal* by James Brockway); Louis Couperus, *Old people and the things that pass*, 1963, 265p. (a reprint of an earlier translation by Alexander Teixeira de Mattos of *Van oude menschen. De dingen die voorbijgaan*); Simon Vestdijk, *The garden where the brass band played*, 1965, 312p. (a translation by A. Brotherton of *De koperen tuin*); Frans Coenen, *The house on the canal* (*Onpersoonlijke herinneringen*), translated by James Brockway and J. van Oudshoorn; and *Alienation* (Willem Mertens' *Levensspiegel*), translated by N. C. Clegg, 1965, 220p.; *Medieval Netherlands religious literature*, 1965, 226p., a translation by E. Colledge of writings by Beatrice of Nazareth, Hadewijch, Ruysbroek, *Beatrijs* and *Mariken van Nimweghen*; Multatuli, *Max Havelaar*, 1967, 337p., translated by Roy Edwards (q.v.); *'Reynard the fox' and other medieval Netherlands secular literature*, 1967, 194p., edited and translated by E. Colledge, including translations of *Karel ende Elegast*, parts of *Walewein* and *Lanceloet van Denemarken* (*Charles and Elegast* and *Lancelot of Denmark*).

736 **Willem Frederik Hermans: an English sampler.**
Paul F. Vincent. *Dutch Crossing*, vol. 16 (1982), p. 19–53.

These translations, Vincent says, are intended to give some impression of a few aspects of this highly distinguished and original contemporary author. He has chosen as his sample 'A tourist' (1979), the 'Monologue of an Anglophobe' from *Het sadistische universum* (The sadistic universe) (1964), an extract from the postscript to *Onder professoren* (Among professors) (1975), and an extract from *De raadselachtige Multatuli* (The enigmatic Multatuli) (1976).

Comparative literature

737 **Anger and isolation: Dutch and English fiction in the fifties.**
Ton Anbeek. *Dutch Crossing*, vol. 24 (1984), p. 3–12.

In comparing the writing of Wain, Amis and Osborne with that of Van het Reve and Hermans, Anbeek sees a clear distinction between the well-directed angles of the English novelists and the hopeless isolation of the Dutch protagonists who have much more similarity with the characters described in Colin Wilson's *The Outsider*.

738 **Literary relations between the Low Countries, England and Germany, 1400–1624.**
Leonard Forster. *Dutch Crossing*, vol. 24 (1984), p. 16–31. bibliog.

Reynard the Fox, *Everyman* and *Mary of Nijmegen* are discussed as early texts emanating from the southern Netherlands and ending up in German and/or English versions, and the English or German relations of d'Heere, Van der Noot, Gruter and Daniel Heinsius who likewise published in Dutch are similarly reviewed.

739 **Dutch dawn poetry.**

Leonard W. Forster. In: *Eos: an enquiry into the theme of lovers' meetings and partings at dawn in poetry*. Edited by Arthur T. Hatto. The Hague: Mouton, 1965, p. 473–504. bibliog.

The chapter on the Dutch contribution to this comparative study of a theme throughout world literature covers the period up to the mid-17th century, with translations of a number of medieval and Renaissance songs. See also *Dawn poetry in the Netherlands* (q.v.).

740 **The common origins of English, German and Dutch Reynard iconography.**

Jan Goossens. *Dutch Crossing*, vol. 21 (1983), p. 29–53. bibliog.

A close comparison of the woodcut illustrations in the various Dutch and German editions of the Reynard tale with those previously recorded by Kenneth Varty in the English versions leaves interesting speculation on the origin of four blocks in the 'Wynkyn de Worde'-cycle that do not appear anywhere else. The article is amply illustrated. It summarizes the main conclusions in his *Die Reynaert–ikonografie* (Darmstadt: Wissenschaftlich Buchgesellschaft, 1983. 120p.). Contains 180 illustrations.

741 **Text to reader.**

Theo d'Haan. Amsterdam: Benjamin, 1983. 162p. bibliog. (Utrecht Publications in General and Comparative Literature).

This includes a chapter on L–P. Boon's *De Kapellekensbaan* (Chapel Road), which compares the self-reflexive aspect (implicating the reader with the author by the use of the second-person pronoun) with similar features in Barth, Fowles and Cortazar. The quotations, some of them lengthy, are taken from the Dutch text rather than the English translation. See also *Chapel road* (q.v.).

742 **Dawn poetry in the Netherlands.**

Peter K. King Amsterdam: Polak and Van Gennep, 1971. 176p. bibliog. (Literair–Wetenschappelijke Serie).

An amplification of Leonard Forster's chapter in *Eos* (q.v.), providing a comparative study of the development of a specific theme in Dutch poetry from the Middle Ages to the present day. It relates the poetry to contemporary social conditions and the history of ideas.

743 **The trial in heaven in the *Eerste bliscap* and other European plays.**

P. Meredith, L. Muir. *Dutch Crossing*, vol. 22 (1984), p. 84–92. bibliog.

This notes differences between the English and the continental treatment of the trial in heaven, and since the continental plays were presumably influenced by their antecedent, the *Eerste bliscap* (The first joy of Mary), there may have been a different tradition for the English plays.

744 **Dramatisations of social change: Herman Heijermans' plays as compared with selected dramas by Ibsen, Hauptmann and Chekhov.**
H. van Neck Yoder. The Hague: Nijhoff, 1978. 81p. bibliog.

A disappointing essay challenging the received opinion that Heijermans was the socialist author of static drama, arguing that he is a realist rather than an idealist.

745 **Morality play and *Spel van Sinne*: what are the connections?**
R. A. Potter. *Dutch Crossing*, vol. 22 (1984), p. 5–16. bibliog.

A generous acknowledgement of the errors in his references to Dutch moralities in his *The English morality play*, now rectified by the discussion of the differences between a specific and very productive genre in the Netherlands and a much smaller production in England commonly classed as moralities. Moreover, while the English examples can be dated, the *Rederijker* plays in Dutch cannot be given a clear chronology. But the indications are, Potter concludes, that the two traditions appear to develop in parallel with similar themes at corresponding times.

746 **On translating *Elckerlijc*, then and now.**
Jan Pritchard. *Dutch Crossing*, vol. 22 (1984), p. 38–48.

A consideration of the problems of translating a text rich in imagery, popular sayings and of a powerful yet simple idiom leads on to a discussion of the respects in which the English *Everyman* fails to convey what is in the original Dutch text, and which, in turn, explains the differences between the subsequent literatures on both texts.

747 **The Dutch 'Elckerlyc' is prior to the English 'Everyman'.**
E. R. Tigg. Privately printed [n.d.]. 44p.

This reiterates the earlier case made by Tigg, adding further evidence in reviewing the whole debate and discrediting H. de Vocht's case for the priority of *Everyman*.

748 **Dutch novels translated into English: the transformation of a minority literature.**
Ria Vanderauwera. Amsterdam: Rodopi, 1985. 170p. bibliog. (Approaches to Translation Studies, no. 6).

A study of some fifty Dutch novels, 1961–80, translated into English and published in Britain or America. The aesthetic aspects of the translations are not discussed since the review concentrates on the marketing aspects and the commercial results, in order to assess the impact of a 'minority' literature on the world market.

749 **Fiction in translation: policies and options.**
Ria Vanderauwera. Antwerp: University of Antwerp, Department of Germanic Philology, 1983. 297p. bibliog.

This doctoral dissertation is a 'case study of the translation of Dutch novels into English over the last two decades.' It represents an original approach to reception studies with respect to a single corpus of literature, investigating cultural transfer, reception aesthetics, marketing aspects, translation theory and practice, promotion and review. Her conclusion is that the failure of the Dutch novel to make a greater impact in English translation must be attributed to commercial caution and an unsympathetic 'target taste'.

750 **Vision and form in the poetry of Albert Verwey.**
Theodoor Weevers. London: Athlone Press, 1986. 280p.

A substantial anthology of poems from Verwey's collected verse in metrical translations of remarkable accuracy and resonance is preceded by a critique of Verwey's work and his relationship to Wordsworth, Stefan George and Southey.

751 **Albert Verwey and English romanticism.**
Manfred Wolf. The Hague: Nederlandse Boek-en Steendrukkerij, n.d. [1977]. 151p. bibliog.

This is a doctoral dissertation providing a comparative and critical study, with original translations. It traces in Verwey's poetry the development of the relations between himself and the world, in four phases of dichotomy, reconciliation, harmonization and finally complete identification with both, corresponding respectively to the types represented by the early Shelley, Wordsworth, Blake and the later Shelley.

The Arts

The visual arts in general

752 **The art of describing: Dutch art in the seventeenth century.**
Svetlana Alpers. Chicago, Illinois: University of Chicago Press, 1983. 271p. bibliog.

A new approach to the meaning of realism in Dutch genre art which discusses the relationship of the new science to contemporary theories of art and the importance of accurate cartographic reproduction and the verbal text in Holland at that time. This rightly draws attention to aspects of this art that have been overlooked in the recent concentration on the emblematic interpretation.

753 **Documentary studies in Leiden art and crafts 1475–1575.**
Jeremy D. Bangs. Leiden: Leiden University, 1976. 202p. bibliog.

This doctoral dissertation is a study of tapestry weaving at Leiden, 1500–75, with a number of appendixes, including substantial documents on De Raet, and sections on the furnishings of Rijnsburg Abbey and the organ of St Peter's Church in Leiden (previously published respectively in *Bulletin van de KNOB*, no. 74 (1975), and *Oud Holland*, no. 88 (1974)).

754 **Beeldende kunst in Limburg.** (Visual art in Limburg.)
Venlo, The Netherlands: Uitgeverij Spijk; Maastricht, The Netherlands: Stichting Trajecta 83, 1983. 357p.

An illustrated description (in Dutch, English, French and German) of plastic art in Limburg.

755 **Graffiti.**
Edited by Wim Beeren, Talitha Schoon. Rotterdam: Museum Boymans–Van Beuningen, 1983. 64p. (Catalogue Museum Boymans–Van Beuningen, no. 407).

Dutch and English catalogue of the exhibitions at Rotterdam (22 October to 4 December 1983) and Groningen (14 January to 26 February 1984). Can graffiti legitimately be shown in a gallery, where they most certainly do not belong? On the other hand, this exhibition demonstrates that the fraternity of graffiti artists have reason for identifying themselves as such, and how else if not in an exhibition?

756 **Dutch landscape: the early years: Haarlem and Amsterdam 1590–1650.**
Christopher Brown. London: The National Gallery, 1986. 239p. bibliog.

A catalogue of an exhibition in 1986, with an introduction by Brown on three contemporary discussions of landscape painting (Van Mander, Ampzing, Huygens). Also included are essays by David Bornford on the techniques of these painters, E. K. J. Reznicek on Goltzius and his conception of landscape, Margarita Russell on seascape into landscape, M. A. Schenkeveld–Van der Dussen on nature and landscape in contemporary Dutch literature, and Jan de Vries on the Dutch rural economy and the landscape. The catalogue illustrates precursors in Antwerp and Rome, the Flemish immigrants and the first and second generations in Haarlem and Amsterdam.

757 **The Dutch cityscape in the seventeenth century and its sources.**
Bentveld–Aerdenhout, The Netherlands: Landshoff, 1977. 272p. bibliog.

This catalogue of an exhibition in both Ontario and Amsterdam has a miscellaneous collection of introductory essays on the town behind the picture, on the topographical tradition in northern Holland, on the sources for the cityscape and on the draughtsman's and painter's representation of the city. There are notes and commentaries on the paintings, biographies of the artists and a topographical index.

758 **De Stijl: 1917–1931.**
Edited by Mildred Friedman, introduction by Hans L. C. Jaffé. Oxford: Phaidon, 1982. 255p. bibliog.

This is a collection of essays on painting and sculpture in the context of *De Stijl*, on Van der Leck and *De Stijl*, on Mondriaan, on *De Stijl* and architecture and neoplasticism, on Rietveld's furniture and his Schröder House, and on the influence of *De Stijl* on typography, the city and later art.

759 **Van Gogh: a documentary biography.**
Abraham Marie Hammacher, Renilde Hammacher. London: Thames & Hudson, 1982. 240p. bibliog.

An introduction and commentary linking original documents, some not previously published in English.

760 **The complete Van Gogh: paintings, drawings, sketches.**
Edited by J. Hulsker. Oxford: Phaidon, 1980. 498p. bibliog.

This is as much an artistic record of Van Gogh's life as it is a biographical commentary on his art, since Hulsker's purpose is to use Van Gogh's extensive correspondence to enable the reader to retrace his daily development, as marked by the almost complete collection of paintings, drawings and sketches reproduced in this magnificent edition.

761 **The Dutch arcadia: pastoral art and its audience with the Golden Age.**
Alison McNeil Kettering. Montclair, New Jersey: Allanheld & Schram, 1983. 339p. bibliog.

A scholarly work, based on a doctoral dissertation, on pastoral art and literature in the 17th century. This opens up a new field in a historical period that offers a great deal to comparative studies, nowhere more so than in the similarities and cross-references between art and literature. Dr Kettering looks at pastoral rogues and poets, courtesans and courtiers, the Dutch *Concert Champêtre* and pastoral narrative. There are 113 pages of plates and an index of personal names.

762 **Iconography of the Counter-Reformation in the Netherlands: heaven on earth.**
J. B. Knipping. Nieuwkoop, The Netherlands; Leiden: Sijthoff, 1974. 2 vols. bibliog.

This standard work is of value to all historians of this period, especially to art and church historians, and investigates the phenomenon of the Counter-Reformation and the themes of Humanism, asceticism in the Renaissance, piety and devotion, the biblical sources of symbols and icons, the saints and hagiography, the sacraments, and the church militant. Finally, the general characteristics of Counter-Reformation art are discussed and placed in the mainstream of art history.

763 **Jacques de Gheyn: three generations.**
I. Q. van Regteren Altena. The Hague; London: Nijhoff, 1983. 3 vols. (Vol. I: Text and bibliog.; vol. II: Catalogues; vol. III: Plates).

A substantial and authoritative work not only on the three gifted Jacques de Gheyn, but on the social and cultural backgrounds of the period spanned by the three generations, though concentrating on the life and work of Jacques II, on which this author had published a study in 1936.

764 **Karel Appel: street art, ceramics, sculpture, wood reliefs, tapestries, murals, Villa El Salvador.**

Pierre Restany, Allen Ginsberg. Amsterdam: Becht, 1985. 256p. bibliog.

Over 300 large colour reproductions of work by the artist with his own sparse comments on them, with an article on street art (collages assembled from materials found on the streets of Amsterdam, Paris and New York), and an interview with Frederic de Towarnicki with whom he discusses what he means by street art and what he hopes to achieve by it. There are also lists of biographical data and exhibitions.

765 **Vincent van Gogh: the letters.**

Selected, edited and introduced by Mark W. Roskill. London: Fontana, 1983. 2nd ed. 352p.

A selection of Van Gogh's letters to his brother, with illustrations.

766 **A guide to Dutch art in America.**

Peter C. Sutton. Grand Rapids, Michigan: Eerdmans; Kampen, The Netherlands: Kok, 1986. 350p.

This lists by location and museum(s) within the United States the most important art works (including ceramics, etc.) in collections available to the public. A commentary places the collections in their historical context and the named items are shown in reproduction. There is a list of painters and the location(s) of their work.

767 **Hieronimus Bosch.**

Charles de Tolnay. London: Reynal and William Morrow, 1966. 451p. bibliog.

The standard work, containing 288 very fine reproductions (many in colour) of Bosch's paintings and drawings, with an introduction on his early life, his asceticism and later harmony, *catalogues raisonés* of the paintings and drawings, and an appendix of plates illustrating related topics.

768 **The expressionists.**

D. Welling. Amsterdam: Meulenhoff, 1969. 32p. bibliog. (Art and Architecture in The Netherlands).

A short essay on the shift from modernism to impressionism – in Bergen, Rotterdam, Groningen and South Limburg, with biographical notes on the expressionists – introduces reproductions in colour and monocrhome from 1901 (Johan Prikker) to 1948 (Hendrik Chabot and Edmond Bellefroid).

Synthese: twelve facets of culture and nature in South Limburg.
See item no. 23.

The Netherlands: an historical and cultural survey, 1795–1977.
See item no. 141.

Mental, religious and social forces.
See item no. 318.

Nijhoff, Van Ostaijen, 'De Stijl'.
See item no. 700.

Studies in cultural history: Cornelis Engebrechtsz's Leiden.
See item no. 835.

Dutch Art and Architecture Today.
See item no. 934.

Dutch Arts.
See item no. 935.

Ons Erfdeel. (Our Heritage.)
See item no. 963.

Bibliography of the Netherlands Institute for Art.
See item no. 983.

Bibliographie Néerlandaise historique-scientifique des ouvrages importants dont les auteurs sont nés aux 16e, 17e et 18e siécles, sur les sciences mathématiques et physiques, avec leur applications. (Dutch historical-scientific bibliography of the major works of authors born in the 16th, 17th and 18th centuries on the mathematical and physical sciences, and their applications.)
See item no. 984.

Arts and economics.
See item no. 1017.

The visual arts: painting

769 **Frans Hals.**
H. P. Baard. London: Thames & Hudson; New York: Abrams, 1981. 167p. bibliog. (Library of Great Painters).

Forty-nine fine colour reproductions with commentaries on them are preceded by a critical, illustrated account of Hals' art and its relationship to previous, contemporary and later work.

770 **Ferdinand Bol 1616–1680: een leerling van Rembrandt.**
(Rembrandt's pupil.)
Albert Blankert. Doornspijk, The Netherlands: Davaco, 1982. 2nd imp. 382p. bibliog. (Aetas Aurea, no. 2).

A doctoral dissertation in Dutch with an English summary, covering Bol's life and a critique of the 200 works positively identified as his. The discussion of his work is divided between his historical subjects and his portraits, tracing the development in his style from the classical to the baroque.

771 **The impact of a genius: Rembrandt, his pupils and followers in the seventeenth century.**

Albert Blankert, Ben Broos, Ernst van de Wetering, Guido Jansen, Willem van de Wetering. Amsterdam: Waterman, 1983. 240p. bibliog.

The articles, which are illustrated with plates of paintings from museums and private collections, are by Albert Blankert on 'Rembrandt's pupils and followers in the 17th century', Ben Broos, who questions the indiscriminate use of the term 'Rembrandt's school', and Ernst van de Wetering on 'Isaac Jouderville, a pupil of Rembrandt's.' The catalogue itself is written by Guido Jansen and Willem van de Wetering.

772 **Vermeer of Delft: complete edition of the paintings.**

A. Blankert. Oxford: Phaidon, 1978. 176p.

This translation of the original Dutch text of 1975 is rather a commentary on his work than a biography, and takes us from the emergence of the Delft School through the middle period to his late style. The concluding chapter considers Vermeer and his public, including a discussion of the Van Meegeren forgeries and two questionable Vermeers. There are sixty-three pages of plates, several in colour, and a catalogue.

773 **Rembrandt: the complete edition of the paintings.**

A. Bredius, revised by H. Gerson. London: Phaidon, 1969; New York: Praeger, 1971. 4th rev. ed. 636p.

Although originally published in 1935, this is still the standard work on Rembrandt which has been substantially revised and rewritten by H. Gerson. Its value lies more in its illustrations than in its text, consisting only of explanatory notes, because it contains reproductions of all of Rembrandt's paintings, albeit unfortunately only in monochrome. It is conveniently arranged according to subjects: portraits, genre, landscape, history, and biblical topics. An appendix contains small reproductions of paintings of questionable authorship and there is a concordance.

774 **Dutch genre painting.**

Christopher Brown. *Dutch Crossing*, vol. 4 (1978), p. 21–26.

A brief survey of some of the salient themes in 17th-century paintings – merry companies, astronomy and alchemy, vanitas, the militia, sexual morality and proverbs.

775 **A corpus of Rembrandt paintings.**

J. Bruyn, B. Haak, S. H. Levie, P. J. J. van Thiel, E. van de Wetering. The Hague; Boston; London: Nijhoff, 1982– . bibliog. (Vol. I, 1982; vol. II, 1986).

Published on behalf of the Foundation Rembrandt Research Project, the first volume (of the twenty-eight planned) covers the period 1625–31, the second takes the account to 1634, but, as the authors point out, a long-term and vast project of this nature entails some further commentary on the earlier volume because of shifts of opinion and developments in research since 1979 (when vol. I went to press). Each volume offers an introductory chapter on the characteristic features of the period and extensive commentaries on each of the paintings, finishing with a concordance.

776 **All the paintings of the Rijksmuseum in Amsterdam.**

Edited by Marianne Buikstra–De Boer, G. Schwartz, Margaret Roche, foreword by A. van Schendel. Amsterdam: Rijksmuseum; Maarssen,The Netherlands: Gary Schwartz, 1976. 911p.

A completely illustrated catalogue compiled by the painting department at the museum.

777 **Mondrian Studies.**

Kermit S. Champa. Chicago, Illinois; London: University of Chicago Press, 1985. 150p. bibliog.

The author, Professor of Art History in Brown University, traces the development from Mondriaan's earliest Dutch impressionism through Parisian influences and cubism back to the Netherlands of the *De Stijl* period, back again to Paris and the further development of neoplasticism. There are detailed commentaries on his 'Painting 2' (1925), his 'Composition with blue and yellow' (1935) and his 'Broadway Boogie-Woogie', with notes, and an index.

778 **Dutch church painters: Saenredam's great church at Haarlem in context.**

Edinburgh: Trustees of the National Galleries of Scotland, 1984. 64p.

An exhibition catalogue centred around the painting of the interior of St Bavo's Church. There are illustrated essays on other painters of the same church, on contemporary artists and their paintings of other churches and on the place of the organ in Dutch churches.

779 **The lie of the land: the foundations of painting and the history of art.**

Charles Ford. *Dutch Crossing*, vol. 26 (1985), p. 10–32. bibliog.

An essay on the so-called realism in Dutch Renaissance landscapes, concentrating on the association of Goltzius and Van Mander at Haarlem and developing into a tradition of painting familiar (or quasi-familiar) scenes to satisfy the growing market in the rapidly expanding towns.

780 **The comedians in the work of Jan Steen and his contemporaries.**
S. J. Gudlaugsson. Soest, The Netherlands: Davaco, 1975. 70p.

The comic figures of doctors, dandies, captains, quacks, dentists and so on in the paintings are shown to be derived from the Comedia dell'arte characters of the dottore, pantalone, capitano, etc.

781 **G.H. Breitner.**
P. H. Hefting. Amsterdam: Meulenhoff, 1969. 32p. bibliog. (Art and Architecture in the Netherlands).

A short biography of the artist, a selected list of his exhibitions, and a broad sampling of his work in four colour and twenty-four monochrome plates.

782 **The examination and restoration of The Last Judgement by Lucas van Leyden.**
P. F. J. M. Hermesdorf, J. P. Filedt Kok. *Nederlandsch Kunsthistorisch Jaarboek*, vol. 29 (1978), p. 311–424. bibliog.

An important article for art historians and curators of museums in particular, because it is an interdisciplinary statement of the collaboration between experts that should be undertaken before embarking on the restoration of any fine work of art. Lucas' painting is therefore merely a model to demonstrate a general principle.

783 **Willink.**
H. L. C. Jaffé. Amsterdam: Meulenhoff/Landshoff, 1983. 3rd ed. 257p.

An illustrated biography of the painter Albert Carel Willink, which supersedes Rene H. Dubois' earlier monograph of 1940.

784 **Catalogue of paintings by artists born before 1870**, vol. VII: **Seventeenth-century North Netherlandish still lifes.**
Onno ter Kuile. The Hague: Staatsuitgeverij; Amsterdam: Meulenhoff/ Landshoff, 1985. 223p. bibliog.

The Netherlands Office for Fine Arts holds one of the largest collections of old masters, which is the subject of this catalogue. This is the first in a series of 17 volumes providing a descriptive catalogue of 3,500 paintings by artists born before 1870. This volume includes a short description of the Netherlands Office and a description of the concept of the catalogue. There is an introduction on the genre, followed by reproductions with short biographies, internal and external information, provenance, location, literature and exhibitions, indexes and concordances.

785 **The Hague School: Dutch masters of the 19th century.**
Edited by Ronald de Leeuw, John Sillevis, Charles Dumas.
London: Weidenfeld & Nicolson, 1983. 336p. bibliog.

Illustrations of every picture in the Royal Academy summer exhibition in 1983, some in colour, and over fifty that were not in the exhibition, and ten essays. The catalogue is the most comprehensive work on the school available in English. Bosboom, the Maris brothers, Mauve, Israel, Gabriel, Mesdag, Artz, Bilders, Roelofs, Van Gogh and Mondriaan are among the many painters represented.

786 **Dutch and Flemish painters.**
Carel van Mander. New York: Arno Press, 1969. 560p.

Constant van de Wall's translation of *Het Schilder–Boeck* of 1604. This is the earliest and most influential of the theories of painting written in northern Europe. Van Mander, as a Humanist painter and poet, travelled from his native Flanders to Italy and Austria and later founded with Goltzius a drawing academy in Haarlem.

787 **The Dutch world of painting.**
Gary Schwartz. Maarssen, The Netherlands: Gary Schwartz, 1986. 167p.

This is a catalogue of an exhibition in the Vancouver Art Gallery and it is included here because of the author's familiarity with Dutch art in general, and because it is recent and is reasonably illustrated. The aim of the exhibition was to relate painting to its social environment, and in this it is largely successful.

788 **Dutch double and pair portraits.**
D. R. Smith. London; Ann Arbor, Michigan: University Microfilms International, 1978. 501p. bibliog.

'This dissertation deals with one of the major genres of Dutch portraiture, the marriage portrait, and its relationship to some of the dominant social ideals of the seventeenth-century Netherlands'. In addition to a general consideration of the development of the double and pair portrait, there is a chapter devoted to the iconography in marriage portraiture and particular studies of Frans Hals and Rembrandt. Unfortunately the seventy-eight pages of plates are valueless since the reprographic method used cannot reproduce two-tone prints.

789 **Masters of seventeenth century Dutch genre painting.**
Organized by Peter Sutton, edited by Jane Watkins.
Philadelphia: Philadelphia Museum of Art, 1984. 397p. bibliog.

An exceptionally fine catalogue reproducing in colour the 127 paintings in the exhibition held in Philadelphia, Berlin and London, with introductory essays by Peter Sutton on 'Masters of Dutch genre painting' and 'Life and culture in the Golden Age', and a fully documented catalogue of the paintings.

790 **Pieter de Hooch: complete edition.**
Peter C. Sutton. Oxford: Phaidon, 1980. 168p. bibliog.

The first seventy-two pages give an account of his life and consider De Hooch and the tradition of Dutch genre painting, and his followers and critical reception. The catalogue (p. 73–144) lists the accepted works, tentatively accepted and questionable works, works known only through descriptions and works wrongly attributed to De Hooch. The majority of the reproductions are in monochrome. There is a list of collections, and a concordance.

791 **The Dutch painters: 100 seventeenth century masters.**
Christopher Wright. London: Orbis Books, 1984. rev. ed. 180p. bibliog.

An introduction on the history of Dutch painting according to location and notes on 104 artists with many colour plates and lists of museums housing their work, with a general bibliography and bibliographies relating to individual artists.

The visual arts: graphics

792 **Escher: with a complete catalogue of the graphic works.**
F. H. Bool, B. Ernst, J. R. Kist, J. L. Locher, F. Wierda. London: Thames & Hudson, 1982. 349p. bibliog.

An essential reference work which, in its 570 black-and-white and thirty-six colour illustrations includes a very large number of lesser known and rarely reproduced works by the artist. It includes Escher's essay 'on the regular division of the plane', notes on the illustrations, and a concordance.

793 **Maurits Cornelis Escher: the graphic work, introduced and explained by the artist.**
M. C. Escher, translated by John E. Brigham. London: Pan Books, 1978. 78p.

This contains the artist's own introduction to his work and short commentaries on the seventy-six prints that are reproduced here.

794 **Trends in Dutch drawing 1945–1985.**
Doris Wintgens Hötte. Leiden: Stedelijk Museum de Lakenhal, 1985. 73p.

Catalogue of drawings by Ben Akkerman, Karel Appel, Armando, Frank van den Broeck, Rene Daniels, Ad Dekkers, Marlene Duman, Rob van Koningsbruggen, Lucassen, Lucebert, Ouborg, Martin Rous, Jan Schoonhoven, Itta Smeets, Rob Smit, Kees Smits, Peter Struyken, Toon Verhoef, Henk Visch, and Co Westerik.

795 **Dutch figure drawings from the seventeenth century.**
P. Schatborn. The Hague: Government Publishing Office, 1981. 152p. bibliog.

An entertaining introduction discusses the ways in which figure-drawing was learned in the 17th century. The remainder of the study surveys work of individual artists from Goltzius and Averkamp in the earlier period, to the Italianates, the genre, history and portrait artists, the Haarlem group and the figures of landscape painters.

The visual arts: architecture and sculpture

796 **Theo van Doesburg.**
J. Baljeu. London: Collins/Macmillan, 1979. 232p. bibliog.

This presentation of the life and work of a complex artist and architect sees him as part of a creative process that is still influential. His development and relationship to Mondriaan and the *De Stijl* group is nicely illustrated. There is a bibliography of the complete writings of Van Doesburg and a select bibliography of the literature on him.

797 **Dutch architecture after 1900.**
R. Blijstra. Amsterdam: Van Kampen, 1966. 143p.

A useful general monograph on the subject taking the reader as far as the introduction of systems building and the (re-)introduction of prefabrication. There are constant and necessary references to the specifically Dutch problems and traditions in planning, environment and design. There are forty photographs and a list of buildings completed since 1945.

798 **Sculptures of the Rijksmuseum Kröller–Müller.**
Edited by C. de Dood, A. Henriquez, M. Jansen–Sheuring. Otterlo, The Netherlands: Rijksmuseum Kröller–Müller, 1970. 3rd imp. 156p. + 86p.

Though this museum specializes in modern art, its extensive collection of sculptures, in a special sculpture park, contains some Dutch medieval and early work as well as a substantial representation by Dutch sculptors in its international exhibition of modern work.

799 **Sculpture 1983.**
Edited and compiled by Cees van der Geer, Gosse Oosterhof. Rotterdam: Rotterdamse Kunststichting, 1983. 133p.

An illustrated catalogue of the exhibition in Rotterdam.

800 **Old houses in Holland.**
Sydney R. Jones. London: Studio Editions, 1986. 2nd imp. 160p.

A survey of early domestic architecture illustrated with the author's pen-drawings and colour reproductions of Vermeer's and De Hooch's paintings to exemplify the charm of a tradition based on the widespread use of Dutch bricks, whose form and colour impose their particular character on Dutch architecture.

801 **Dutch classical architecture.**
Wouter Kuyper. Delft, The Netherlands: Delft University Press, 1980. 615p. bibliog.

This is a 'survey of Dutch architecture, gardens and Anglo–Dutch architectural relations from 1625 to 1700'. An interesting chapter in the first part on classicism and 17th-century churches discusses the Dutch influence on Wren churches, and English influences on the Dutch, and this is further discussed in the consideration of the classicist revolution in Holland and its effect on Wren and his contemporaries. The formal country house garden is described with (fortunately) less influence on Britain, and Dutch influence on the flat style of later English work is also discussed. There is an extensive catalogue of printed sources, 265 pages of illustrations and an index.

802 **Unbuilt Netherlands.**
Cees Nooteboom. London: Architectural Press, 1986. 118p.

A survey of 130 years of visionary projects by Berlage, Oud, Duiker, Van der Broeck, Van Eyck, Hertzberger and others of buildings that never left the drawing board in a country that played a seminal role in the development of modern architecture. The schemes and design prototypes investigated were never executed because they were too visionary or technically advanced for their times.

803 **American influences on late nineteenth century architecture in the Netherlands.**
A. W. Reinink. *Journal of the Society of Architectural Historians*, vol. 29 (1970), p. 163–74. bibliog.

H. H. Richardson's influence on Berlage had earlier been noted. This contributes further to the discussion and argues that Berlage's conception, while influenced by earlier American architecture, also found inspiration in Viollet le Duc.

804 **H. P. Berlage: idea and style: the quest for modern architecture.**
P. J. P. Singelenberg. Utrecht: Herentjens, Dekker & Gumbert, 1972. 274p. bibliog.

This monograph falls broadly into two parts: a biography, and a discussion of Berlage's work on the Amsterdam exchange. A final section looks at contemporary and recent criticism of Berlage and influences (of Hegel and Schopenhauer) on him.

805 **Kijken naar monumenten in Nederland.** (Looking at monuments in the Netherlands.)
Compiled and edited by A. P. Smaal. Baarn, The Netherlands: Bosch & Keuning, 1979. 2nd imp. 144p. bibliog.

Photographs and drawings with Dutch texts describing monuments in towns and villages, residences, castles and country houses, churches, farms, mills, stations, water towers, pumping stations and lighthouses, with an address list and an index of place names.

806 **G. Rietveld architect.**
István L. Szénâssy. Amsterdam: Stedelijk Museum, 1971; London: Arts Council, 1972. 44p. (Catalogue Stedelijk Museum Amsterdam, no. 516).

Illustrated catalogue of the exhibition in the Civic Museum at Amsterdam and the Hayward Gallery, London, in 1972.

Design and crafts

807 **Design from the Netherlands.**
G. Bakker. The Hague: Staatsuitgeverij, 1980. 66p.

An exhibition catalogue in English and German illustrating designs in clothing, textiles, furnishing, ornaments, electrical and other equipment by leading Dutch designers and firms.

808 **Dutch silver 1580–1830.**
Edited by A. L. den Blaauwen. The Hague: Staatuitgeverij, 1979. 390p. bibliog.

The catalogue of an extensive exhibition in the Rijksmuseum, and in Toledo and Boston (Massachusetts) in 1980. J. Verbeek provides the introductory chapter on the history of the craft and its trade, J. H. Leopold writes on silver, the silversmiths and the hallmarks. There is a list of earlier exhibitions of silverware and the descriptive and illustrated catalogue of 168 items has a list of repertoria.

809 **The clay tobacco pipe in seventeenth-century Netherlands.**
P. H. Duco. Oxford: Oxford University Press, 1981. 163p. bibliog. (Bar International Series, vol. 106, no. 2. The Archaeology of the Clay Tobacco Pipe, V, Europe: 2, part II, p. 305–468).

A historical and archaeological review of the shapes, marks and decorations of Dutch clay pipes, and accounts of the pipe-makers in the various towns in Holland and northern Belgium. There are numerous pen-drawing illustrations with full descriptions.

810 **Carolingian jewellery with plant ornament.**
N. Fraenkel–Schoorl. *Berichten van de ROB*, vol. 28 (1978), p. 346–97. bibliog.

For the artist, craftsman and art historian, this nicely illustrated article will demonstrate the skill and artistry of the Carolingian craftsmen. The historian will also be struck by the wide distribution of the finds, showing that the Scandinavian trade routes were more important than the eastward routes.

811 **Dutch silver.**
J. W. Frederiks. The Hague: Nijhoff, 1952–61. 4 vols. bibliog.

This monumental work on silver from the Renaissance to the end of the 18th century gives a general descriptive history of embossed plaquettes, tazze and dishes (vol. 1), of wrought plate in North and South Holland (vol. 2), of wrought plate in the central, northern and southern provinces (vol. 3), and embossed and ecclesiastical and secular plate (vol. 4).

812 **Dutch firearms.**
Arne Hoff, edited by Walter A. Stryker. London: Philip Wilson, 1978. 252p. bibliog.

A standard work, well illustrated, on the earliest firearms, matchlocks, flintlocks, blunderbusses, extra long and short guns and pistols, magazine guns and airguns.

813 **Delft ceramics.**
Caroline H. de Jonge. London: Pall Mall, 1970. 168p. bibliog.

A complex subject involving confusing doubts about artists, manufacturers and identification marks is placed in its relationship to the early techniques and the popularity of designs transferred from the Orient to the European continent.

814 **Dutch tiles.**
Caroline H. de Jonge. London: Pall Mall, 1971. 337p. bibliog.

This substantial study of the tile industry from 1350 to the present day obviously concentrates on the 17th and 18th centuries. The text is fully annotated. There is a list of literature and collections, 158 pages of fine plates, a list of illustrations and their sources, a list of museums and private collections, and an index.

815 **Embroidery motifs from Dutch samplers.**
Albarta Meulenbelt–Nieuwburg. London: Batsford, 1984. 2nd imp. 192p.

A well-illustrated account of eighteen different groups of motifs with instructions on making the stitches, with patterns and clear colour codes for the reader who may want to copy some of the examples illustrated.

816 **Roentgenatlas of old Dutch clocks.**
T. de Roo, with advice for restoration and technical matters by P. Vel. Alkmaar, The Netherlands: Hopman, 1974. 165p. bibliog.

As well as being a very interesting and lavishly illustrated history of clock making in the Netherlands, this also explains the author's technique of making an X-ray examination to discover fakes and mala fide restorations and to investigate the original state of the piece before starting to restore it.

Music and dance

817 **Electronic music: its development in the Netherlands.**
Henk Badings. *Delta*, vol. 1, no. 4 (winter 1958–59), p. 85–93.

The composer of electronic music writes about the infinite range of possibilities available in electronic sound production and describes some of the techniques with illustrations of the notation, tracing the evolution of this kind of composition from its introduction as *musique concrète* by Pierre Schaeffer in 1948.

818 **The sixteenth-century organ of the Pieterskerk Leiden.**
J. D. Bangs. *Oud Holland*, vol. 88 (1974), p. 220–31.

An account of the St Peter's organ of 1553, very similar to the contemporary organ built for St John's church in Gouda (now in Abcoude), with illustrations of the original case and later (17th century) minor additions to it.

819 **Sweelinck's keyboard music.**
Alan Curtis. Leiden: University Press, 1969. 2nd ed. 243 p. bibliog. (Publications of the Sir Thomas Browne Institute, General Series, no. 5).

A commentary on Sweelinck's music is extended to discuss English elements in 17th-century Dutch composition.

820 **Godmother to composers: the story of Donemus.**
Lex van Delden. *Delta*, vol. 1, no. 3 (autumn 1958), p. 101–05.

Donemus (Foundation for the Documentation of Dutch Music) took over and enlarged the functions of the Music Copyright Bureau not only ensuring that musical manuscripts were photographed and stored, but that they were also printed and distributed, with agencies among music publishers abroad.

821 **The technique of singing.**
J. B. van Denise, W. R. O. Goslings. The Hague: Government Publishing Office, 1982. 79p.

An illustrated account of Dutch singing techniques compared with other systems.

822 **Componisten van de Lage Landen.** (Composers of the Low Countries.)
Willem Elders. Utrecht: Bohn, Scheltema and Holkema, 1985. 183p.

The Dutch school of the 15th and 16th centuries is set in its cultural context, with a discussion of the musical influences on the composers and performers, the blending of text and music and short biographies of some fifty composers.

823 **The dancing Dutch: ballet in the Netherlands.**
David Koning. *Delta*, vol. 11, no. 2 (summer 1968), p. 41–54.

The head of the television drama department at Hilversum describes the struggle to establish the two internationally recognized companies, the National Ballet and the Netherlands Dance Theatre, against a Protestant ethic that had scorned ballet as a trivial art form for two centuries.

824 **Een eeuw Nederlandse muziek 1815–1915.** (A century of Dutch music 1815–1915.)
Eduard Reeser. Amsterdam: Querido, 1986. 2nd rev. ed. 163p. bibliog.

A revised and expanded version of the original publication of 1950, this surveys the lives and music of composers in a European context, written by an authority on Diepenbroek, at one time Professor of Music in Utrecht and President of the Society for the History of Dutch Music. The book includes lists of composers, musical quotations and recordings.

825 **Zeventig jaar Nederlandse muziek 1915–1985.** (Seventy years of Dutch music 1915–1985.)
Leo Samama. Amsterdam: Querido, 1986. 323p. bibliog.

This is in effect a continuation of Reeser's history (see previous entry), and it similarly concentrates on musical life and composition with particular reference to Matthijs Vermeulen, Willem Pijper, Henk Badings, Rudolf Escher and Ton de Leeuw. Unlike the history of the 19th century it makes no pretensions of completeness, but there are ample quotations from the music, lists of recordings and composers, and an index.

826 **Willem Pijper and the renascence of Dutch music.**
Paul F. Sanders. *Delta*, vol. 1, no. 1 (spring 1958), p. 87–95.

Willem Pijper (1894–1947) gradually acquired a personal style, independent of foreign influences, developing from 'the familiar idiom of the 19th century to a new contemporary idiom' identifiable in his polyphonic counterpoint. He wrote a number of essays on his work and edited a monthly journal.

827 **Master Jan Pieterszoon Sweelinck: phoenix of music.**
Robert L. Tusler. *Delta*, vol. 2, no. 4 (winter 1959–60), p. 74–82.

A short biography of the 16th-century composer and contemporary opinions of his music (with translations of the quotations) which appears to have found such favour that even the strict Calvinist city council did not restrain him in his organ and choral composition.

Arts in research: the structural position of research in post-secondary music and drama education.
See item no. 665.

Dances of the Netherlands.
See item no. 870.

Theatre and film

828 **Bert Haanstra: a poet of the documentary.**
Jan Blokker. *Delta*, vol. 1, no. 2 (summer 1958), p. 94–100.

Haanstra's work is distinguishable from that of the other outstanding post-war film-maker, Herman van der Horst, because of the poetic quality of his factual shooting. His early film *Panta Rhei* clearly shows his lyrical tendencies which have been restrained to good effect in his later documentaries.

829 **Dutch cinema: an illustrated history.**
Peter Cowie. London: Tantivy Press; South Brunswick; New York: A. S. Barnes; The Hague: Ministry of Culture, Recreation and Social Welfare, 1979. 154p. bibliog.

This short history of film-making in Holland traces Iven's influence in the 1930s and Haanstra's and Rademaker's since the war. Chapters are devoted to the mixed fortunes of the 'Long New Wave' and to experimental cinema. There is an index of the film titles cited.

830 **Joris Ivens: filmer committed to humanity.**
Hans Keller. *Delta*, vol. 15, no. 1 (spring 1972), p. 14–29.

A review of the films, with their political Marxist ideology, from his earliest, 'The bridge' (1927), to 'Le peuple et ses fusils' of 1968.

831 **Dutch cinema: old guard, new guard, avant-garde.**
Hans Saaltink. *Delta*, vol. 10, no. 4 (winter 1967–68), p. 37–49.

A review of Dutch films since 1965, an era with government subidies, better training facilities and the opportunities provided by television, which has produced disappointing results, except in documentary filming.

832 **The play, the players and the game: contemporary Dutch drama.**
Johan Snapper. *Delta*, vol. 13, no. 2 (summer 1970), p. 83–92.

A personal view of post-war stage, radio and television drama as a game in which man adopts the role he plays in the theatre, in which communication is noticeably lacking, conventional attitudes are satirized, anti-semitism and racial friction are dominant, and social themes and characters are caricatured.

Arts in research: the structural position of research in post-secondary music and drama education.
See item no. 665.

Philosophy and the History of Ideas

833 **Studies in the posthumous work of Spinoza: on style, earliest translation and reception, earliest and modern edition of some texts.**
F. Akkerman. Groningen, The Netherlands: Bouman, 1980. 280p. bibliog.

This doctoral thesis for the University of Groningen (1980) contains four essays on Spinoza already published elsewhere; the major unpublished section, chapter 5, is a painstaking examination of the translations (by others) of Spinoza's *Ethics*.

834 **Sir Constantine Huygens and Britain 1596–1687**, vol. I: **1596–1619.**
Alfred G. H. Bachrach. Leiden: University Press; London: Oxford University Press, 1962. 238p. bibliog. (Publications of the Sir Thomas Browne Institute, Leiden, General Series, no. 1).

The poet and diplomat Huygens' early years, first in a home and circle intricately involved in English affairs and later in England itself. British high society is seen and judged through the eyes of the young man whose father, Christiaan, was Secretary of the Dutch Council of State, moving in diplomatic circles where British affairs dominated foreign policy. The subtitle 'A pattern of cultural exchange' aptly sums up this scrutiny of personalities and ideas during twenty-three years of Anglo–Dutch history.

835 **Studies in cultural history: Cornelis Engebrechtsz's Leiden.**
J. D. Bangs. Assen, The Netherlands: Van Gorcum, 1979. 259p. bibliog.

A biography of Engebrechtsz and his circle, religion, art and letters in Leiden in the late 15th and early 16th centuries. Particular paintings are discussed: the Van der Does–Van Poelgeest panels, 'The Babylonian Captivity of the Church' and the 'Preaching of the Lord's Prayer'. Appendixes describe selected drawings and provide genealogical tables. There are inventories, lists of abbreviations, and extensive indexes.

836 **Caspar Barlaeus: from the correspondence of a melancholic.**
F. F. Blok. Assen, The Netherlands; Amsterdam: Van Gorcum, 1976. 197p. (Republica Literaria Neerlandica, no. 2).

An unusual biographical study which, as the subtitle indicates, derives a case-history on melancholia from a study of that part of Barlaeus' correspondence referring to his dominant mood. It is a pity that the English translation is based, not on the original Latin of the many letters quoted, but on a Dutch translation of the original.

837 **'Teyler' 1778–1978: studies en bijdragen over Teylers stichting naar aanleiding van het tweede eeuwfeest.** ('Teyler' 1778–1978: studies and essays on Teyler's foundation on the occasion of its bicentenary.)
J. C. Boogman (et al.). Haarlem, The Netherlands; Antwerp: Schuyt, 1978. 328p. bibliog.

Pieter Teyler was a banker-philanthropist of Haarlem who founded two parallel societies for theology and general learning in 1778. This account of the societies' history includes contributions on the foundation, its buildings, and its activities, and is copiously illustrated. There are English abridgements of the Dutch text.

838 **Dutch popular culture in the seventeenth century.**
Peter Burke. Rotterdam: Erasmus University, 1978. 25p. bibliog. (Centrum voor Maatschappijgeschiedenis, Mededelingen, no. 3).

This paper on cultural 'mobility' in the Golden Age recognizes the difficulty of defining popularity and of discrimination in the cultural movement prompted by Calvinist teaching or the economic consequences of urbanization. It also recognises the conservative nature of popular culture.

839 **Spinoza's political and theological thought.**
Edited by C. de Deugd. Amsterdam; Oxford; New York: North Holland, 1984. 248p. bibliog.

The twenty-four papers read by international scholars at the symposium to mark the 350th anniversary of Spinoza's birth range widely from his theory of politics and natural law to his Jewish relations and the concepts of theological and philosophical freedom.

840 **The radical arts: first decade of an Elizabethan Renaissance.**
J. A. van Dorsten. Leiden: University Press, 1973. 146p. bibliog. (Publications of the Sir Thomas Browne Institute, Special Series, no. 4).

A study of cosmopolitan interrelationships in the 1560s when immigrants from France and the Low Countries were largely responsible for the establishment of the new art and learning in England. The scholarly enquiry into the complex relationships between individuals, many of them members of the 'Domus Charitatis', reveals an impressive exchange of international learning.

841 **Ten studies in Anglo–Dutch relations.**
Edited by Jan van Dorsten. Leiden: University Press; London: Oxford University Press, 1974. 271p. bibliog. (Publications of the Sir Thomas Browne Institute, General Series, no. 5).

This contains Gordon Kipling's essay on John Skelton's close association with Burgundian letters; Anna Simoni's description of the three editions of Jacob de Gheyn's *The exercise of armes* dedicated to Prince Henry, son of James I; Paul R. Sellin's discussion of the Leiden 'Ordo Aristoteles', a treatise on Aristotle's *Poetics*; Alice Carter's comparison of English and Dutch marriage counselling in the early 17th century; C. W. Schoneveld's study of the reception in the Netherlands of Sir Thomas Browne's *Religio Medici*; R. G. Collmer's essay on the reception of Bunyan's works in the Netherlands; Leonard Forster's account of De Schoolmeester's period of residence in Highgate.

842 **Baruch Spinoza and western democracy.**
Joseph Dunner. New York: Philosophical Library, 1955. 142p. bibliog.

A short monograph stressing, as the title implies, Spinoza's political thought, and his concern for contemporary human affairs.

843 **Erasmus of Rotterdam.**
George Faludy. London: Eyre & Spottiswoode, 1970. 298p.

A nicely illustrated biography of a man whose source materials (collected works and letters amounting to some 16 million words) and two hundred biographies leave nothing original to be said. This, then, is a reassessment of Erasmus' place in history by an author in sympathy with his religious position, who is particularly interested in Erasmus' efforts for peace and tolerance.

844 **Janus Gruter's English years.**
Leonard W. Forster. Leiden: University Press; London: Oxford University Press, 1967. 167p. bibliog. (Publications of the Sir Thomas Browne Institute, Special Series, no. 3).

'Studies in the continuity of Dutch literature in exile in Elizabethan English' is the apt subtitle of a monograph on a little-known Dutch poet who exemplifies the close relations between Dutch and English scholars in the late 16th century and who was one of the pioneers of the sonnet form in Dutch.

845 **The myth of Venice and Dutch Republican thought in the seventeenth century.**
Eco O. G. Haitsma Mulier. Assen, The Netherlands: Van Gorcum, 1980. 237p. bibliog.

Examines the ideas held by Dutch thinkers of the Venetian Golden Age, and the effect it had on the development of political and constitutional ideas in the 17th century.

846 **Hugo Grotius, a great European 1583–1645.**
Delft, The Netherlands: Meinema, 1983. 103p.

Translation of the articles abridged for the exhibition catalogue *Het Delfts orakel 1583–1645* (The Delft oracle), with portraits. The biographical contributions cover Grotius' life in Holland and in exile, whilst the remaining articles discuss Grotius as a jurist, a theologian and Bible exegetist, as a frustrated statesman, a historiographer and a poet and philologist.

847 **Erasmus of Rotterdam.**
Johan Huizinga. London: Phaidon, 1952. 266p.

This is one of the best-known and certainly most attractive of the biographies because its scope and treatment is popular among students as well as specialists and particularly because of the author's stimulating essay style and insights. There are translations of twenty-two of his letters, a number of plates and an index of names.

848 **Humanists and Humanism in Amsterdam.**
Amsterdam: Universiteitsbibliotheek, 1973. 80p.

A catalogue of an exhibition in the Trippenhuis in Amsterdam organized by the Library staff of Amsterdam University Library and the Institute of Neophilology and Neo-Latin in the University on the occasion of the second International Congress of Neo-Latin Studies. The illustrated list of titles in the exhibition provides an excellent setting for the two papers on Barlaeus and Vossius included in this catalogue.

849 **The life of Desiderius Erasmus.**
Albert Hyma. Assen, The Netherlands: Van Gorcum, 1972. 140p.

A straightforward, shorter account by the author of *The youth of Erasmus* (1931, reprinted 1968).

850 **The idea of the civic triumph: drama, liturgy and the Royal Entry in the Low Countries.**
Gordon Kipling. *Dutch Crossing*, vol. 22 (1984), p. 60–83. bibliog.

The political and historical importance of the manifestations organized by the literary guilds of Rhetoricians as propaganda for the ruler is exemplified by the religious and biblical themes involving not only the glories and power of the city but also the holiness of the sovereign to whom homage is paid in the tableaux and triumphal arches displayed on his visits to his cities.

851 **The triumph of honour: Burgundian origins of the Elizabethan renaissance.**
Gordon Kipling. Leiden: University Press; London: Oxford University Press, 1977. bibliog. (Publications of the Sir Thomas Browne Institute, General Series, no. 6).

The Burgundian influence, which amounted to the milieu of the early Tudor court in England, is derived from substantial references to source materials.

852 **The Dutch case: a national or a regional culture?**
E. H. Kossmann. *Transactions of the Royal Historical Society*, vol. 29 (1979), p. 155–68. bibliog.

Looking back from the undesirable awareness of nationhood in the 19th century, the author discusses the evolution of this awareness from its regional, North Holland, origins. For this he consults 17th-century literary sources and posits, against J. L. Price's book (q.v.), that however much national awareness and achievement may seem from the outside to have declined in the 18th century, there was within the country little change in the collective awareness.

853 **Intertraffic of the mind.**
C. W. Schoneveld. Leiden: Brill, 1983. 270p. bibliog. (Publications of the Sir Thomas Browne Institute, Leiden, New Series, no. 3).

The subtitle 'Studies in seventeenth-century Anglo–Dutch translation with a checklist of books translated from English into Dutch, 1600–1700' is somewhat misleading. No attempt is made to cover the whole area of translation activity, though some idea of its scope is given in the checklist. In the first chapter Thomas Browne's *Religio Medici* is reviewed in its Dutch, Latin and French translations. The second chapter discusses Thomas Hobbes and the reception of his *Leviathan* and *De Cive* in Holland. The third chapter outlines the life of one translator, Johannes Grindal, and reviews his work as a translator, and the concluding chapter examines trends in Anglo–Dutch translation of this period.

854 **Daniel Heinsius and Stuart England.**
Paul R. Sellin. Leiden: University Press; London: Oxford University Press, 1968. 263p. bibliog. (Publications of the Sir Thomas Browne Institute, General Series, no. 3).

'Since Heinsius has been most patently neglected in England', the author writes, his study will 'sketch only his most relevant personal relationships with the island kingdom under the early Stuarts and trace the impact of his editorial and critical activities on some English literary theorists.' He examines Ben Jonson's indebtedness to Heinsius, claims Heinsius as the most important source for Milton's theory of tragedy, and contrasts Heinsius' theory with Dryden's interpretation of it.

855 **Power, state and freedom.**
Douglas J. den Uyl. Assen, The Netherlands: Van Gorcum, 1983. 172p. bibliog.

This interpretation of Spinoza's political philosophy examines his views on the origin of the state, on reason, sociality and contract, on freedom, peace and power and on the nature and foundation of political authority, with appendixes on Hobbes and Spinoza and on Spinoza's view of democracy. There is a bibliography of primary and secondary sources (in English and French).

856 **Selections from the letters of Erasmus (1529–1536): translation and commentary.**
Mary R. Williams. PhD thesis, Saint Louis University, 1969. 350p. bibliog.

A large selection from Erasmus' 3,000 letters in the original and in translation is preceded by an introduction assessing the significance of the vast correspondence and is followed by a reference index, with commentaries and notes on the letters themselves.

857 **The Anglo–Dutch contribution to the civilization of early modern society: an Anglo–Netherlands symposium.**
Charles H. Wilson (et al.). London: Oxford University Press for the British Academy, 1976. 72p. bibliog.

The proceedings of a symposium held in June 1974 sponsored by the Royal Society, the British Academy, and the Royal Netherlands Academy. Charles Wilson's paper is on the Dutch and Huguenot bankers of 18th-century England, and the other contributions are on Copernicanism, Huygens and Newton, and Erasmus.

858 **Holland and Britain.**
Charles H. Wilson. London: Collins [n.d.]. 127p.

Though written in the 1940s and now difficult to obtain, it is the only comparative general and historical work on Anglo–Dutch relations, and it is very readable, reliable and well illustrated. An introduction traces evidence of this relationship in Britain today, and subsequent chapters discuss trading relations, maritime concerns, literary influences, painting, architecture and design, science, Dutch influence on the English countryside, and exploration and colonial trade. Unfortunately there are no reference notes or bibliography.

859 **The world of Hugo Grotius (1583–1645: proceedings of the International Colloquium organised by the Grotius Committee of the Royal Netherlands Academy of Arts and Sciences, Rotterdam 6–9 April 1983).**
Amsterdam: APA–Holland University Press, 1984. 214p. bibliog.

English, French and German texts of twelve papers on Grotius as a lawyer, historian, philologist, poet, playwright and biblical exegetist.

The ideological origins of the Batavian Revolution: history and politics in the Dutch Republic 1747–1800.
See item no. 116.

Studies on Christiaan Huygens.
See item no. 691.

Descartes et le cartesianisme hollandais. (Descartes and Dutch Cartesianism.)
See item no. 693.

Darwin and our forefathers: Dutch reactions to the theory of evolution 1860–1875: a field survey.
See item no. 694.

Boerhaave's correspondence.
See item no. 696.

Herman Boerhaave: the man and his work.
See item no. 697.

Life and works of Gerardus Joannes Vossius (1577–1649).
See item no. 717.

Graffiti.
See item no. 755.

Dutch catchpenny prints: three centuries of pictorial broadsides for children.
See item no. 869.

Rudolf Agricola: a bibliography of printed works and translation.
See item no. 1000.

Bibliography of Dutch seventeenth century political thoughts: an annotated inventory, 1581–1710.
See item no. 1001.

Sports, Recreation and Cuisine

860 **Sport and physical education in the Netherlands.**
Jan Broekhoff. In: *Sport and physical education around the world*. Edited by William Johnson. Champaign, Illinois: Stipes, 1980, p. 431–47. bibliog.

Physical education in the Netherlands moved from Swedish and German gymnastics with games (track and field) to Austrian 'free-style' expression in the 1930s. At universities, however, sports were neglected until, after the Second World War, a sports centre was built at Delft. The most popular sports are tennis, swimming, water polo, table tennis, athletics, soccer, judo, badminton, hockey and volleyball. There is a listing of the membership of the ten largest sporting associations in 1976.

861 **Masters and men: chess in the Netherlands.**
Jan Hein Donner. *Delta*, vol. 2, no. 1 (spring 1959), p. 91–96.

Very late in starting, the Netherlands suddenly moved into the world class when the wealth of the country attracted great chess players to settle there after the First World War. The true founder of the contemporary interest in chess in that country is Euwe, who beat Aljechin at the peak of his power.

862 **Daughters of wind and waves: yachting in the Netherlands.**
Niels A. Douwes Dekker. *Delta*, vol. 12, no. 1 (spring 1969), p. 30–43.

A description, with excellent line-drawings, of twelve boat designs from the Flying Dutchman to an 81-foot motor yacht.

863 **Dutch cooking.**
Heleen A. M. Halverhout. Amsterdam: De Driehoek, 1982. 3rd rev. ed. 144p.

A number of generally simple Dutch recipes with comparative tables of English and American terms and measurements.

864 **Cricket in the Netherlands.**
T. J. O. Hickey. *Delta*, vol. 7, no. 3 (autumn 1964), p. 30–36.

An outline of the spread of cricket from 1845 to 1964 when there were fifty-one clubs that were members of the Royal Netherlands Cricket Association. It remains, however, a somewhat élitist game.

865 **The Bumble filmbook.**
Rob Houwer, Marten Toonder. Antwerp: Scriptoria, 1983. 90p.

An adaptation of the feature film cartoon 'If you know what I mean'; a translation, with illustrations of *Het Bommelfilmboek*.

866 **The art of Dutch cooking.**
C. Countess van Limburg Stirum. London: André Deutsch, 1962. 192p.

A book of recipes following the pattern of most cookery books, with a section on recipes for left-overs, on beverages for parties, for 'Sinterklaas', children's parties, and on Indonesian dishes. Imperial weights and measures are used, and there is an index.

867 **The Dutch on ice.**
Dietert Molonus. *Delta*, vol. 9, no. 4 (winter 1966–67), p. 73–81.

An account of the skating tradition in which skating in one locality is considered greatly inferior to travelling long distances along the canals, through villages and stopping for Dutch fare at stalls on the way. This means that speed skating is Holland's contribution to skating events, though Sjoukje Dijkstra, of course, proved an eloquent exception to this rule.

868 **Hot pants in Holland: Dutch football.**
Nico Scheepmaker. *Delta*, vol. 14, no. 2 (summer 1971), p. 5–23.

An illustrated account of the successes of some of the better-known Dutch teams, and profiles of some of the best known players.

869 **Dutch catchpenny prints: three centuries of pictorial broadsides for children.**
C. F. van Veen. The Hague: W. van Hoeve, 1971. 91p.

An excellent collection of full-size reproductions of (sometimes coloured) woodcuts and engravings of biblical subjects, portraits, animals, literature, soldiers, the world upside down, topography, caricatures, children's games, vehicles, foreigners, fashions, and varia. The index gives details of the titles, publishers, a description of the prints and their provenance.

870 **Dances of the Netherlands.**

E. van der Ven–Ten Beusel. London: Parrish, 1949. 40p. bibliog.

A description of regional and national dances with illustrations of costumes and with music notation alongside an account of the steps and formations for four national dances.

The myth of Sinterklaas.
See item no. 12.

The kingdom of the Netherlands: facts and figures.
See item no. 14.

Siertuinen van Nederland en Belgie. (Flower gardens of the Netherlands and Belgium.)
See item no. 77.

WVC Documentatie. (WVC Documentation.)
See item no. 975.

Archives, Libraries, Galleries and Museums

Archives

871 **Libraries and archives 8: The Netherlands.**
H. Dunthorne. *History*, vol. 57 (1972), p. 217–20.

A short and helpful introduction to Dutch archives. Inevitably some points are now dated.

872 **Manual for the arrangement and description of archives.**
T. A. Fruin. New York: H. W. Wilson, 1968. 225p. bibliog.

Originally commissioned by the Netherlands Association of Archivists, and published in 1898, this is a reprint of the 1940 translation of the second edition with a new foreword by K. Munden.

873 **Archives in the Netherlands.**
H. Hardenburg. *Acta Historiae Neerlandicae*, vol. 3 (1968), p. 266–87. bibliog.

Hardenburg was Archivist General until 1966. He deals with the development of archive administration in the Netherlands, and then explains how archives are organized today.

874 **Overzichten van de archieven en verzamelingen in de openbare archiefbewaarplaatsen in Nederland.** (Surveys of the archives and collections in the public archive depositories in the Netherlands.) Edited by L. M. T. L. Hustinx, F. C. J. Ketelaar, H. J. H. A. G. Metselaars, J. J. Temick, H. Uil. Alphen, The Netherlands: Samsom, 1979– . 13 vols, in progress.

This indispensable series, published under the auspices of the Dutch Society of Archivists, describes the state and contents of Dutch public archives in about 1980, and is now near completion, with one volume for each province, plus one for Amsterdam (vol. VIII (1981)) and one – probably the most useful – for the General State Archives in The Hague (vol. IX (1982)). A list of the archives and collections in the depositories is given, together with the author, title and number of the inventory or list of contents. Perhaps the most important feature of this series is that the collation of material for its publication has caused a major rationalization of the archives in the Netherlands.

875 **Guide to the archives of the Spanish inquisitions in or concerned with the Netherlands (1556–1706).**
Geoffrey Parker. *Archives et Bibliothèques de Belgique*, special issue III (1971). bibliog.

An authority on Spain and the Dutch Revolt, Parker has been through Spanish, Italian, French, Swiss and English archives to produce this most helpful listing of these widely dispersed sources.

876 **Guide to the sources of the history of Africa south of the Sahara in the Netherlands: Netherlands State Archives Service.**
Marius P. H. Roessingh, W. Visser. New York: K. G. Saur; Munich: Verlag Dokumentation Saur KG, 1978. 241p. bibliog.

An annotated list of archive sources dealing with both public and private depositories. Provides ample indexing.

877 **Sources of the history of Asia and Oceania in the Netherlands: Netherlands State Archives Service and Royal Institute of Linguistics and Anthropology. Part I. Sources up to 1796. Part II. Sources 1796–1949.**
Marius P. H. Roessingh Munich: K. G. Saur, 1982–83. 2 vols. bibliog.

Covers sources in national, provincial and municipal archives, and also non-government and private collections. The entries are annotated, and there is ample indexing.

Libraries

878 **The library of the Mennonite Church of Amsterdam.**
J. L. Beijers. Utrecht: Beijers, 1970. 183p.

This is an auction catalogue of the sale of the library of the Mennonite Church in 1971.

879 **Special libraries and documentation centres in the Netherlands.**
Jack Burkett. Oxford: 1968. 103p.

An illustrated account (sometimes reminding us of the rapid changes in technology when bibliophones are here displayed as the latest thing in information technology) of government library and information services, libraries at the technological universities at Delft, Wageningen and Eindhoven, and specialist industrial and research libraries and documentation services. There are useful lists of abbreviations and a cross-reference index. Obviously much of the information given (e.g. in holdings, budget, services) is now dated, but the general descriptions are still very useful.

880 **Internationaal Instituut voor Sociale Geschiedenis: Alfabetische catalogus.** (Alphabetical catalogue.)
Boston, Massachusetts: G. R. Hall, 1970. 12 vols plus supplements.

Catalogue of the Institute's library in Amsterdam. It is concerned as much with the history of socialist ideas and movements as with social history, and is international in scope. The collection lists over 350,000 volumes.

881 **Libraries and documentation centres in the Netherlands.**
The Hague: Nederlandse Bibliotheek en Lektuurcentrum, 1978. 78p.

A description of library organizations, of research, public and special libraries, of information services and the training process for librarianship.

882 **The Rooklooster register evaluated.**
P. F. J. Obbema. *Quaerendo*, vol. 7 (1977), p. 326–53. bibliog.

The importance of this register, which has never been published, is as a reliable and extensive catalogue showing the location of early manuscripts throughout the Low Countries and the German border area.

883 **Venadam bibliotheekgids 1982.** (Venadam library guide 1982.)
Malden, The Netherlands: Venadam, 1982. 276p.

This gives libraries according to alphabetical listing of their localities. It also lists library organizations and associations, and has a subject cross-reference index.

Leiden imprints 1483–1600 in Leiden University Library and Bibliotheca Thijsiana.
See item no. 987.

Galleries and museums

884 **History en scène: the Amsterdam Theatre Museum.**
Ben Albach. *Delta*, vol. 10, no. 4 (winter 1967–68), p. 21–29.

The museum, opened in 1960, covers four centuries of theatre in the Netherlands. It owes much to Hartkamp's important collection of prints, décor, costume designs, portraits, programmes, posters, press-clippings and photographs which were acquired on his death in 1927. It is accommodated on all the floors of a 17th-century house on the Herengracht and has a number of model reconstructions of earlier stages and modern sound and video recordings of actors.

885 **Jewish Historical Museum.**
J. C. E. Belifante. Haarlem, The Netherlands: Enschedé, 1978. 96p. (Dutch Museums, no. 3).

A description of the museum, opened in 1932, reassembled from what remained after the Germans had stolen the collection during the Second World War, and re-opened in 1955. Fine colour plates of the present exhibits, with descriptions in Dutch and English, include a prayer book of the 13th century and Couzijn's sculpture of the 'Jews in Flight' of 1951.

886 **Delta**, vol. 5, no. 1 (spring 1962).
Amsterdam: Delta International Publications Foundation, 70p. [Special issue].

This is a special museum number with many shorter articles on individual museums, on types of museum throughout the country and on recent trends in museum design and restoration. The following museums are described: Teyler's Museum, opened in 1793 at Haarlem 'to promote the arts and sciences', the Frans Hals Museum in Haarlem, the National Museum of Antiquities in Leiden, the Rotterdam Museum of Ethnology and the Rotterdam Museum of Ethnography, the Netherlands Open Air Museum (of folklore) at Arnhem, the sculpture park at the Kröller–Müller Museum (Otterlo) and the Literary Museum in The Hague. There are also general articles on modernizing old, and designing new museums, the requirements of a museum of contemporary art, temporary exhibitions, museums of science and technology and regional museums.

887 **From Van Eyck to Van Gogh: the Van Beuningen Collection.**
J. C. Ebbinge Wubben. *Delta*, vol. 1, no. 4 (winter 1958–59), p. 43–50.

The Boymans Museum, after failing in the 19th century to acquire important collections, restored its reputation in 1958 when it purchased the Koenigs and Van Beuningen collections, including Van Eyck, Bosch, Brueghel, Rubens, Memlinc, Metsys, Lucas van Leyden, Steen and numerous other Dutch, Flemish and Italian masterpieces up to the more recent work of French (Courbet, Gauguin) and Dutch artists.

888 **Groot museumboek.** (Greater museum book.)
Compiled by Joost Elffers, Mike Schuyt, text by the editor, Annemieke Overbeek. Amsterdam: Meulenhoff/Landshoff, 1980. 432p.

A fully colour-illustrated Dutch description of 660 museums, giving their precise addresses, opening hours and entry charges, arranged alphabetically by location. There are proper name and key-word indexes.

889 **Fries Museum.**
Haarlem, The Netherlands: Enschedé, 1978. 110p.

This guide is published in English and Frisian, since the second language in the Netherlands is Frisian. This itself demonstrates an important fact that may not be obvious: Frisian is a distinct and separate language spoken within the kingdom of the Netherlands and nurtured these days in much the same way that Welsh is nurtured in Wales.

890 **Kröller–Müller Museum.**
Haarlem, The Netherlands: Enschedé, 1981. 2nd ed. 159p. (Dutch Museums, no. 1).

A guide with monochrome and colour illustrations of the paintings, drawings, sculptures and open-air sculpture park in the museum of modern art at Otterlo, near Arnhem.

891 **Dutch museums.**
Remmet van Luttervelt. London: Thames & Hudson, 1960. 319p.

A member of the staff of the Rijksmuseum in Amsterdam introduces Dutch art collections through short chapters on the genesis and history of group portraits and family portraits. He describes the history of the museums themselves from the earliest 16th-century cabinets of paintings to post-war developments. The remainder of the work (p. 80–303) provides commentaries on colour and monochrome reproductions of painting from the museums, with lists of the paintings and their locations.

892 **National Museum of Antiquities.**

Edited by H. D. Schneider. Haarlem, The Netherlands: Enschedé, 1981, 128p. (Dutch Museums, no. 6).

Parallel Dutch and English texts (a mediocre translation of the Dutch) describing this museum at Leiden that houses collections of Mediterranean and Western Asian art alongside collections of prehistoric, ancient and medieval art from the Netherlands. The catalogue of some of the exhibits is accompanied by fine colour photographs.

893 **State museum Het Catharijne Convent.**

Haarlem, The Netherlands: Enschedé, 1983. 100p.

An illustrated guide to the museum of ecclesiastical appurtenances in Utrecht.

894 **Van Abbe museum Eindhoven.**

Haarlem, The Netherlands: Enschedé, 1982. 204p. (Dutch Museums, no. 4).

The civic museum at Eindhoven, donated by the industrialist and art collector, H. van Abbe, contains contemporary art which is represented here in a large number of colour illustrations with biographical and descriptive appreciations by members of the museum's staff.

895 **Museum guide for Amsterdam.**

H. Vogels. Baarn, The Netherlands: Bosch & Keuning, 1981. 128p.

A description, with information on addresses, opening times etc., of the thirty-six museums in Amsterdam, including museums containing archives relating to particular persons, and on history, zoology, the Bible, spatial planning, geology, botany, Jewish history, industry and technology, the press, fine arts, marine history, handwriting, typewriters, theatre, and the tropics.

Sculptures of the Rijksmuseum Kröller–Müller.
See item no. 798.

Books

896 **The book through five thousand years.**
Fernand Baudin (et al.), edited by Hendrik D. L. Vervliet, postscript by Ruari McLean. London: Phaidon, 1972. 496p.

A handsomely illustrated general survey with references to manuscript and book production in the Netherlands in chapters on 'Gothic manuscripts in Belgium and the Netherlands', 'Printing in the fifteenth and sixteenth centuries', 'Development of the fine book after 1600' and 'Bookbinding from the 16th century to the present'.

897 **A short introduction in the binding of books, followed by a note on the gilding of the edges by Ambrosius Vermerck.**
Dirk de Bray, with an introduction and paraphrase by K. van der Horst, C. de Wolf. Amsterdam: Nico Israel, 1977. 87p.

A facsimile of the original Dutch manuscript is included with the translation.

898 **Brinkman's [Cumulatieve] Catalogus van Boeken.** (Brinkman's [Cumulative] Catalogue of Books.)
Alphen, The Netherlands: Samson, 1833– . monthly, with annual cumulations.

This lists all the books published or reprinted in the Netherlands and Flanders that have been received by the Royal Library (copyright library) in The Hague. Its three parts contain author and title lists, alphabetically ordered and cross-referenced where necessary, foundations and societies and a subject index. It is a continuation of R. Arrenberg's *Alphabetische naamlijst van boeken*, 1790–1832 and J. van Abkoude and R. Arrenberg's *Naamregister van Nederduitsche boeken 1600–1761*.

899 **J. Allart: printer, publisher and bookseller 1754–1816.**
Ton Broos. *Dutch Crossing*, vol. 14 (1981), p. 27–35.

This very substantial Amsterdam printer published 708 editions between 1774 and 1816, equalling the largest publishers in Europe. His lists were dominated by literature, followed by theology, natural science and medicine and history.

900 **A century of Dutch manuscript illumination.**
L. M. J. Delaissé. London: Cambridge University Press; Berkeley: University of California Press, 1968. 102p. bibliog.

This follows developments in Dutch manuscript decoration from its probably French origins in the earliest period to greater independence and realism in the 14th century, up to the finest period in the mid-15th century when the Dutch style (centred on Utrecht) shows that it can be clearly distinguished from the Flemish, with its stronger French influence.

901 **Thomas Basson 1555–1613.**
J. A. van Dorsten. Leiden: University Press, 1961. 126p. bibliog.

A biography of the English printer who owned a bookshop in Cologne before moving to the Netherlands, where he finally became University Printer at Leiden and a member of the scholarly fraternity of the 'familists'.

902 **Dutch–American bibliography, 1693–1794.**
H. Edelman. Nieuwkoop, The Netherlands: De Graaf, 1974. 125p. bibliog.

This is a descriptive catalogue of Dutch-language books, pamphlets and almanacs printed in America. There is a historical introduction describing the social circumstances of the Dutch settlers and the printers. The list of imprints, in chronological order, includes very short English summaries of the contents. Titles, names and places are indexed.

903 **Hebrew typography in the northern Netherlands, 1585–1815: historical evaluation and descriptive bibliography.**
L. Fuks, R. G. Fuks-Mansfeld. Leiden: Brill, 1984. 232p.

A descriptive chronological listing of titles printed at Leiden, Franeker and Amsterdam and including indexes of names, titles, subjects, financial backers, etc.

904 **Copy and print in the Netherlands: an atlas of historical bibliography.**
Wytze G. S. Hellinga. Amsterdam: North Holland Publishing Co., 1962. 254p. bibliog.

A fine, well-illustrated production of a scholarly standard work on the subject. It covers book production and the book trade from the 15th century to the present day. The second half of the book is entirely devoted to superb (and normally full-size) reproductions of copy and plates which illustrate the author's conclusion that book production in the Netherlands has maintained a standard reflecting the requirements of a widely literate and cultured people.

905 **The fifteenth century printing types of the Low Countries.**
Wytze G. S. Hellinga, Lotte Hellinga–Querido. Amsterdam: Hertzberger, 1966. 2 vols. bibliog.

A work of substantial scholarship by the two leading authorities in this field. There is a detailed introduction on types and presses, tables of types, an account of the derivation of the types used by printers in the Netherlands, a general index, an index in the Proctor–BMC order, a synoptical table of illustrations of types plates (giving full-size reproductions), an index of type measurements, a chronological survey of the use of types and an index in the Campbell order.

906 **Early printing in the Low Countries: its survival and its importance.**
L. Hellinga–Querido. *Delta*, vol. 4, no. 1 (spring 1973), p. 24–43. bibliog.

A description of a research project on the origins of printing in Haarlem and a bibliographical analysis of the earliest editions at Haarlem, with a number of illustrative plates.

907 **Boek, bibliotheek en geesteswetenshappen.** (Book, library and the humanities.)
Edited by W. R. H. Koops. Hilversum, The Netherlands: Verloren, 1986. 383p. bibliog.

A collection of essays in German, French and English, in honour of C. Reedijk on his retirement as Librarian of the Royal Library in The Hague, ranging from Erasmus and Belle de Zuylen to the future of the National Library.

908 **Treasures of the Royal Library, The Hague.**
Compiled by A. S. Korteweg, C. A. Chavannes–Mazel, preface by R. E. O. Ekkart. The Hague: The Royal Library, 1980. 121p.

A catalogue of the exhibition in the Meermanno–Westreenianum Museum and the Museum of the Book in The Hague, 17 December 1980–14 March 1981.

909 **On designing and devising type.**
J. van Krimpen. London: Sylvan Press, 1957. (Typophile Chap Book, no. 32).

The famous hand punch-cutter, who designed type and lay-out for J. Enschedé for thirty-five years, describes his work and explains the problems involved in transferring to machine monotype casting.

910 **Letter and image.**
's-Hertogenbosch, The Netherlands: Offsetdrukkerij Bilbo, 1976. 48p.

Typographical and illustration exercises from the illustration department of the Royal Academy of Art and Design.

911 **The Haarlem legend of the invention of printing by Laurens Janszoon Coster, critically examined.**

A. van der Linde. Haarlem, The Netherlands: De Vriesebosch, 1981. 170p.

This is a reprint of the 1968 edition (Naarden, The Netherlands: Van Bekhoven) which was first published in London in 1871, consisting of an introduction and a classified list of the Costerian incunabula.

912 **Printed in the Netherlands: Dutch book production.**

Guus Sötemann. *Delta*, vol. 4, no. 4 (winter 1961–2), p. 67–84. bibliog.

A comparison of book production in the Netherlands, the United States, the United Kingdom, the Soviet Union and Japan in 1959 places the Netherlands just behind Scandinavia and Switzerland with a production of over 750 titles per million inhabitants. The article then traces the development of the book trade in the Netherlands from Gutenberg to the present day (1960).

913 **Incunabula in Dutch libraries.**

Edited by Gerard van Thienen. Nieuwkoop, The Netherlands: De Graaf, 1983. 2 vols. (Vol. I: Catalogue; vol. II: Indexes and concordances).

The first volume contains a census of 15th-century printed books in Dutch public collections – 4,746 entries are alphabetically listed. The second volume lists reference works, libraries, abbreviations, places with printers and publishers, printers and publishers and concordances.

The burning fen.
See item no. 67.

Quaerendo.
See item no. 966.

Leiden imprints 1483–1600 in Leiden University Library and Bibliotheca Thijsiana.
See item no. 987.

A short-title catalogue of books printed at Hoorn before 1701.
See item no. 998.

Atlantes Neerlandici: bibliography of terrestrial, maritime and celestial atlases and pilot books, published in the Netherlands up to 1880.
See item no. 1003.

Fable-books printed in the Low Countries: a concise bibliography until 1800.
See item no. 1008.

Nederland: een selectief overzicht leverbare titels, U aangeboden door Broese Kemink b.v. (The Netherlands: a selective survey of available titles, presented by Broese Kemink b.v.)
See item no. 1013.

Nederlandse bibliografie van 1500–1540. (Dutch bibliography from 1500–1540.)
See item no. 1016.

Short title catalogue of books printed in the Netherlands and Belgium and of Dutch and Flemish books printed in other countries from 1470 to 1600 now in the British Museum.
See item no. 1020.

Mass Media

914 **Radio Nederland Wereldomroep: the Dutch world broadcasting system.**
J. W. Acda. *Delta*, vol. 10, no. 1/2 (spring/summer 1967), p. 117–23.

The director of this system outlines its history and activities, indicating the wide range of programmes that are either beamed direct on short wave or distributed in foreign language tapes and discs for transmission from local stations abroad, winning awards for the high standard of its programmes and the objectivity and scope of its reporting.

915 **AVRO Televizier Magazine – to the bitter end: the polio drama of Staphorst.**
Delta, vol. 15, no. 3 (autumn 1972), p. 60–72.

An illustrated description of the award-winning documentary on the results of the strict Calvinist resistance to vaccination in Staphorst during the polio epidemic in 1971. Despite violent local hostility to the cameras, the crew managed to film the village and even to obtain an interview with the leading elder of the local church.

916 **The cable and satellite yearbook 1985.**
London: Cable and Satellite Information Systems, 1985. 240p.

A survey of current developments in the provision of cable and satellite television in fifteen European countries including the Netherlands. There is a list of addresses of telecommunications offices.

917 **Broadcasting in the Netherlands.**
Kees van der Haak, Joanna Spicer. London: Routledge & Kegan Paul, 1977. 93p. bibliog. (Case Studies on Broadcasting Systems).

A description of the Dutch environment for broadcasting, its evolution up to the Broadcasting Act of 1967 and its development since then, showing a shifting basis in the system with a prediction of future changes. Useful appendixes give a translation of the 1969 act, lists of broadcasting organizations, transmission allocations, revenues and expenditure, TV output and consumption, jobs in broadcasting and a summary of the memorandum on mass-media policy.

918 **Netherlands world broadcasting.**
Robert D. Haslach. Philadelphia: Lawrence Miller Publishing, 1983. bibliog.

Follows the fortunes of Dutch overseas broadcasting from its early days as a colonial service run by Philips, through the difficulties experienced in the Second World War.

919 **Help to people in hiding.**
Louis de Jong. *Delta*, vol. 8, no. 1 (spring 1965), p. 36–79.

The full text, with illustrations, of the last of 21 programmes on the history of the German occupation shown on Dutch television, each one of which lasted from 70 to 100 minutes.

920 **ETV in the Netherlands: specifically ETV programmes.**
D. A. De Korte. In: *Television in education and training*. Eindhoven, The Netherlands: Philips Gloeilampenfabrieken, 1967, p. 60–70. bibliog.

A brief survey of the genesis of Dutch schools broadcasting and television (Educational TV) is followed by a description of the provision in the 1960s with pupil and teacher reactions to the programmes, a note on postgraduate training in television, and a description of the television academy, TELEAC.

921 **The Dutch press adjusts to the future.**
Maarten Rooij. *Delta*, vol. 16, no. 4 (winter 1973–74), p. 56–66.

The financial crisis facing two newspapers, *De Tijd* and *Trouw*, in the 1970s is described in some detail as typifying the struggle of most national newspapers at that time. The result has been concentration caused by mergers, though this has coincided with the social and political change in the country in which religious and political pluriform structure of the population has undergone rapid change and a shift in loyalties. Government support, first by means of direct subsidy and then through the Press Fund, has proved insufficient to prevent a severe reduction in the range of daily newspapers.

922 **Publish or perish: Dutch press under pressure.**
G. J. van Roozendaal. *Delta*, vol. 14, no. 3 (autumn 1971), p. 66–77.

The threat to the nine surviving national newspapers came (in 1971) from the instability of advertising revenue which accounts for two-thirds of the total (the remaining third comes from readers' subscriptions) and the escalating costs of printing and investment in new technology. Despite government subsidization, the papers are expected to continue merging and the subscription rate is likely to have to provide more than one-third of the revenue.

923 **Mirror of a pillarized society: broadcasting in the Netherlands.**
Henk Schaafsma. *Delta*, vol. 9, no. 4 (winter 1966–67), p. 57–69.

'Of the five broadcasting associations, all of which have now been in existence more than forty years, only AVRO (General Broadcasting Association) calls itself "neutral"'. This, the writer states, is an antiquated and untenable adherence to the devolving pluralist structure of Dutch society, which fragments and dilutes the quality of broadcasting on all stations.

924 **Holland: the shaky pillars of Hilversum.**
Herman Wigbold. In: *Television and political life: studies in six European countries*. Edited by Anthony Smith. London: Macmillan, 1979, p. 191–231.

Covers the history of television in the Netherlands, with its unique system of ideologically based broadcasting organizations, a system which is now in steep decline in the ideological neutrality of the 1970s and 1980s.

Dutch Film.
See item no. 937.

Newspapers in microform: foreign countries 1948–1972.
See item no. 1014.

Periodicals

925 **A. A. G. Bijdragen.** (Contributions from the Department of Rural History).

Wageningen, The Netherlands: Agricultural University, 1958/59– . irregular.

This series is a publication vehicle for the staff and associates of the Department of Rural History of the Agricultural University of Wageningen. Over the years it has been the mouthpiece of the so-called 'Wageningen School' of economic-social-demographic history, with its pioneering work on local history. The subject matter is Dutch social and economic history.

926 **Aarts' letterkundig almanak.** (Aarts' literary almanac.)

Amsterdam: Aarts, 1979– . annual.

An annual publication containing addresses of living authors, a calendar of literary events, short biographies of recently deceased writers and a special section varying from year to year (e.g. lists of available reprints of a particular period or movement).

927 **Acta Historiae Neerlandicae/Low Countries History Yearbook.**

Leiden: Brill; The Hague: Nijhoff, 1966–82. annual.

This journal was administered by the Nederlands Historisch Genootschap (Dutch History Society) and consisted largely of translations into English of the best articles to have appeared recently in Dutch. Now discontinued, it has not been replaced, and is much missed. From 1973 to 1982 it also contained a regular critical survey of new work on Dutch and Belgian history.

928 **Acta Politica: Tijdschrift voor Politicologie.** (Acta Politica: Journal for Political Science.)
Meppel, The Netherlands: Boom, 1965– . quarterly.

A political science journal with anything up to half of the articles in English. When in Dutch, the contributions have summaries in English. The subject matter is Dutch politics, although international matters are also examined.

929 **Britain and the Netherlands.**
Various publishers, 1959– . irregular.

This series is approximately biennial, and is the record of the proceedings of the Anglo–Dutch historical conferences which have been held roughly every two years since 1959. The papers included are usually originals, rather than translations from Dutch material already in print, and cover every aspect of Dutch, English, and Anglo–Dutch history.

930 **Canadian Journal of Netherlandic Studies/Revue Canadienne d'Études Néerlandaises.**
Edited by Dorothy Howard, Hendrika Ruger. Windsor, Ontario: University of Windsor, Department of French, 1979– . biennial.

A publication of the Canadian Association for the Advancement of Netherlandic Studies, containing articles in English and French on 'Netherlandic culture in the broader sense of the word' and including creative writing in Dutch, and book reviews.

931 **Counterpart: The International Dimension of Higher Education in the Netherlands: Bulletin of the Netherlands Universities Foundation for International Co-operation (NUFFIC).**
The Hague: NUFFIC, 1956– . biennial.

This contains scholarly articles on all aspects of research activities in the Netherlands and reports on ongoing research. It is a continuation of the original publication, *Higher Education and Research in the Netherlands*.

932 **Current Research in the Netherlands.**
The Hague: Netherlands Organization for the Advancement of Pure Research (ZWO), various starting dates. occasional.

There are separate volumes listing and describing research in progress under the headings: physical sciences (mathematics, physics, geology, astronomy); technological science; humanities; biological and medical sciences; language and literature. Their value is somewhat reduced by the irregularity in the appearance of the volumes and their supplements.

933 **Delta: a Review of Art, Life and Thought in the Netherlands.**
Edited by J. H. Bannier (1961–74), Frances Daendels–Wilson (1968–74), E. J. Dijksterhuis (1958–59), Dick Elffers (1961–74), Dick Hiltenius (1971–71), James S. Holmes (1958–65), Ed. Hoornik (1958–70), Karel Jonckheere (1958–74), Louis de Jong (1958–74), Daniël de Lange (1966–74), Hans van Marle (1966–74), Aad Nuis (1971–74), H. M. van Randwijk (1966), Maarten Rooij (1959–74), J. W. Schulte Nordholt (1966–74), Mels Sluyser (1971–74), J. J. M. van der Ven (1958–60), Elizabeth Willems–Treeman (1966–67). Amsterdam: Delta International Publications Foundation, 1958–74. quarterly.

A high-quality journal with finely illustrated articles on a very considerable range of aspects of Dutch life, past and present, generally written by specialists for the general informed reader. Though it ceased publication in 1974, it was widely distributed due to generous financial support. A complete cumulative index, 1958–74, was published in 1975.

934 **Dutch Art and Architecture Today.**
The Hague: Ministry for Cultural Affairs, Recreation and Social Welfare. June 1977–May 1982. three times a year.

This replaced the English-language *Museum* (a Dutch periodical for modern art, which ran to six issues). The contents of this journal cover major developments in painting, sculpture, drawing and graphics, architecture, film and video, applied art and intermedia, as well as reporting on government policy on museums and the visual arts. The journal was distributed free to fine art departments and institutions abroad.

935 **Dutch Arts.**
The Hague: Government Publishing Office. 1985– . occasional.

A series published at irregular intervals, each issue of which contains short essays outlining the history and current state of the visual arts, music, dance, theatre, film and literature. The contributions provide a straightforward introduction to the topics discussed, with pleasing colour illustrations.

936 **Dutch Crossing: a Journal of Low Countries Studies.**
Edited by Jane Fenoulhet, Charles Ford, Theo Hermans, Jonathan Israel, Paul Vincent, Roel Vismans, Michael Wintle. London: Department of Dutch, Bedford College, 1977–83; University College, 1983– . three times a year.

This journal, now published almost entirely in English, contains scholarly articles, progress reports on research, translations and reviews. Since the expansion of the editorial team in 1985, the subject-matter has included history, art history, and the social sciences: the journal now functions as a focus outside the Netherlands for Dutch studies in the widest sense of the term.

937 **Dutch Film.**
The Hague: Government Publishing Office, 1969– . annual.

Though production standards have improved as the series has progressed, it has maintained its basic format – a critical introduction on any significant developments in the year or years under survey and short reviews of the films under the headings of features and low-budget features, documentaries, shorts, animations and experimental films.

938 **Dutch Heights.**
The Hague, Ministry for Cultural Affairs, 1987– . three times a year.

This provocative title to a journal from the Low Countries belongs to a new magazine on arts and culture in the Netherlands. The first issue does not indicate the frequency of publication, but its introduction states that the term 'culture' covers far more than artistic production embracing 'all products of human work and thought characteristic of a community or population'.

939 **Dutch Studies.**
Edited by P. Brachin, J. Goossens, P. K. King, J. de Rooij. The Hague: Nijhoff, 1974–76. annual.

'An annual review of the language, literature and life of the Low Countries'. The first volume includes J. Goossens, 'Germanic studies in Germany and their relation to the study of German and Dutch'; H. Schultink, 'Modern Dutch grammar as a science'; W. A. P. Smit, 'The Dutch theatre in the Renaissance – a problem and a task for the literary historian'; C. A. Zaalberg, 'Studies in Hooft'. Vol. 2 includes Nienke Bakker, 'The Dutch dictionary'; Joris Duytschaever, 'James Joyce's impact in Simon Vestdijk's early fiction'; J. Fleerackers, 'The historical force of the Flemish Movement in Belgium – past aims, present achievements and future cultural aspirations'; C. van Bree, 'Bibliographical aids in Dutch language studies'. Vol. 3 includes W. Blok, 'Ergocentric analysis of the novel and the history of literature'; A. L. Sötemann, 'Some suggestions concerning two modernist traditions in European poetry'; and F. Haarsma, 'Development in the spiritual life of Holland, particularly in the Roman Catholic church in the last ten years'.

940 **Dutch Theses: a List of Titles of Theses Submitted to Dutch Universities.**
Utrecht: Bibliotheek der Rijksuniversiteit, 1975– . annual.

This journal lists titles of theses by subject, with a list of institutions offering higher degrees, a tabular analysis of degrees conferred, a glossary of words and abbreviations, corrections and addenda to earlier volumes, and an index of names.

941 **De Economist: Driemandelijks Tijdschrift – Quarterly Review.**
Leiden: Stenfert Kroese, 1852– . quarterly.

Founded in 1852 by the political economist J. L. de Bruyn Kops, this journal now carries mainly English-language articles on theoretical economics and empirical economic studies of the Netherlands, as well as reviews.

942 **European Economic Review.**

Amsterdam: Elsevier Science Publishers (North-Holland), 1969– . 3 vols (9 issues) annually.

An international journal for theoretical economics, but which attracts a large number of articles by Dutch economists who inevitably use Dutch material to illustrate their models.

943 **Historia Agriculturae.**

Groningen, The Netherlands: Nederlands Agronomisch–Historisch Instituut, 1953– . annual.

This annual periodical contains only Dutch-language material on the development of agriculture in the Netherlands, but much of the material is statistical and documentary data. Volumes 12 (1978) and 15 (1983) are bibliographies of agricultural history by H. van Zon covering publications in the period 1975–80.

944 **Holland Herald.**

Weert, The Netherlands: Roto Smeets International Publications, 1965– . monthly.

A 'colour supplement' type of magazine with a large number of short, illustrated articles on a wide range of topics of general interest about the Netherlands.

945 **Holland Industrial.**

The Hague: Export Publishers Netherlands. ca. 1986/87– . occasional.

This very high quality magazine 'to promote the Dutch industry world wide', in co-operation with the Netherlands Foreign Trade Agency, is well written, beautifully illustrated and an attractive means of keeping in touch with design and production developments in the Netherlands.

946 **Holland Quarterly.**

The Hague: Netherlands Foreign Trade Agency, 1978– . quarterly.

A nicely produced trade magazine written and illustrated for the layman as well as the industrialist and businessman.

947 **In Touch with the Dutch.**

London: Netherlands–British Chamber of Commerce, 1969– . monthly.

A trade magazine which contains shorter articles on new ventures, successful enterprises and the potential for new trading links with Holland.

948 **International Review of Social History.**

Assen, The Netherlands: Van Gorcum, 1956– . three times a year.

This is the journal of the International Institute of Social History (IISG) in Amsterdam, devoted to social history in the widest thematic and geographical sense, but with a preponderance of articles on Dutch history, and especially on the Dutch labour movement. It succeeds the yearbook published by the Institute before the Second World War, entitled *International Review for Social History* (1936–39).

949 **Internationale Spectator.**
The Hague: Nederlands Genootschap voor Internationale Zaken 'Clingendael', 1947– . monthly.

Most of the material in this foreign affairs journal is in the Dutch language, but short English abstracts are provided. The subject matter is foreign affairs, through Dutch eyes.

950 **Jaarcijfers voor het Koninkrijk der Nederlanden, Rijk in Europa.**
(Annual Statistics for the Kingdom of the Netherlands, European Division.)
The Hague, etc.: publisher varies, 1881– . annual.

This annual publication covers the years between the *Résumé statistique* (q.v.), and the foundation of the Central Bureau of Statistics (CBS) in 1899. There are data on all aspects of the economy and the public sector, with the limitations usual in 19th-century statistics. Publication continued well into the 20th century, and was indeed taken over by the CBS in 1899.

951 **Keesing's Contemporary Archives.**
London: Longman, 1931– . weekly.

A weekly diary of important events in all countries including the Netherlands, with texts of speeches and documents, obituaries, statistics, etc. A subject index accumulates quarterly, annually and biennially.

952 **Low Countries Newsletter.**
Edited by S. B. Wolinetz, R. Wakefield. Minneapolis, Minnesota: University of Minnesota, 1981– . biennial.

A short, sometimes irregular, but useful publication with theme articles on all aspects of Low Countries Studies, news of relevant events in the North America academic world, and reviews. Covers the social sciences particularly well.

953 **Maandschrift van het CBS.** (Monthly Bulletin of the CBS.)
The Hague: Staatsuitgeverij, 1905– . monthly.

This is the monthly organ of the Central Bureau of Statistics (CBS) in Voorburg, and contains the latest monthly figures for statistics on nearly all aspects of public affairs. Although published in Dutch, much help is given to foreign readers by the translation of symbols, titles and the like into English.

954 **Maandstatistiek van de Industrie.** (Monthly Bulletin of Industrial Statistics.)
Voorburg, The Netherlands: Central Bureau of Statistics, 1953– . monthly.

A monthly statistical abstract on Dutch industry, grouped into annual volumes, with English translations of headings.

955 **Netherlands International Law Review.**
Leiden; The Hague: Nijhoff, 1954– . quarterly.

This specializes in public and private international law, conflicts of law and, since 1982, comparative law. It is published on behalf of the T. M. C. Asser Instituut (20–22 Alexanderstraat, The Hague), an interuniversity institute representing eight Dutch universities offering courses in international law.

956 **Netherlands Journal of Agricultural Science.**
Wageningen, The Netherlands: Royal Netherlands Society for Agricultural Science, 1953– . quarterly.

Every aspect of agricultural science is covered, especially that which is carried on at the Agricultural University at Wageningen. All the contributions are in English.

957 **Netherlands Journal for Legal Philosophy and Jurisprudence and Proceedings of the Netherlands Association for the Philosophy of Law.**
Zwolle, The Netherlands: Tjeenk Willink, 1971– . biennial.

A biennial of approximately 170 pages devoted to general studies on the philosophy and theories of law and research into the principles of particular legal disciplines. Articles are generally in Dutch, but all contributions (except English) are preceded by English summaries.

958 **Netherlands Journal of Plant Pathology: Tijdschrift over Planteziekten.**
Wageningen, The Netherlands: Netherlands Society for Plant Pathology, 1945– . bimonthly.

The journal covers the whole field of plant diseases and pests, including weed and plant protection in general. Aspects of practical application or local importance are dealt with in the society's Dutch-language journal *Gewasbescherming* (Crop Protection). Only articles submitted by members of the Society of Plant Pathology are published.

959 **Netherlands Journal of Sea Research.**
Executive editor, J. W. de Blok. Texel, The Netherlands: Nederlands Instituut voor Onderzoek der Zee. 1966– . quarterly.

This journal publishes papers dealing mainly with the various fields of marine science, but primarily those concerned with pure research. All articles are written in English. It has an international editorial board.

960 **The Netherlands' Journal of Sociology.**
Amsterdam: Elsevier, 1976– . biennial.

Published for the Netherlands Sociological and Anthropological Society, this journal 'primarily aims to publish translations of selected studies that have previously appeared in the Netherlands.'

961 **Netherlands Journal of Zoology.**
General editor, C. D. N. Barel. Leiden: Brill, 1950– . quarterly.

This contains scientific papers, short notes and communications on zoology in its widest sense, normally by Dutch zoologists writing in English, French or German, preceded by summaries. Each issue contains about fifty pages.

962 **Netherlands Official Statistics: Quarterly Journal of the Central Bureau of Statistics.**
Voorburg, The Netherlands: Central Bureau of Statistics, 1986– . quarterly.

This periodical was launched in 1986 and is intended as an international channel on the development of Dutch official statistics. It contains articles on presentation of official statistics, and brief 'communications' on statistical matters.

963 **Ons Erfdeel.** (Our Heritage.)
Rekkem, Belgium: Stichting Ons Erfdeel, 1957– . bimonthly.

This Dutch-language journal, on general literary, linguistic and cultural topics in the Netherlands and Flanders, includes, annually, a listing of Dutch-language books in translation, and hence provides a continuation of the *Bibliographia Neerlandica* (q.v.).

964 **Planning and Administration.**
Edited by E. M. Harlof. The Hague: International Union of Local Authorities (IULA) and the International Federation for Housing and Planning (IFHP), 1973– . biennial.

A journal which includes articles on the Netherlands among its coverage of planning and administration in countries worldwide.

965 **Planning and Development in the Netherlands: a Periodical on the Initiative of the Netherlands Universities Foundation for International Co-operation (NUFFIC).**
Assen, The Netherlands: Van Gorcum, 1968–82 (with gaps and delays). biennial.

The general subject area is planning, but since the Dutch plan everything, all aspects of modern society were included in the articles of this excellent journal.

966 **Quaerendo.**

Amsterdam: Theatrum Orbis Terrarum, 1971– . quarterly.

A quarterly journal from the Low Countries devoted to manuscripts and printed books. The scholarly articles, which are normally written in English, cover subjects throughout Europe, though favouring the Low Countries.

967 **Rotterdam Europoort Delta.**

Chief editor, Willem C. N. van Horssen. Rotterdam: Municipal Port Authority, 1962– . 5 times a year.

A magazine for the general reader with short, illustrated articles on developments, events and personalities connected with the area from Rotterdam to the coast, and south to the Zeeland coast.

968 **Sociologia Neerlandica.**

Assen, The Netherlands: Van Gorcum, 1962–75. biennial.

Contained translations and English summaries of the most salient Dutch sociological work. There are theoretical articles, and survey articles on the discipline in the Netherlands, but most of the periodical is taken up with empirical studies of social conditions and social policies in the Netherlands.

969 **Statistical Yearbook of the Netherlands.**

The Hague: Staatsuitgeverij; Voorburg, The Netherlands: CBS Publications, 1969– . annual.

Since 1969–70 this compendium of quantitative information has appeared in English. Comparative figures are provided from approximately ten or fifteen years previously. Every aspect of public life is briefly covered. There is an index, and a list of publications by the CBS (Central Bureau of Statistics), with the titles translated into English.

970 **Statistisch Zakboek.** (Statistical Pocketbook.)

The Hague: Staatsuitgeverij; Voorburg, The Netherlands: CBS Publications. 1899– . annual.

This publication is finalized in the autumn of each year, and includes data available up to August of the current year. Every quantifiable aspect of Dutch life is briefly referred to.

971 **Summary of the Annual Report of the National Physical Planning Agency.**

The Hague: Ministry of Housing and Physical Planning. annual.

These annual summaries report on physical planning developments in Europe in general and the Netherlands in particular.

972 **Tijdschrift voor Economische en Sociale Geografie/Journal of Economic and Social Geography.**
Amsterdam: Koninklijk Nederlands Aardrijkskundig Genootschap, vol. 40 (1949)– . five times a year.

Prior to 1949 this was published under the title *Tijdschrift voor Economische Geografie* (Journal of Economic Geography). About one half of the articles nowadays are in English, and the subject matter covers the whole field of economic and social geography. There is a substantial section each year on the Netherlands itself.

973 **Tijdschrift voor Nederlands en Afrikaans.** (Journal for Dutch and Afrikaans.)
Edited by H. Vekeman. Cologne: Lukassen, 1983– . quarterly.

A journal on the language, literature and culture of the Netherlands and South Africa with German and English as the dominant languages of its contributors.

974 **Writing in Holland and Flanders.**
Amsterdam: Foundation for the Promotion of the Translation of Dutch Literary Works, 1960–82. irregular.

This occasional publication (originally a quarterly bulletin, from 1956–59 under the title *Literary Holland*) reviewed current or recent writing in Dutch which was available or could be offered in English translation. Earlier issues generally provided translated excerpts with a short résumé of the whole work. Later issues have featured one or two writers in particular. Economies forced cessation of publication in 1982.

975 **WVC Documentatie.** (WVC Documentation.)
The Hague: Staatsuitgeverij. 1966– . twice monthly.

A systematic survey of books, articles and official publications concerning the very varied areas within the operating field of the Dutch Ministry of Welfare, Health and Cultural Affairs (WVC). Each year a cumulative index (jaarregister) is published covering the twenty-four issues in the preceding twelve months. A useful bibliography on social, cultural and health matters in the Netherlands.

Rijkswaterstaat Communications. (Public Works Communications.)
See item no. 56.

Parlement en kiezer: jaarboek. (Parliament and voter: yearbook.)
See item no. 410.

Central Economic Plan.
See item no. 515.

The Economist (London).
See item no. 519.

Periodicals

The Economist Intelligence Unit Analysis of Economic and Political Trends Every Quarter: Country Report: Netherlands. (Title prior to 1986: EIU Quarterly Economic Review of the Netherlands.)
See item no. 520.

The Economist Intelligence Unit: Country Profile: Netherlands 1986–87.
See item no. 521.

De Nederlandsche Bank n.v.: Quarterly Bulletin.
See item no. 526.

De Nederlandsche Bank n.v.: Annual Report Presented to the General Meeting of Shareholders.
See item no. 527.

Review of the Netherlands Economy: Bank Mees and Hope N.V.
See item no. 533.

The Netherlands Budget Memorandum (Abridged).
See item no. 553.

The Netherlands–British trade directory 1985.
See item no. 568.

The port of Rotterdam in figures.
See item no. 570.

Rotterdam Europoort: general information.
See item no. 574.

Brinkman's Catalogus van Boeken.
See item no. 898.

Centrale catalogus van periodieken en seriewerken in Nederlandse bibliotheken. (Central catalogue of periodicals and serials in Dutch libraries.)
See item no. 991.

Directories

976 **Biografisch woordenboek der Nederlanden.** (Biographical dictionary of the Netherlands.)
Abraham J. van der Aa. Haarlem, The Netherlands: Van Brederode, 1852. 7 vols; reprinted Amsterdam: Israel, 1969.

An absolutely indispensable reference work for biographies up to 1850, since later dictionaries build on it. The author describes it as containing biographies of 'such people as have in any way contributed to the fame of our country'. That 'in any way' is not far from the truth, for he has been remarkably conscientious in researching minor as well as major figures. There are supplements and indexes in the final volume. See also *Biografisch woordenboek van Nederland* and *Nieuw Nederlandsch biografisch woordenboek* (q.v.).

977 **Cassell's encyclopaedia of world literature.**
Edited by J. Buchanan Brown, S. A. Steinberg. London: Cassell, 1973. 2nd ed. 3 vols.

Vol. 1 contains outline literary histories of countries throughout the world and articles on literary subjects. Vols 2 and 3 list biographies of authors and commentaries on anonymous works in alphabetical order. Each volume includes a key to the contributors who are identified in vol. 1. The Dutch contributions are by A. van Elslander, A. M. Barkey Wolf–Berkelbach van der Spenkel, R–F. Lissins, J. J. Mak, R. P. Meijer, J. J. Oversteegen, J. Smit, J. W. Weevers and Th. Weevers. The Frisian contributions are by K. Dykstra and W. E. Collinson.

978 **Biografisch woordenboek van Nederland.** (Biographical dictionary of the Netherlands.)
Edited by J. Charité. Vol. I: The Hague: Nijhoff, 1979; vol. II: Amsterdam: Elsevier, 1985. in progress.

A multi-volume reference work, at present in the process of being published, which will complement the two other main biographical dictionaries, *Biografisch woordenboek der Nederlanden* and *Nieuw Nederlandsch biografisch woordenboek* (q.v.). This version concentrates on those whose deaths occurred after 1910. The listing is alphabetical, from A to Z in each volume. There is no index to vol. I, but vol. II carries an index to both volumes.

979 **Dutch medical biography: a biographical dictionary of Dutch physicians and surgeons 1475–1975.**
G. A. Lindeboom. Amsterdam: Rodopi, 1984. 2243p.

A comprehensive reference book, listing alphabetically the very large number of medical specialists whose biographies are included. A great value of the encyclopaedia is its detailed listing of sources.

980 **Nieuw Nederlandsch biografisch woordenboek.** (New Dutch biographical dictionary.)
P. C. Molhuysen, P. J. Blok, F. K. H. Kossmann. Leiden: Sijthoff, 1937. 10 vols.

The listing is by surname alphabetically from A to Z in each volume. Only those whose deaths occurred before 1910 are included. There is an index. See also *Biografisch woordenboek der Nederlanden* and *Biografisch woordenboek van Nederland* (q.v.).

981 **Benelux abbreviations and symbols: law and related subjects.**
Compiled by Adolf Sprudzs. New York: Oceana, 1971. 129p.

This comprehensive listing gives only the expanded (Dutch or French) version of the items, so that a substantial Dutch–English law dictionary will be needed by the English user.

Aardrijkskundig woordenboek der Nederlanden. (Geographical dictionary of the Netherlands.)
See item no. 27.

Lijst van docenten in de neerlandistiek aan buitenlandse universiteiten en ledenlijst IVN. (List of teachers of Dutch Studies at foreign universities and membership list IVN (International Association for Dutch Studies).)
See item no. 674.

Jewish physicians in the Netherlands, 1600–1940.
See item no. 695.

A guide to Dutch art in America.
See item no. 766.

Venadam bibliotheekgids 1982. (Venadam library guide.)
See item no. 883.

Aarts' letterkundig almanak. (Aarts' literary almanac.)
See item no. 926.

Bibliographies

982 **Bibliografie van de Nederlandse taal- en literatuurwetenschap.** (Bibliography of Dutch language and literature.) Hilda van Assche (et al.). The Hague: Bureau voor de Bibliografie van de Neerlandistiek (BBN), 1975– .

Annual publications are collected in quinquennial volumes: vol. 23, 1965–69; vol. 24, 1970–74; vol. 25, 1975–79. Each volume consists of a systematic listing, including works in Frisian, according to groups identified by decimal classification, and indexes listing journals, subjects and authors. The editorial board, assisted by the staffs of the Archief en Museum voor het Vlaamse Cultuurleven in Antwerp, the Royal Libraries in Brussels and The Hague, and the Nederlandse Letterkundig Museum en Documentatiecentrum in The Hague, produce the bibliography for the Werkgroep voor de Documentatie der Nederlandse Letteren.

983 **Bibliography of the Netherlands Institute for Art.** The Hague: Rijksbureau voor Kunsthistorische Documentatie, 1946– .

With the title 'The bibliography of the Rijksbureau voor Kunsthistorische Documentatie' up to vol. 8, this has now reached the seventeenth volume covering 1973 and 1974. It is divided into four parts: painting, old art; sculpture, old art; arts and crafts, old art; personalia. There is a section on 'sources and bibliography' and a short list of 'general' titles.

984 **Bibliographie Néerlandaise historique-scientifique des ouvrages importants dont les auteurs sont nés aux 16e, 17e et 18e siècles, sur les sciences mathématiques et physiques, avec leur applications.** (Dutch historical-scientific bibliography of the major works of authors born in the 16th, 17th and 18th centuries on the mathematical and physical sciences, and their applications.)
D. Bierens de Haan. Nieuwkoop, The Netherlands: De Graaf, 1965. 424p.

A reprint of the original edition of 1883, in which the entries are arranged alphabetically by author, with a cross-reference index by subject (mathematics, physics, chemistry, mechanics, engineering, astronomy, naval architecture, music, graphics, armaments, philosophy).

985 **Lijst van verkorte titels van boeken gedrukt in de Nederlanden en van Nederlandse boeken tot 1800 in Bedford College Library.**
(Short-title list of books printed in the Low Countries and of Dutch books before 1800 in Bedford College Library.)
Karel Bostoen, Jeannette Huizing. *Dutch Crossing*, vol. 2 (July 1977), p. 26–35.

The books listed here have now been moved to the new location of the Dutch department at University College, London. They are described according to a simplified system that is intended for non-specialists and is summarized under twelve headings (p. 28).

986 **Signalement van boeken gedrukt in de Nederlanden en van Nederlandstalige boeken voor 1800 in de Dutch Church Library te Londen.** (List of books printed in the Low Countries and of Dutch books before 1800 in the Dutch Church Library in London.)
Karel Bostoen. *Dutch Crossing*, supplement to vol. 16 (1982). 53p.

A short-title list of about half of the complete collection of early texts (including manuscripts) in that library, with the recently added classification which runs consecutively on from that given to the early texts in Bedford College Library (see previous item). There is also an index of authors, editors, previous owners and translators, and an index of printers and booksellers.

987 **Leiden imprints 1483–1600 in Leiden University Library and Bibliotheca Thijsiana.**
Compiled by R. Breugelmans. Nieuwkoop, The Netherlands: De Graaf, 1974. 127p.

This is a short-title catalogue modelled on those of the British Library. It has an alphabetical listing of towns and the printers and publishers who are established there.

988 **Bibliografie van de Nederlandse landbouwgeschiedenis.** (Bibliography of Dutch agricultural history.)
W. D. Brouwer. Wageningen, The Netherlands: Centrum voor Landbouwpublikaties en Landbouwdocumentatie, 1975. 2 vols.

The first volume covers work published from 1875 to 1939, and the second from 1940 to 1970. The entries are not annotated, but clearly arranged in thematic sections for easy reference.

989 **Bibliografie der geschiedenis van Nederland.** (Bibliography of the history of the Netherlands.)
H. de Buck. Leiden: Brill, 1968. 712p.

The standard bibliographical work on Dutch history, and the initial point of departure for most research projects. The cut-off date is 1963; classification is by subject, with indexes of authors' names, other personal names, and place-names.

990 **Historical research in the Low Countries 1970–1975: a critical survey.**
Edited by Alice C. Carter, Rosemary Jones, Johanna Kossmann–Putto, K. W. Swart. The Hague: Nijhoff, 1981. 275p. bibliog. (Bibliografische reeks van het Nederlands Historisch Genootschap, no. 1).

A collection of reprints from *Acta Historiae Neerlandicae* (1973–77). Each is a review article of works appearing in a period of one, two or three years, with a full list of references. Full indexes complete this indispensable survey of Dutch historiography, with the emphasis on works in English.

991 **Centrale catalogus van periodieken en seriewerken in Nederlandse bibliotheken.** (Central catalogue of periodicals and serials in Dutch libraries.)
The Hague: Koninklijke Bibliotheek, 1978. 2nd ed. 7 vols.

Contains about 160,000 descriptions of periodicals and serials, including dailies, annuals, and almanacs. It does not include publishers' series and accession lists of libraries. It is not restricted by time or place (the earliest title dates from 1539). International serial numbers could not be included since these were not available when work was started on this catalogue. Annual supplements are published, and there is a cumulative supplement on the years 1978–80 (1981. 2nd ed. 2 vols).

992 **A bibliography of Netherlandic dictionaries: Dutch–Flemish.**
Compiled by Frans M. Claes, foreword by F. de Tollenaere. Munich: Kraus International Publications, 1980. 314p. (World Bibliography of Dictionaries, no. 5).

A comprehensive listing of monolingual, bilingual and multilingual dictionaries, including abbreviations, synonym, rhyming, reverse, technical and slang dictionaries with an author and language index, from the earliest publications up to 1979.

993 **A critical survey of studies on Dutch colonial history.**
W. P. Coolhaas, revised by G. J. Schutte. The Hague: Nijhoff, 1980. 2nd ed. 264p. (Koninklijk Instituut voor Taal-, Land- en Volkenkunde Bibliographical Series, 4).

The first edition of 1960 has been thoroughly revised and updated. The bibliography is analytical-descriptive in form, grouped by subject, while three indexes by year, personal names and placenames provide excellent access. This is an indispensable source of reference.

994 **A survey of Dutch drama before the Renaissance.**
H. van Dijk, W. M. H. Hummelen, W. Hüsken, E. Strietman. *Dutch Crossing*, vol. 22 (1984), p. 97–131.

There are two sections on (a) Hummelen's *Repertorium van het rederijkersdrama 1500–c.1620* (Catalogue of Rhetoricians drama) (1968), and (b) plays discovered since 1968. They introduce a supplement to the *Repertorium*, following the same format with alphabetical lists of locations of the texts, authors, copyists and owners, *dramatis personae*, technical terms, systematic groupings, consulted works and titles of plays.

995 **Bibliografie van het Nederlandse belastingwezen.** (Bibliography of the Dutch tax system.)
Emma Dronckers. Amsterdam: Veen, 1954–55. 2 vols.

This bibliography of works mainly in the Dutch language covers taxation in the periods 1940–46 (vol. 1) and 1947–52 (vol. 2). The arrangement is systematic, with indexes for access.

996 **Labor relations in the Netherlands: a bibliography.**
Donald P. Goodman. Monticello, Illinois: Vance Bibliographies, 1979. 16p. (Public Administration Series: Bibliography P–261).

An unannotated list of books and articles of the 1960s and 1970s. Most entries are in English. Goodman is with the Business Administration College at Niagara University.

997 **Select bibliography of works in English on the economic history of the Netherlands from the sixteenth to the nineteenth century.**
R. T. Griffiths, J. I. Israel, M. J. Wintle. *Dutch Crossing*, vol. 30 (Dec. 1986), p. 112–27.

An unannotated alphabetical listing of English-language publications on this subject: a handy starting point for those launching into the subject, and a checklist for those already well versed in the material. The authors intend to publish occasional updates.

998 **A short-title catalogue of books printed at Hoorn before 1701.**
J. A. Gruys, C. de Wolf. Nieuwkoop, The Netherlands: De Graaf, 1979. 125p. (Bibliotheca Neerlandica: 12).

An introduction describes the short-title catalogue, Netherlands (STCN) of which this is an example. This is an ambitious plan to extend the work of Campbell, Nijhoff and Kronenberg which should be completed in two stages: the 17th century within ten years, the remainder within a further fifteen years.

999 **Bibliografie van de stedengeschiedenis van Nederland.**
(Bibliography of the urban history of the Netherlands.)
G. van Herwijnen, W. G. van der Moer, M. Carasso–Kok, M. J. J. G. Chappin. Leiden: 1978. 355p. map.

This listing of over 3,000 books and articles on Dutch towns and urban development is divided into sections according to province, preceded by a general section, which includes recent general histories specifically dealing with urban history. There are indexes of places and personal names.

1000 **Rudolf Agricola: a bibliography of printed works and translation.**
Gerda C. Huisman. Nieuwkoop, The Netherlands: De Graaf, 1985. 262p.

To commemorate the quincentenary of the famous humanist Agricola's death (1444–85). This bibliography, with indexes, date and place of publication and names of printers, does not always include the present location of the works listed.

1001 **Bibliography of Dutch seventeenth century political thoughts: an annotated inventory, 1581–1710.**
G. O. van de Klashorst. Amsterdam: APA/Holland University Press, 1986. 162p.

This remedies the lack of publications on important contributors to this field other than Grotius and Spinoza. It contains a listing of 361 publications, annotated and chronologically arranged, with references to the libraries holding copies of the publications, and an index.

1002 **Bibliografie van de geschriften op het gebied van de Nederlandse taalkunde uit de periode 1691–1804.** (Bibliography of writings on Dutch language from the period 1691–1804.)
Compiled by J. Knol (vol. 2), M. Maas (vols 1 and 2). Vol. 1: Nijmegen, The Netherlands: Katholieke Universiteit, 1977; vol. 2: Amsterdam: Amsterdam Free University, 1978.

A provisional listing of publications 1550–1690 (vol. 1) and 1691–1804 (vol.2), excluding dissertations. A final version will add those articles from journals not so far included.

1003 **Atlantes Neerlandici: bibliography of terrestrial, maritime and celestial atlases and pilot books, published in the Netherlands up to 1880.**
Compiled by C. Koeman. Amsterdam: Theatrum Orbis Terrarum, 1967. 5 vols. Vol. VI (compiled by C. Koeman and H. J. A. Homan): Alphen, The Netherlands: Canaletto, 1985.

The listings are alphabetical, giving the location of rare items. The fifth volume indexes the following subjects in separate sections: terrestrial atlases, sea-atlases, rutters and pilot books (all in chronological order), personal names of cartographers, engravers, map-authors and publishers, and geographical names. Vol. VI brings the listing up to 1940, provides corrections and a supplement to vols I–V and a bibliography of atlases, 1880–1940.

1004 **Historical research in the Low Countries 1981–1983: a critical survey.**
Edited by Joanna Kossmann–Putto, E. Witte. Leiden: Brill, 1985. 117p. bibliog.

From 1973 to 1982 a critical survey of the latest historical work on the Netherlands and Belgium appeared in the journal *Acta Historiae Neerlandicae/ Low Countries History Yearbook*. This volume carries on that survey, after the demise of the journal, for the years 1981, 1982 and 1983.

1005 **The Netherlands: a selective bibliography of reference works.**
Margritt B. Krewson. Washington, DC: Library of Congress, 1986. 42p.

A very brief and fleeting glimpse, especially considering that the Library of Congress claims to have 100,000 volumes in its Dutch collections. Some extraordinary exclusions and mystifying inclusions. There is no comment on the 166 items listed, and no cross-referencing, but an index and a useful list of institutions (in the United States) dealing with the Netherlands are included. A lightweight but useful starting point.

1006 **Guide to Netherlandic studies: bibliography.**
Walter Lagerwey. Grand Rapids, Michigan: Calvin College, 1964. mimeographed. 169p.

This is a revision of the author's earlier 'Guide to Dutch Studies' of 1961, and as well as a general update it includes books on Northern Belgium, or Flanders: hence the change from 'Dutch' to 'Netherlandic'. The titles are not annotated, and include both Dutch and English material. The largest section is on the Dutch language, although all subjects are covered. The list is now very dated, and was never very available, being mimeographed rather than published. Useful nevertheless.

1007 **Emblem books in the Low Countries, 1554–1949.**
John Landwehr. Utrecht: Haentjens Dekker & Gumbert, 1972.

A listing, alphabetically by author (preceded by a chronological list of titles), of emblem books by authors of any nationality and in any language, printed in the Low Countries during four centuries.

1008 **Fable-books printed in the Low Countries: a concise bibliography until 1800.**
John Landwehr. Nieuwkoop, The Netherlands: De Graaf, 1963. 43p.

This is a first, and hence not exhaustive listing of fable-literature up to the time that it became primarily children's reading. It does not include political fables, most of which are published in pamphlet form. There is an index of publishers, printers, booksellers and illustrators.

1009 **Splendid ceremonies: state entries and royal funerals in the Low Countries, 1515–1791.**
John Landwehr. Nieuwkoop, The Netherlands: De Graaf; Leiden: Sijthoff, 1971. 206p.

This bibliography lists the royal persons concerned, with biographical notes and plates, the cities taking part and the dates of their ceremonies, a chronological listing of the contemporary descriptions and full-page contemporary engravings of the ceremonies.

1010 **Referentiewerken voor de studie van de hedendaagse samenleving.**
(Reference works for the study of present-day society.)
C. Lis, P. vanden Eeckhout. Zutphen, The Netherlands: Terra, 1982. 319p.

A guide to reference works in the social sciences, with strong emphasis on Belgian and Dutch material. Arrangement by form, e.g. bibliographies, encyclopaedias, is unhelpful, forcing the user to rely heavily on the subject index. But a useful aid to finding information on Dutch studies.

1011 **National population bibliography of the Netherlands, 1945–1979.**
Edited by Han G. Moors. The Hague: published for the International Union for the Scientific Study of Population by the Netherlands Interuniversity Demographic Institute, 1981. 647p.

This huge listing covers every aspect of demography. The entries are briefly annotated, there are indexes by author and place-name, and the chapter division provides a thematic inroad to the material.

1012 **Bibliographia Neerlandica.**
Compiled by P. M. Morel, A. M. P. Mollema. The Hague: Nijhoff, 1962. 598p.

This contains books on the Netherlands in foreign languages, 1940–57, and translations of Dutch books, 1900–57. A shortcoming of this volume is the absence of Dutch literature from Belgium, and this is remedied in the sequels to this, published as: *Het Nederlandse boek in vertaling* (q.v.). Thereafter, lists of translations are published annually in *Ons Erfdeel* (q.v.).

1013 **Nederland: een selectief overzicht leverbare titels, U aangeboden door Broese Kemink b.v.** (The Netherlands: a selective survey of available titles, presented by Broese Kemink b.v.)
Utrecht: Broese Kemink, 1986. 51p.

A useful checklist of books on the Netherlands offered for sale by Broese Kemink b.v. (Stadhuisbrug, Utrecht), one of the largest booksellers in the country. Titles in all languages are included. The division into sections is thematic, including history, geography, politics, law, art, reference works, etc.

1014 **Newspapers in microform: foreign countries 1948–1972.**
Washington, DC: Library of Congress, 1973. 269p.

Lists are by country and by title; Dutch newspapers current in 1973 are also listed here.

1015 **Molenbibliografie.** (Bibliography on mills.)
P. Nijhof. Zutphen, The Netherlands: Walberg Pers, 1982. 219p.

The last word on mills of all shapes and sizes. It is, though, only a listing, without annotation. The chapters deal firstly with thematic, then with regional listings.

1016 **Nederlandse bibliografie van 1500–1540.** (Dutch bibliography from 1500–1540.)
Wouter Nijhoff, M. E. Kronenberg. The Hague: Nijhoff, 1965–71. 3 vols and supplements.

Lists by printer and publisher, and provides addresses where no name of the printer/publisher is given, and pseudonyms with systematic and alphabetical indexes. There is an introduction to the third volume (175p.) with emendations showing dubious titles, those printed before 1500 or after 1540, and other errata and supplements (in six fascicules).

1017 **Arts and economics.**
Tineke Pronk. Amsterdam: Boekman Foundation, 1982. 111p.

This compilation marks the government's support of the Boekman Foundation library to establish a special collection of books in this field and also the International Conference on Cultural Economics and Planning. The alphabetical listing of authors and titles is by subject, under six headings: 'Theory of economics and culture', 'Government support for the arts; theory and practice',

'Fundraising/private support', 'Management', 'Economics and the arts', and 'Bibliographies'. There is a reference index of authors' names.

1018 **Het Nederlandse boek in vertaling.** (The Dutch book in translation.)
Compiled by E. van Raan. The Hague: Staatsuitgeverij, 1958–67, 1968–72, 1973– .

In 1962 *Bibliographia Neerlandica* (q.v.) contained translations of Dutch works 1900–57 into foreign languages. The bibliography has subsequently been maintained as a rubric in *Ons Erfdeel* (q.v.), and annual volumes are published by the Staatsuitgeverij at The Hague. The subject headings are: general; libaries and book production; philosophy; religion; social sciences; politics; law; fine art; music; theatre; dance; film; language and literature; childrens literature; history; folklore; education; sport; and miscellaneous.

1019 **Repertorium van boeken en tijdschriftartikelen betreffende de geschiedenis van Nederland.** (Repertorium of books and periodical articles concerning the history of the Netherlands.)
Publication varies. Lately, The Hague: Nijhoff. 1941– . irregular. The most recent issue, compiled by T. S. H. Bos, covered publications in 1984 (The Hague: Nijhoff, 1986. 456p.).

A classified listing of publications on Dutch history, with full indexes. An indispensable research tool.

1020 **Short title catalogue of books printed in the Netherlands and Belgium and of Dutch and Flemish books printed in other countries from 1470 to 1600 now in the British Museum.**
London: British Museum, 1965. 274p.

An author catalogue, with the headings of the General Catalogue of Printed Books (in the British Library). Anonymous books are listed under any proper name in the title or, failing this, under the first noun in the title. Titles are simplified by rational abbreviation. There is an index of printers and publishers.

1021 **Science research and public policy making.**
The Hague: Foundation for Educational Research (SVO), 1981. 49p.

This is a bibliography prepared for the international Foundation for Educational Research workshop on this topic held in 1981. It lists publications 1970–81 in English, French, German, Spanish and Dutch. An appendix gives abstracts of all the bibliographical entries.

1022 **Vondel in English: a bibliography.**
Paul F. Vincent. *Dutch Crossing*, vol. 8 (1979), p. 87–89.

This gives precise details of whole works and fragments translated in various publications from 1824 to 1978.

1023 **Godsdienst en kerk in Nederland, 1945–1980; een geannoteerde bibliografie van sociaal-wetenschappelijke en historische literatuur over de godsdienstige en kerkelijke ontwikkelingen in Nederland.** (Religion and church in the Netherlands, 1945–1980: an annotated bibliography of social-scientific and historical literature on the religious and ecclesiastical developments in the the Netherlands).

J. P. A. van Vugt. Baarn, The Netherlands: Ambo, 1981. 400p.

This useful handbook has two opening chapters concerning the developments in the sociology of religion since the Second World War, and then presents a review of the major publications in each thematic area of the subject in the period 1945–80. A short chapter points to the lacunae in the published work, and then the main bibliography follows in the form of a more or less complete listing, year by year. Indexes to author and subject make this chronological listing easily accessible.

1024 **Een voorlopige bibliografie over het thema 'verzuiling'.** (A provisional bibliography on the theme 'vertical pluralism'.)

J. P. A. van Vugt. Nijmegen, The Netherlands: 1980. 13p.

This unannotated list is more or less a collection of the references cited in various papers and essays produced by staff and students in Nijmegen University, 1978–80. Not exhaustive, nor very informative, but a good starting point for anyone wishing to work on topics related to 'verzuiling'.

1025 **A guide to foreign language grammars and dictionaries.**

Edited by A. J. Walford. London: Library Association, 1977. 3rd rev. ed. 240p.

The Dutch section, p. 124–30, though now seriously dated, contains a number of technical dictionaries not separately included in this survey.

Collections of maps and atlases in the Netherlands.
See item no. 64.

Doctoraal scripties geschiedenis 1980–1984. (Dissertations for the degree of Doctorandus in history 1980–1984.)
See item no. 97.

Zigeuners, woonwagenbewoners en reizenden: een bibliografie. (Gypsies, caravan-dwellers and travellers: a bibliography.)
See item no. 240.

Overzicht onderzoek minderheden, deel I: onderzoek minderheden 1980–1985: een geselecteerde bibliografie. (Survey of research on minorities, part I: research on minorities 1980–1985: a select bibliography.) **Deel II: samenvattingen van verslagen van achttien interdepartmentale onderzoeksprojecten met betrekking tot minderheden.** (Part II: Summaries of reports from eighteen interdepartmental research projects concerning minorities.)
See item no. 246.

Dutch and Afrikaans.
See item no. 273.

Rural community studies in the Netherlands.
See item no. 361.

Current issues in anthropology: the Netherlands.
See item no. 363.

Health in the Netherlands: publications in foreign languages.
See item no. 384.

Systematic list of publications 1986.
See item no. 646.

Dutch–American bibliography, 1693–1794.
See item no. 902.

Copy and print in the Netherlands: an atlas of historical biography.
See item no. 904.

Incunabula in Dutch libraries.
See item no. 913.

Acta Historiae Neerlandicae/Low Countries History Yearbook.
See item no. 927.

Historia Agriculturae.
See item no. 943.

Ons Erfdeel. (Our Heritage.)
See item no. 963.

WVC Documentatie. (WVC Documentation.)
See item no. 975.

Index

The index is a single alphabetical sequence of authors (personal and corporate), titles of publications and subjects. Index entries refer both to the main items and to other works mentioned in the notes to each item. Title entries are in italics. Numeration refers to the items as numbered.

For personal names with a prefix, e.g. J. de Jong, see under the main stem of the name, viz. Jong, J. de (this applies to all prefixes: van, den, van den, uit den, 't, etc.).

A

A. A. G. Bijdragen 925
Aa, A. J. van der 27, 976
Aardrijkskundig woordenboek der Nederlanden 27
Aarts' letterkundig almanak 926
Abbe, H. van 894
Abbreviations 256, 981
Abcoude 818
Abele spelen 726
Abert, J. G. 510
Abkoude, J. van 898
Abma, R. 626
Absenteeism 397
Academic economics in Holland 1800-1870 154
Accentuation 286, 293, 300
Access to justice: a world survey 441
Accounting 537, 548, 557
Acda, J. W. 914
Achterhoek 223
1899-1979: tachtig jaren statistiek in tijdsreeksen 643
Acidification in the Netherlands: effects and policies 471
Acronyms 256
Acta Historiae Neerlandicae 927, 990, 1004
Acta Politica: Tijdschrift voor Politicologie 928
Adam in ballingschap 711
Adam International Review 723
Adaptation of migrants from the Caribbean in the European and American metropolis 232
Adat law in Indonesia 436
Adjustment after migration: a longitudinal study of the process of adjustment by refugees to a new environment 238
Administration 964
Adult education 291, 647, 651, 661, 668, 671
Adversary politics and electoral reform 402
Advertising 529
Adviescommissie Onderzoek Minderheden 246
Africa 197-198, 876, 973
Afrikaans 273, 305, 973
Aged, The 7, 350, 368, 393
Agricola, R. 1000
Agricultural geography 603
Agricultural science in the Netherlands (including the former guide 'Wageningen: Centre of Agricultural Science') 1985-1987 601
Agriculture 13, 30, 39, 82, 169, 174, 176, 179, 223, 254, 259, 355, 601-613, 943, 956, 988

Air force 619
Air photography and Celtic field research in the Netherlands 82
Air transport 616, 620, 622-623, 625, 685
Airports 625
Akkerman, B. 794
Akkerman, F. 833
Albach, B. 884
Albert Verwey and English romanticism 751
Alexander I of Russia 580
Algemene geschiedenis der Nederlanden 88
Alienation 735
Aljechin, A. A. 861
All of one company: the VOC in biographical perspective 182
All the paintings of the Rijksmuseum in Amsterdam 776
Allart, J. 899
Allochtonen in Nederland: beschouwingen over de gerepatrieerden, Molukkers, Surinamers, Antilleanen, buitenlandse werknemers, Chinezen, vluchtelingen, buitenlandse studenten in onze samenleving 249
Almanacs 410, 902, 926, 991
Almere 19
Almere-Haven 19
Aloofness and neutrality: studies on Dutch foreign relations and policy-making institutions 509
Alpers, S. 752
Alphen, O. van. 1
Ambassadors and secret agents: the diplomacy of the first Earl of Malmesbury at The Hague 106
Ambonese 241
American law 453
Americans 230
Amersfoort, H. van 228, 239
Amersfoort Evangelical College 326
Amis, K. 737
Ampzing, S. 756
Amro Bank 564
Amsterdam 1, 6, 8, 22, 25, 34, 48, 103, 120, 148, 161, 171, 187, 228, 232, 243, 322, 338, 365, 369-370, 443, 456, 460, 474, 556, 558, 582, 614, 615, 625, 683, 720, 727, 756-757, 764, 804, 848, 874, 878, 884, 891, 895, 899, 903
Amsterdam canal guide 25
Amsterdam Historical Museum 187, 243
Amsterdam 1950-1959 1
Amsterdam: the planning and development in a nutshell 456
Amsterdam School 804
Amsterdam Theatre Museum 884
Amsterdam University 228, 474, 848
Amsterdam University Library 848
Anabaptism 309, 329, 331
Anarchism 415
Anatomy 76
Anbeek, T. 721, 737
Anderen 362
Anderson, Gavin & Co. 530, 534
Andeweg, R. B. 371
Anglo-Dutch contribution to the civilization of modern society: an Anglo-Netherlands symposium 857
Anglo-Dutch relations 108, 111, 124, 494, 566, 819, 834, 841, 844, 851, 853-854, 857-858, 929
Anglo-Dutch relations and European unity, 1940-1948 494
Anglo-Dutch trade flows 1955-75: their effects on, and consequences for, Dutch port development and planning 566
Anglo-Dutch Wars 124
Animals 76
Anker, M. C. in 't 485
'Annales' School 99
Anne Frank: the diary of a young girl 727
Anne Frank Foundation 239
Annotata anatomica 683
Annoyance in the dwelling environment due to cumulative environmental noises: a literature study 479
Anthropology 362-363, 960
Anti-Catholicism 319
Anti-Semitism 131, 832
Antilleans 247, 249
Antilles 191-192
Antiquities 892
Antwerp 161, 582, 614, 756, 982
Appel, K. 794
Apprenticeship 661

Arabic 279
Archaeology 70, 78-85, 606, 809-810
Archief en Museum voor het Vlaamse Cultuurleven 982
Architecture 22-23, 25, 29, 183, 563, 758, 796-797, 801, 805, 837, 934
marine 984
Archives 820, 871-877, 882, 895
Aristotle 841
Armando 794
Arminians 308, 336, 675
Arminius 308, 317
Arminius: a study in the Dutch Reformation 317
Army 382
Arnhem 132, 886, 890
Arrenburg, R. 898
Art 6, 21, 23, 72, 119-120, 318, 752-832, 835, 858, 934, 963, 983-984
modern 764, 777, 794, 798, 890
Art of describing: Dutch art in the seventeenth century 752
Art of Dutch cooking 866
Art history 756, 762-763, 765-768, 776, 779, 782, 784, 786-788, 791, 795, 806, 810-811, 891, 936, 983
Arts 13, 141, 310, 752-832, 935, 938, 1012, 1017-1018
Arts and economics 1017
Arts in research: the structural position of research in post-secondary music and drama education 665
Artz, A. 785
Ashton, R. K. 537
Ashworth, G. J. 38
Asia 189, 205, 579, 877, 892
Asimov, I. 730
Assche, H. van 982
Asser, T. M. C. 955
Asser Institute 440
Association Internationale d'Histoire des Mers Nordiques de l'Europe 582
Association for the Preservation of Windmills 686
Astronomy 682-683, 691, 984
At spes non fracta: Hope & Co., 1717-1815: merchant bankers and diplomats at work 541
Athenae Batavae: the University of Leiden 1575-1975 670
Atlanta 398
Atlantes Neerlandici: bibliography of terrestrial, maritime and celestial atlases and pilot books published in the Netherlands up to 1880 1003
Atlas 60-61, 63-66, 1003
Atlas van Nederland/Atlas of the Netherlands 60
De atlas van Nederland 61
Attman, A. 150
Austin Friars 333, 986
Austin Friars: history of the Dutch Reformed Church in London 333
Australia 199-200, 388
Australia unveiled: the share of the Dutch navigators in the discovery of Australia 200
Austria 388, 414, 786, 860
Automatic semantic interpretation: a computer model of understanding national language 284
Averkamp, A. 795
Aymard, M. 151
AIDS 398

B

Baard, H. P. 769
Bachrach, A. G. H. 834
Badings, H. 817, 825
Baehr, P. R. 487, 500
Bagley, C. 229
Bakel, J. van 284
Bakels, C. C. 78
Baker, V. J. 230
Bakhuizen van den Brink, R. C. 73
Bakker, G. 807
Bakker, J. A. 79
Bakker, N. 939
Bakker, W. T. 50
Bakvis, H. 399
Baljeu, J. 796
Ballegeer, F. J. A. 271
Ballet 823
Baltic 582
Bangs, C. 317
Bangs, J. D. 753, 818, 835
Bank, J. 325, 341
Bank Mees and Hope N. V. 533
Bank solvency regulation and deposit insurance in the U. S. and the Netherlands 544

Banking 453, 524, 526-527, 533, 538, 540-542, 544-545, 564, 567, 574, 857
Bannier, J. H. 933
Barel, C. D. N. 961
Barents, R. 511
Barkey Wolk-Berkelbach van der Spenkel, A. M. 977
Barlaeus, C. 836, 848
Barnouw, A. J. 726
Baroque 675, 762
Bartels, C. P. A. 512
Bartels, D. 231
Barth, J. 741
Baruch Spinoza and western democracy 842
Basia 719
Bassand, J. B. 696
Basson, T. 901
Batavian Revolution 116
Bath, B. H. Slicher van 176
Baudet, H. 152, 156, 181
Baudin, F. 896
Bavinck, H. 318
Bax, J. 562
Baysse, M. 729
Beardsmore, H. B. 250
Beast epic 726, 738, 740
Beatrice of Nazareth 735
Becker, J. W. 458, 485
Bedford College, London 985
Beek, B. van 539
Beek, B. L. van 80
Beek, J. M. van der 453
Beek, L. 690
Beekman, E. M. 75, 699, 716, 734
Beeldende kunst in Limburg 754
Beeren, W. 755
Begijnhof Church 322
Beijer, G. 349
Beijers, J. L. 878
Belcampo 730
Beld, C. A. van den 517
Belgic Confession 313
Belgium 6, 31, 38, 86, 88, 92-93, 161-163, 169-170, 209, 306, 367, 411, 421, 424, 463, 488, 505-506, 539, 583, 593, 612, 644, 689, 700, 722, 809, 882, 896, 900, 905, 927, 992, 1004, 1006, 1010, 1020
Belifante, J. C. E. 885
Bellefroid, E. 768
Benelux 31, 38, 92, 381, 408, 411, 508, 583, 644, 689, 981
Benelux abbreviations and symbols: law and related subjects 981
Benelux conference: September 1977 411
Benelux countries: an historical survey 92
Benelux: an economic geography of Belgium, the Netherlands and Luxembourg 38
Benelux statistieken/statistiques: tijdreeksen/series retrospectives 1948-1974 644
Die Beneluxstaaten: eine geographische Länderkunde 31
Bennis, H. 294
Benthem Jutting, W. S. S. van 480
Bergeijk, G. A. van 427
Bergen 768
Bergen, J. E. J. van 664
Bergh, S. van den 598
Berlage, H. P. 802-804
Berlin 133, 789
Bernlef, J. 729
Bertelsmeier, E. 49
Bertin, E. C. 730
Beukema, F. 294
Beuningen, D. G. van 887
Bible 315, 762
Bible and theology in the Netherlands: Dutch Old Testament criticism under modernist and conservative auspices 1850 to World War I 315
Bibliografie der geschiedenis van Nederland 989
Bibliografie van de geschriften op het gebied van de Nederlandse taalkunde uit de periode 1691-1804 1002
Bibliografie van het Nederlandse belastingwezen 995
Bibliografie van de Nederlandse landbouwgeschiedenis 988
Bibliografie van de Nederlandse taal- en literatuurwetenschap 982
Bibliografie van de stedengeschiedenis van Nederland 999
Bibliographia Neerlandica 1012
Bibliographie Néerlandaise historique-scientifique des ouvrages importants dont les auteurs sont

nés aux 16e, 17e 18e siècles, sur les sciences mathématiques et physiques, avec leur applications 984
Bibliographies 64, 97, 240-241, 246, 273, 361, 384, 386, 421, 433-434, 508, 642, 687, 701, 721, 731-732, 791, 796, 902, 904, 913, 927, 943, 963, 975, 982-1025
Bibliography of Dutch seventeenth century political thoughts: an annotated inventory, 1581-1710 1001
Bibliography of Netherlandic dictionaries: Dutch-Flemish 992
Bibliography of the Netherlands Institute for Art 983
Bibliology 986, 998
Bibliotheca Neerlandica 735
Bibliotheca Thijsiana 987
Bierens de Haan, D. 984
Bierstadt, O. B. 89
Biervliet, W. E. 232
Bijdragen en Mededelingen betreffende de Geschiedenis der Nederlanden 626
Bilders, A. G. 785
Bi-lingual codebooks of the questionnaire Dutch member of parliament 1979/80 446
Bilingual education in Friesland 663
Bilingualism 299, 663
Bindoff, S. T. 28, 488
Bing, V. 2
Binneveld, H. 378
Binneveld, J. M. W. 627
Biografisch woordenboek van Nederland 978
Biografisch woordenboek der Nederlanden 976
Biographies 26, 105-106, 111, 121, 125, 129, 691, 693, 695, 697-699, 705, 710, 713, 717, 719, 722, 728, 759-760, 764, 768, 770, 781, 783-784, 790, 804, 822, 827, 846, 859, 901, 904, 926, 976-980
Biology 53, 70, 480
Bird, R. B. 281
Birnbaum, E. 53
Birth of New York: Nieuw Amsterdam: 1624-1664 187
Blaauwen, A. L. den 808
Black economy 232, 514, 549
Blaeu, J. 65
Blake, W. 751
Blaman, A. 724
Blancquaert, E. 295
Blanken, M. 379
Blankert, A. 770-722
Bläsing, J. F. E. 576
Blijstra, R. 730, 797
Bloch, D. A. 242
Blockmans-Delva, A. 101
Blockmans, W. P. 101
Blok, D. P. 88
Blok, F. F. 836
Blok, J. W. de 959
Blok, P. J. 89, 91, 980
Blok, W. 939
Blokker, J. 828
Blom, I. 563
Blom, J. C. H. 127
Blume, S. S. 679
Blussé, L. 182
Bodenheimer, S. J. 489
Boek, bibliotheek en geesteswetenschappen 907
Boeke, W. 730
Boer, H. de 251
Boer, J. 361
Boer, P. M. C. de 513
Boerhaave, H. 687, 690, 696-698
Boerhaave's correspondence 696
Boerhaave's men, at Leyden and after 698
Boeschoten, W. C. 514
Boëthius, A. M. S. 704
Bogaard, H. van den 8
Bol, F. 770
Het bommelfilmboek 865
Bone, R. C. 400
Bontekoe, W. 732
Bood, E. G. de 251
Boogaart, E. van den 183
Boogaart, P. C. uit den 252
Boogman, J. C. 128-129, 490, 837
Booij, G. 285
Book of tulips 72
Book through five thousand years 896
Bookbinding 896-897, 904
Books 869, 896-913, 926, 966, 985, 987, 1013
Bool, F. H. 792

Boon, L.-P. 724, 730, 741
Boon, M. 665
Boorsma, P. B. 380
Bornewasser, J. A. 319-320, 325
Bornford, D. 756
Bos, H. J. M. 691
Bos, R. W. J. M. 153
Bos, T. S. H. 1019
Bosboom, J. 785
Bosch, H. 767, 887
Bosch, S. van den 666
Bosman, H. W. J. 540
Bostoen, K. 985-986
Boston 808
Botany 71, 77, 254, 696-698, 958
Boutens, P. C. 718
Boxer, C. R. 184
Boymans-Van Beuningen Museum 887
Boymans, F. J. O. 887
Braak, M. ter 703
Braam, G. P. A. 350
Brachin, P. 305-306, 939
Brandt Corstius, J. 700
Brandt, R. 81
Brandt, R. W. 80
Bratt, J. D. 321
Bray, D. de 897
Brazil 183
Bredero, G. A. 725, 733
Bredius, A. 773
Bree, C. van 939
Breitner, G. H. 781
Breugelmans, R. 987
Bridges 688
Brigham, J. E. 793
Brinkman's Catalogus van Boeken 898
Britain 91, 95, 106, 108, 150, 155, 189, 192, 205, 229, 322, 339, 370-371, 388, 391, 428, 442, 455, 457, 489, 494, 504, 537, 566, 594, 598, 602, 691, 694, 698, 714, 737-738, 743, 745-746, 748-749,751, 801, 819, 834, 840, 844, 851, 853-854, 857-858, 912, 929
Britain and the Netherlands 91, 127-128, 136, 147, 165, 181, 205, 319, 325, 341, 490, 929
British Academy 857
British law 453
British Library 987, 1020
British Overseas Trade Board 569
Broadcasting 914, 917-920, 923-924
Broadcasting in the Netherlands 917
Broadsides 869
Brockway, J. 735
Broeck, F. van den 794, 802
Broecke, M. van den 286
Broekhoff, J. 860
Broese Kemink 1013
Bromley, J. S. 128, 147, 165, 181, 205, 319, 490
Bronckhorst, A. van 433
Brongers, J. A. 82
Broos, B. 771
Broos, T. 705, 899
Brotherton, A. 735
Brouwer, W. D. 988
Brown University, Rhode Island 777
Brown, C. 756, 774
Browne, Sir T. 841, 853
Brueghel, P. 887
Bruggenkate, K. ten 253
Bruijn, J. R. 577
Brumble, H. D. 725
Brunt, L. 342
Bruyn Kops, J. L. de 941
Bruyn, J. 775
Buchanan Brown, J. 977
Buck, H. de 989
Buddingh', C. 728-729
Budget 553, 661
Buikstra-De Boer, M. 776
Buissink, J. D. 208
Buist, M. G. 541
Buiting, B. 382
Bulb-growing 355
Bulgaria 503
Bulhof, F. 272, 700
Bulletin van de KNOB 753
Bullion 150
Bumble filmbook 865
Bunyan, J. 841
Bureaucracy 395
Burg, H. van der 628
Burggraaff, M. 485
Burgundian Netherlands 101
Burgundians 99, 101-102, 841, 851
Burial rites 85
Burke, G. L. 29
Burke, P. 103, 838
Burket, J. 879
Burkunk, W. 730
Burnchurch, R. de 90
Burning fen 67

Business code 439, 455
Business law 453
Business management 452-453, 455
Buskes, J. J. 130
Butot, L. J. M. 480
Butter, I. H. 154
Buyten, L. van 161

C

Cabinets 410
Cable and satellite yearbook 1985 916
Cahen, J. J. 22
Calvin, J. 313, 335
Calvinism 18, 107, 172, 310-311, 315-317, 321-323, 325, 332, 336, 339, 342, 348, 378, 838, 915
Calvinism: six Stone Lectures 310
Calvinist preaching and iconoclasm in the Netherlands 1544-1569 107
Cambridge 308
Campbell, M. F. A. G. 998
Campen, S. I. P. van 491
Camper, P. 76
Campert, R. 1
Campfens, H. 233
Canada 218, 222, 227, 233, 388, 930
Canadian Journal of Netherlandic Studies/Revue Canadienne d'Études Néerlandaises 930
Canals 25, 42
Cape of Good Hope, 1652-1702: the first fifty years of Dutch colonisation as seen by callers 198
Capital 95, 153, 204, 453, 533
Capital markets 538, 541-543, 551, 556, 581-582
Cappalletti, M. 441
Carasso-Kok, M. 999
Caravan-dwellers 240
Caribbean 190-191
Carlson-Thies, S. W. 337
Carmiggelt, S. 730
Carriers of Europe: a concise history of Holland 98
Carter, A. C. 104, 155, 322, 492, 841, 990
Cartesianism 691, 693
Cartography 65, 67, 1003
Casimir, H. B. G. 667
Caspar Barlaeus: from the correspondence of a melancholic 836
Cassell's encyclopaedia of world literature 977
Catalogue of paintings by artists born before 1870, vol. VII: seventeenth-century North Netherlandish still lifes 784
Catechism 312
Catharijne Convent 893
Catholic power in the Netherlands 399
Catholics 319, 325, 341, 343-344, 346-347, 399
Cats, J. 733
Cauwenberghe, E. van 612
Cazaux, Y. 105
CBS (Central Bureau of Statistics) 219, 535, 570, 643, 646, 950, 954, 962, 969-970
Celibaat 735
Celtic fields 82
Central America 67
Central Bureau of Statistics *see* CBS
Central Economic Plan 515
Central Planning Office 515, 517
Centrale catalogus van periodieken en seriewerken in Nederlandse bibliotheken 991
Centre for the History of Europe 182
Centre for Information on Language Teaching and Research *see* CILT
Century of Dutch manuscript illumination 900
Ceramics 764, 766, 813-814
Ceremonies 850, 1009
Chabot, H. 768
Chamber of Commerce 567-568
Champa, K. S. 777
Chang, T. M. 668
Changing countryside: proceedings of the first British-Dutch symposium on rural geography 30
Changing economy in Indonesia: a selection of statistical source material from the early nineteenth century up to 1940 196
Chantepie de la Saussaye, D. 323
Chapel road 724
Chapkis, R. 730
Chappin, M. J. J. G. 999
Characteristics and recognizability of verbal expressions of emotion 289

Charité, J. 978
Chavannes-Mazel, C. A. 908
Chekhov, A. 744
Chemical Substances Act 472
Chess 861
Chester, M. G. 455
Child benefit 387
Child care 431
Child care and protection in the Netherlands 431
Child spacing and family size in the Netherlands 220
Children's books 869
China 182, 188
Chinese 249
Chivalry 99
Chorus, J. M. J. 434
Christian Democrats 311, 332
Church and state since the Reformation: papers delivered to the seventh Anglo-Dutch historical conference 325
Church music 827
Church painting 778
CILT (Centre for Information on Language Teaching and Research) 273
Cinema 829, 937
Cityscape 757
Civil code 450-451
Claes, F. M. 992
Claessen, H. J. M. 363
Clark, G. 30
Clark, Sir G. 124
Clason, A. T. 70
Classes, Social 147, 210, 342, 350, 352, 355-356, 368, 371, 376, 416, 425
Classicism 801
Claus, H. 729-730
Clay pipes 809
Clay tobacco pipe in seventeenth-century Netherlands 809
Clegg, N. C. 735
Climate 52, 58, 60, 63, 259, 269
Clio's mirror: historiography in Britain and the Netherlands 91
Clocks 816
Clogs 591
Clubs 10, 17
Co-operative movement in the Netherlands: an analysis 629
Co-operatives 610-611, 629
Coal industry 43, 635
Cobban, A. 106
Coenen, F. 735
Coetzee, J. M. 724
Cohen, A. 286
Cohen, B. 542
Coins 539
Coleman, D. C. 156
Coleman, J. A. 343
Colie, R. L. 308
Colijn, H. 3
Collaboration 134, 145
Collage 764
Collections of maps and atlases in the Netherlands 64
Colledge, E. 726, 735
Collège Wallon 675
Collette, B. J. 692
Collins, B. 287
Collinson, W. E. 977
Collmer, R. G. 841
Cologne 901
Colonies 183-187, 192, 196, 198, 201, 206-207, 231, 241, 504-506, 509, 585, 732, 734, 918, 993
Comedians in the work of Jan Steen and his contemporaries 780
Commerce and industry in the Netherlands: a base for business operations in Europe 564
Commission for Emancipation 377
Communications 10, 916
Community attitude as a limiting factor in port growth: the case of Rotterdam 572
Commuting 211
Compact geography of the Netherlands 32
Company law 439, 449-450, 452, 455
Comparative law 432, 451, 453, 455
Comparative literature 714, 737-751
Comparative social policy and security: a ten-country study 388
Complete Van Gogh: paintings, drawings, sketches 760
Componisten van de Lage Landen 822
Comprehension 278, 292
Conduct unbecoming: the social construction of police deviance and control 369
Congo 206
Conrad, P. 730

Conservation 469
Consociationalism 401, 403, 416-417, 421-422, 1024 (See also Verzuiling)
Constandse, A. K. 40
Constitution 412, 434, 444-447
Consular service 509
Consumer behaviour and economic growth in the modern economy 152
Contraception 357
Cookery 3, 10, 73, 863, 866
Coolhaas, W. P. 993
Cooper, J. 428-429
Coornhert, D. V. 704
Copernicus, N. 857
Copy and print in the Netherlands: an atlas of historical bibliography 904
Corporal punishment 443
Corporate law of the Netherlands and of the Netherlands Antilles 450
Corporatism 422
Corpus of Rembrandt paintings 775
Correspondence 760, 765, 836, 847, 856
Corruption 369
Cortazar, J. 741
Cosimo III of Florence 507
Costa, F. J. 458
Coster, L. J. 911
Costumes 2, 18, 21, 24
Cottaar, A. 246
Council of State 834
Counter-Reformation 762
Counterpart 669
Counterpart: The International Dimension of Higher Education in the Netherlands: Bulletin of the Netherlands Universities Foundation for International Co-operation (NUFFIC) 931
Country houses 77, 801
Country monograph 1982 on the human settlements situation and related trends and policies in the Netherlands 351
Country profile: Netherlands: export Europe 565
Couperus, L. 735
Courbet, G. 887
Court 26, 99
Couzijn, W. 885
Cowie, D. 4
Cowie, P. 829
Craanen, T. 675
Crafts 753, 764, 808-809, 815, 858
Crankshaw, E. 724
Creutzberg, P. 196
Crew, P. M. 107
Crime 369-370, 394, 427, 549
Criminal law 434
Criminology 427, 430
La crise religieuse en Hollande: souvenirs et impressions 323
Critical survey of studies on Dutch colonial history 993
Crombag, H. F. 668
Cubism 777
Cuijpers, P. 730
Cultivation system 185
Cultural property and air pollution 477
Culture 110, 113, 119-120, 126, 141, 838, 852, 930, 938, 975, 1017
Culture and society in the Dutch Republic during the seventeenth century 119
Currency 539, 550
Current issues in anthropology: the Netherlands 363
Current Research in the Netherlands 932
Curtis, A. 819
Cycles, Economic 512
Czechoslovakia 355

D

Daalder, H. 324, 401-403
Daalder, S. 294
Daendels-Wilson, F. 933
Dalstra, K. 382
Dam, J. E. van 676
Dance 823, 870
Dances of the Netherlands 870
Daniel Heinsius and Stuart England 854
Daniels, R. 794
Darwin, C. 694
Daubenton, F. 76
Davies, D. W. 578
Dawn poetry in the Netherlands 742
De . . . For personal names with the prefix 'de', e.g. J. de Jong, see under the main stem of the name,

De . . . *contd.*
viz. Jong, J. de (this also applies to other prefixes: van, den, van den, uit den, 't, etc.).
De cive 853
Dèr Mouw, J. A. 718
Deakin, F. 566
Debije, P. J. W. 690
Deckers, P. H. 83
Decolonization 159, 181, 195, 207
Decorte, B. 729
Deelname aan het lager onderwijs in Nederland gedurende de negentiende eeuw 652
Deeply rooted: a study of a Drenthe community in the Netherlands 362
Defence 13, 353, 491, 495, 619
Deferred revolution: social experiment in church innovation in Holland, 1960-1970 344
Dekker, E. D. *see* Douwes Dekker, E.
Dekkers, A. 794
Delaissé, L. M. J. 900
Delden, L. van 820
Delft 279, 772, 813, 846, 860, 879
Delft ceramics 813
Delft University 879
Delft, A. van 458, 516
Het Delfts orakel 846
Delta 46, 53, 130, 458, 886, 933, 967
Delta Plan 688
Delta: a Review of Art, Life and Thought in the Netherlands 933
Democratic parties in the Low Countries and Germany: origins and historical development 424
Demographic research and spatial policy: the Dutch experience 213
Demography 13, 32, 34-35, 44, 85, 208-227, 245, 349, 367-368, 392, 643-645, 676, 925, 953, 1011
Denise, J. B. van 821
Denmark 388
Depression (1930s) 166
Deprez, P. 209
Deregulation 622
Derivation of spatial goals for the Dutch land consolidation programme 604
Derksen, J. B. D. 157
Dermoût, M. 732
Descartes, R. 687, 693
Descartes et le cartesianisme hollandais 693
Design 758, 807, 815, 910, 945-946
Design from the Netherlands 807
Determinants of transport mode choices in Dutch cities: some disaggregate stochastic models 615
Deugd, C. de 839
Development of Dutch Anabaptist thought and practice from 1539-1564 309
Development of Dutch science policy in international perspective, 1965-1985 679
Development of the economies of continental Europe 1850-1914 169
Development of socio-medical care in the Netherlands 392
Dialectology 295
Dickinson, C. 701
Dictionaries 27, 250-251, 253-254, 256, 258-266, 273, 992, 1025
Dictionary of electrical engineering 261
Dictionary of scientific and technical terminology: English, German, French, Dutch, Russian 262
Diederiks, H. 430
Dien, A. van 5
Diepenbrock, A. J. M. 824
Diffusion 214-215, 221
Dijk, H. van 210, 352, 614, 702, 994
Dijksterhuis, E. J. 693, 933
Dijkstra, S. 867
Dik, S. C. 267
Dilemmas in regional policy 525
Diminutives 301
Diplomacy 104, 106, 111, 124, 488, 498, 505, 509, 541, 834
Disability 383, 397
Discipline communautaire et politiques économiques nationales 511
Distance higher education and the adult learner 671
Distance learning: on the design of an open university 668
Dittrich, K. 493
Dixon, A. 713, 724, 730
Doctoraal scripties geschiedenis 1980-1984 97
Documentary 828, 914-915, 919
Documentary studies in Leiden art and crafts 1475-1575 753

Documentation centres 654, 879
Documents of the persecution of the Dutch jewry, 1940-1945 131
Doek, J. E. 431
Does, J. van der 835
Doesburg, T. van 700, 796
Dolman, D. 444
Domestic equipment 807
Domingo, V. A. 234
Donaldson, B. C. 268, 306
Donckels, R. 630
Donemus 820
Donnea, F. X. de 615
Donner, J. H. 861
Dood, C. de 798
Dordrecht 335, 717
Dorestad 84
Dorna, M. 723
Dorp in Drenthe 361
Dorsten, J. A. van 840-841, 901
Douwes Dekker, E. 710, 734
Douwes Dekker, N. A. 862
Downes, D. 432
Drainage 13, 19, 47, 55-59
Drama 665, 702, 708-709, 711, 725-726, 743-747, 780, 832, 850, 884, 935, 939, 994
  history of 884
  medieval 702, 708-709, 726, 743, 745-747
Dramatisations of social change: Herman Heijermans' plays as compared with selected dramas by Ibsen, Hauptmann and Chekhov 744
Drawings 21, 25, 805
Dredge drain reclaim: the art of a nation 57
Dredging 53, 57
Drenthe 361-362
Drewe, P. 211
Driehuis, N. 517
Driel, G. A. van 381
Drift, K. F. J.M. van der 668
Drinking water 486
Dronckers, E. 995
Dryden, J. 854
Dubois, R. H. 783
Duc, V. le 803
Duco, P. H. 809
Duden Dictionaries 266
Duijn, J. H. van 512
Duiker, J. 802
Duke, A. C. 91, 127, 136, 325, 341
Duman, M. 794
Dumas, C. 785
Dunford, M. 6
Dunham, D. M. 457
Dunnen, E. den 543
Dunner, J. 842
Dunthorne, H. 108, 871
Durand-Drouhin, J-L. 361
Dutch and Afrikaans 273
Dutch in America: immigration, settlement, and cultural change 225
Dutch-American bibliography, 1693-1794 902
Dutch-American relations 501-502, 902
Dutch Anabaptism: origin, spread, life and thought (1450-1600) 331
Dutch arcadia: pastoral art and its audience with the Golden Age 761
Dutch architecture after 1900 797
Dutch Art and Architecture Today 934
Dutch Arts 935
Dutch-Asiatic shipping in the 17th and 18th centuries 577
Dutch-Asiatic trade 1620-1740 579
Dutch business law 453
Dutch Calvinism in modern America: a history of a conservative subculture 321
Dutch capitalism and world capitalism: capitalisme hollandais et capitalisme mondial 151
Dutch in the Caribbean and in the Guianas, 1680-1791 191
Dutch in the Caribbean and on the Wild Coast 1580-1680 190
Dutch catchpenny prints: three centuries of Dutch broadsides for children 869
Dutch church painters: Saenredam's great church at Haarlem in context 778
Dutch cinema: an illustrated history 829
Dutch cityscape in the seventeenth century and its sources 757
Dutch civilisation in the seventeenth century and other essays 113
Dutch classical architecture 801
Dutch colonial policy and the search for identity in Indonesia 1920-1931 201

Dutch come to Korea 194
Dutch community: social and cultural structure and process in a bulb-growing region of the Netherlands 355
Dutch companies and their financial details 567
Dutch company law 452
Dutch contribution to the European knowledge of Africa in the seventeenth century: 1595-1725 197
Dutch contribution to replacement value accounting theory and practice 557
Dutch cooking 863
Dutch course 272
Dutch Crossing: a Journal of Low Countries Studies 936
Dutch dissenters: a critical companion to their history and ideas 329
Dutch double and pair portraits 788
Dutch economy: recent developments and prospects: March 1986 518
Dutch education system 647
Dutch 'Elckerlyc' is prior to the English 'Everyman' 747
Dutch elm disease 609
Dutch elm disease: aspects of pathogenosis and control 609
Dutch emigration to North America 1624-1860: a short history 227
Dutch/English company law 455
Dutch enterprise and the world bullion trade 1550-1800 150
Dutch explorations, 1605-1756, of the north and northwest coast of Australia: extracts from journals, log-books and other documents relating to these voyages 199
Dutch family in the 17th and 18th centuries: an explorative-descriptive study 366
Dutch figure drawings from the seventeenth century 795
Dutch Film 937
Dutch firearms 812
Dutch and Flemish painters 786
Dutch foreign policy since 1815: a study in small power politics 506
Dutch under German occupation, 1940-1945 149
Dutch Heights 938
Dutch immigrant memoires and related writings 218
Dutch impact on Japan (1640-1853) 188
Dutch interior: post-war poetry of the Netherlands and Flanders 728
Dutch–Italian relations 507
Dutch Jewish history: proceedings of the [second] symposium on the history of the Jews in the Netherlands 334
Dutch landscape: the early years: Haarlem and Amsterdam 1590-1650 756
Dutch language: a survey 305
Dutch: the language of twenty million Dutch and Flemish people 307
Dutch in London: the influence of an immigrant community 95
Dutch medical biography: a biographical dictionary of Dutch physicians and surgeons 1475-1975 979
Dutch military aviation 619
Dutch morphology 285
Dutch museums 891
Dutch novels translated into English: the transformation of a minority literature 748
Dutch organised agriculture in international politics 608
Dutch painters: 100 seventeenth century masters 791
Dutch parliamentary election study 1982: an enterprise of the Dutch political science community 404
Dutch pioneers of science 690
Dutch planning pioneers and the conservation movement: a forgotten tradition in urban and regional planning in the interwar period 469
Dutch plural society: a comparative study in race relations 229
Dutch popular culture in the seventeenth century 838
Dutch Puritanism: a history of English and Scottish Churches of the Netherlands in the sixteenth and seventeenth centuries 339
Dutch reader 283
Dutch reference grammar 268
Dutch Reformed Church 333

Dutch regional economic policy: a review of contents and an evaluation of effects 522
Dutch Republic and the civilisation of the seventeenth century 126
Dutch Republic in Europe in the Seven Years War 104
Dutch Republic and the Hispanic world 1606-1661 114
Dutch Revolt 118
Dutch rural economy in the Golden Age, 1500-1700 179
Dutch School 752, 756, 769-770, 772-775, 779-780, 789-791, 795
Dutch seaborne empire 1600-1800 184
Dutch in the seventeenth century 110
Dutch shipbuilding before 1800: ships and guilds 596
Dutch silver 811
Dutch silver 1580-1830 808
Dutch Society of Archivists 874
Dutch Studies 939
Dutch Theses: a List of Titles of Theses submitted to Dutch Universities 940
Dutch tiles 814
Dutch trade with Russia from the time of Peter I to Alexander I: a quantitative study in eighteenth century shipping 580
Dutch welfare state 382
Dutch windmill 686
Dutch world of painting 787
Dutchmen on the bay: the ethnology of a contractual community 202
Dutt, A. K. 458
Duytschaever, J. 939
Duyvetter, J. 24
Dykstra, K. 977

E

Early-medieval Dorestad, an archaeo-petrological study 84
East India Company 182, 189, 194, 577
East Indies 73, 75, 156, 181-182, 185-186, 189, 196, 201, 203, 205-206, 504, 577, 732, 734
Eastern Europe 696
Ebbinge Wubben, J. C. 887
Ecclesia reformata: studies on the Reformation 335
Econometrics 513, 535, 615
Economic development 152-153, 157-158, 160, 162, 164-165, 167, 169-170, 173, 175-176, 178, 209, 226, 244, 411, 518, 613
Economic and financial reporting in England and the Netherlands: a comparative study over the period 1850-1914 561
Economic history of the Low Countries, 800-1800 163
Economic policy 166, 411, 423, 510-512, 515, 522, 525, 532, 536, 583, 595, 600, 611
Economic policy and planning in the Netherlands, 1950-1965 510
Economic policy in practice: the Netherlands 1950-1957 536
Economic thought 154, 172
Economics 154, 170, 180, 512-514, 516, 519-520, 532, 535, 551, 559, 941-942, 1017
Economisch- en Sociaal-Historisch Jaarboek 635
Economist 519
De Economist: Driemandelijks Tijdschrift – Quarterly Review 941
Economist Intelligence Unit (EIU) 520-521
Economist Intelligence Unit Analysis of Economic and Political Trends Every Quarter: Country Report: Netherlands 520
Economist Intelligence Unit: Country Profile: Netherlands 521
Economy 9, 13, 35, 37, 80, 196, 260, 379, 411, 452, 510-536, 549, 568-569, 643-644, 941-942, 953
Economy and politics of the Netherlands since 1945 159
Ecumenicalism 328, 345
Edelman, H. 902
Education 10, 13, 17, 310, 356, 364, 379, 433, 574, 632, 638-639, 931, 940, 1012, 1021
  adult 393
  higher 664-678, 920
  non-university 660
  primary and secondary 652-663, 860, 920

Education and training for migrants in the Netherlands 648
Educational developments in the Netherlands, 1984-1986 649
Educational reform 656, 677
Edwards, R. 734-735
EEC 36, 159, 449, 453, 489, 494-495, 504, 511, 608, 634
Eeckhout, P. vanden 1010
Eeden, F. van 718, 724
Eerste bliscap 743
Een eeuw Nederlandse muziek 1815-1915 824
Eijk, C. van der 404-405
Eijkman, C. 690
Eindhoven 210, 879, 894
Eindhoven University 879
Eisen, J. 494
Eizenga, W. 544-545
Ekkart, R. E. O. 670, 908
Elckerlijc 746-747
Elders, W. 822
Eldersveld, S. J. 406
Elections 96, 159, 399, 402, 404-405, 409, 414, 418-419, 422, 426, 445
Electoral change in the Netherlands: empirical results and methods of measurement 405
Electoral participation: a comparative analysis 422
Electrical engineering 261
Electronics industry 588, 592
Elffers, D. 933
Elffers, J. 888
Elite images of Dutch politics: accommodation and conflict 406
Elites 103, 406, 414, 420
Elizabeth I of England 95
Ellemers, J. E. 235
Elm disease 609
Elslander, A. van 977
Elsloo 78
Emancipation 347, 359, 373, 377, 399, 413
Emants, M. 724
Emanuel, H. 383
Embarrassment of riches: a history of Dutch civilisation in the Golden Age 123
Emblem books in the Low Countries, 1554-1949 1007
Embroidery motifs from Dutch samplers 815
Emergence of science in Western Europe 681
Emigration 3, 95, 202, 216, 218, 222, 225, 227, 321, 493, 502
Emmeloord 40
Emotion 289
Employment 452, 455, 536, 567, 632, 637, 640
Enckervoort, G. van 671
Encyclopedia of sacred theology: its principles 311
Energy 351, 463, 465, 600, 676
Energy conservation 351
Enforced marriage in the Netherlands: a statistical analysis in order to test some sociological hypotheses 364
Engebrechtsz, C. 835
Engels woordenboek 253
Engineering 56, 263, 684, 688, 984
English diplomat in the Low Countries: Sir William Temple and John de Witt 1665-1672 111
English morality plays 745
English Reformed Church in Amsterdam in the seventeenth century 322
English self-study supplement to Levend Nederlands 277
Enklaar, H. 672
Enlightenment 705
Enschedé, J. 909
Enterprise and history: essays in honour of Charles Wilson 156
Entzinger, H. B. 236-237
Environment 13, 31-32, 41, 70, 78, 213, 254, 259, 375, 379, 453, 459, 461, 464, 469-486, 525, 572, 589, 618, 620-621, 625, 676
Environmental hygiene and urban and village renewal 473
Environmental innovation in small firms 474
Environmental program of the Netherlands 475
Environmental programme of the Netherlands, 1985-1989, concerning waste substances 476
Eos: an enquiry into the theme of lovers' meetings and partings at dawn in poetry 739, 742
Erasmus, D. 843, 847, 849, 856-857, 907

Erasmus of Rotterdam 843, 847
Ernst, B. 792
Erosion 50
Escher, M. C. 792-793
Escher, R. 825
Escher: with a complete catalogue of the graphic works 792
Espionage 106
Essen, J. L. van 326
Est, J. van 459
Establishment of an open university in the Netherlands 673
Estuarine studies 480
Ethical Movement 323
Ethical Policy 201
Ethics 833
Ethnic minorities and Dutch as a second language 288
Ethnic minorities: A. Report to the government. B. Towards an overall ethnic minorities policy 247
Ethnography 886
Ethnology 886
Etiquette 10, 16-17
Eucharist 314
Eurasian Indonesians 228-229, 235, 238, 249
Europe 34-35, 118, 153, 161, 176, 197, 242, 349, 397, 408, 489, 494, 500, 504-505, 508, 523, 608, 824, 971
European demography and economic growth 209
European Economic Review 942
European electoral systems handbook 445
European immigration policy: a comparative study 237
European Monetary System 550
Europoort 46, 562, 574, 967
Euwe, M. 861
Evaluation of dredging in the western Scheldt (the Netherlands) through bioessays 53
Evert, G. van 458
Everts, P. P. 353, 496
Everyman 738, 746-747
Evolution 694
Evolution of Dutch Catholicism, 1958-1974 343
Ex horreo: IPP 1951-1976 80
Ex, J. 238
Examinations 273
Exchange rate policy, monetary policy, and Dutch-German cooperation 550
Exercise of armes 841
Exploration 858
Expressionism 768
Expressionists 768
Extra, G. 288
Eyck, A. van 802
Eyck, F. G. 92
Eyck, H. van 887

F

Faber, J. A. 212
Fable-books printed in the Low Countries: a concise bibliography until 1800 1008
Fact sheet on the Netherlands, series E 7
Failed transitions to modern industrial society: Renaissance Italy and seventeenth century Holland 167
Fairlee, J. 132
Falk Plan: Nederland autokaart/carte routière/autokarte/road map 1:250.000 62
Faludy, G. 843
Familists 840, 901
Family 219-220, 224, 360, 366-367, 376, 388
Family life in the Netherlands 360
Family of Love 325
Farces 708, 726
Fascism 133, 146
Fase, M. M. G. 514
Fasseur, C. 185
Fauna 21, 75-76
Feature service 460
Federal Reserve System 545
Federation of Netherlands Industry 518
Feenstra, J. F. 477
Feenstra, R. 433
Feminism 359, 373, 376-377
Fenoulhet, J. 274, 936
Ferdinand Bol 1616-1680: een leerling van Rembrandt 770
Ferdinandusse, R. 8
Feyter, C. A. de 584

Fiction in translation: policies and options 749
Fiege, S. 514
Fieldhouse, D. K. 585
Fifteenth century printing types of the Low Countries 905
Fifty Dutch and Flemish novelists 722
Fifty years of Unilever 1930-1980 594
Figure-drawing 795
Filedt Kok, J. P. 782
Film 828-831, 865, 934-935, 937
Finance 453, 521, 528, 537-561
public 13, 155, 380, 521, 537-561, 637, 645
Financial relationship between central and local government 546
Finer, S. E. 402
Firearms 812
Fiscal law 434
Fisher, D. 346
Fishing 13, 42, 440
Flaman, D. J. 485
Flanders 724
Fleerackers, J. 939
Flemish language 305-306
Flemish Movement 939
Flevoland 40
Flexibility and commitment in planning 468
Flora 21, 71-75, 77, 958
Florence 507
Flowers 72, 74
Fluctuations and growth in a near full employment economy: a quarterly economic analysis of the Netherlands 517
Fokkema, D. C. 434
Fokkema, D. W. 703
Fokker aircraft 685
Folklore 12, 869-870
Folmer, H. 522
Food consumption 152
Food industries 585, 594, 598
Football 868
'Force of order and methods': an American view into the Dutch directed society 379
Ford, C. 779, 936
Foreign exchange 543, 550, 569, 582
Foreign policy 13, 104, 111, 127, 140, 155, 411, 487, 490-492, 495-496, 499, 500-501, 504-506, 508-509, 949
Foreign policy adaptation 504
Foreign policy of the Netherlands 500
Foreign relations 188, 440, 487-509, 576, 608, 841, 857, 949
Foreigners in our community: a new European problem to be solved 239
Fornier, J. W. 485
Forster, L. W. 738-739, 742, 841, 844
45 years with Philips: an industrialist's life 592
Foundation for Educational Research 660
Foundation for the Scientific Atlas of the Netherlands 60
Four linearbandkeramik settlements and their environment: a paleoecological study of Sittard, Stein, Elsoo and Hienheim 78
Fowles, J. 741
Fraenkel-Schoorl, N. 810
France 99, 381, 691, 696, 840, 900
Franeker 903
Frank, A. 727
Franks, H. G. 586
Frans Hals 769
Frans Hals Museum 886
Fraud 549
Frederiks, J. W. 811
Free farmer in a free state: a study of rural life and industry 607
Free trade and protection in the Netherlands 1816-30: a study of the first Benelux 583
Fremdherrschaft und Kollaboration: die Niederlande unter deutscher Bezatzung 1940-1945 134
French language 279, 981
French Revolution 116, 143
Fried, R. C. 407
Friedman, M. 758
Fries Museum 889
Friesland 9, 59, 663
Frisian language 270, 299, 663, 889, 982
Frisian islands 49
Frisian Movement 9
Frisian reference grammar 270
From Wolfram and Petrarch to Goethe and Grass 704
Fruin, R. 91
Fruin, T. A. 872

Fry, E. H. 408
Fuks-Mansfeld, R. G. 903
Fuks, L. 903
Functionalism 758
Funnel Beaker Peoples 79
Furnishings 753, 758, 807
Furnivall, J. S. 186
Future of old housing stock in the Netherlands 354
Future of Randstad Holland: a Netherlands scenario study on long-term perspectives for human settlement in the western part of the Netherlands 41

G

G. Rietveld architect 806
G. H. Breitner 781
Gaastra, F. S. 577
Gabriël, P. J. C. 785
Gadourek, I. 355-356
Gans, M. H. 327
Garden where the brass band played 735
Gardens 74, 77, 801
Garth, B. 441
Gas 159, 453, 595, 600
Gaugin, P. 887
Gazaleh-Weevers, S. 11
Geer, C. van der 799
Geest, A. van der 275
Geld door de eeuwen heen: geschiedenis van het geld in de Lage Landen 539
Gelder, R. van 187
Gelderman-Curtis, C. 10
General State Archives 874, 876-877
Genre painting 752, 774, 780, 789-790, 795
Geographical study of the Dutch-German border 49
Geography 27-69, 1003
economic 35-39, 44, 972
historical 27
physical 50-53, 55
regional 40-49
Geological history of the Netherlands: explanation to the general geological map of the Netherlands on the scale of 1:200,000 54
Geology 54, 56, 58, 60, 692, 932
George, S. 750
Georgel, J. 445
German factor: a survey of sensitivity and vulnerability in the relationship between the Netherlands and the Federal Republic: summary of the twenty-third report to the government 497
German language 305
Germany 49, 132-134, 144-145, 149, 223, 381, 388, 424, 463, 491, 493, 497, 506, 550, 571, 576, 696, 738, 860, 882
Gerretson, F. C. 587
Gerritsen, J. 253
Gerritsen, M. 294
Gerritsen, W. P. 704
Gerson, H. 773
Geschiedenis van de Nederlandse arbeiders beweging in de negentiende eeuw 627
Geschiedenis van de Nederlandse stam 109
Geschlossene und offene Form im Drama 709
Getting off to a good start in European trade 562
Getting, spending and investing in early modern times: essays on Dutch, English and Huguenot economic history 155
Geurtsen, W. 276
Gewasbescherming 958
Geweld in onze samenleving 427
Geyl, P. 91, 109, 113
Gezelle, G. 712
Gezelle and Multatuli: a question of literature and social history 712
Gheyn, J. de 763, 841
Giddy, I. H. 544
De Gids 721
Gijsen, M. 724
Ginsberg, A. 764
Gladdish, K. 409
Glamann, K. 579
Glossary of land resources: English, French, Italian, Dutch, German, Swedish 259
Goddijn, W. 344

Godsdienst en kerk in Nederland, 1945-1980: een geannoteerde bibliografie van sociaal-wetenschappelijke en historische literatuur over de godsdienstige en kerkelijke ontwikkelingen in Nederland 1023
Goen, B. van der 730
Gogh, T. van 765
Gogh, V. van 759-760, 765, 785
Das goldene Delta und sein eisernes Hinterland 1815-1851: von niederländisch-preussischen zu deutsch-niederländischen Wirtschaftbeziehungen 576
Goltzius, H. 756, 779, 786, 795
Good Hope, Cape of 198
Goodman, D. P. 996
Goodman, G. K. 188
Goor, J. van 189
Goos, P. 67
Goossen, P. 410
Goossens, J. 740, 939
Gordon, P. 11
Gorkum, P. H. van 631
Gorter, H. 718
Gorter, I. 5
Goslinga, C. C. 190-192
Goslings, W. R. O. 821
Gouda 112, 818
Gouda in Revolt: particularism and pacifism in the Revolt of the Netherlands 1572-1588 112
Goudsmit, S. A. 680
Governia van Bezooijen, R. A. M. 289
Goyvaerts, D. 250
Graffiti 755
Grammar 267-270, 273
Grammars 1025
Graphics 792-793
Gravensande, W. J. S. van 's- 690
Greek 707
Green, D. H. 704
Greenwood, C. 15
Greunsven, N. J. J. van 357
Griffiths, R. T. 158-160, 997
Grindal, J. 853
Groen van Prinsterer, G. 326
Groendijk, J. 30
Groenhuis, G. 325
Groenman-Van Waateringe, W. 80
Groningen 152, 323
Groot museumboek 888
Groot, A. D. de 12
Groot, A. H. de 498
Groot, H. de 632
Groot, J. P. 361
Grotius, H. 435, 846, 859, 1001
Groundwater flow systems in the Netherlands: a groundwater-hydrological approach to the functional relationship between the drainage system and the geological and climatical conditions in a quarternary accumulation area 58
Gruter, J. 704, 738, 844
Gruys, J. A. 998
Gudlaugsson, S. J. 780
Guest labour 228, 235, 243, 247-249
Guianas 191
Guide to Dutch art in America 766
Guide to foreign language grammars and dictionaries 1025
Guide to Jewish Amsterdam 22
Guide to Netherlandic studies: bibliography 1006
Guide to the sources of the history of Africa south of the Sahara in the Netherlands: Netherlands State Archives Service 876
Guilds 596
Guillaume le Taciturne de la 'Généralité' de Bourgogne à la République de Sept Provinces-Unies 105
Guttenberg 912
Gypsies 240

H

H. P. Berlage: idea and style: the quest for modern architecture 804
Haak, B. 775
Haak, K. van der 917
Haan, T. d' 741
Haanstra, B. 828, 829
Haar, B. ter 436
Haarlem 756, 778-779, 786, 795, 837, 886, 906, 911
Haarlem legend of the invention of printing by Laurens Janszoon Coster, critically examined 911

Haarsma, F. 939
Hackmann, W. D. 681
Hadermann, P. 700
Hadewijch 733, 735
Haga, C. 498
Hague, The 106, 230, 458, 624, 886, 908
Hague School, The 781, 785
Hague School: Dutch masters of the nineteenth century 785
Haitsma Mulier, E. O. G. 845
Haley, K. H. D. 110-111
Hall, P. 458
Hals, F. 769, 788, 886
Halverhout, H. A. M. 863
Hambloch, H. 31
Hamel, H. 194
Hamelink, J. 730
Hammacher, A. M. 759
Hammacher, R. 759
Hammar, T. 237
Hamnett, S. 458
Hand, G. 445
Handboek der geografie van Nederland 33
Hannay, M. 277
Hanon, A. J. 705
Hansen, E. 133, 633
Hardenburg, H. 873
Harduyn J. de 733
Harlof, E. M. 964
Harris, Sir J. 106
Harry, K. 671
Hart, M. 't 723, 706
Hartkamp, A. T. 884
Hartog, J. A. 381
Haslach, R. D. 918
Hasselt, K. van 568
Hatto, A. T. 739
Hauptmann, G. 744
De haventolk 265
Hayward Gallery 806
Health 7, 13, 378, 384, 392, 398, 473, 676, 975
Health care 379, 383, 389, 392-393, 397-398, 427, 632
Health in the Netherlands: publications in foreign languages 384
Hebly, J. A. 345
Hebrew typography in the Northern Netherlands, 1585-1815: historical evaluation and descriptive bibliography 903
Hedendaagse Nederlandse leesteksten voor volwassen buitenlanders 276
Heeger, H. P. 358
Heerding, A. 588
Heere, L. d' 738
Heere, W. P. 440
Heerlen 671
Hefting, P. H. 781
Hegel, G. W. F. 804
Hegeman, J. G. 694
Heide, H. ter 213
Heidelberg Catechism 313
Heijermans, H. 718, 744
Heinsius, D. 715, 738, 854
Heldring, J. L. 411
Hellinga, G. 730
Hellinga, W. G. S. 904-905
Hellinga-Querido, L. 905-906
Hendriks, G. 385
Henriquez, A. 798
Herck, P. van 730
Herengracht 884
Herik, M. J. M. van 13
Herman Boerhaave: the man and his work 697
Hermans, T. J. 307, 707, 729, 936
Hermans, W. F. 703, 723, 736-737
Hermesdorf, P. F. J.M. 782
Herreweghen, H. 729
Herwijnen, G. van 999
Herzen, F. 730
Hes, H. S. 695
Hetzel, O. J. 386
Heuven, V. van 286
Hibben, C. C. 112
Hickey, T. J. O. 864
Hienheim 78
Hieronimus Bosch 767
Higher education 664-678, 931
Higher education in the Netherlands 678
Higher education and research in the Netherlands 931
Highgate 841
Hiltenius, D. 933
Hilversum 823
Hints to exporters: the Netherlands 569
Hirschfeld, G. 134
Hirschfeld, H. M. 523
Historia Agriculturae 943

Historical research in the Low Countries 1970-1975: a critical survey 990
Historical research in the Low Countries 1981-1983: a critical survey 1004
Historiography 91, 113, 136, 145, 334, 990, 1004
History 6, 21, 88-90, 92-94, 96-98, 113, 135, 137, 243, 427, 488, 509, 837, 857-858, 876-877, 880, 936, 989, 1009, 1019
  19th century 128-129, 137, 141-142, 147-148, 202, 206, 208, 216, 218, 225, 242, 378, 390, 400-401, 413, 415, 424, 490, 505-506, 561, 576, 583, 602, 610, 613-614, 627, 633, 641, 645, 652, 656, 712, 950
  20th century 26, 127, 130-141, 144-146, 149, 225, 390, 400-402, 408, 413, 415, 424-426, 506, 597, 610, 633, 635, 641-642
  bibliography 988-990, 993, 997, 999, 1004, 1012, 1019, 1024
  Burgundian 99-102, 438, 582, 851
  colonial 75, 156, 181-196, 198, 201, 203-207, 436, 993
  commercial 101, 120, 150, 206, 563, 576-583
  economic 95, 130, 150-180, 196, 204, 226, 529, 541, 552, 556, 558, 561, 576-584, 586-588, 591, 596-598, 602, 606-607, 612-613, 814, 925, 943, 988, 997
  Jews 22, 885
  medieval 29, 84, 99-102, 438, 582, 742, 810, 850-851
  periodicals 925, 927, 929, 936, 943, 948, 950
  Republic 15, 29, 91, 95, 103-104, 106, 108-111, 113-114, 116-117, 119-126, 143, 188, 197, 199-200, 227, 242, 366, 401, 430, 433, 443, 492, 498, 507, 558, 577-582, 596, 675, 681, 687, 717, 757, 761, 838, 840, 845-846, 859, 1001
  Revolt 91, 95, 105, 107, 112, 114-115, 117-118, 120, 122, 125, 840, 875
History of the Dutch coast in the last century 50
History of ideas 742, 833-859, 1000
History of N. V. Philips' Gloeilampenfabrieken, vol. I: The origin of the Dutch incandescent lamp industry 588
History of the people of the Netherlands 89
History of religion 107, 130, 172, 308-309, 315, 317-340 345-348, 762, 893, 1023
History of the Royal Dutch 587
History of science 681, 683
History of Unilever: a study in economic growth and social change 598
Hobbes, T. 853, 855
Hoe leer je een taal? De Delftse methode 279
Hoebel, E. A. 436
Hoed, P. den 461
Hoekveld, G. A. 35
Hoff, A. 812
Hoff, J. H. van 't 690
Hofmann, M. 331
Hofstee, E. W. 214-215, 221
Hofstra, H. J. 547
Hogeweg-De Haart, H. P. 359
Hohenberg, P. M. 167
Holford, W. 29
Holland 15
Holland (Michigan) 216
Holland (province) 45, 165, 596, 757
Holland, J. 6
Holland and Britain 858
Holland in close-up 21
Holland Herald 944
Holland Industrial 945
Holland: the land and the people 4
Holland Quarterly 946
Holland's industries stride ahead: the new Netherlands of the 1960s 586
Holland transport 616
Holland on the way to the forum: living in the Netherlands 5
Holmes, J. S. 728, 933
Holocene sea level changes in the Netherlands 51
Holsbergen, S. 5
Holt, S. 412
Holtgrefe, A. A. A. 617
Holzer, H. P. 548
Homan, G. D. 413
Homan, H. J. A. 1003

Homosexuality 374
Hondius, E. H. 434
Hong Lee, O. 241
Hooch, P. de 790, 800
Hooft, P. C. 733, 939
Hoogerwerf, A. 462
Hoogovens 597
Hoorn 998
Hoornik, E. 933
Hope & Co. 541
Hopman, F. 99
Horgan, J. 328
Horssen, W. C. N. van 967
Horst, H. van der 828
Horst, I. B. 329
Horst, K. van der 897
Horticulture 611
Hortus Floridus: the four books of spring, summer and winter flowers 74
Hötte, D. W. 794
House on the canal 735
Housing 5, 13, 17, 25, 30, 41, 55, 246, 351, 354, 358, 368, 379, 386, 473, 621, 644, 964
Houska, J. J. 414
Houtappel, J. C. 441
Houte, H. van 239
Houtman, C. 577
Houtte, J. A. van 161-163
Houwer, R. 865
Hovens, J. 240
Hovens, P. 240
Howard, D. 930
Hudson, R. 470
Hugenholtz, F. W. N. 113
Huggett, F. E. 135
Hugo Grotius, a great European 1583-1645 846
Hugo's Dutch in three months: simplified language course 274
Huguenots 155, 857
Huisman, G. C. 1000
Huisman, H. 463
Huitenga, T. 254-255
Huizing, W. P. 387
Huizinga, J. 99, 113, 847
Huizinga, L. 718
Hulsker, J. 760
Hulsman, L. H. C. 437
Hulst, H. van der 290
Hulst, H. C. van de 682
Hulstijn, J. H. 277, 291
Human rights 508
Humanism 183, 675, 715, 717, 719, 762, 786, 840, 846, 848, 859, 1000
Humanists and Humanism in Amsterdam 848
Hummelen, W. M. H. 709, 994
Hunebeds 79
Hunters 87
Hüsken, W. 708, 994
Hustinx, L. M. T.L. 874
Huygens, Christiaan 687, 690-691, 834
Huygens, Constantijn 693, 756, 834, 857
Hyma, A. 849

I

Ibsen, H. 744
Iconoclasm 107, 118
Icononography 740, 762
Iconography of the Counter-Reformation in the Netherlands: heaven on earth 762
Ideeën 710
Ideological origins of the Batavian Revolution: history and politics in the Dutch Republic 1747-1800 116
Idiomata Neerlandica 271
Idioms 255
IFHP (International Federation for Housing and Planning) 964
IISG (International Institute of Social History) 948
IJ (Y) 42
IJmuiden 597
IJssel 47
IJsselmeer 19, 40, 55, 458
IJsselmeerpolders 56
Illumination 900
Illustrated dictionary of mechanical engineering: English, French, German, Dutch, Russian 263
Immigration 237, 243-244
Immigration and the formation of minority groups: the Dutch experience 1945-1975 228
Impact of a genius: Rembrandt, his pupils and followers in the seventeenth century 771

Implementation of international sanctions: the Netherlands and Rhodesia 499
Import of labour: the case of the Netherlands 244
Impressionism 777
In so many words 260
In Touch with the Dutch 947
Income distribution 168, 352, 559
Income distribution: analysis and policies 559
Incunabula 911, 913, 987, 1016, 1020
Incunabula in Dutch libraries 913
Independence of the Federal Reserve System and of the Netherlands Bank: a comparative analysis 545
India 182, 186
Indicative multi-year programme to control air pollution, 1985-1989 478
Indonesia 195-196, 203, 207, 231, 238, 365, 436, 504, 716, 724, 732, 734, 866
Indonesian language 279
Industrial democracy in the Netherlands: a seminar 631
Industrial mobility and migration in the European Community 590
Industrial policy and shipbuilding: changing economic structures in the Low Countries 1600-1980 584
Industrial relations 524, 564, 631, 634-635, 641-642, 996
Industrial retardation in the Netherlands 1830-1850 160
Industrial waste 474
Industrialization 138, 164, 167, 170, 175, 210
Industrialization in the Low Countries, 1795-1850 170
Industrialization without national patents: the Netherlands, 1869-1912: Switzerland, 1850-1907 175
Industry 21, 37, 43, 48, 80, 95, 160, 164-165, 175, 260, 397, 439, 453, 463, 528, 548, 561, 564-568, 572-573, 584-600, 630, 641, 685, 805, 809, 814, 945-946, 954, 1015
Industry in the Netherlands: its place and future. Reports to the Government 18, 1980 589
Inflation 547, 922
Inflation-adjusted tax system: a summary of the report on the elimination from the Dutch tax system of the distorting effects of inflation 547
Influencing mass political behaviour: elites and political subcultures in the Netherlands and Austria 414
Information, General 4, 7, 10-11, 13-15, 17, 21, 944
Information and Documentation Centre for the Geography of the Netherlands 66
Information services 459, 881
Information systems for integrated regional planning and policy making in the Netherlands 459
Information technology 650, 676
Input-output analysis 513, 532, 535
Input-output experiments: the Netherlands 1948-1961 535
Inside information 10
Insignia 16
Instruments of money market and foreign exchange market policy in the Netherlands 543
Insulinde: selected translations from Dutch writers of three centuries on the Indonesian archipelago 732
Insurance 17, 388, 453, 544, 558, 567, 574
Integration of ethno-cultural minorities: a pluralist approach: the Netherlands and Canada: a comparative analysis of policy and programme 233
Interactions of Amsterdam and Antwerp with the Baltic region, 1400-1800: De Nederlanden en het Oostzeegebied, 1400-1800 582
Internationaal Instituut voor Sociale Geschiedenis: Alfabetische catalogus 880
International Agricultural Centre 601
International Geographers Union 39
International government finance and the Amsterdam capital market 1740-1815 556
International law 434, 440
International law in the Netherlands 440
International Review of Social History 948

Internationale Spectator 949
Interpreting and valuing transport's role in social well-being: an international conference held 12-15 April 1983, Noordwijk, Netherlands 618
Interregional input-output analysis and Dutch regional policy problems 532
Intertraffic of the mind 853
Intonation 286, 289
Introduction to Dutch 269
Introduction to Dutch law for foreign lawyers 434
Introduction to the sources of European economic history 1500-1800 161
Investment 39, 204, 453, 524, 530, 534, 556, 640
Investment guide to the Netherlands 524
Iongh, D. de 333
IPP (Institute for Prae- and Protohistory) 80
Ireland 388
Irian 195
Irish Times 328
Ishwaran, K. 360
ISMO 549
ISMO 1985: fraud and abuse in relation to taxation, social security and government subsidies in the Netherlands: a summary of the ISMO report 1985 549
Israel 144, 391
Israel, J. I. 114, 936, 997
Italy 133, 167, 696, 780, 786
Itterbeek, E. van 729
IULA (International Union of Local Authorities) 964
Ivens, J. 829-830
IVN (International Association for Dutch Studies) 674

J

Jaarcijfers voor het Koninkrijk der Nederlanden, Rijk in Europa 950
Jackson, P. A. 619
Jacobi, H. 539
Jacques de Gheyn: three generations 763
Jaffé, H. L. C. 758, 783
James I of England 841
James-Gerth, W. 724
Jansen-Scheuring, M. 798
Jansen, A. J. 361
Jansen, G. 771
Jansen, H. P. H. 93, 100
Jansen, K. 539
Jansenism 330
Jansma, L. G. 329
Janssen, D. 256
Janus Gruter's English years 844
Janus Secundus 719
Japan 182, 188-189, 289, 912
Japanese camps 203
Java 185, 189
Jelgersma, S. 51
Jenkins, H. M. 602
Jeptha 711
Jewelry 810
Jewish Historical Museum 131, 885
Jewish Historical Museum 885
Jewish physicians in the Netherlands, 1600-1940 695
Jews 22, 131, 140, 144, 324, 327, 334, 695, 727, 839, 885
Jitta, J. W. J. 440
Joan Blaeu and his grand atlas 65
Jög, N. 382
Johan Maurits van Nassau-Siegen 1604-79: a Humanist prince in Europe and Brazil: essays on the tercentenary of his death 183
John de Witt: statesman of the 'true freedom' 121
Johnson, B. 854
Johnson, L. P. 704
Johnson, W. 860
Jonckheere, K. 729, 933
Jones, D-D. 634
Jones, R. 990
Jones, S. R. 800
Jong, E. D. de 257
Jong, L. de 136, 919, 933
Jong, R. de 415
Jonge, C. H. de 813-814
Jonge, H. J. de 382
Jonge, J. A. de 164-165
Jongman, R. W. 427
Jons, R. 729
Joosten, B. 278
Jordan, J. S. 588
Jordanhill College 132
Joseph in Dothan 711
Jouderville, I. 771
Joustra, D. S. 50
Joyce, J. 939

Judicial violence in the Dutch Republic: corporal punishment, executions and torture in Amsterdam 1650-1750 443
Judiciary 412, 441, 443
Jung, C. 12
Jurgens, A. 598
Jurisprudence 435, 957
Jurisprudence of Holland 435
Jurriens, R. 635
Justice 382, 430, 437, 441

K

Kaim-Caudle, P. R. 388
Kalendarium: geschiedenis van de Lage Landen in jaartallen 93
De Kapellekensbaan 741
Karel Appel: street art, ceramics, sculpture, wood reliefs, tapestries, murals, Villa El Salvador 764
Karel ende Elegast 726
Kars, H. 84
Keeney, W. E. 309
Keesing's Contemporary Archives 951
Kelk, C. 382
Keller, H. 830
Kentie, Y. M. D. 620
Kerkhoff, A. 288
Ketelaar, F. C. J. 874
Kettering, A. M. 761
Keuls, M. 364
Keur, D. L. 362
Keur, J. Y. 362
Kieve, R. A. 416
Kijken naar monumenten in Nederland 805
Kilburn, G. 730
King, P. K. 704, 710-712, 742, 939
Kingdom of the Netherlands: facts and figures 14
Kingston Papers 193
Kipling, G. 841, 850-851
Kirk, G. W. 216
Kirsner, R. S. 292
Kist, J. R. 792
Klaassen, L. H. 590
Klashorst, G. O. van de 1001
Klederdrachten 24
Klein, P. W. 156, 166
Het klimaat van Nederland gedurende de laatste twee en een halve eeuw 52
Klimaatatlas van Nederland 63
Kloeke, G. G. 295
Kloos, P. 363
Klotz, V. 709
Knaap, G. A. van der 217
Knap, G. H. 42
KNIL (Dutch Colonial Army) 231
Knippenberg, H. 652
Knipping, J. B. 762
Knol, J. 1002
Knoppers, J. V. T. 580
Koeman, C. 64-65, 67, 1003
Koenraadt, F. 382
Kok, A. de 389
Kok, M. 330
Kok, R. H. M. 15
Koning, D. 823
Koningsbruggen, R. van 794
Konjunktur, Krise, Gesellschaft: wirtschaftliche Wechsellagen und soziale Entwicklung im 19. und 20. Jahrhundert 157
Kooi, P. B. 85
Kooiman, D. A. 713
Kooiman, J. 406
Koopmans-Van Beinum, F. J. 293
Koops, W. R. H. 907
Kooy, G. A. 364
De koperen tuin 735
Kopland, R. 729
Korea 194
Korte, D. A. de 920
Korteweg, A. S. 908
Korteweg, P. 550-551
Kossmann-Putto, J. 990, 1004
Kossmann, E. H. 94, 128, 147, 165, 167, 181, 205, 319, 490, 852
Kossmann, F. K. H. 980
Kouwenaar, G. 729
Kraak, A. 292, 294
Kraemer, P. E. 390
Krahn, C. 331
Kramer, R. M. 391
Kramer's Nederlands woordenboek 258
Krantz, F. 167
Krashuis Monitor Theory 291
Krewson, M. B. 1005
Krimpen, J. van 909
Krispyn, E. 700, 724
Kristensen, I. 480

Kroef, J. M. van der 332
Kroes, R. 365
Krol, G. 703
Kröller-Müller Museum 798, 886, 890
Kronenberg, M. E. 998, 1016
Kuile, O. ter 784
Kuipers, S. K. 628
Kuklinski, A. 525
Kuyper, A. 310-311, 316, 322
Kuyper, P. J. 499
Kuyper, W. 801
Kuznets, S. 168
Kwaak, A. 458

L

Labor relations in the Netherlands 642
Labor relations in the Netherlands: a bibliography 996
Labour 39, 148, 236, 242-245, 248, 531, 637
Labour laws 434, 634, 640
Labour market 628, 630, 676
Labour movement 626-627, 629, 631, 635, 641-642
Labour Party 425
Labour Plan 626
Labrijn, A. 52
Laer, A. J. F. van 193
Laerhoven, B. van 730
Laet, S. J. de 86
Lagerwey, W. 1006
Lake IJssel 47
Lamb to the slaughter 713
Lambooy, J. G. 525
Lampo. H. 730
Lamur, H. E. 232
Lanceloet van Denemarken 726
Land consolidation 604-605
Land papers 193
Land reclamation 13, 51
Land of Stevin and Huygens 687
Landscape 756, 779, 795
Landwehr, J. 1007-1009
Lange, D. de 933
Language 6, 9, 141, 246, 250-307, 707, 932, 936, 939, 963, 973, 982, 1002, 1006, 1012, 1018
  history of 302, 305-307, 1002
  courses 271-283
  games 275
Language and language attitudes in a bilingual community: Terherne (Friesland) 299
Language learning 288, 291
Language is my world 729
Language usage 257
Lans, C. 730
Larkin, G. 138
Lasco, J. à 333
Latin 707
Laut, P. 603
Law 17, 427-455, 511, 625, 839, 846, 859, 957, 981
  company 439
  comparative 432
  constitutional 434, 444-448
  criminal 434
  fiscal 434
  history of 433, 438
  international 434, 955
  labour 434
  maritime 440
  private 434
Law of obligations 451
Law and order 382
Lawrence, D. H. 734
Lawrence, G. R. P. 43-44
Leck, B. van der 758
Ledyard, G. 194
Lee, O. H. 241
Lee, R. W. 435
Lee, W. R. 209
Leeb, I. L. 116
Leeuw, R. de 785
Leeuw, T. de 825
Leeuw, W. C. de 71
Leeuwarden 663
Leeuwenhoek, A. van 690
Legal administration 454
Legal aid 428-429
Legal reform 437
Legal services 428
Legal system 427-443
Legislation 449-455, 560, 649, 655, 917
Leiden 96, 171, 323, 468, 717, 753, 818, 886, 892, 901, 903
Leiden imprints 1483-1600 in Leiden University Library and Bibliotheca Thijsiana 987
Leiden University 96, 182, 230, 670, 675, 698, 987

Leiden University in the seventeenth century: an exchange of learning 675
Leiden University Library 987
Leigh-Loohuizen, R. 730
Lely, J. 19
Lelystad 19
Leopold, J. M. 808
Lessen Kloeke, W. U. S. van 294
Letter and image 910
Lettering 910
Leupen, P. 438
Leurdijk, J. H. 500
Levant 498
Levend Nederlands 280, 282
Lever Brothers 598
Leviathan 853
Levie, S. H. 775
Levie, T. 334
Lewis, G. 693
Lewis, J. R. 470
Lexicon 297
Liberalism 128-129, 147, 323, 424
Liberals 320
Libraries 507, 820, 871, 878-883, 907, 986, 991, 1005
Libraries and documentation centres in the Netherlands 881
Library of Congress 1005
Library of the Mennonite Church of Amsterdam 878
Library of Netherlandic Literature 724
Lieftinck, P. 552
Liet, J. van der 15
Life of Desiderius Erasmus 849
Life and works of Gerardus Joannes Vossius (1577-1649) 717
Light and enlightenment: a study of the Cambridge Platonists and the Dutch Arminians 308
Lijphart, A. 195, 417, 421
Lijst van docenten in de neerlaandistiek aan buitenlandse universiteiten en ledenlijst IVN 674
Limburg 23, 43, 635, 754, 768
Limburg Stirum, C. van 866
Limits to the welfare state: an enquiry into the realizability of socioeconomic desiderata in a highly industrialized society 381
Limperg, T. 557
Lindblad, T. J. 581
Linde, A. van der 911
Lindeboom, G. A. 683, 696-697, 979
Lindeboom, J. 333
Linearbandkeramik 78
Linguistic history of Holland and Belgium 306
Linguistic theory 267, 303
Linguistic theory and the function of word order in Dutch: a study of the interpretive aspects of the order of adverbial and noun phrases 303
Linguistics 284-304
Linguistics in the Netherlands 294
Lipschits, I. 418
Lipsius, J. 675
Lis, C. 1010
Lissens, R-F. 977
Lisser, E. C. 434
Literary history, modernism, and post-modernism 703
Literary Holland 974
Literary Museum 886
Literary theories of Daniel Heinsius: a study of the development of his views on literary theory and criticism in the period from 1602 to 1612 715
Literature 6, 9, 72, 101, 119, 141, 318, 321, 699-751, 899, 926, 930, 932, 935-936, 939, 963, 973-974, 977, 982, 1007-1008, 1012, 1018
  comparative 714, 737-751
  history of 714-716, 718, 977
  medieval 738
  modern 701, 718, 723, 730, 737
  Renaissance 761
  sociology of 712
Literature of the Low Countries 714
'Livability' of the environment in terms of traffic in the Netherlands 621
Living in the Netherlands 17
Local elites and the structure of political conflict: parties, unions and the action groups in the Netherlands 420
Local government 20, 448, 462, 468, 546
Locher, J. L. 792
Lodder, P. 570
Lodewijk, T. 72
Loggem, E. van 730
Loggem, M. van 730

Logie, G. 259
London 95, 333, 369, 789
Lonely but not alone 26
Loo, P. D. van 551
Loof, B. H. 260
Looy, J. van 718
Lorentz, H. A. 690
Loss of inflection in the Dutch language 302
Lovelock, Y. 731
Low Countries 86
Low Countries in early modern times: selected documents 122
Low Countries Newsletter 952
Low Countries 1780-1940 137
Lowland highlights: church and oecumene in the Netherlands 345
Lubbers, R. 159
Lucas van Leyden 782, 887
Lucas, H. S. 218
Lucassen 794
Lucassen, J. 242-243
Lucebert 794
Lucifer 711
Luginsky, Y. N. 261
Lunsingh Scheurleer, T. H. 675
Luttervelt, R. van 891
Luxembourg 6, 31, 38, 92, 411, 539, 583, 644, 689
Lyng, R. 228

M

Maandschrift van het CBS 953
Maandstatistiek van de Industrie 954
Maas, M. 1002
Maass, W. B. 139
Maastricht 669
Maasvlakte 516
McGeehan, C. 724
McLean, R. 896
Macro, C. 696
Maeijer, J. M. M. 449
Main lines of the informatics stimulation plan 650
Mak, J. J. 977
Making of Dutch towns: a study in urban development from the tenth to the seventeenth centuries 29
Malmesbury, Earl of 106
Man in the mirror 735
Man, H. de 626
Managerial accounting and analysis in multinational enterprises 548
Mander, C. van 756, 779, 786
Manifestoes 418
Manpower 636, 638-639
Manpower and social policy in the Netherlands 636
Mansvelt, W. M. F. 196
Manual for the arrangement and description of archives 872
Manuscripts 882, 900, 966
Maps 54, 60-69
Margaret of Austria 733
Marine biology 480
Maris, J. 785
Maris, M. 785
Maris, W. 785
Maritime law 440
Maritime powers, 1721-1740: a study of Anglo-Dutch relations in the age of Walpole 108
Maritime research 959
Market for money and the market for credit: theory, evidence and implications for Dutch monetary policy 551
Marketing 564-565, 569
Markov, A. S. 262
Marlan, A. J.van 446
Marle, H. van 933
Marquenie, J. M. 53
Marriage 364, 366-367
Marriage 735
Marshall Plan 523
Marshall, A. 244
Marsman, H. 718
Martin, W. 264
Marxism 416
Mary of Nijmegen 738
Masters of seventeenth century Dutch genre painting 789
Mathematics 932, 984
Mathias, P. 156
Matter, J. 282
Maurits Cornelis Escher: the graphic work, introduced and explained by the artist 793
Maurits, J. 183
Mauve, A. 785
Max Havelaar or the coffee auctions of the Dutch Trading Company 710, 734

Mead, R. 696
Meaning and lexicon: proceedings of the second international colloquium on the interdisciplinary study of the semantics of natural language held at Cleves, 30 August – 2 September 1983 297
Medals 16
Media 7, 13, 671, 914-924
Medicine 696-698, 899, 932, 979
Mediterranean 498, 892
Meegeren, H. van 772
Meer, S. W. van der 450
Meere, J. M. M. de 168
Meermanno-Westreenianum Museum 908
Mees and Hope N. V. 533
Mees, I. 287
Meijer, H. 32, 45-47
Meijer, H. G. 16
Meijer, H. R. 723
Meijer, J. N. 630
Meijer, R. P. 714, 977
Meijlink, J. 17
Meilink-Roelofsz, M. A. P. 182
Meinesz, V. 692
Melancthon, P. 313
Melgert, W. 239
Mellink, A. F. 115
Memlinc, H. 887
Memorbook: a history of Dutch Jewry from the Renaissance to 1940 327
Mennonites 331, 878
's-Menschen sin en verganckelijk schoonheid 709
Mental health 378, 393
Mental, religious and social forces 318
Mercator 690
Meredith, P. 743
Mesdag, H. W. 785
Mesolithic settlement systems in the Netherlands 87
Meter, J. H. 715
Methodology 404-405
Metrics 290
Metselaars, H. J. H. A. G. 874
Metsys, G. 887
Meulen, H. van der 152
Meulenbelt-Nieuwburg, A. 815
Michigan 216
Michman, J. 334
Middeleeuwse geschiedenis der Nederlanden 100
Miedema, H. M. E. 479
Migrant labour in Europe 1600-1900: the drift to the North Sea 242
Migration 211, 213, 223, 225, 229, 242, 245-246, 349, 590, 648
Migration, minorities and policy in the Netherlands: recent trends and developments 245
Migration and settlement 5: Netherlands 211
Military 365
Miller, W. E. 419
Millioenen-studiën 710
Mills 686, 1015
Mills, D. G. 48
Milton, J. 854
Milward, A. 169
Ministry of Agriculture 608, 650
Ministry of Culture 7, 385
Ministry of Economic Affairs 524, 530, 534, 650
Ministry of Education 647-651, 653, 655, 657-658, 661, 673, 677
Ministry of Finance 546, 553, 555, 560
Ministry of Foreign Affairs 523
Ministry of Housing 41, 351, 354, 375, 467, 471-473, 475-478, 481-484, 621, 971
Ministry of Justice 451
Ministry of Transport 19, 616, 618, 623-624
Ministry of Welfare 7, 384, 389, 975
Minnebrieven 710
Minorities 7, 9, 207, 228-249, 288, 350
Minshull, G. N. 36
Mirror of the Indies: a history of Dutch colonial literature 716
Mobilization, center-periphery structures and nation-building: a volume in commemoration of Stein Rokkan 401
Models of contemporary Dutch family building 224
Modern European company law system: a commentary on the 1976 Dutch legislation 449
Modern music 825-826
Modern Netherlands 135
Modern novel 706, 721-722, 749
Modernism 315, 700, 703, 768, 939
Modernization 214-215, 221

Moer, W. G. van der 999
Moerings, M. 382
Mokyr, J. 170
Molenbibliografie 1015
Molhuysen, P. C. 980
Moll, J. J. van 255
Molle, W. T. M. 590
Mollusca 480
Molonus, D. 867
Moluccans 228, 231, 235, 241, 247, 249, 382
Moluccas 75
Monarchy 26, 412
Mondriaan, P. 758, 777, 785, 796
Mondrian Studies 777
Monetary policy 540, 543, 545, 550, 552
Monetary policy in the Netherlands in the post-Smithsonian era 540
Money 526-527, 531, 533, 538-540, 542, 551, 582
Monitor use by adult second language learners 291
Montens, F. 279
Montyn, J. 713
Monuments 805
Mook, B. 366
Moonen, J. M. 668
Moore, B. 140
Moore, C. N. 732
Moors, H. G. 219-220, 367, 1011
Mootz, M. 368
Moralities 709, 745-746
Morel, P. M. 1012
Morin, P. 671
Moroccan workers in the Netherlands 248
Moroccans 228, 248, 288, 367, 648
Morphology 285
Morris, A. E. J. 458
Morris, P. 733
Mortimer, C. 696
Mörzer Bruijns, M. F. 480
Motley, J. L. 117, 502
Mout, N. 325
Movement of 1880 718
Muir, L. 743
Mulder, C. P. 16
Mulder, G. A. M. 33
Mulisch, H. 723, 730
Muller, F. 64
Multatuli 710, 712, 734-736
Multatuli 710
Multi-criteria analysis and regional decision-making 516
Multinationals 542, 548, 585, 587-588, 592, 594, 598-599
Munden, K. 872
Munters, E. J. 960
Museum 934
Museum of the Book 908
Museum guide for Amsterdam 895
Museums 766, 782, 791, 798, 884-895, 908, 934
Music 665, 691, 817-827, 935, 984
Music Copyright Bureau 820
Mussert, A. 146
Muus, P. J. 245
Muusland 348
Muysken, J. 628
Myth of Venice and Dutch Republican thought in the seventeenth century 845

N

Naaman prinche van Sijrien 709
Nassau-Siegen, J. M. van 183
National Ballet 823
National income 178
National Museum of Antiquities 886, 892
National Museum of Antiquities 892
National population bibliography of the Netherlands 1945-1979 1011
National Socialist Union 146
Nationale Co-operatieve Raad 629
Nationalism 852
NATO 495, 500
Natural history 75
Natural science 899
Naturalism 721
Naval Intelligence Division 28
Navy 28
Nazism 133, 140, 146
Neck Yoder, H. van 744
Nederland: een selectief overzicht leverbare titels, U aangeboden door Broese Kemink b.v. 1013
Nederlands Economisch Cultureel Archief 529
Nederlands-Engels woordenboek voor landbouwwestenschappen 254

Nederlands Historisch Genootschap 927
De Nederlandsche Bank 526-527, 543, 545
De Nederlandsche Bank n.v.: Annual Report Presented to the General Meeting of Shareholders 527
De Nederlandsche Bank n.v.: Quarterly Bulletin 526
Nederlandsche prijsgeschiedenis 171
Nederlandse bibliografie van 1500-1540 1016
Het Nederlandse boek in vertaling 1018
Nederlandse Letterkundig Museum 982
Nederlandse ondernemingen en hun financiële kenmerken 528
Nederlandse Spoorwegen 617
Nederlandse teksten met verklaring en oefeningen 278
De Nederlandse Unie 145
Nelson, J. W. 571
Neo-Calvinism 332
Neo-Latin 848
Netherlands 28, 37
Netherlands adjusting to change: supplement to 'Euromoney', October 1986 542
Netherlands Antilles 192, 450
Netherlands Association of Archivists 872
Netherlands Association for Sexual Reform: a study in the sociology of social movements 357
Netherlands Bank 526-527, 540, 543, 545
Netherlands in brief 13
Netherlands-British Chamber of Commerce 568
Netherlands-British trade directory 1985 568
Netherlands budget memorandum (abridged) 553
Netherlands-Bulgaria: traces of relations through the centuries: material from Dutch archives and libraries on Bulgarian history and on Dutch contacts with Bulgaria 503
Netherlands Business Corporation code 439
Netherlands Civil Code, book 6: the Law of Obligations 451
Netherlands Corporate Tax Act 1969 554
Netherlands Dance Theatre 823
Netherlands economic and cultural documentation 529
Netherlands Economic Institute 590
Netherlands economy in the twentieth century: an examination of the most characteristic features in the period 1900-1970 180
Netherlands as an environment for plant life 71
Netherlands Foreign Trade Agency 945-946
Netherlands: an historical and cultural survey, 1795-1977 141
Netherlands India: a study of a plural society 186
Netherlands indicative multi-year programme for chemical waste 481
Netherlands International Law Review 955
Netherlands Investment News 530
Netherlands Journal of Agricultural Science 956
Netherlands Journal for Legal Philosophy and Jurisprudence and Proceedings of the Netherlands Association for the Philosophy of Law 957
Netherlands Journal of Plant Pathology 958
Netherlands Journal of Sea Research 959
Netherlands' Journal of Sociology 960
Netherlands Journal of Zoology 961
Netherlands: OECD economic survey 1985/1986 531
Netherlands Office for Fine Arts 784
Netherlands Official Statistics: Quarterly Journal of the Central Bureau of Statistics 962
Netherlands in one hundred maps 69
Netherlands Open Air Museum 886
Netherlands Scientific Council for Government Policy (WRR) 393, 497, 589, 637
Netherlands: a selective bibliography of reference works 1005
Netherlands in the seventeenth century 109

Netherlands Society of Criminology 427
Netherlands Society for Plant Pathology 958
Netherlands survey on fertility and parenthood motivation 1975: Country Report, World Fertility Survey 219
Netherlands taxes 555
Netherlands at war: 1940-1945. 139
Netherlands Works Councils Act 640
Netherlands world broadcasting 918
Neubourg, C. de 628
Neutrality or commitment: the evolution of Dutch foreign policy 1667-1795 492
New Cambridge modern history 94
New catechism: Catholic faith for adults 312
New educational provision for the 16 to 18 age group in the Netherlands 653
New Europe: an economic geography of the EEC 36
New Guinea 195, 207
New Left 425
New Netherland 338
New trends in social welfare policy in the Netherlands 385
New worlds from the lowlands 730
New York 187, 193, 369, 764
New York historical manuscripts: Dutch 193
New York Historical Society 187
New Zealand 388
Newspapers 915, 921-922, 991, 1014
Newspapers in microform: foreign countries 1948-1972 1014
Newton, G. 141
Newton, I. 857
Next twenty-five years: a survey of future developments in the Netherlands 464
Niagara University 996
Nicholas, Saint 12
Die Niederlande und das deutsche Exil 1933-1940 493
Niemöller, B. 405
Nieuw Amsterdam 187
Nieuw Nederlandsch biografisch woordenboek 980
Nieuwenhuys, R. 716, 724
Nieuwkamp, J. 458
Nieuwkomers: immigranten en hun nakomelingen in Nederland 1550-1985 243
Nijenhuis, W. 335-336
Nijhof, P. 1015
Nijhoff, M. 700, 998
Nijhoff, Van Ostaijen, 'De Stijl' 700
Nijhoff, W. 1016
Nijkamp, P. 465, 516
Nijmegen 314, 1024
Nijmegen University 1024
Niks-Corkum, R. 10
Nobel Prize 724
Noise 479
Nooit meer slapen 723
Noordergraaf, A. 501
Noordwijk 618
Noorlander, H. 591
Noot, J. van der 733, 738
Nooteboom, C. 703, 802
North-East Polder 40
North Holland 852
North Sea 242, 684
Novelists 701, 737
Novels, Modern 748
NSB (National Socialist Union) 133, 146
Nu noch 726
Nuclear weapons 353, 496
NUFFIC (Netherlands Universities Foundation for International Co-operation) 669, 672, 931, 965
Nuis, A. 933
Numismatics 539
Nutrition 152
NVSH (Netherlands Association for Sexual Reform) 357

O

Obbema, P. F. J. 882
Observationes anatomicae 683
Observationes anatomicae collegii privati Amstelodamensis 683
Observations upon the United Provinces of the Netherlands 124
Oceania 877
Ochse, J. 73
OECD (Organisation for Economic Co-operation and Development) 245, 531, 636, 671

Oecumene 345
OEEC (Organization for European Economic Co-operation) 523
Of Dutch ways 3
Oil industry 48, 192, 453, 587, 593, 684
Old Catholic Church of the Netherlands 330
Old Catholics 330
Old houses in Holland 800
Old people and the things that pass 735
Oldenbarnevelt, J. van 125
Oldenbarnevelt 125
Olga, L. 730
Olthuis, M. 730
On designing and devising type 909
Onder professoren 736
Onpersoonlijke herinneringen 735
Ons Erfdeel 963
Ontario 757
Oost-Indische spiegel 716
Oosterhaven, J. 522, 532
Oosterhof, G. 799
Open University 668, 671, 673, 678
Optimizing medium-term planning for the Netherlands railways 617
Opzoomer, C. W. 694
Orabel, J. 693
Ordeal 735
Orders and decorations of the Netherlands 16
Ordo Aristoteles 841
Organisation for Economic Co-operation and Development *see* OECD
Organization for European Economic Co-operation *see* OEEC
Organization and structure of education in the Netherlands 651
Organs 753, 778, 818, 827
Orient 150
Ormrod, D. 95, 156, 167
Orthodox Calvinism 348, 915
Osborne, J. 737
Osselton, N. E. 253
Ostaijen, P. van 700
Other Western Europe: a political analysis of the smaller democracies 408
Otterlo 886, 890
Ottervanger, T. R. 640
Ottoland 348
Ottoman Empire 498
Ottoman Empire and the Dutch Republic: a history of the earliest diplomatic relations 1610-1630 498
Ouborg, P. 794
Oud, J. J. P. 802
Oud Holland 753
Oudshoorn, J. van 735
Outline of Dutch history 90
Outsider 737
Ouwinga, M. T. 197
Overbeek, A. 888
Oversteegen, J. J. 977
Overzicht onderzoek minderheden, deel I: onderzoek minderheden 1980-1985: een geselecteerde bibliografie 246
Overzichten van de archieven en verzamelingen in de openbare archiefbewaarplaatsen in Nederland 874
Oxford 468
Oxford Dictionaries 266

P

Pais, A. 666
Pais, R. M. 640
Palaeoecology 78
Palm, C. H. M. 18
Pamphlets 902
Panhuys, H. F. van 440
Pannekoek, A. J. 54
Panta Rhei 828
Paridon, C. W. A. M. van 571
Paris 151, 764, 777
Parker, G. 118, 161, 875
Parker, W. N. 178
Parlement en kiezer: jaarboek 410
Parliament 410, 444, 446-447
Parliament of the Kingdom of the Netherlands 447
Parliament in the Netherlands 444
Parties, Political 142, 147, 402, 407, 409, 418, 420, 424-426, 626-627, 633
Party re-alignment in the Netherlands 426
Pass, C. van de 74
Pastimes 861
Patents 175
Pathology 958

Patriot Movement 106, 116, 143
Patriots and liberators: revolution in the Netherlands 1780-1813 143
Patterns of European urbanisation since 1500 34
Patterson, W. E. 425
Pauw, J. L. van der 446
PBO (Publiekrechtelijk Bedrijfsorganisatie) 631
Peace movement 353, 496
Peace, profits and principles: a study of Dutch foreign policy 508
Penal system 432
Penninx, M. J. A. 236, 243, 247
Penninx, R. 236, 243, 247
Pennsylvania, University of 501
Pensions 388
Periander 723
Periodicals 519-520, 925-975, 991
  agriculture 958
  arts 926, 934-935, 937-938, 963, 966
  bibliography 975
  economics 521, 561, 941-942
  education 932, 940
  finance 553, 561
  foreign relations 949
  geography 972
  history 925, 927, 929, 936, 943, 948
  language 973
  law 955, 957
  literature 926, 930, 973-974
  planning 964-965, 971
  politics 928, 951-952
  science 932, 940, 956, 958-959, 961
  sociology 960, 968
  statistics 950, 953, 962, 969-970
  trade 947
Perron, E. du 703, 718
Perspective on governmental housing policies in the Netherlands 386
Peter I of Russia 580
Peters, K. I. L. M. 654
Petersen, W. 221-222
Petrarch, F. 704
Petrology 84
Petzina, D. 157
Philadelphia 789
Philanthropy 837
Philip of Leyden: a fourteenth century jurist 438
Philips n.v. 548, 588, 592, 918, 920
Philips, F. 592
Philology 675, 846, 859
Philosophy 316, 957, 984
Phonetics 286-287, 293, 296
Photographs 1, 5, 8, 21, 24, 66, 82, 686, 805
Phrase books 255
Physicians 695
Physics 984
Pictorial atlas of the Netherlands 66
Pieter de Hooch: the complete edition 790
Pijper, W. 825-826
Pillars of piety: religion in the Netherlands in the nineteenth century 340
Pilotage 67, 1003
Pinder, D. A. 37, 572, 593, 604-605
Planned migration: the social determinants of the Dutch-Canadian movement 222
Planning 13, 29, 30, 32, 40-41, 44-45, 55-56, 159, 211, 213, 351, 354, 358, 375, 379, 454, 456-470, 485, 510, 515-517, 525, 572-573, 589, 604-605, 617, 620-621, 625, 638-639, 647, 649, 654-655, 657, 660, 662, 664, 667, 679, 964-965, 971, 1021
Planning and Administration 964
Planning and the creation of an environment: experience in the Ysselmeerpolders 40
Planning and Development in the Netherlands 55, 965
Plas, M. van der 346
Platonists 308
Platt, J. 313
Platt, R. S. 49
Pluralism 229, 233-234, 341, 347
Poel, J. M. G. van der 606
Poetry 704, 719, 726, 728-729, 731, 733, 739, 761, 844, 846, 859
  medieval 726, 733, 739
  modern 728, 731
  neo-Latin 719
  pastoral 761
  Renaissance 733, 739
Poison tree: selected writings of Rumphuis on the natural history of the Indies 75
Police 369-370, 394-395
Policing the inner city: a study of

Amsterdam's Warmoesstraat 370
Policy development: a study of the Social and Economic Council of the Netherlands 423
Policy-oriented survey of the future: towards a broader perspective 466
Political thought 115-116, 842, 845, 855, 1001
Political union: a microcosm of European politics 1960-1966 489
Politics 13, 15, 30, 142, 147, 159, 195, 337, 341, 347, 371, 382, 395, 399-426, 489, 496, 608, 633, 656, 839, 928
local 407, 412, 420
Politics of accommodation: pluralism and democracy in the Netherlands 417
Pollution 471-486
Pomerans, A. J. 113, 327
Popular culture 755, 838
Population and Family in the Low Countries 367
Population growth and urban systems development: a case study 217
Population history of Britain 226
Population and history from the traditional to the modern world 226
Population mobility in the Netherlands, 1880-1910: a case study of Wisch in the Achterhoek 223
Port of Amsterdam 42
Port of Rotterdam in figures 570
Portraiture 788, 795, 891
Ports 42, 46, 48, 265, 563, 566, 573, 593, 614
Portugal 150, 696
Pos, H. J. 693
Post-modernism 703, 731
Post-war financial rehabilitation of the Netherlands 552
Posthuma, F. 573
Posthumus, N. W. 171
Posthumus Meyjes, G. H. 675
Potter, G. R. 94
Potter, R. A. 745
Pottery 79, 85
Poverty 154
Powell, R. B. 125
Power, state and freedom 855
Praatpaal 280
Prakken, T. 382
Pre-Roman urnfields in the north of the Netherlands 85
Prehistory 23, 70, 78-87, 100, 606
Press 915, 921-922, 1014
Prevenier, W. 101
Price, J. L. 119, 852
Price, T. D. 87
Price effects in input-output relations: a theoretical and empirical study for the Netherlands, 1949-1967 513
Prices 171, 513, 518, 534, 536, 559, 612
Prikker, J. 768
Primary Education Act (Netherlands) 655
Primer of Dutch seventeenth century overseas trade 578
Principles of sacred theology 311
Prins, R. 397
Prinsterer, G. G. van: see Groen van Prinsterer, G. van
Printing 65, 67, 899, 901, 903-906, 909, 911, 913, 966, 985-987, 998, 1016
Prints 1009
Prison reform 382, 437, 442
Pritchard, J. 746
Private law 434
Problem of popularising land consolidation in the Netherlands: thirty years of legislative change, 1924-54 605
Problem of presentative sentences in modern Dutch 292
Productivity of land and agricultural innovation in the Low Countries (1250-1800) 612
Profile of Dutch economic geography 39
Promise of American life: social mobility in a nineteenth century immigrant community, Holland, Michigan, 1847-94 216
Pronk, T. 1017
Pronunciation 286-290, 293, 296, 298, 300
Proportional representation 402
Prospects for reforming the labour system: summary of the twenty-first report to the government 637
Protestantism 172
Prussia 576
Psychology 405

PTT (Postal and Telecommunications Service) 532
Public legal services: a comparative study of policy, politics and practice 428
Public opinion 201, 207, 353, 487, 496, 663
Public opinion, the churches and foreign policy: studies of domestic factors in the making of Dutch foreign policy 496
Public planning in the Netherlands 458
Public spending cuts 380, 389
Public works 56
Publishing 899, 901, 926, 1016
Punch, M. 369-370
Punishment 430
Puritans 339

Q

Quaerendo 966
Quaternary sector 632
Querido, A. 392
Quest for security: some aspects of Netherlands foreign policy 1945-1950 491
Quintana, A. 730
Quispel, H. V. 684

R

De raadselachtige Multatuli 736
Raalte, E. van 447
Raan, E. van 1018
Raap, B. K. 453
Raasveld, J. C. 730
Rabb, T. K. 226
Raben, H. 622
Racism 229, 241, 244, 246, 832
Rademaker, C. S. M. 717
Rademaker, F. 829
Radical arts: first decade of an Elizabethan Renaissance 840
Radicals 142
Radio 914, 917-919, 923
Raes, H. 730
Raet, W. A. de 753
Rail transport 617
Rallings, C. S. 371
Randstad 34, 36, 41, 44-45
Randstad Holland 44-45
Randwijk, H. M. van 933
Raven-Hart, R. 198
Ravenzwaaij, C. van 381
Raymond, G. A. 408
Raymond, K. 537
Reader, W. J. 594
Readers 276, 278, 281, 283
Reading Dutch: fifteen annotated stories from the Low Countries 281
Realism 752, 763, 779
Reappraisal of welfare policy: summary of the twenty-second report to the government 393
Reclamation 19, 47, 51, 55, 57, 59
Reconnaissance Corps 132
Recreation 15, 259, 860-871
Recycling and clean technologies 482
Rederijkers 708, 745, 850, 994
Reedijk, C. 907
Reen, T. van 730
Reeser, E. 824-825
Referentiewerken voor de studie van de hedendaagse samenleving 1010
Reformation 107, 313, 317, 325, 329, 335, 345
Reformed thought and scholasticism: the arguments for the existence of God in Dutch theology, 1575-1650 313
Refugees 140, 238, 249, 493
Refugees from Nazi Germany in the Netherlands 1933-1940 140
Regin, D. 120
Regional costumes in the Netherlands 2
Regional imbalances 37, 158-159, 208, 210, 214-215, 352, 525, 532, 590
Regional information systems and impact analysis for large-scale energy development 465
Regional planning in Europe 470
Regional policy 37, 39, 211, 512, 516, 522, 525, 532
Regteren Altena, C. O. van 480
Regteren Altena, I. Q. van 763
Regulations concerning protection of the soil 483
Reichenbach-Consten, M. J. G. 501
Reinders, A. 448
Reinink, A. W. 803

Relations in civil aviation between the Netherlands and the United States 623
Religio Medici 841, 853
Religion 18, 208, 220, 222, 225, 308-348, 364, 412, 419, 425, 496, 762, 843, 846, 859, 893, 1012, 1023
Religion and trade in New Netherland: Dutch origins and American development 338
Religious factors in early Dutch capitalism 1550-1650 172
Rembrandt 770-771, 773, 775, 788
Rembrandt: the complete edition of the paintings 773
Remember Arnhem 132
Remonstrants 308, 313
Renaissance 167, 327, 675, 707, 711, 738, 779, 811, 844
Repertorium van boeken en tijdschriftartikelen betreffende de geschiedenis van Nederland 1019
Repertorium van de rederijkersdrama 994
Research 665, 667, 669, 676, 679, 931-932, 940, 945-946, 959, 1021
Residential environment 358
Restany, P. 764
Résumé statistique des Pays-Bas 1850-1881 645
Reve, G. K. van het 737
Review of the Netherlands Economy: Bank Hope and Mees N. V. 533
Reynaert-ikonografie 740
Reynard the Fox 726, 738, 740
Reynard the Fox and other medieval Netherlands secular literature 726
Reznicek, E. K. J. 756
Rheenen, P. van 394
Rhetoricians *see* Rederijkers
Rhine 49, 516, 563, 570, 575-576
Rhode, E. S. 74
Rhodesia 499
Richardson, H. H. 803
Riemersma, J. C. 172
Rietveld, G. 758, 806
Right in the center: the Netherlands foreign investment review 534
Rijksbureau voor Kunsthistorische Documentatie 983
Rijksmuseum 776, 891
Rijkswaterstaat 56
Rijkswaterstaat Communications 56
Rijnsburg Abbey 753
Riley, J. C. 173, 556
Riley, R. C. 38
Rise of the Dutch Republic: a history 117
Risks at sea: Amsterdam insurance and maritime Europe, 1766-1780 558
Ritzen, J. M. M. 638
Road to recovery: the Marshall Plan, its importance for the Netherlands and European co-operation 523
Roaming 'round Holland 11
Robert, W. C. H. 199
Robertson-Scott, J. W. 607
Robijns, M. J. F. 142
Robinson, A. D. 608
Robinson, R. 724
Roche, M. 776
Rochon, T. R. 420
Rodenko, P. 730
Roelofs, W. 785
Roemer-Visscher, A. 733
Roentgenatlas of old Dutch clocks 816
Roessingh, H. K. 174
Roessingh, M. P. H. 876-877
Roggeveen, A. 67
Rokkan, S. 401
Roland Holst-Van der Schalk, H. 718
Roland Holst, R. 718
Rollins, S. 729-730
Roltschäfer, K. F. 485
Roman Catholics 208, 312, 314, 328, 341, 343-344, 346-347, 399, 413, 426, 635
Roman and native in the Low Countries: spheres and interaction 81
Romans 23, 81, 84
Rome 344. 756
Romein-Verschoor, A. H. M. 718
Roo, T. de 816
Rooij, J. J. de 295-296, 939
Rooij, M. 921, 933
Room at last! The Ysselmeer polders described and illustrated 19
Roon, G. van 157
Roos, T. de 382
Roosevelt family 502
Roozendaal, G. J. van 922
Rose, R. 422
Rosenau, J. N. 504

Rosenthal, U. 395
Roskill, M. W. 765
Rotberg, R. I. 226
Rothfeld, E. 441
Rotterdam 20, 36, 46, 210, 234, 323, 542, 562-563, 566, 570, 572-575, 593, 614-615, 768, 799, 847, 886-887, 967
Rotterdam Europoort Delta 967
Rotterdam Europoort: general information 574
Rotterdam: the gateway to Europe 575
Rotterdam with a green thumb 20
Rotterdam Information Department 20
Rotterdam Museum of Ethnology 886
Rotterdam, Rijnmond, Poort van Europa 563
Rough guide to Amsterdam and Holland with a chapter on Luxembourg and selected Belgian cities 6
Rous, M. 794
Rowen, H. H. 121-122
Royal Academy 785, 910
Royal Dutch Company 587
Royal Family 16, 26, 1009
Royal Library, Brussels 982
Royal Library, The Hague 898, 907-908, 982
Royal Meteorological Institute 63
Royal Netherlands Academy 857, 859
Royal Netherlands Cricket Association 864
Royal Society 698, 857
RSV 584, 595
Rubens, P. P. 887
Rudge, J. 730
Rudolf Agricola: a bibliography of printed works and translation 1000
Rudwick, M. J. S. 691
Ruffles on the calm 519
Ruger, H. 930
Ruiter, N. C. de 40
Ruiter, R. 639
Rules of physical planning in the Netherlands 467
Rumphuis, G. E. 75
Rural community studies in Europe: tends, selected and annotated bibliographies, analyses 361
Rural conditions 30, 473
Rural migrants in urban setting 349
Russel, M. 756
Russia 580, 912
Rutten, F. J. T. 238
Ruysbeek, E. van 729
Ruysbroek 735
Ruyslinck, W. 730
Ruyter, P. de 458

S

Saaltink, H. 831
Het sadistische universum 736
Saenredam, P. J. 778
Sahara 876
Saint Nicholas 12
Samama, L. 825
Samplers 815
Samson, G. 223
Sanctions 499
Sanders, P. 452
Sanders, P. F. 826
Sandor, K. 730
Santow, G. 224
Sasse, C. 445
Sassenheim 355
Saul, S. B. 169
Saussaye, D. C. de la 323
Savage, S. 74
Savings through innovative care provision in the Dutch welfare state 389
Saxonhouse, G. 178
Scandinavia 810, 912
Scaron, A. G. 279
Schaafsma, H. 923
Schaeffer, P. 817
Schama, S. 123, 143, 656
Scharloo, M. 539
Schatborn, P. 795
Scheepmaker, N. 868
Scheffer, R. J. 609
Scheldt 53, 202, 488, 688
Scheldt question to 1839 488
Schendel, A. van 718, 735, 776
Schendelen, M. C. P. M. van 382, 421
Schenk, M. G. 372
Schenkeveld-van der Dussen, M. A. 756
Scherer, K. 15, 21
Scheurwater, J. 459
Schierbeek, B. 724

Schiff, E. 175
Het schilder-boeck 786
Schilder, G. 200
Schillebeeckx, E. 314
Schiller, A. A. 436
Schiphol 625
Schmal, H. 34
Schmid, R. A. 557
Schmutzer, E. J. M. 201
Schneider, H. D. 892
Schoenmakers, A. 280
Schöffer, I. 96, 577
Schofield, R. S. 226
Scholten, I. 422
Schoneveld, C. W. 841, 853
Schoolfield, G. 719
Schoolmeester, De 841
Schools 647, 651-663
  pre-primary 658
  curriculum 659
Schools inspectorate in the Netherlands 657
Schoon, T. 755
Schooneboom, I. J. 373
Schoonhoven, J. 794
Schopenhauer, A. 804
Schraver, J. 575
Schrijnen-Van Gastel, A. 665
Schuit, S. R. 453, 640
Schulte Noordholt, J. W. 502, 933
Schultink, H. 286 939
Schutte, G. J. 993
Schütze, H. G. 671
Schuyt, M. 888
Schwartz, G. 776, 787
Schwartz, V. V. 263
Science 310, 601, 609, 676, 679-699, 858, 886, 932, 956, 984, 1021
Science research and public policy making 1021
Scotland 126, 339
Scott, K. 193
Sculpture 754, 758, 764, 798-799, 806
Sculpture 1983 799
Sculptures of the Rijksmuseum Kröller-Müller 798
Sea defences 50-51, 53, 59
Sea-level 51
Secularization 138, 419
Secundus, J. 719
Security 491, 500, 504, 508
Seip, D. 445
Selection of early Dutch poetry 733
Selections from the letters of Erasmus (1529-1536): translation and commentary 856
Sellin, P. R. 841, 854
Semantic analysis of temporal elements in Dutch and English 304
Semantics 284, 304
Sensory assessment and chemical composition of drinking water 486
Sentences 292
Serials 991
Service levels of urban public transport: a series of documents on a study commissioned by the Ministry of Transport and Public Works of the Netherlands 624
Seuren, P. A. M. 297
Seven Years War 104
Seventeenth-century Leyden law professors and their influence on the development of civil law: a study of Bronchorst, Vinnius and Voet 433
Sevrurier, C. 693
Sex 220, 224, 357, 364, 374
Shadid, W. A. 248
Shell Oil 587
Shelley, P. B. 751
Sherard, W. 696
Shetter, W. Z. 269, 281
Shipbuilding 582, 584, 596, 616
Shipping 42, 558, 562, 570, 574, 577, 579-580, 967
Short history of the Netherlands 96
Short history of the Netherlands Antilles and Surinam 192
Short introduction in the binding of books, followed by a note on the gilding of the edges by Amrosius Vermerck 897
Short-title catalogue of books printed at Hoorn before 1701 998
Short title catalogue of books printed in the Netherlands and Belgium and of Dutch and Flemish books printed in other countries from 1470 to 1600 now in the British Museum 1020
Siertuinen van Nederland en Belgie 77
Sijes, B. A. 144
Sik, K. S. 440

Sillevis, J. 785
Silt and sky: men and movements in modern Dutch literature 718
Silverware 808, 811
Simhoffer, K. 730
Simmers, J. W. 53
Simoni, A. 841
Simons, M. 329, 331
Singelenberg, P. J. P. 804
Singh, W. 423
Singing 821
Sinterklaas 866
Sir Constantine Huygens and Britain 1596-1687, vol. I: 1596-1619 834
Sittard 78
Six European states 412
Skating 867
Skelton, J. 841
Skillen, J. W. 337
Slagter, S. 431
Slauerhoff, J. J. 699
Slicher van Bath, B. H. 176
Slis, I. H. 298
Sloane, H. 696
Slofstra, J. 81
Slot, J. 503
Sloten, P. J. van 557
Sluys, F. van der 458
Sluys, H. van der 454
Sluyser, M. 933
Smaal, A. P. 805
Smeets, I. 794
Smidt, M. de 39
Smit, H. J. 97
Smit, J. 977
Smit, R. 794
Smit, W. A. P. 939
Smith, A. 924
Smith, D. R. 788
Smith, G. L. 338
Smith, J. F. 299
Smith, M. L. 145
Smith, N. D. 314
Smith, R. 442
Smith, S. M. 504
Smith, W. J. 728
Smyth, K. 312
Snapper, J. 832
Snelders, H. A. M. 691
Snellius, W. 690
Sociaal-Economische Raad 423
Social and Economic Council 423
Social change as redefinition of roles: a study of structural and causal relationships in the Netherlands of the 'seventies' 356
Social classes 147, 210, 342, 350, 352, 355-356, 368, 371, 376, 416, 425
Social conditions 5, 7, 349-377, 565, 569, 618, 644, 742, 965, 968, 972, 975
Social democracy 425, 633
Social democratic parties in western Europe 425
Social Democratic Workers' Party 626
Social movements 357, 359, 373, 377
Social policy 7, 13, 233-237, 247, 351, 354, 358, 373, 382, 385-389, 396-397, 423, 525, 549, 604, 636, 965, 968, 975
Social security 383, 387-388, 396, 549, 634
Social services 379, 392, 428-429, 431, 437
Socialism 141, 419, 425, 626-627, 633, 635, 880
Societal state: the modern osmosis of state and society as representing itself in the Netherlands in particular: a case study of a general trend 390
Society for the History of Dutch Music 824
Sociologia Neerlandica 968
Sociologische Gids 342
Sociology 356, 960
Sociology of religion 341-348, 355, 364, 1023
Soeters, J. 397
Soldiers and students: a study of right- and left-wing radicals 365
Somberg, H. A. 685
SOPEMI 245
Sötemann, A. L. 700, 704, 912, 939
Sound structures: studies for Antonie Cohen 286
Sounds of English and Dutch 287
Sources of the history of Asia and Oceania in the Netherlands 877
South Africa 198, 876, 973
South America 150
South-west Netherlands: Rotterdam Europoort Delta 46
Southey, R. 750

Spain 114, 150, 192
Spaniards 648
Spanish Brabanter: a seventeenth Dutch social satire in five acts 725
Spanish Inquisition 875
Sparks, M. 59
Special libraries and documentation centres in the Netherlands 879
Speckmann, J. D. 232
Speech 287, 296
Speech punctuation: an acoustic and perceptual study of some aspects of speech prosody in Dutch 296
Spelen met taal 275
Spicer, J. 917
Spices 73
Spierenburg, P. C. 443
Spies, M. 720
Spinoza, B. 308, 833, 839, 842, 855, 1001
Spinoza's political and theological thought 839
Splendid ceremonies: state entries and royal funerals in the Low Countries 1515-1791 1009
Splunteren, C. van 22
Spooner, F. C. 558
Sport 7, 13, 15, 860-862, 864, 867-868, 1012
Sport and physical education around the world 860
Spreektaal: woordfrequenties in gesproken Nederlands 257
Sprudzs, A. 981
Sprunger, K. L. 339
Stadlander, M. 398
Standard of living 152
Staphorst 18, 915
Stassaert, L. 729
State museum Catharijne Convent 893
States General 447
Statistical Society 645
Statistical Yearbook of the Netherlands 969
Statistics 25, 196, 209, 570, 643-646, 950, 953-954, 962, 969-970
Statistisch Zakboek 970
STCN 998
Stedelijk Museum Amsterdam 806
Steel industry 597
Steen, J. 780, 887
Steenstra, S. J. 427
Stein 78
Steinberg, S. A. 977
Stevin, S. 687, 690
De Stijl 700, 758, 777, 796
De Stijl: 1917-1931. 758
Stikker, A. 595
Still life 752, 763
Stock exchange 538, 542
Stokes, L. D. 146
Stokhuyzen, F. 686
Stokvis, P. 225
Stoutenbeek, J. 22
Stouthard, P. C. 419
Straver, C. J. 374
Stress 290
Streuvels, S. 724
Strietman, E. 994
Strikes 635
Struik, D. J. 687
Struyken, P. 794
Stryker, W. A. 812
Stryker-Rodda, K. 193
Stuarts 854
Students 249, 365
Studies on Christiaan Huygens 691
Studies in cultural history: Cornelis Engebrechtsz's Leiden 835
Studies in functional grammar 267
Studies in the posthumous work of Spinoza: earliest translation and reception, earliest and modern edition of some texts 833
Study of the spatial planning process in Britain and the Netherlands 457
Stuijvenberg, J. A. van 610
Der Sturm 700
Stuvel, H. J. 688
Stuyt, A. M. 440
Subject technology in Dutch education 659
Suèr, H. 346
Summary of the Annual Report of the National Physical Planning Agency 971
Summary of the report on urbanization in the Netherlands 375
Surinam 192
Surinamese 228-229, 232, 234-235, 239, 247, 249
Sutton, P. C. 766, 789-790
SVO (Foundation for Educational

Research) 1021
Swammerdam, A. 690
Swart, K. W. 167, 990
Sweden 581, 675, 860
Sweden's trade with the Dutch Republic 1738-1795: a quantitative analysis of the relationship between economic growth and international trade in the eighteenth century 581
Sweelinck, J. P. 819
Sweelinck's keyboard music 819
Swierenga, R. P. 225, 502
Switzerland 175, 403, 696, 912
Swüste, W. 275
Syllable 290, 301
Syllable in Dutch: with special reference to diminutive formation 301
Syllable structure and stress in Dutch 290
Symonds, R. R. 611
Synod of Dordrecht 335
Syntax 284, 303
Synthese: twelve facets of culture and nature in South Limburg 23
Systematic list of publications 1986 (CBS) 646
Szénâssy, I. L. 806
Szwengrub, L-M. 361

T

Het 80.000 stratenboek: met plattegronden van 122 steden en een register van 80.000 straaten 68
Taiwan 289
Tak, T. van der 406
Tamse, C. A. 91, 127, 136, 325, 341, 505
Tamsma, R. 69
Tariffs 583
Tavecchio, L. W. C. 376
Taxation 165, 352, 387, 453, 524, 546-547, 549, 553-555, 560, 564, 995
Taylor, L. J. 202
Technique of singing 821
Technique, spirit and form in the making of the modern economies: essays in honour of William N. Parker 178
Technology 56, 254, 260-262, 659, 679, 682, 684, 686, 688, 879, 886, 932, 945-946
Teirlinck, H. 735
Teixeira de Mattos, A. 735
Telecommunications 532
Telephones 532
Television 217, 831-832, 915-917, 919-920, 923-924
Television in education and training 920
Television and political life: studies in six European countries 924
Teminck, J. J. 874
Tempel, N. J. 676
Temple, Sir W. 111, 124
Ten studies in Anglo-Dutch relations 841
Terken, J. M. B. 300
Terrorism 231
Tex, J. den 125
Text to reader 741
Texts concerning the Revolt of the Netherlands 115
Teyler, P. 837, 886
'Teyler' 1778-1978: studies en bijdragen over Teylers stichting naar aanleiding van het tweede eeuwfeest 837
Teyler's Museum 886
Theatre 823, 832, 884, 935
Theo van Doesburg 796
Theology 172, 308-317, 323, 335-336, 340, 345, 348, 399, 837, 839, 899
Thiel, P. J. J. van 775
Thienen, F. W. S. van 24
Thienen, G. van 913
Thijssen-Schoute, C. L. 693
Third world 585, 669
Thissen, F. 30
Thissen, G. G. J. 410
Thomas Basson 1555-1613 901
Thomas, A. H. 425
Thomas, D. 468
Thorbecke, J. R. 128-129, 320
Those Dutch Catholics 346
Three seaports of the Low Countries in the nineteenth century, Amsterdam, Antwerp and Rotterdam 614
Thurlings, J. M. G. 347
Tiefstich pottery 79
Tiersma, P. M. 270
Tigg, E. R. 747

De Tijd 921
Tijdschrift voor Economische en Sociale Geografie 69, 972
Tijdschrift voor Nederlands en Akrikaans 973
Tijn, T. van 147-148, 641
Tilanus, C. B. 535
Tiles 814
Timmenga, S. J. 485, 625
Timmermans, J. M. 368, 458
Tinbergen, J. 559
Tobacco 174
Toledo 808
Tolerance 374, 843, 847
Tollenaere, F. de 992
Tolnay, C. de 767
Toonder, M. 865
Tops, G. A. J. 264
Torsvik, P. 401
Tourism 13
Tourist guides 3-4, 6, 10-11, 15, 20-22, 25
Towards a reformed philosophy: the development of Protestant philosophy in Dutch Calvinistic thought since the time of Abraham Kuyper 316
Towarnicki, F. de 764
Town planning 19, 797, 999
Trade 42, 46, 80, 84, 156, 184, 188-189, 206, 260, 338, 439, 452-453, 497, 503, 507, 520-521, 524, 528, 531, 554, 562-583, 589, 630, 858, 945-947, 967
Trade unions 148, 627, 633-635, 641-642
Traders, artists, burghers: a cultural history of Amsterdam in the 17th century 120
Trading companies in Asia 1600-1830 189
Traffic 621
Tragoediae constitutione 715
Training teachers and head teachers for pre-primary schools in the Netherlands 658
Translation 255, 707, 836, 974, 992
Translation guide: Dutch English 255
Translations 710, 722-751, 853, 963, 1012, 1018, 1022
Transport 13, 158, 177, 217, 265, 358, 473, 567, 570, 574, 614-625
Trauma of decolonization: the Dutch and West New Guinea 195
Travels through the lexicon 250
TRB West group: studies in the chronology and geography of the makers of hunebeds and Tiefstich pottery 79
Treasures of the Royal Library, The Hague 908
Trends in Dutch drawing 1945-1985 794
Trends in research and development in the Netherlands 676
Trim, J. L. M. 282
Trippenhuis 848
Triumph of honour: Burgundian origins of the Elizabethan renaissance 851
Trommelen, M. 301
Trouw 921
Trouwen 735
Tudors 851
Tulips 72, 74
Tulleners, H. 25
Turkey 498
Turkish language 279
Turks 228, 288, 367, 648
Tuscany 507
Tuscany and the Low Countries: an introduction to sources and an inventory of four Florentine libraries 507
Tusler, R. L. 827
Twente University 380
24 hours Amsterdam 8
Two hundred years of Netherlands-American interaction 501

U

Uerberfeldt, B. van 2
Uhlenbeck, G. 680
Uil, H. 874
Unbuilt Netherlands 802
Underdevelopment of ex-colonial immigrants in the metropolitan society: a study of Surinamers in the Netherlands 234
Underwood, E. A. 698
Unemployment 628, 637
Unger, R. W. 596
Unilever 585, 594, 598-599

Unilever 1945-1965: challenge and response in the post-war industrial revolution 599
Unilever overseas: the anatomy of a multinational 1895-1965 585
Union of Netherlands Municipalities 462
United Nations 351, 499
United Nations Association 239
United States 3, 216, 218, 225, 227, 230, 310, 321, 338-339, 388, 391, 398, 407, 428, 489, 501-502, 530, 534, 544-545, 623, 694, 748, 766, 902, 912, 1005
Universities 97, 154, 638, 647, 651, 664, 666, 668, 670-671, 674-675, 677-678, 860
Universities abroad 672, 674
University College 985
University education in the Netherlands 677
Urban conditions 29, 34, 217, 375, 407, 473, 615, 624, 999
Urban planning 456, 460
Urbanization 34, 36, 41, 44-45, 217, 349, 364, 375, 838, 999
Urnfields 85
Use and extent of replacement value accounting in the Netherlands 537
Use and function of accentuation: some experiments 300
Use of a health education planning model to design and implement health education interventions concerning AIDS 398
Utrecht 171, 219, 601, 893, 900
Utrecht University 219, 601
Uyl, D. J. den 855

V

Vaccination 915
Valk, A. van der 469
Vallen, T. 288
Valois Burgundy 102
Value-added tax in the Netherlands 560
Van . . . For personal names with the prefix 'van', e. g. J. van Goor, see under the main stem of the name, viz. Goor, J. van (this also applies to other prefixes: de, den, van den, uit den, 't, etc.).
Van AAB tot ZOO 256
Van Abbe museum Eindhoven 894
Van Dale, groot woordenboek Engels-Nederlands, groot woordenboek Nederlands-Engels 264
Van Gogh: a documentary biography 759
Van oude mensen. De dingen die voorbijgaan 735
Vancouver Art Gallery 787
Vanden Vos Reynaerde 726
Vandenbosch, A. 506
Vandeputte, O. 307
Vanderauwera, R. 748-749
Varty, K. 740
Vatican Council II 346
Vaughan, R. 102
Veen, C. F. van 869
Veen, H. T. van 507
Veen, J. van 57
Vegetables 73
Vegetables of the Dutch East Indies 73
Vekeman, H. 973
Vel, P. 816
Veld-Langeveld, H. M. in 't 373
Velde, J. van der 302, 659
Velden, D. van 203
Veldkamp, H. 660
Veldman, J. 611
Ven-Ten Beusel, E. van der 870
Ven, J. J. M. van der 933
Venadam bibliotheekgids 1982 883
Venice 103, 845
Venice and Amsterdam: a study of seventeenth-century élites 103
Verbeek, J. 808
Verduyn, J. 730
Verhagen, A. 303
Verheijen, L. 13
Verhoef, R. 448
Verhoef, T. 794
Verkade, W. 424
Verkiezingsprogramma's 1986: verkiezingen voor de tweede kamer der Staten-Generaal, 21 mei 1986 418
Vermeer of Delft: complete edition of the paintings 772
Vermeer, A. 288
Vermeer, J. 772, 800
Vermeer, W. 704

Vermerck, A. 897
Vermeulen, M. 825
Verrips, J. 348
Versnel, P. 265
Vertical pluralism *see* Verzuiling
Vervliet, H. D. L. 896
Verwey, A. 750-751
Verwey-Jonker, H. 249
Verzuiling 138, 324, 341, 343, 347, 382, 401, 403, 416-417, 421-422, 923-924, 1024
Vestdijk, S. 718, 735, 939
Vigeveno, P. 22
Vincent van Gogh: the letters 765
Vincent, P. F. 305, 307, 721, 736, 936, 1022
Vinnius, A. 433
Violence 427
Visch, H. 794
Vision and form in the poetry of Albert Verwey 750
Vismans, R. 936
Visser, J. 210
Visser, R. P. W. 76, 691
Visser, W. 876
Vissink, H. G. A. 561
VNO (Federation of Netherlands Industry) 518
VOC (East India Company) 182
Vocational education in the Netherlands 661
Vocational training 647, 651, 653, 661
Vocht, H. de 747
Voer voor psychologen 723
Voet, P. 433
Vogelaar, F. O. W. 455
Vogels, H. 895
Voiced-voiceless distinction and assimilation in Dutch 298
Voicing 298
Vollmann, W. 678
Volume and composition of structural unemployment in the Netherlands, 1950-1980 628
Volume of payments and the informal economy in the Netherlands 1965-1982: an attempt at quantification 514
Voluntary agencies in the welfare state 391
Vondel, J. van den 707, 711, 720, 733, 1022
Voogd, H. 459, 470
Voorhoeve, J. J. C. 508
Een voorlopige bibliografie over het thema 'verzuiling' 1024
Voort, J. P. de 204
Vossius, G. J. 717, 848
Vowel contrast reduction: an acoustic and perceptual study of Dutch vowels in various speech conditions 293
Voyages of discovery 194, 199-200
Vries, J. H. de 311
Vries, J. J. de 58
Vries, Jan de 177-179, 226, 756
Vries, Johan de 130, 180, 597
Vries, S. J. de 315
Vugt, J. P. A. van 1023-1024
Vuyst, J. de 304

W

Waal, C. J. D. de 433
Waals, J. D. van der 690
Wabeke, B. H. 227
Wagenaar, B. W. 16
Wageningen University 361, 601, 613, 669, 879, 925, 956
Wages 170, 178, 226, 510, 518, 521, 534, 634, 637
Wages and employment in the E. E. C. 634
Wagret, P. 59
Wain, J. 737
Wakefield, R. 952
Wal, C. van der 458
Wal, S. L. van der 205
Walewein 726
Walford, A. J. 1025
Walgate, R. 689
Wall, C. van der 786
Wallerstein, W. 151
Walschap, G. 735
Waning of the Middle Ages: a study in the forms of life, thought and art in France and the Netherlands in the fourteenth and fifteenth centuries 99
Warfield, B. B. 311
Warmbrunn, W. 139, 149
Warmoesstraat 370
Wassen-Van Schaveren, P. 377

Waste disposal 472, 475-476, 481-482, 484
Waste Substances Act 484
Water control 32, 47, 51, 53, 55-57, 59, 688
Water flows 50, 58
De waterman 735
Watkins, J. 789
Wealth and property in the Netherlands in modern times 352
Weber, M. 172
Wee, H. van der 612
Weerman, F. 294
Weevers, J. W. 977
Weevers, T. 750, 977
Wegman, F. W. 77
Wel, F. J. van 98
Welfare state 380-383, 385, 387-391, 396, 549, 559, 975
Welling, D. 768
Wels, C. B. 509
Welsh, R. P. 700
Werkgroep voor de Documentatie der Nederlandse Letteren 982
Werkman, E. 21
Wesseling, H. L. 206-207
West India Company 191, 338
West Indians 239
West Indies 190-191, 204, 229
West Irian 195
West Sayville 202
Westerik, C. 794
Westow, T. 346
Weststrate, C. 536
Wetering, E. van de 771, 775
Wetering, W. van de 771
Wever, E. 39
Weyerman, J. C. 705
White-collar workers 371
Wierda, F. 792
Wieringa, W. J. 582
Wieringen, A. L. M. van 662
Wieringermeer 40
Wigbold, H. 924
Wijers, L. 40
Wild Coast 190
Wilhelmina, Queen 26
Willekens, F. J. 213
Willem Mertens' levensspiegel 735
Willems, W. 246
Willems-Treeman, E. 933
William the Silent 105
William I, King 128
William II, King 142
Williams, J. K. 283
Williams, M. R. 856
Willink 783
Willink, A. C. 783
Wilmots, J. 278
Wilson, C. 737
Wilson, C. H. 126, 156, 161, 598-599, 857-858
Windmills 686, 1015
Windmuller, J. P. 642
Wintle, M. J. 340, 936, 997
Wisch 223
Wit, C. H. E. de 143
Wit, J. de 722
Witt, J. de 111, 121-122
Witte, E. 1004
Woerkom, F. J. H. van 595
Wolf, C. de 897, 998
Wolf, M. 751
Wolff, P. 600
Wolinetz, S. B. 425-426, 952
Wolkers, J. 730
Wolst, E. 210
Wolters, G. J. R. 485
Wolters' beeld-woordenboek Engels en Nederlands 266
Wolters' ster woordenboek Nederlands/Engels en Engels/Nederlands 251
Women 141, 359, 367, 372-373, 376-377, 630
Women in the Netherlands: past and present 372
Women in small business: focus on Europe 630
Woodcuts 740
Wooden shoes and baseball bats: a study of the sociocultural integration of Americans in The Hague 230
Wooden shoes: their makers and their wearers 591
Woonerf 358
Woordfrequenties in geschreven en gesproken Nederlands 252
Word frequencies 252, 257
Word order 303
Wordsworth, W. 750-751
Works councils 452, 631, 640
World of Hugo Grotius (1583-1645) 859

World Service 914
World War Two 26, 28, 91, 127, 131-132, 134, 136, 139, 144-146, 149, 203, 324, 493-494, 540, 575, 619, 727, 918-919
Woutertje Pieterse 710
Wren, Sir C. 801
Wright, C. 791
Wright, G. 178
Wright, H. R. C. 583
Wrigley, E. A. 226
Writing in Holland and Flanders 722, 974
WRR (Netherlands Scientific Council for Government Policy) 247, 393, 497, 589, 637
Würzner, H. 493
Wuttke, D. 704
WVC Documentatie 975
Wynkyn de Worde 740

Y

Y *see* IJ
Yachting 862
Yemen 182
Young, W. 316
Youth 7, 360, 366, 426
Youth of Erasmus 849
Yperen, M. J. L. van 191
Yssel *see* IJssel
Ysselmeer *see* IJsselmeer

Z

Zaalberg, C. A. 939
Zanden, J. L. van 613
Zandvoort, R. W. 253
Zeeland 59, 202, 596
Zeeman, P. 690
Zelfportret of het galgemaal 735
Zeventig jaar Nederlandse muziek 1915-1985 825
Zigeuners, woonwagenbewoners en reizenden: een bibliografie 240
Zoeteman, B. C. J. 486
Zon, A. H. van 628
Zon, H. van 943
Zondag, K. 663
Zonneveld, W. 286, 294
Zoological work of Petrus Camper (1722-1789) 76
Zoology 76, 961
Zuyder Zee 19, 47, 55, 59, 458
Zuyder Zee: Lake IJssel 47
Zuylen, B. de 907
Zweelo 361
ZWO (Netherlands Organisation for the Advancement of Pure Research) 932

Map of the Netherlands

This map shows the more important towns and other features.